*Limited Classical Reprint Library*

# A COMMENTARY ON PAUL'S FIRST AND SECOND EPISTLES TO THE CORINTHIANS

by

## Hermann Olshausen

Foreword by Dr. Cyril J. Barber

*KLOCK & KLOCK CHRISTIAN PUBLISHERS, INC.*
*2527 Girard Ave. N.*
*Minneapolis, Minnesota 55411*

Originally published by
T. & T. Clark
Edinburgh, 1855

ISBN:  0-86524-184-8

Printed by Klock & Klock in the U.S.A.
1984 Reprint

# FOREWORD

A few years ago, on the cover of one of his book catalogs, Richard Owens Roberts, the well-known second-hand book dealer from Wheaton, Illinois, inscribed the following: *"The choice of books--like the choice of friends--will be either a great blessing or a tragic blight. Nowhere is greater wisdom needed or more foolishness manifested."* With these wise words, few will disagree. Careful selection, however, needs to be made so that the discerning reader may avail himself of the best of the past as well as the present.

Among those fine studies which continuously commend themselves to modern readers, there stand the writings of Hermann Olshausen (1796-1839), a noted German exegete, who following studies in the universities of Kiel and Berlin, achieved distinction in the areas of historical and exegetical theology. Such was his erudition that, following graduation in 1821, he was elected extraordinary professor at Konigsberg where he taught until 1834, at which time he was called upon to accept a theological professorship at Erlangen. Unfortunately, he had never enjoyed robust health, and he died in Erlangen five years later.

Among Dr. Olshausen's numerous works there is his *Commentar uber sammtliche Schriften des Neuen Testaments*, which began publication in Konigsberg in 1830 and was completed by two of his colleagues after his death.

Of the volumes in this series, Dr. Philip Schaff had this to say:

> The principal merit and greatest charm of Olshausen's exegesis lies in its spirit. He excells beyond most commentators in what we may call the art of organic reproduction of the sacred text, and the explanation of Scripture by Scripture. The philological portions are often too brief and unsatisfactory for the advanced scholar [though they may be read with real profit by the discerning seminarian]; . . . for Olshausen pays more careful attention to the thelolgical exposition, entering into the marrow of religious idea, and introducing the student to the spirit and inward unity of the divine revelation in its various stages of development under the old and new dispensations. He has an instinctive power of seizing, as if by a sacred sympathy, the true meaning of the inspired writer, and bringing to light the hidden connections and transitions, the remote allusions and far reaching bearing of the text. There is nothing mechanical and superficial about him. He is always working in the mines and digging at the roots. . . Pious students will read him with delight and profit, and regard the spiritual depth and the warm glow of a profoundly pious heart as the sweetest charm and highest recommendation of his work. He approaches the Bible with devout reverence as the Word of the living God, leads the reader into the sanctissimum and makes him feel that here is the gate of heaven.

Olshausen's commentaries were originally translated into English for Clark's *Foreign Theological Library* and are well deserving of continued reading today.

Cyril J. Barber
Author, *The Minister's Library*

033374

# TRANSLATOR'S PREFACE.

In preparing an English version of Olshausen's valuable exposition of St Paul's Epistles to the Corinthians, no pains have been spared to render its exegetical and critical language into such plain and simple phraseology, as may present ample means to the English reader for appreciating the Author's capabilities as a Commentator upon the infallible truths of Holy Scripture.

The chief difficulty in preparing this version has been found to arise from the impossibility—acknowledged by all students—of infusing the genius of the German language into the expressions of our own, and of adopting phraseology as simple, yet as comprehensive,—as copious, yet as emphatic as the original. The peculiarities of the author's style have also added very considerably to the labour,—whilst his originality of thought has, in many instances, appeared almost to defy anything like an adequate rendering. However, notwithstanding all these impediments, they have yielded before an earnest desire to make the value of Dr Olshausen's Scriptural investigations still further known, than they have been already by the previous translation of his Commentaries on the four Gospels, and on the Epistle to the Romans.

In attempting to elucidate the causes for the divisions of the church at Corinth, the author has assumed that the οἱ τοῦ Χρίστου, whom divines of our own country for the most part have supposed to be the true believers in Christ, were a distinct schismatical party, and as such he has treated them throughout his

Exposition.   As no known term equivalent to that which he uses
for his designation of this party exists in our language, the
German appellation has been retained, so that wherever the
*Christianer*, or the *Christus parthei* is mentioned in the original,
it is rendered by the former of these words in the translation.   It
is hoped that this explanation will remove a difficulty which might
otherwise have been felt had an English word, or words, been
employed to give expression to the Author's meaning.

In bringing this English version to a close, the translator feels
that he should be deficient both in gratitude and courtesy were
he not to acknowledge the valuable assistance he has had, and
the obligation he is under, to J. E. TAYLOR, Esq., the learned
translator of several German works of deep research, who has
kindly revised the proof-sheets as they have passed through the
press.   Without the aid of this friend, the work would have been
far less complete in its several parts.


LONDON, *December* 31, 1850.

# TABLE OF CONTENTS.

———◆———

## INTRODUCTION.

## FIRST EPISTLE.
### PART FIRST (i. 1—iv. 21).

### PART SECOND (v. 1—xi. 1).

### PART THIRD (xi. 2—xiv. 40).

### PART FOURTH (x. 1—xvi. 24).

# SECOND EPISTLE.

## PART FIRST (i. 1—iii. 18.)

## PART SECOND (iv. 1—ix. 15).

## PART THIRD (x. 1—xiii. 13.

# INTRODUCTION.

## § 1. CHARACTER OF THE CORINTHIAN COMMUNITY.

In the Epistle to the Romans, doctrine decidedly predominates; in the Epistles to the Corinthians, practical directions, on the contrary, prevail. The Epistles of Paul to the Christians at Corinth arose out of the pressure of circumstances; and while displaying to us the wisdom of the great apostle of the Gentiles, they make us especially acquainted with his power of arranging and controlling involved and difficult questions. To the *second* Epistle we are indebted for our acquaintance with St Paul as an individual; to the *first*, for an account of the condition of the ancient church. Without the possession of the latter, any idea which we are enabled to collect of the important movements in the apostolic church would be much more general, as it gains more life and form from this Epistle than from the remaining Epistles of Paul collectively. This is to be accounted for by the character of the Corinthian community—that is to say, although a powerful and living principle animated the entire church from the period of the assumption of man's nature by the Son of God, by which light and darkness, good and evil, were aroused from their inmost depths, to array themselves against each other, yet Corinth was the spot in which this principle manifested the most striking appearances.

The city of Corinth stood on the confines of both west and east, blending internally the peculiar properties of each; her wealthy trade, and industrious pursuit of objects connected with science and art, drew within her walls men of every degree,* and

---

* Compare Wilkens Specimen antiquitatum Corinthiacarum selectarum ad illustrationem utriusque epistolae Paulinae ad Corinthios. Bremae 1747. J. Ernest. Imm. Walch antiquitates Corinthiacae. Jenae 1761.

upon this stirring and intelligent mass Christianity exercised the most powerful influences, and thus produced the most varied effects. The Christian church in that city may be viewed as a prefiguration of the Apostolic church; all the directions put forth by the latter were already to be found in the former; the rules which served to direct them, at the time Paul made his appearance in Corinth, were drawn from the same spiritual source, although those charged with the work had not been able fully to emancipate themselves from their early errors, in order to dedicate themselves in all purity to the novelty of the Gospel; they rather mingled what was new with the elements of the old, and thus perverted the nature of that doctrine whose professed principles are ever at variance with error and corruption. This blending of the new and the old gave occasion to the formation of sects in the church of Christ, and their appearance is referred to, even in the first Epistle to the Corinthians, which is a brief history of the sects from the earliest moment of the existence of such schisms.

One of the principal questions to which the Introduction to these Epistles has to reply, and a right understanding of which must be of primary importance, is this—" *What were the doctrines already propagated in the Corinthian Church?*" The obscurity of expression used by the apostle in describing these doctrines, and the various hypotheses to which this consequently gave rise, render it a most difficult question to approach, inasmuch as it requires a satisfactory and clear explanation to enable us to understand the contents of the Epistles, which principally refer to the disputes and controversies which then agitated the church of Corinth.

We propose, therefore, first to explain the opinions we have adopted, upon what appears to be just grounds, and then to institute a comparison of the same, with the most important views of others upon the same subject.

Paul distinctly points out four different parties in Corinth,— those of Peter, Apollos, Paul, and οἱ τοῦ Χριστοῦ (1 Cor. i. 12, iii. 4, iv. 3, 22, 2 Cor. x. 7), and we have as little reason to suppose that there existed more than these four parties, as that there were less (compare the remarks upon i. 12). In the passages quoted the apostle does not simply name several parties, as if for the sake of exemplification, but he gives many historical particulars relative to their condition as members of the Corinthian church, so that there is no difficulty in discovering the tendencies of some of them. They who said *I am of Paul* were orthodox in belief; to this Paul assents, but chiefly blames them for attaching themselves too much to his person, and for depending on his human characteristics; for which reason, and to prevent any misuse of human authority, he continually enjoins them to have faith in the Lord. (i. 1, 13, et sqq.) Very closely allied to the party attached to Paul, was that of Apollos. This man "eloquent and mighty in the Scriptures," (Acts xviii. 24), himself taught in Corinth, (Acts xix. 1), finding there, as might have been expected, willing hearers, and as Paul was intimately associated with Apollos himself in the work, (i. 4, 6, xvi. 12), he had nothing of more importance to reprove in the followers of Apollos than this same respect to his human individuality. This involuntary adherence may have occasioned a formal difference between the followers of the two teachers, they being probably both inclined to put forth a claim for their own manner of interpreting the Old Testament, of which the Epistle to the Hebrews (which, if not written by Apollos, proceeded from a completely analogous order of mind), affords an example; at all events they vied with each other in striving to obtain a deeper knowledge of evangelical truth, in the form of a more perfect Jewish Gnosis, with a bias towards the views of the Alexandrian school. The third party, which called itself after Peter, is doubtless the Pharisaic Jewish sect, which Paul so strongly opposes in his Epistle to the Galatians. Peter partook neither of their errors nor of their enmity to Paul; but this party took advantage, nevertheless, of the position of Peter, as the chief of the apostles, appointed for the people of Israel, and used his name in order to sanction their proceedings.* At the time the first Epistle was written, this party was yet weak, or its ultimate character was not entirely developed; but in the second Epistle, especially in chap. xi., it is distinctly pointed out and opposed, together with the fourth party. We now come to in-

---

* This party did not assume the name of Peter in consequence of the presence of Peter in Corinth (for the abode in Corinth mentioned by Eusebius [Hist. Eccl. ii. 25] occurred long after the Epistles to the Corinthians were drawn up), but on account of the public position which he occupied in the church of Christ.

quire who were meant under the name οἱ τοῦ Χριστοῦ, and this question is as difficult to decide as the inquiry, with reference to the three first named sects, is easily to be disposed of. From the name itself nothing with certainty can absolutely be deduced, since members of the Corinthian church may have taken occasion, under a variety of circumstances, to name themselves "of Christ," just as in the same manner, from the word Jesuit, nothing of the spirit or regulation of the order could possibly be learned, unless we possessed some other information upon the point. It appears, therefore, that the only way to arrive at a well-grounded reply to the question, is to ascertain if anything may be inferred concerning the condition of those who esteemed themselves direct disciples of Christ, from the manner in which the apostle expresses himself in the Epistles with regard to them. The apostle expressly wrote with reference to existing sects in Corinth, and mention is made of these throughout the whole Epistle; it is therefore natural to suppose that he viewed their errors in a polemical light. Now, against which of the sects already mentioned did Paul especially argue? Evidently not against the followers of Paul and Apollos, for at the most, erroneous or ill-directed striving after knowledge is imputed to the latter, in the passages wherein Paul at once mentions and preaches against it, (compare 1 Cor. chap. i.–iii.) Then possibly against the followers of Peter? But of this not a trace is to be found in the first Epistle to the Corinthians, inasmuch as it does not contain a single argument similar to these which abound in the Epistle to the Galatians. All that appears to be directed against the adherents of Peter occurs in 1 Cor. ix., concerning the anxiety of those who sought to avoid the use of meats offered to idols; but the reference to this error is merely incidental, for the real argument in this chapter is directed against those who, by wandering into a by-path, had fallen into a state of false liberty. In the second Epistle, however, the case is quite different; and had we this Epistle alone, without the first, doubtless all the antitheses against false and presumptuous teachers, of which it contains so large a number (see 2 Cor. iii. 1, iv. 2, v. 12, xi. 13, sqq., xii. 11, sqq.), must have been held to refer to the Judaists, who were everywhere opposers of, and hostile to, the apostle; and it is possible that the teachers and representatives of this party, then in Corinth, might have been included. But, taking the first Epistle for our guide, we can only understand 2 Cor. x. 7 to refer to the οἱ τοῦ Χριστοῦ, and accordingly the preaching in the second Epistle against false teachers, must include the heads of this party also, (which is likewise the opinion of Baur—see his Comm., 2 Cor. x. 7), not to say that it is entirely directed against them. Beyond this, the second Epistle touches only upon personal circumstances, avoiding doctrinal or ethical disputes; therefore the first Epistle is the only source which remains to us for investigation, the most prominent contents of which appear to be entirely directed against the *Christianer*.[*] It is true that Paul does not expressly indicate this sect, but speaks as if he addressed all the *Christianer* in Corinth without distinction, but the sole motive for this was in order to preserve a recollection of their unity in the church. To have addressed one party alone would have been to regard the division as perfected, and thus to have made the evil without remedy.[†] But by the form of remonstrance which Paul adopted, he promoted a spirit of concord, and encouraged as long as possible the hope of leading back the misguided. From this circumstance it is so much the more indispensable to the correct understanding of the first Epistle, that he should become intimately acquainted with the character of the sect who named themselves of Christ. From a consideration of the character of the city of Corinth as the centre of heathen life generally, and heathen art and science particularly, it appears probable that if in any place the coalition of Christianity with these elements was probable it would take place in this city.[‡] Further, if we endeavour to take a comprehensive view of all the dogmatic and ethic points adverted to by

[*] As in Galatia, the followers of Peter became afterwards the most dangerous, so were the *Christianer* now in Corinth. In 1 Cor. i. 12, a climax is therefore to be observed in which the most threatening party takes the last place.

[†] Even in the second Epistle, where the division had now more strongly exhibited itself, the parties were not separately distinguished, although the different character of the first and second part of this Epistle strongly displays its reference to them. (Compare further § 3).

[‡] Had the party named by Paul οἱ τοῦ Χριστοῦ been designated by the name of an apostle, they must have been called οἱ τοῦ Ἰωάννου, for John preached the doctrine in the true, which this party put forth in the erroneous form. By the name οἱ τοῦ Χριστοῦ, which these sectarians doubtless applied to themselves (2 Cor. x. 7), they wished to make themselves noted above all others as the true πνευματικοί, the real and peculiar Christians.

the apostle in the first Epistle, it shews us that it is exactly the
over-estimation of human science and art, together with the endeavour to establish independence of, and freedom from, the burdensome fetters of the law, which discloses itself in heathenism.   In
the first four chapters Paul plainly speaks against the foolishness
of human wisdom, which without doubt refers to the Greek philosophy and science so highly prized among the Corinthians; and
it is possible that the followers of Apollos are incidentally included among those to whom the apostle addresses himself.   In
the 5th chapter the special reference is to the existence of incest
among them; and the reason that the Corinthians themselves,
from their own sense of morality, had not repressed the practice, is
to be found in the very lax opinions of the Gentile Christians relative to the sexes, as may be plainly seen in 1 Cor. x. 8, 2 Cor.
xii. 21, while, on the contrary, the Jews and Jewish Christians were
very strict on the subject.   Yet their immorality can excite no
astonishment when we are told that belonging to the temple of
the Isthmia Dione, upon the Acrocorinth, there were more than
a thousand votaresses whose excesses, far from being forbidden,
were regarded as an acceptable offering to the goddess.   The new
Christians naturally renounced all gross offences upon their
entrance into the church; yet it was natural that a more refined
feeling should only gradually arise in both sexes, as to their
mutual relation to each other; for which reason Paul felt himself constrained (xi. 5, sqq., xiv. 35), to address several precepts
to the women regarding their conduct.   The contents of the
succeeding chapters refer to law proceedings before heathen
judges, to marriage, and to the use of meats offered to idols,
the apostle enjoining that all false liberty in such things should
be avoided.   In the tenth chapter the evil consequences of this
licence is distinctly described and exemplified from the Old
Testament.   It will be perceived that these articles bear reference not to doctrine, but to the manner of life, and the exhortations which follow concerning the Lord's Supper, its worthy
celebration (xi. 17, sqq.), and the right use of spiritual gifts (xii.
1, sqq., xiv. 1, sqq.), possess no dogmatic character; nevertheless, the arguments referring to the resurrection (cap. xv.),
in which the ideal error is distinctly refuted that the resurrection was only to be received in a spiritual sense (xv. 12), are

equally applicable to the doctrine of the Lord's Supper. This precise error (*i. e.* respecting the doctrine of the resurrection) was one which agreed exactly with the principles of philosophic Gentile Christians,* who cultivated this opinion, as well as the materialism of the Jewish Christians, leaving us no room to doubt who were to be understood under the name οἱ τοῦ Χριστοῦ, for to neither of the other three parties can this error be attributed. Paul, in Romans, chaps. xiv. xv., describes certain persons in Rome who appeared under precisely similar circumstances to the *Christianer* in Corinth, asserting their freedom in opposition to a strict Jewish practice, and differing only from the latter in adopting less extreme opinions. The supposition that these opponents of the doctrine of the resurrection had formerly belonged to the Sadducees is by no means tenable : not a trace exists of any coalition between Sadduceism and Christianity. Like Epicureanism among the heathen, the principles of the sect were so completely at variance with the spirit of the Gospel, that it was utterly impossible for the converted Sadducee to unite the elements of his former belief with those of his new faith. In addition to this, the Sadducees entirely denied the existence of a spiritual world (Acts xxiii. 8), therefore they could not interpret the doctrine of the resurrection spiritually, they could only entirely reject it.

This view of the Corinthian *Christianer*, which to us seems the only correct one, has also been put forth by Neander[†] in its most important points, and the conviction of its accuracy does not rest alone upon the evidence adduced in its favour, but also upon the impossibility of sustaining any other. The conjecture of Eichhorn is that, by the *Christianer*, the neutral party was meant; that is to say, it signified those who, not receiving Christianity me-

* It is as well to remark, that in this place the weakness of Baur's hypothesis strikingly exhibits itself (compare the leading observations of this learned man, 79 sqq.), which, setting aside the followers of Peter, as well as the *Christianer*, considers the reference is to Greek influence. But is it not more natural to suppose that, in a city like Corinth, this influence would not have shown itself with regard to the doctrine of the resurrection alone, but may rather be supposed to have been concentrated in the *Christianer*, leaving to that of Peter the strict ceremonial observance of the Jewish Christians, together with the opposition to the apostolic authority of Paul, exactly as we see it in the Epistle to the Galatians?

† Geschichte der Pflanzung und Leitung der christlichen Kirche durch die Apostel. Hamburg, 1832. Part i. p. 296, sqq. Jäger also declares himself in favour of this view in its main points. See his work (über die Korinthierbriefe) upon the Epistles to the Corinthians, page 36.

diately through the apostles, had drawn it from the primitive
Gospel (!). The hypothesis, the foundation of which had already
been laid by the fathers, especially Chrysostom, and afterwards defended by Pott, Schott, Einleitung ins Neue Testament (Introduction to the New Testament), and Rückert, Commentar zum
ersten Briefe an die Korinthier (Commentary upon the first
Epistle to the Corinthians, pp. 43, 447), may be regarded as
long since refuted, for, according to 1 Cor. i. 12, 2 Cor. x. 7, it is
clear that Paul blamed the *Christianer*, regarding them as the
cause of division, which, if they remained neutral in the proper
sense of the word, certainly could not have occurred.* There
remains, consequently, only the hypothesis of Storr and Baur
which may claim a closer examination. The substance of Storr's
hypothesis is,† that the expression οἱ τοῦ Χριστοῦ refers to the
disciples of James, the brother of our Lord; as followers of this
kinsman of Christ, Storr considers that they had added the appellation, "belonging especially to Christ," as a mark of superiority.
Billroth and Baur have already proved that to this the name
οἱ τοῦ Χριστοῦ is in no degree suitable. The brothers of Christ,
and especially James, are never called οἱ ἀδελφοὶ τοῦ Χριστοῦ,
but τοῦ κυρίου. It follows, therefore, that the *Christianer* in
Corinth must be termed οἱ τοῦ κυρίου, or οἱ τοῦ Ἰησοῦ, for οἱ τοῦ
Χριστοῦ could not possibly be applied to the brothers of Jesus;
and we may further infer, that the followers of James were not to
be distinguished from those of Peter, consisting as they did of
strict Christian Jews. In short, all positive grounds for this
hypothesis fail, not only in the original form as laid down by
Storr, but also in the modification adopted by Bertholdt, who
considers the reference to be made not to James alone, but to
several brothers of our Lord. That the brethren of Christ and
James are mentioned 1 Cor. ix. 5, xv. 7, signifies nothing, inasmuch as this mention of them has no connexion with any ani-
madversion against the *Christianer*, or indeed against any
one in particular, the allusion to them being merely incidental.

* The hypothesis of Eichhorn, which Pott ranks before all others, is best supported by 1 Cor. iii. 22. Here all the four parties seem to be mentioned, and
that of the *Christianer* with praise. But that this is only in appearance, the explanation of the passage will show.

† This is detailed in the treatise Notitiæ historicae epistol. ad Cor. interpreta-
tioni servientes. It is printed in Storr's Opusc. Acad., vol. ii.

(Compare the Commentary on this place). But had a polemic reference existed in this passage, we should have been far more justified in attributing it to the adherents of Peter, if it had not been expressly directed against the *Christianer*, for the whole of chapter ix. agrees with their character; and as the doctrine of James, the brother of our Lord, was likewise Christian Jewish, he may certainly be placed, together with Peter, at their head. The γινώσκειν Χριστὸν κατὰ σάρκα (2 Cor. v. 16) bears other reference (as the further exposition of the passage will shew) than to the family circumstances of the Redeemer; this expression places Christ's entire human nature in opposition to his everlasting and heavenly being. The supposition of Baur (very ingeniously developed in the Tübinger Zeitschrift, 1831, pt. iv.), and for which also Billroth, with some slight modification, has decided, is so far identified with that of Storr, in that it connects the sect of Christ with that of Peter; so that Paul, in 1 Cor. i. 12, only indicates two principal parties, viz., that of Paul, including also the followers of Apollos, and that of Peter, in which the peculiar disciples of Peter and the *Christianer* have to be numbered. But Baur attributes a very different derivation from Storr to the name οἱ τοῦ Χριστοῦ, and besides defines much more closely the character of those who bore it. First of all, the distinguishing characteristic of the Judaists was a strict fulfilling of the outward law; according to Baur, this was the criterion by which the followers of Cephas were known.* Then they placed themselves in a polemic position with regard to Paul, attacking not only his teaching, but his apostolic authority, asserting that he was not a genuine disciple of Christ, but an apostate, styling themselves real disciples, because converted by those apostles who were chosen by Christ himself. Fundamentally, therefore, the party of Cephas and that of Christ were one and the same, though circumstances in Corinth seem to have been less favourable to those who held strict views. But if the question should occur, why, under these circumstances, any distinction should be made between the party of Cephas and that of Christ—why both should not have been included under the latter appellation—

* When Heidenreich considers the *Christianer* in the same light as these Judaists, he sets aside any distinction between the adherents of Cephas and the τοῦ Χριστοῦ, and takes up Storr's position, that no difference between these two parties was evident.

it may be replied that, by admitting this, the first Epistle contains nothing against the *Christianer*, for Paul does not therein explicitly defend his apostolic authority, and, besides this, the greater proportion of the subjects which are brought under consideration would thereby have no reference to the sects mentioned 1 Cor. i. 12, none of the latter having the particular tendency which, as we have shown above, so strongly marked the party of Cephas.* By admitting the supposition, however, that all the points touched upon in the Epistle have no reference to the particular divisions of the church, it requires a somewhat unconnected and inconsequent character, not to say that it is psychologically quite improbable, that such errors as the apostle opposes in the first Epistle were what might be termed sporadic, or without connexion with those fundamental doctrines, from which they might rather be considered to emanate, as branches from one stem. Upon these grounds we cannot decide in favour of Baur's hypothesis, without acknowledging that more can be urged in its favour than for Eichhorn's or Storr's, and Billroth justly remarks that some passages in the second Epistle appear to support it. In 2 Cor. iii. a literal as well as a spiritual parallel is instituted between the Old and New Testaments, in order to convince those persons who had as yet gained no view of the specific peculiarity of the Gospel. The important passage, x. 7, stands in such connexion with the controversy against false apostles (xi. 13, sqq., xii. 11), that the whole train of argument is very similar to that in the Epistle to the Galatians.† Paul here, as there, defends strongly his apostolic authority against false and treacherous apostles, who had attacked and cast suspicion upon it, and precisely because the expressions are so strong (especially in chap. xi. 13), one cannot conceive that they are applied to the real apostles (which are understood in Galatians ii. under δοκοῦντες),

---

* Except a few general remarks upon 1 Cor. i.–iv., Baur only quotes from the first Epistle, ix. 1, in which Paul says of himself τὸν κύριον ἑώρακα, which he considers may be referred to the opponents of the apostle, who made it a subject of reproach to him that he had *not* seen the Lord. (See reference already mentioned, p. 85–88). From the second Epistle, on the contrary, he deduces arguments which occupy from p. 89–114. But can that hypothesis be considered valid, which, casting aside the first and most important Epistle, rests for support upon the second alone?

† I pass over the passage 2 Cor. v. 16, so copiously treated, because the proof deduced therefrom by Baur appears very precarious. (See exposition of the passage).

for it is impossible that Paul could call these ψευδαπόστολοι. Besides, this name is equally applicable to the usurping heathen heterodox teachers, as to the Jewish, since they both alike contested Paul's authority, as may be seen in the Epistle to Timothy, (2 Tim. i. 15), and it is certain the opponents there named were not of Judaised, but rather heathen heretical opinions. Should it be attempted to prove anything for Baur's hypothesis as modified by Billroth, from 2 Cor. x. 7, in connexion with cap. xi. and xii., it can only be done by asserting that the passages quoted are applicable solely to Jewish heterodox teachers;* this is, however, impossible, and Baur himself allows (p. 99) that in 2 Cor. x. 7, not only the *Christianer*, but all the sects in Corinth collectively are intended; his views, therefore, derive no corroboration from the passages indicated. In short, weighing well the improbability of narrow-minded Jewish opinions predominately asserting themselves in a city like Corinth, whilst the more lax heathen principle (so much more acceptable) made no approach to an extreme point, we feel called upon to declare that, as no decided grounds for this view exist in the Epistles themselves, we do not feel inclined to entertain it. But by the supposition that the *Christianer* were an Ethnic party, the first Epistle especially gains an internal coherence which any other conjecture would fail to bestow. In the second Epistle, according to Baur, this harmony of connexion is not so deficient, and his theory appears considerably clearer, *by admitting the correctness of our conjecture that the apostle opposes equally the representatives of both the false sects, and directs his reproofs against the Christianer*

---

* The use that Baur makes of the vision, mentioned by Paul in the 12th chap. in defending his hypothesis, is very ingenious. He considers that Paul intended to oppose to the materialist opinions of the Jewish Christians, who asserted a personal instruction through Christ, the ideal effect—viz., the immediate production of faith by the working of the Spirit. But I fear that this would prove too much! It is by no means the intention of the apostle to say, that the spirit is able to raise at pleasure the church of Christ in any spot. "Faith comes only out of preaching." (See my Exposition, Rom. x. 14). Paul himself did not become a member of the church by the appearance of the Lord to him at Damascus; he was only led thereby to desire to be received into the church, and for this reception the word of Ananias and baptism were necessary. (See Comm., Acts ix. 17, sqq.) The parallels likewise which Baur quotes from the Clementines do not appear to me entirely applicable. It is probable Paul's motive for appealing to his vision was, that his opponents did the same; he will, consequently, as it were, say, "Behold, I can allege the same, and yet greater." The manner in which Paul speaks, in 1 Cor. xii.—xiv., of the misuse of the gifts, renders this not improbable.

*and likewise the adherents of Peter*, who, whatever their internal differences, were yet linked together in the attempt to obtain
opportunity for the propagation of their errors, by undermining
the authority of the great apostle of the Gentiles.    It is true
that Baur has likewise expressed his dissent from this view in
the Tübing. Zeitschr., 1836, part iv.; and though this learned
man may assert, with some show of reason, that Rückert errs in
stating that the identity, which the former supposes to exist between the partisans of Peter and Christ, is injurious to his own
hypothesis, his remarks, nevertheless, upon the views of Neander and myself must be considered to have failed.    He has evidently misunderstood Neander when he states that he ascribed
to the *Christianer* similar views to those entertained by the followers of Carpocrates* at a later period—that is to say, they
ranked Christ with Socrates as a great investigator of truth, and
therefore did not deserve the name of a Christian sect.    That
this was by no means the position of the *Christianer* is so apparent that it could not be Neander's opinion, for under such circum-

---

* [The philosophy of this schismatic did not differ in its general pirnciples from
that of the other Egyptian Gnostics.  For he admitted one supreme God, *Æons*,
the offspring of God, eternal and malignant matter, the creation of the world from
evil matter by angels, divine souls unfortunately enclosed in bodies, and the like.
But he maintained that *Jesus* was born of *Joseph* and *Mary*, in the ordinary course
of nature, and that he was superior to other men in nothing but fortitude and greatness of soul.    He also not only gave his disciples licence to sin, but imposed on
them, besides, a necessity of sinning, by teaching that the way to eternal salvation
was open to those souls only which had committed all kinds of enormity and wickedness.    But it is utterly beyond credibility that any man who believes that there
is a God, that *Christ* is the Saviour of mankind, and who inculcates any sort of
religion, should hold such sentiments.    Besides, there are grounds to believe that
*Carpocrates*, like the other Gnostics, held the Saviour to be composed of the man
*Jesus*, and a certain Æon called *Christ;* and that he imposed some laws of conduct
on his disciples.    Yet, undoubtedly, there was something in his opinions and precepts that rendered his piety very suspicious.    For he held that concupiscence
was implanted in the soul by the Deity, and is therefore perfectly innocent; that
all actions are in themselves indifferent, and become good or evil only according to
the opinions and laws of men; that in the purpose of God all things are common
property, even the women, but that such as use their rights are by human laws
counted thieves and adulterers.    Now, if he did not add some corrective to the
enormity of these principles, it must be acknowledged that he wholly swept away
the foundations of all virtue, and gave full licence to all iniquity.  See Irenæus,
*contra Hæres.* l. i. c. 25 ; Clemens Alex. *Stromat.* l. iii. p. 510, and the others.
(Mosheim *de Rebus Christi*, &c., p. 361—371 ; C. W. F. Walch, *Histore der Ketzer*,
vol. i. p. 309—329 ; A. Neander, *Kirchengesch.* vol. i. pt. ii. p. 767—773 ; Mosheim's *Institutes of Eccl. Hist.*, vol. i. pp. 198, 9.   Ed. (Soames) Lond. 1845].

stances Paul would not have troubled himself to maintain the unity of the church, but would have immediately required the expulsion of the heterodox teachers from their body. (See Gal. v. 4; Tit. iii. 10). Neander doubtless intends only to say (p. 301) that the *Christianer* were willing to profess the doctrine of Christ, omitting the Jewish form; and indefinite as the expression may be, it is probable that the words of Neander, " Christ appeared to them a second, perhaps more perfect, Socrates," would only declare that they had looked upon Christ as something more than human. In the more recent article of Baur's, before alluded to, there occurs nothing of weight or consequence affecting the correctness of the supposition that the *Christianer* entertained Ethnic opinions. The members of this sect were very likely converted by those who looked to Paul as their head, and believing themselves called upon to free themselves from all human attachments and national prejudices, they consequently shaped for themselves a course of living and doctrine, without however as yet touching upon the limits of heresy. It would be surprising if, in the ancient church, and especially in a city like Corinth, such a party had not formed itself. The Marcionites and other Gnostic sects prove the early existence of such tendencies, from which their own rise at a subsequent period may be dated. What, therefore, more natural than to perceive here a trace of their existence, especially as the supposition of the identity with the followers of Cephas, only a slight difference laid down by Baur and Billroth, is undeniably something very like a forced conclusion?

According to this view it is irrefragable that the Epistles to the Corinthians were excited by circumstances which had reference purely to the apostolic time, while in the Epistle to the Romans the contents of the Gospel as objective are brought under consideration. Not that we are justified in inferring from them that the former have only an historical importance; many passages are pregnant with meaning for the later periods of the church, and especially for the present age. In the condition of the Apostolic church the state of the church at every period is reflected, and above all under its present circumstances. The principal danger which threatened so many members of the existing church in Corinth is likewise the chief evil of our own times —an over-estimation of human wisdom, instead of godly ever-

lasting truth, an universal laxity and indifference in the most important social ties, viz., in the relation between the sexes, a
neglect of powerful biblical realism, and a predominance of the
subjective restraints assigned to them instead of the objective.
For this reason, precisely at the present moment, the Epistles
to the Corinthians possess an inclusive and palpable importance,
and this will be daily more acknowledged as the conviction
spreads, that for everything contained in the Scriptures the final
norm is given.   The weighty discussion of the Charismata (1 Cor.
xii. 14) only remains as unintelligible to our times as to earlier
ages, since, from the period of the apostles, these gifts are lost,
and even the intuition of many among them—for example, the
gift of tongues has long since vanished.   But as the looking for
these has begun again to exhibit itself, it may be inferred that the
gifts themselves may be restored to the church of Christ as the
final development of the same draws nigh, by which the end is to
be made conformable to the beginning in the chief points.   The
internal development of the church will therefore also in this respect assist to perfect the exposition.


§ 2. CONNEXION OF PAUL WITH THE CORINTHIAN CHURCH.

The question which occurs next in order to that referring to
the position of the various parties in Corinth is, how Paul conducted himself towards the Corinthian church,—that is to say,
how often he visited them, and how many Epistles he wrote
to them.   The Acts of the Apostles, and the accounts contained in the Epistles to the Corinthians, convey to us the following
particulars.
The old city of Corinth, as is well known, was destroyed by
Mummius B.C. 146, and remained in ruins until Julius Cæsar
planted a Roman colony in it, endowing it with great privileges.
Paul first appeared in Julius Cæsar's newly-restored city, while
prosecuting his second journey in connexion with his mission
(Acts xviii. 1, sqq.)   He found there Aquila and Priscilla, who,
by the command of the Emperor Claudius, had been driven out
of Rome (Suet. Claud. c. 25), and preached one year and six
months, after receiving in a vision the assurance that in this city
a large number were to be found, of whom God was known, and

whom it was his purpose to protect. The consequences of his preaching were so extraordinary, that, deeply sunk as that city was in pleasures and excess, a large Christian community arose therein, and even Crispus, the ruler of the synagogue, included himself therein. In consequence of this a tumult, directed against Paul, arose among the Jews, which required the wisdom and mildness of Gallio, the proconsul, a brother of the celebrated philosopher Seneca, to allay (Tacit. Annal. xvi. 7). After the lapse of a year and a half, taking Aquila and Priscilla with him, Paul passed over into Ephesus, where he left them, on his way to Jerusalem; but the apostle himself stayed there only a short time, promising before long to return thither, (Acts xviii. 18, sqq.) In the meantime there came to Ephesus a learned Alexandrian Jew, the famous Apollos, a true disciple of John the Baptist, viz., one who viewed him only as the forerunner of the Messiah, and not as the Messiah himself, as some of John's disciples falsely asserted him to be. This man, convinced by Aquila of the Messiahship of Jesus, and filled with the new faith, passed over into Corinth, taking with him written commendations to the disciples there, and soon distinguished himself. While Apollos was thus labouring in Corinth, Paul came back to Ephesus from Jerusalem, to which place Apollos also returned at a later period (Acts xix. 1 ; 1 Cor. xvi. 12) ; and here the apostle remained two years and three months (Acts xix. 8, 10). During this time Paul received sorrowful information respecting the condition of the church in Corinth. A member of this body was living in illicit intercourse with his father's wife, consequently his own stepmother; and the other members had so little right or moral feeling relative to such matters, that they nevertheless suffered the offender to continue one of their body. This impelled the apostle to address an epistle to the Christians in Corinth, in which he exhorts them to avoid the company of sinners and the dissolute (1 Cor. v. 9). This *first* Epistle is lost. It is true that there exists another Epistle to the Corinthians, differing from either of those we possess, as well as one from the latter to Paul, both in the Armenian language, but Carpzov (Leipsic 1776) has already triumphantly proved that they are not genuine.* More

* The Epistles of Paul first appeared in "Histoire Critique de la Republique des Lettres," Amsterd. 1714, tom. x., but incomplete. William Whiston pub-

recently Rink, who was long an evangelic preacher in Venice, edited the Epistles (Heidelberg, 1823. 8.), and the Armenian Monk Aucher, of the Convent of San Lazaro, near Venice, at the conclusion of his Armenian Grammar, has critically revised and republished the Armenian text (Venice, 1819); but Rink's attempt to defend the authenticity of the Epistles has been fundamentally confuted by Ullman (Heidelberger Jahrbuch, 1823, pt. vi.) The first Epistle of Paul therefore remains lost to us. The Corinthians replied to it, and it is probable that this was delivered to the apostle by the hands of Stephanus, Fortunatus, and Achaicus (1 Cor. xvi. 18, 19). Partly by means of this reply, and the verbal information of the messengers specified, and partly through the slaves of the Corinthian matron Chloe (1 Cor. i. 11), Paul received further intelligence of the circumstances of the Corinthian church, which drew from him the second Epistle, preserved in our *first* Epistle of Paul to the Corinthians. When the apostle composed it he was still in Ephesus, purposing to remain there until Pentecost (1 Cor. xvi. 8), and it is probable that the season in which he wrote was either spring or autumn, and undoubtedly in the year 59. But Paul had scarcely dispatched our first Epistle to Corinth when the tumult occasioned by the goldsmith Demetrius broke out in Ephesus, which compelled the apostle to leave the city before Pentecost and to depart into Macedonia (Acts xix. 1, sqq.), where he anxiously awaited intelligence of the effect produced by the letter referred to (2 Cor. ii. 13, 14), being desirous of ascertaining the feeling of the various parties in reference to this before he himself appeared in Corinth as he proposed. Paul, therefore, was expecting the return of Timotheus to Macedonia from Corinth, whither he had sent him (1 Cor. iv. 17). But whether it was that Timotheus had already quitted that city before the arrival of Paul's Epistle, or that he had not yet reached it, it is certain that the apostle did not receive the desired intelligence through him, for which reason he sent Titus to Corinth, and during the interval of his absence journeyed through Macedonia (2 Cor. ii. 13). Upon the return of Titus, Paul wrote *our second* Epistle,

lished them entire, together with the pretended letter of the Corinthians to Paul, at the end of his Historia Armeniæ Mosis Choronensis. Lond. 1736, 4. Carpzov's Work bears the title: Epistolae duae apocryphae, altera Corinthiorum ad Paulum, altera Paula ad Corinthios. Lips. 1776. 8.

in order to awaken the frame of mind which he desired to behold among the Corinthians when he himself should visit them (2 Cor. vii. 7, sqq.), and in it the apostle praises the well-intentioned members of their church (viz., the followers of Paul and Apollos) for their obedience to his commands, and likewise for their repentant spirit; but, on the contrary, he strongly reproves the contumacious (viz., the adherents of Peter, and the *Christianer* above all), because they had despised his most serious exhortations, and their presumption had only increased. This, our second Epistle, was sent by Titus and two brethren, not mentioned by name, (2 Cor. viii. 16, sqq.), to Corinth. The apostle intending shortly to follow, one of these brethren was possibly Luke, and this is inferred partly because the description in the place above indicated is directly applicable to him, and also because his name stands in the subscription at the conclusion of the Epistle; and as Luke, in the Acts of the Apostles (xx. 1), recommences his narration in the third person, having hitherto written in the first, we may conclude that he must have left the apostle in Macedonia.

This is the original account of the occasion upon which the Epistles to the Corinthians were written, as well as the periods at which they were composed. In the most important points it is thoroughly correct, for it rests upon passages to be found in the Acts of the Apostles, as well as in the Epistles themselves. But more recently, the scrutiny instituted by Bleek and Schrader* into the events which, according to our canon, took place between the drawing up of the first and second Epistle, has elicited results which undoubtedly claim a preference over the older and more uncertain account. According to these, at the period the apostle wrote our second Epistle, he had not been again in Corinth, but this supposition is negatived by several places in this Epistle, viz., xii. 14, xiii. 1, in which a third coming is mentioned. It is true that the first of these places is usually explained by the τρίτον being understood of the wish for the coming, and not the coming itself, but this does not agree with the context, which undoubtedly refers to a fact, adverted to in xiii. 1, as decided upon (compare further the exposition of this place); and there is the more reason for taking this view of the passage, as the follow-

* Bleek, in an Article in the Stud. und Kritiken, Jahrg. 1830, page 614, sqq. Schrader Der Apostel Paulus. 1. Pt. p. 95, sqq.

ing verse (xiii. 2) contains an intimation announced during the
second stay, viz., that proofs of forgiveness and indulgence would
not be repeated.

If we assume only one residence of Paul in Corinth, at the
time of the establishment of the church itself, then there could
have arisen no occasion for forgiveness; and this supposition could
by no means be made to agree with the passage ii. 1, xii. 21, in
which mention is made of the renewal of the grief of the Corinthians upon the occasion of his coming, which of course bore no
reference to his appearance among them as an individual.  Consequently, Paul must undoubtedly have made a second journey to
Corinth, but when did it take place?  The original account may
be adopted if we suppose that when Luke mentions a stay of a
year and a half in Corinth made by Paul, he has taken together
two separate periods of residence.  But to this one objection
presents itself, as in this case we must allow that in the short
period which elapsed between the first and second stay, all the
errors which became the subject of reproof had opportunity to
develope themselves.  The only remaining inference, therefore, is,
that the second visit to the Corinthians is perfectly distinct from
the one of a year and a half's duration, and that it occurred either
*before* the writing of the first, or *between* the sending of the first
and second Epistle.  We may imagine the course of events to have
been this.  As soon as Paul had received the intelligence from
the slaves of Chloe as to the condition of the Corinthians, he
wrote our first Epistle, and shortly after quitted Ephesus for
Corinth.  He here expressed himself in strong terms against his
adversaries, but, from some cause unknown to us, he soon left the
city, returning again into Macedonia.  Now, in decided opposition to this view, are the passages 2 Cor. i. 15, 16, 23, which
shew that Paul could not have been in Corinth in the period that
occurs between the writing of our two Epistles.*  The most

---

* This circumstance, it cannot be denied, is unfavourable to the whole hypothesis, since the first Epistle (1 Cor. i. 11, v. 1, xi. 18), supposed to be written after
the second personal abode of the apostle in Corinth, represents the apostle as becoming acquainted with the affairs of the Christian church in that place from report
only, and not from personal inspection.   This is also the opinion of De Wette, in
the criticism upon Billroth's Commentary in the Stud. Jahrg. 1834, part 3, page
683.  An explanation of this is offered by Böttger (Beitr. part 3, p. 28), who supposes that Paul intentionally refrained from going to Corinth, visiting only Achaia
and the churches in the neighbourhood of Corinth.

probable inference, therefore, is, that upon receiving these evil reports, the apostle immediately proceeded from Ephesus to Corinth, and returning to the former place, wrote and sent from thence our first Epistle. Bleek, however, imagines, that before the sending of our second Epistle, the apostle wrote an Epistle from Macedonia to the Corinthians, couched in terms of strong reproof, which has not been preserved, (so that Paul wrote to them in all four Epistles, two being lost and two preserved), and I am much inclined to support this conjecture,* for the apprehension experienced by Paul in regard to the impression produced upon the Corinthians by his Epistle, which the arrival of Titus allayed, (2 Cor. vii. 2—10), is not to be accounted for by the subject of the first Epistle. The contents are by no means of a nature to justify Paul in his fears of an unfavourable reception; but by assuming that Titus was likewise the bearer of the lost Epistle, we account in the most simple manner for the motive of his journey, and all the difficulties relative to this which present themselves by following the old conjecture, at once vanish.

## § 3. GENUINENESS AND INTEGRITY OF THE EPISTLES.

The Epistles to the Corinthians, as well as that to the Romans, may be classed with those in which the spirit of Paul stands forth so pre-eminently, that an attempt to dispute their authenticity has never been made, either in ancient or modern times. Contents and form correspond alike with the ideas and style of Paul, and the strictest coincidence exists between the historical notices of the Acts of the Apostles and those occasionally found

---

\* Rückert (Comm. upon the 2d Epis. Cor. p. 417, sqq.) opposes this hypothesis of Bleek's, relative to the sending of an Epistle between the first and second of our canonical Epistles, and it must be allowed that the grounds upon which this is laid down are not sufficient to furnish any positive proof of the same. Nevertheless, the conjecture itself is by no means improbable, as Rückert admits no internal traces of the condition of mind which Paul describes as existing in himself, characterising the early Epistle in question. But this learned man has inferred too much from 2 Cor. vii. 8, in stating that as Paul wrote ἐλύπησα ἡμᾶς ἐν τῇ ἐπιστολῇ, he could only have written one letter in heaviness of mind, and not two. The expression naturally concerns only the last Epistle, bearing not the slightest reference to an earlier one, otherwise Paul must have used the plural form, for according to 1 Cor. v. 9, he had already written an Epistle whose contents were those of sad reproof.

in these Epistles.   The style of the second Epistle is very striking,
on account of a certain ruggedness of speech, occasioned by the
powerful agitation of spirit under which he wrote, and the
haste with which it was composed during his journeys in various
parts of Macedonia.   But, notwithstanding the roughness of
style, the second Epistle bears too strongly the impress of Paul's
peculiarities to be mistaken, though we are not disposed to proceed as far as Rückert, who views it as a masterpiece of eloquence,
worthy of comparison with the orations of Demosthenes de Corona.
(See his exposition of the second Epistle, p. 427).

But although the genuineness of the Epistles to the Corinthians
is fully established and undisputed, we cannot premise as much
of their integrity, at least of the second.   It was J. S. Semler
who first drew attention to the difference in the first (2 Cor. i.—viii.)
and second division (ix.—xiii.) of the Epistle.   In the first eight
chapters Paul speaks mildly and persuasively, praises his readers
for their repentance and faithful observance of his exhortations,
while in the latter chapters the tone is that of reproach and
severity.   He reprehends the refractory spirit of the Corinthians,
and complains of the charges which they had dared to bring
against him.   Besides this, the same subjects seem to be discussed in the first (cap. viii.) and second part of the Epistle (cap. ix.),
which leads Semler to suppose that an interpolation in the latter
Epistle might have taken place.*   According to him the real
Epistle is formed by the chapters i.—viii. inclusive, to which may
be annexed from the 11—13 ver. of the xiii. cap., and very singularly Rom. xvi. 1—20, and therefore the passages ix. 1—15, and
x. 1—13, 10. are interpolations.   Weber and Dr Paulus, however,
rather consider the second half of the second Epistle as another
letter, agreeing in all necessary points with the usual form;† and
this opinion may stand in connexion with Bleek's views, which
we recently investigated (§ 2) as to Paul's position towards the
Corinthian church.   We see that probably between our first and

* See Semler De duplice appendice epist. ad Romanos.   Halae 1767, and the
Paraphrasis poster. epist. ad Corinthios. Halae 1776.   Ziegler wrote against this
in the Theolog. Abhandl. vol. ii. p. 107, sqq. ; also Gabler in the Neuesten Theolog.
Journal, vol. 1.

† See Weber's work De numero Epistolarum ad Corinthios rectius constituendo.
Wittebergae, 1798.   Weber considered the Epistle to the Hebrews directed likewise to the Corinthians, and therefore reckons four Epistles to the Corinthians in the
canon.  Consult the Heidelberg Chronicle (Heidelberger Jahrbücher, 5, p. 703, sqq.)

second Epistle another had been composed by the apostle. If we consider this to exist in the first half of our second Epistle (2 Cor. i.—viii.), then only one Epistle is lost, that alluded to 1 Cor. v. 9. But the decided admission of this supposition is forbidden by the fact that in 2 Cor. vii. 2—10 the apostle makes allusion to a prior Epistle (which must have been written between our first and second), containing words of strong reproof, while 2 Cor. i.—viii. is distinguished throughout by gentleness and forbearance; and an inversion appears far from probable, which placed the reproving Epistle, 2 Cor. ix.—xiii., and the milder one which succeeded, 2 Cor. i.—viii. Again, this would materially affect the chronological connexion of the Epistles, passing over the additional fact that this fusion of two Epistles, with omission of the greeting and concluding form of one of them, is not by any means to be explained. To this may be added that the repetition alluded to (the exhortation to the collection) in chapters viii. and ix. is nothing more than the continuous exposition of a thought, the tone of the ninth chapter is precisely similar, the change occurring in the tenth. In the meantime the establishment of the integrity of the Epistle is certainly preferable to any attempts at reconciling the various hypotheses, and this would be best promoted by explaining satisfactorily the reason of the difference of tone in the first and second half of it.

This explanation would be furnished by supposing that the apostle was addressing different members in the Corinthian church in the two divisions of the Epistle. His first Epistle had drawn the well-disposed more towards him, while at the same time it aroused in the unfriendly a stronger spirit of opposition, thus occasioning a separation of the elements in Corinth. In the first half of the second epistle he had the better-disposed part of the community in view, viz., the partizans of Paul and Apollos; in the second, on the contrary, he directs himself especially to the adverse party, consisting of partizans of Peter, and, above all, the *Christianer*. Should any one observe upon the improbability that Paul addressed a catholic letter to elements so dissimilar, or that having done so, he should not have plainly indicated the different persons he was addressing, but write as if in both first and second parts he had still the same imdividuals in view, it would be as well to remind such persons, that Paul's compassion and charity restrainel

him from marking out the erring members, or even distinctly
warning them, so long as they abstained from attacking the fundamental articles of the faith.  He rightly judged, too, that such
a particularization would greatly increase the difficulty of freeing them from their errors, and winning them back to the truth
(an object he seems ever to have had in view), and he continued therefore to treat them as an integral part of God's
church, addressing the latter as a united body, without completely distinguishing the composing elements.  Exactly as a wise
pastor would deal with a believing, but in many respects erring
individual, he joyfully acknowledged what was improved in him,
and while reproving what was reprovable, did not on this account
reject the whole man.  The very form of the Epistles to the
Corinthians exhibits strongly the wisdom of the apostle, and his
faithful love towards erring brethren, who so frequently in the
church (and, alas, the same may be observed in our days), were
hindered by an unholy and intemperate zeal in the face of the
brightest Gospel light.  Had Paul commanded the expulsion
from the church of his adversaries in Corinth, either on account
of their Gnostic spiritual views regarding the resurrection, or of
their errors with respect to the holy communion, he would only
with more certainty have given currency to the corruption.*  He
treated them, therefore, as weak members, not knowing what they
said or ventured; bore even with indulgence their opposition
to his apostolic authority (although, had not his humility rendered it impossible, he might easily have persuaded himself that
therein God was resisted), and yielded nothing of the sacred
truths ; but upon the suspicion evincing itself that he commended himself, and boasted of his extraordinary calling, he
openly declared what the Lord had done to and ·by him, and

---

* This is most important in proving that Paul did not hold the opinion concerning the Lord's Supper as fundamental ; for which reason dogmatic differences
concerning the same, and the variation in the theory of Luther and Calvin upon
the same subject, which affect not the dogma itself, but simply a point of the doctrine,
do not justify the exclusion of any one from the community.  Paul declares in the
Epistle to the Galatians that whoever suffered himself to be circumcised in order
thereby to attain salvation, to him Christ had become of none effect (Galat. v. 3, 4),
not so he who erred in the doctrine of the Lord's Supper.  The real ground of the
separation of the reformers from the Catholic church, was not the doctrine of the
Lord's Supper, but the doctrine of free grace in Christ, and the reformers had a
perfect right to separate themselves, on account of the errors in this doctrine.

showed that his care and intention was to preserve the fundamental articles of the Christian faith uninjured.

## § 4. CONTENTS OF THE EPISTLES TO THE CORINTHIANS.

The *first* Epistle is transmitted to us in *four* parts; the *first* of
which extends from i. 1—iv. 21, the *second* from v. 1—xi. 1, the
*third* from xi. 2—xiv. 40, and the *fourth* from xv. 1—xvi. 24.

In the *first division*, which treats of the general condition of
the Corinthians, the apostle mentions the cause of his writing,
the divison of the church into numerous parties, and warns
against a too high estimation of the wisdom of this world, since
all real wisdom rests in the cross of Christ (i. 1—31). Paul
then continues the subject, saying that he has only preached to
them the Lord crucified, as the source of perfect wisdom, but that
the spiritual man alone, and not the natural, is capable of acknowledging His gloriousness (ii. 1—16). That the ground of their
errors was, that this spiritual man was so little developed in them,
that they attached themselves not to Christ himself, but to the
human organ whom Christ had made use of to extend the preaching of the Gospel, and that they were therefore in imminent
danger of building upon a perishable foundation (iii. 1—23). He
himself felt so firmly persuaded of his apostolic calling, that human
judgment produced no effect upon him, and that the numerous
sufferings he was called upon to endure, were evidence in his
favour, instead of the contrary, as tending to his perfectness;
therefore Paul implores the Corinthian Christians not to suffer
themselves to be drawn aside to any other gospel than that which
he, their father in Christ, had preached to them.

In the *second part* (v. 1—xi. 1), which concerns the private
circumstances of several individuals, Paul first exhorts the Corinthians to exclude the incestuous person from their society, and
at the same time defines more closely the command previously
given in the last Epistle, not to have any intercourse with the
dissolute, intending thereby such persons who nevertheless considered themselves believers (v. 1—13). Paul then bestows
advice to the faithful with reference to heathen rulers; and considers it unsuitable to permit the settlement of their differences
before the latter, but he soon returns to the relation of the sexes,

and adds that the sanctification of the body as a temple of the
Holy Ghost, is the Christian's task (vi. 1—20). The various
relations of the married and unmarried state are then brought
under consideration (vii. 1—40), and he concludes with instruc-
tions upon the subject of Christian freedom, having especial
reference to the use of meats offered to idols. The apostle adduces his own course of life as an example to the Corinthians, of
the necessary self-restriction in the use of freedom; and exhibits
the sad consequences of its misuse in the history of the Israelites
in the wilderness (viii. 1—xi. 1).

The *third part* (xi. 2—xiv. 40) concerns the public relations of
the Christians, viz., their conduct in the assemblies; and the apostle
*first* gives directions relative to the appearance of men and women
in their meetings, (xi. 1—16), but especially for the worthy celebration of the holy Sacrament, which the Corinthians had not solemnized
with due dignity (xi. 17—34). *After this* he enters upon the subject of the gift of tongues, and its connexion with the Charismata,
which seems to have displayed themselves in the Corinthian church
under the most varied forms, and were not unfrequently applied in a
measure alien to the design. Paul lays down as a principal rule that
all these gifts originating from one spirit, must be employed to
one great end, viz., the edification of the whole body (xii. 1—31),
and that with an especial regard to the unity in Christ. The
apostle then inculcates the exercise of Christian love as of more
value than all gifts, the latter being, as it were, worthless without
the accompaniment of the former; and Paul defines its nature in
the most animated description, drawn from his own experience,
placing it with faith and hope as the third cardinal virtue (xiii.
1—13). In conclusion, Paul enlarges upon the true use of the
gift of tongues and prophecy, showing that from its nature
the first required a very cautious application, while the quality of
the second was in itself a hinderance to its abuse (xiv. 1—40).

In the *fourth part* (xv. 1—xvi. 24) the apostle finally discourses
upon the doctrine of the resurrection of the body, which the Christians had not been able to receive in its spiritual application,
(xv. 12). He proves the reality of the corporeal resurrection, showing its close connexion with the existence of the Christian faith
(xv. 1—58), and concludes by requesting contributions for the
poor Christians in Jerusalem, and with sundry exhortations and
blessings (xvi. 1—24).

By this it will appear that the points treated by the apostle in his writing are extremely varied in their nature; nevertheless a strong thread of connexion is evident throughout, in the polemic directed against the followers of Peter, and, above all, the *Christianer*, who, by their leaning towards a false freedom and spiritual gnosis, were preparing a dangerous crisis for the church.

The *second Epistle* to the Corinthians divides itself into *three* parts, the *first* of which may be included from i. 1—iii. 18, the *second* from iv. 1—ix. 15, and the *third* from x. 1—xiii. 13.

In the *first part* Paul commences with the comfort he has experienced in his afflictions, referring it to the power of the intercessions of the Corinthian Christians (i. 1—24). He then declares, with reference to the incestuous person already excommunicated, that upon proof of sufficient punishment, he may be received back into the church (ii. 1—17). He next speaks of his own personal position relative to the Corinthians, and entering into a comparison of the ministration under the old and the new law, proves that the latter is far more glorious (iii. 1—18).

In the *second part* (iv. 1—ix. 15) the apostle describes his life and labour as a minister preaching reconciliation through Christ, (iv. 1—18), and draws consolation in all the afflictions and dangers which arise from the office, from the conviction that a resurrection of the body awaits the believer, perhaps even a clothing upon (v. 1—21). In the expectation of this exceeding gloriousness, which renders all earthly persecutions of little moment, the apostle exhorts his readers to deny the world and its lusts, and to dedicate themselves wholly to the Lord (vi. 1–vii. 1). In this he hopes to have prepared them by his former Epistle, the uneasiness which he experienced as to its reception having been allayed by Titus (vii. 2—16). Then follows an ample exhortation to contribute to the collection making for the poor Christians at Jerusalem (viii. 1—ix. 15).

In the *third part* (x. 1—xiii. 13), Paul directs himself against the false teachers, namely, those among the *Christianer*, and defends himself from their attacks (x. 1—18). He then adduces his sufferings and struggles as a proof that he had done more, and effected greater things in God's cause than those arrogant, but treacherous workers who ranked themselves among the apostles of Christ, without being really so (xi. 1—33). He reminds them of the especial instances of favour accorded to him by God, as a proof that he stood in grace, but adds that he would rather glory in his weakness, for thereby he would best know his strength in the Lord. He had therefore a legal right to rank himself with the chiefest apostles, and requires the Corinthians to acknowledge his apostolic authority (xii. 1—21). An exhortation to repentance, love, and peace, concludes the second Epistle to the Corinthians (xiii. 1—13).

## § 5. LITERATURE.

The Epistles to the Corinthians are naturally comprehended in all the preceding general works upon the entire New Testament, and also in the Expositions of Paul's Epistles. But there exist fewer *special* examinations of these Epistles than of the Epistles to the Romans and Galatians, for example, and those which we do possess leave us much to desire. A favourable period for the interpretation of the Epistles to the Corinthians (and the Catholic Epistles likewise) has yet to present itself.

Upon the *two Epistles* to the Corinthians we have commentaries from Mosheim (Flensburg, 1741 and 1762, 2 vols. 4to); Baumgarten (Halle, 1761, 4to); Semler (Halle, 1770 and 1766, 2 vols. 8vo); Moldenhawer (Hamburg, 1771, 8vo); Schulz (Halle, 1784, 2 parts, 8vo); Morus (Leipsig, 1794, 8vo); Flatt (Tübingen, 1827); Billroth (Leipsig, 1833), translated in Clarks' Biblical Cabinet, vols. 21 and 23; Rückert (Leipsig, 1836–37); and Jaeger (Tübingen, 1838).

The *first* Epistle only has been treated upon by Sahl (Copenhagen, 1779); Fr. Aug. Wilhelm Krause (Frankfort, 1792, 8vo); Heidenreich (Marburg, 1825 and 1828, 2 vols. 8vo); Pott (in Koppe's Neuen Testament, Göttingen, 1836. But up to the present time only the first half has appeared, containing ch. i.—x.

The *second* Epistle only has been explained by Leun (Lemgo, 1804), and Emmerling (Leipsig, 1823). Treatises upon particular passages of the second Epistle have appeared from Gabler (Göttingen, 1782, upon chap. ix.—xiii.); J. F. Krause (in his Opusc. Acad. Königsberg, 1818); Royaards (Utrecht, 1818); Fritzsche (Leipsig, 1824).

# EXPOSITION

OF THE

# FIRST EPISTLE TO THE CORINTHIANS.

## I.

## PART FIRST.

### (i. 1—iv. 21).

### § 1. OF HUMAN WISDOM.

### (i. 1—31).

AFTER the greeting (1—3) the apostle mentions immediately
the reason of his writing, namely, the divisions in Corinth; he then
proceeds to warn his readers in the most impressive manner
against that particular worldly wisdom which he considers the
cause of the dissensions, and places before them as a pattern the
true godly wisdom, "Christ crucified," whom he has preached to
them (4—31).

Paul commences the first Epistle to the Corinthians, as usual,
with a salutation and blessing (1–3); but if we compare this
salutation with that which begins the Epistle to the Romans, it
appears far more concise and incomplete than the latter. It is
only in the second verse that the apostle makes some reference
to his readers, and even this is wanting in the second Epistle, as
well as in the greater part of the lesser Epistles of Paul. Theophylact considers, and with reason, that in the διὰ θελήματος
Θεοῦ, a reference, though slight (compare the stronger expressions
in Galatians i. 1), may be found to the opposition offered to his
apostolic authority. The addition of the epithet κλητὸς in
this place is less difficult to account for, than its omission in
A.D.E. would be, where it is not to be found; and this leads us

to entertain doubts of its genuineness, for we cannot conclude
with Heidenreich that κλητὸς should immediately join διὰ θελήματος Θεοῦ; had this been intended κλητὸς would have been
placed before these words, and after Χριστοῦ. In addition to
which the expression κλητὸς has not here, as in ver. 2, the peculiar
dogmatic signification, according to which the Christians, as elect,
are described as called to an entrance into the kingdom of God;
but it rather stands in opposition to those who on their own
authority gave themselves out as apostles (2 Cor. xi. 13). Paul
must undoubtedly have already felt that he had received a mission,
and that he likewise was called to fulfil it, but he probably also remembered that such a charge might be self-assumed by men, as the
Old Testament shows, by speaking of those who prophesied in their
own spirit (Ezek. xiii. 1, sqq.), and were yet distinguished from
those evil prophets out of whom the spirit of darkness spake.—
Sosthenes, whom the apostle names with himself in the salutation,
is probably the writer of the Epistle, to whom Paul dictated. He is
sometimes considered to be the chief ruler of the synagogue, mentioned in Acts xviii. 17, who must then have been subsequently converted; but as we find no further trace of this individual, nothing
certain can be concluded as to the identity of the persons. By supplying χαίρειν λέγουσι, in the second verse, it becomes unnecessary
to admit with Billroth an anacoluthon in the χάρις and εἰρήνη of
ver. 3, as if the accusative must be placed, and is therefore to be
preferred. All the apostle's salutations are arranged to comprehend himself in the blessing, by supplying ἔστω, and Paul again
distinguishes the church of God* in Corinth (i. e. those belonging

* Calvin very strikingly remarks in this place: " Mirum forsan videri queat,
cur eam hominum multitudinem vocet ecclesiam Dei, in qua tot morbi invaluerant,
ut Satan illis potius regnum occuparet, quam Deus.    Respondeo, utcunque multa
vitia obrepsissent, et variae corruptelae tam doctrinae quam morum, exstitisse tamen
adhuc quaedam verae ecclesiae signa.    Locus diligenter observandus, ne requiramus
in hoc mundo ecclesiam omni ruga et macula carentem, aut protinus abdicemus hoc
titulo quemvis coetum, in quo non omnia votis nostris respondeant.    Est enim haec
periculosa tentatio, nullam ecclesiam putare, ubi non appareat perfecta puritas.
*Nam quicunque hac occupatus fuerit, necesse tandem erit, ut, discessione ab aliis omni-
bus facta, solus sibi sanctus videatur in mundo, aut peculiarem sectam cum paucis
hypocritis instituat.*    Quid ergo causae habuit Paulus, cur ecclesiam Dei Corinthi
agnosceret? nempe quia evangelii doctrinam, baptismum, coenam Domini, quibus
symbolis censeri debet ecclesia, apud eos cernebat."    Most important words! which
in these times we have great reason to lay much to heart.—[See Calvin's Comment. on 1 Cor. cap. i. 2, pp. 50, 1.—Ed. Calv. Transl. Soc.]

to God, whom he hath purchased with his own blood (Acts xx. 28) as ἡγιασμένοις ἐν Χριστῷ, and as κλητοὶς ἁγίοις, upon which the necessary observations have been made at Rom. i. 7.* It might appear that the placing together ἡγιασμένοις and ἁγίοις was tautology,† but the second expression is first in concrete opposition to the abstract ἐκκλησία τοῦ Θεοῦ, and then it is to be so connected with what follows, that the idea of sanctification, especially as extended to believers, again presents itself. The text might be thus translated, "Those sanctified in Christ, by communion with him, who, as likewise all who call upon the name of the Lord, are called to be saints;" that is to say, according to the apostle's meaning, " should be," for the following remark involves an exhortation to the Corinthians (as shall be presently shewn), to make manifest their calling by their works. The phrase σὺν πᾶσι κ.τ.λ., is, however, quite peculiar to the commencement of this Epistle. First, it is clear that the words are not to be understood as if Paul wrote primarily to the Christians in Corinth, and secondly, it also was intended for the instruction of others elsewhere; for the whole contents of the Epistle are specially addressed to the Corinthian Church.‡ The phrase only represents, by the repetition of κλητοὶς ἁγίοις and its connexion with σὺν πᾶσι, the universal Christian character of sanctification, and describes the calling thereunto as familiar to and common to them all. Ἐπικαλεῖσθαι ὄνομα=קָרָא בְּשֵׁם is, however, a very usual mode of expressing a life of faith, the necessary expression§ of which is continual calling upon God.

The question now occurs, as to the reasons which led the apostle to enter upon the subject precisely in this place? With-

* [See Olshausen's Exposition of the Epistle to the Romans, p. 69, F.T. Lib.]

† Lücke (Gött. Pfingstprogramm, vom J. 1837) considers ἡγιασμένοις might be removed as simply gloss, but we see no reason to adopt his supposition.

‡ Billroth considers that the words may be connected with the whole salutation, and thus construed, " to you, and to all believers, mercy and peace," without inferring that the Epistle is addressed to all; but certainly the supposition is untenable, the greeting of an Epistle can only be directed to those to whom the Epistle is written. It would be better to place the words κλητοῖς ἁγίοις—αὐτῶν τε καὶ ἡμῶν in brackets, as in the additions to the greeting of the Epistle to the Romans.

§ The supposition of Mosheim, that in ver. 2 three distinct classes of Corinthian Christians are indicated, viz., in the expression ἡγιασμένοι ἐν Χριστῷ the old approved Christians, in κλητοί ἁγιοι, the newly baptized, and in ἐπικαλουμένοις, those who were so in appearance without being virtually so, needs no especial refutation.

o

out doubt he intended to bring to the remembrance of the Corinthians the unity of the church over the whole earth, in order to awaken a spirit of repentance for the divisions among themselves. To this end he reminded them that they, as all believers, were called to manifest a holy unity, and not a church divided by sects. (Upon the use of ὄνομα comp. Comm. pt. 1. Matt. xviii. 21, 22. pt. 2, John xiv. 11—14.—Ὄνομα ἐπικληθὲν ἐφ' ὑμᾶς in Jas. ii. 7. is not to be brought in parallel with these; then the allusion is to the name of the Christians). The words ἐν παντὶ τόπῳ, αὐτῶν τε καὶ ἡμῶν require an especial examination. Ἐν παντὶ τόπῳ conveys only an idea of universality with respect to space, as σὺν πᾶσι does with regard to number. But how is αὐτῶν τε καὶ ἡμῶν to be understood? Eichhorn and other learned men take τόπος in the signification of "place of assembly," and think that the divisions in Corinth had already proceeded so far that the members of the various parties assembled in different localities. Αὐτῶν refers to the antagonists, ἡμῶν to the followers of Paul, (comp. Eichhorn's Introd. pt. 3, p. 110, sqq.) Hug considers that the word τόπος, according to the Hebrew מָקוֹם, signifies party,* and that the passage refers to the dissensions in Corinth, (comp. Hug's Einl. pt. 2, p. 245). But it is evident that this application is highly unnatural and forced; without doubt the αὐτῶν τε καὶ ἡμῶν only signifies the Christians in connexion with the apostle, and those further removed, with a view to impress unity more rigidly upon them, standing as πάντοτε or ἐν πάσῃ τῇ γῇ or οἰκουμένῃ, as Billroth correctly writes after Theophylact. Böttger (Beitr. pt. iii. p. 27, sqq.) mentions places in the neighbourhood of Corinth and Ephesus to which Christianity had already spread from the principal towns. But upon this point we are yet uncertain whether the words αὐτῶν τε καὶ ἡμῶν are better annexed to τόπῳ or to κυρίου ἡμῶν. Grammatically, it were easier to join them to τόπῳ, but the thought contained in them appears to require κυρίου ἡμῶν.† For considerations of locality would occupy little of the attention of believers, while much would be devoted to the identity of the Redeemer of all Christians; the meaning therefore is this, "to all who in any place call upon the

---

* This use of מקום is besides rather doubtful, at least Buxtorf is unacquainted with it (see his Lex. Rabb. p. 2000).

† Lücke is also of this opinion in the Programm already quoted.

name of our Lord Jesus Christ, who is their Lord even as he is ours."—In the blessing the exhortation of εἰρήνη obtains an especial importance through the dissensions in Corinth. It is striking that Paul in this place should desire the χάρις for them, as it is immediately said in ver. 4 that they are rich in grace, but it is with the possession of grace as with that of love, the more one possesses, the more may one receive. Besides this, grace does not remain unchangeable and steadfast; he who grows not in grace loses insensibly what he already possesses; therefore, under every point of view, the increase of God's grace is a suitable wish.

Vers. 4—6. The apostle does not commence immediately with a reproof to the Corinthian Christians (as in Gal. i. 6), but with a hearty thanksgiving unto God for all the grace bestowed upon them, and expresses a confident hope of their final acceptance at the coming of the Lord. He thus appeals to the better feelings of all Corinthian Christians, and so by means of the antithesis (from cap. i. 10, sqq.), brings them to a knowledge of their sins. Further, if we compare the commencement of other Epistles, viz., those to the Philippians, Colossians, and the first to the Thessalonians, in which fellowship in the Gospel, faith, and love are mentioned with commendation, it seems as if here, in exalting knowledge,* a slight intimation were contained, that the striving of some, viz., the Christians, after that which was new, required restraining, as God had already fully opened to them the fountain of true knowledge. With this the aorist ἐπλουτίσθητε of ver. 5, and ὥστε ὑμᾶς μὴ ὑστερεῖσθαι of ver. 7 perfectly agrees. (In ver. 4 Paul writes Θεῷ μου as in Phil. i. 3, as referring to the private prayer which the apostle continually makes to God.—On πάντοτε compare Rom. i. 9.—The thanksgiving is not here made to God for the gift of his grace to himself, but because it was likewise bestowed upon the Corinthians. The ἐν Χριστῷ Ἰησοῦ may be joined with χάριτι τοῦ Θεοῦ, which then points out the grace of God, more especially manifested in the work of Redemption; δοθείσῃ ὑμῖν must however be brought in strict connexion, in order that Christ himself, as preached to them, may clearly appear in and through God's grace. Ἐν is not to be understood in the signification of "through;" we are to conceive Christ filled with grace, and pouring out the same upon the human race.—In ver. 5

* Concerning the relation of γνῶσις to σοφία, see farther on 2, sqq.

ἐν παντὶ is elucidated by λόγῳ and γνώσει.  Both indicate godly
truth, but λόγος objectively as the *subject*, γνῶσις subjectively as
the *wisdom* of the preaching; πᾶς, which finds a place by the two
expressions, adds in some degree to the generality and uncertainty,
for the subject and knowledge of preaching involves an idea susceptible of various degrees of explanation.—Ver. 6 contains only the
opinion that the Gospel was not a temporary work in Corinth, but
would abide, through the power of God, bearing witness to the dominion of grace among the Corinthians, and the ready acceptance of
it on their part.   The expression μαρτύριον τοῦ Χριστοῦ indicates
the preaching of Christ, inasmuch as they testify of him.—Κήρυγμα is correct as an explanation, though objectionable as a reading.  Comp. 1 Cor. ii. 1; 2 Thes. i. 10; 2 Tim. i. 2.   The same
may be observed of μαρτυρία  Compare Rev. xii. 11.—Καθὼς
has here, as in Acts vii. 17, the signification of *siquidem, cum.*

Vers. 7—9.  The appearance of the Charismata, as a result of the
universal possession of godly grace in the Corinthian Church, is
next mentioned.  ὑστερεῖσθαι ἐν μηδενὶ χαρίσματι refers to the
manifold and unusual gifts of grace which even then displayed
themselves in Corinth (comp. on 1 Cor. cap. xii. and xiv.)   In the
apostolic times these gifts, as a consequence, might be always
found the accompaniment of a lively, spiritual life; and possibly the
Charismata in *themselves* did not belong to the *indispensable* appearances in the church.   But upon what grounds does Paul connect the expectation of the coming of the Lord with the gifts?
(Comp. the remarks in Matt. xxiv. 1, upon ἀποκάλυψις κυρίου).
First, if the expectation of Christ's coming is a testimony of inward spiritual life, and to be placed amongst the fruits of faith,
then ἀπεκδέχεσθαι (see on Rom. viii. 19) is not a dry historical
assertion of the fact that the Lord will return again one day, but
becomes the expression of earnest desire for that which is not to
be conceived without love, faith, and hope (1 Cor. xiii. 13).   The
mention of ἀποκάλυψις κυρίου certainly comprehends a slight allusion to the errors of the *Christianer*.  From their peculiar views
they could hardly profess belief in Christ's resurrection or his
second coming.  If the Christians had expressed any real doubts
on the subject, or maintained the doctrine of the second coming
after abandoning the fundamental one of Christ's resurrection, the
apostle might have intended to awaken their perception of the

importance of this latter point by the hope here expressed. And the rather, as in ver. 8, ἡμέρα κυρίου, the day of the Lord, is held forth to view as the decisive period (ἕως τέλους), and the period when all must be decided, and for which therefore there was the most urgent necessity that they should preserve themselves blameless. Billroth justly remarks that ὅς is not to stand in connexion with the Χριστός which immediately precedes it, but with the Θεός of ver. 4; in the former case the apostle would certainly not have been able to write ἐν τῇ ἡμέρα τοῦ κυρίου, but only αὐτοῦ.—The parallel which βεβαιώσει forms with ἐβεβαιώθη, in ver. 6, confirms this, where Θεός is also to be supplied, as if it were that God, in order to reward those who did not resist the operation of grace, approved himself faithful in confirming and maintaining their faith (ver. 9). Βεβαίοω is to be found in the same signification, in 2 Cor. i. 21; Col. ii. 7. Στηρίζω is likewise so used in Rom. i. 11, xvi. 25; 1 Pet. v. 10; 2 Pet. i. 12. As the enemy to all Pelagianism, the apostle refers not only the commencement of the work of man's regeneration, but also its continuation and accomplishment, to God alone, leaving to the individual only the negative fact of non-resistance to grace. (Comp. on Rom. ix. 1).—Πιστὸς ὁ Θεὸς is to be found in 1 Cor. x. 13; 1 Thess. v. 24; 2 Thess. iii. 3. The κλῆσις of God is to be understood as a promise to mankind that God abides by his truth, although man for a season prove untrue, (2 Tim. ii. 13). This unfaithfulness Paul tacitly attributes to many of the Corinthians; and reflecting upon it, and the divisions in Corinth that have possibly been its consequence, he mentions also the κοινωνία. Where a spiritual *communion* with the Redeemer is truly and steadfastly held, there unity with the brethren will always exist with his members; but when insignificant facts are exalted into importance, division will invariably be a necessary consequence.

Ver. 10. After this slight intimation, the apostle, leaving the application to the reader himself, proceeds with more precise reference to the existing contentions, beseeching the Corinthians by the name (*i. e.* the person and existence) of Him with whom, as in ver. 9, all believers, according to the intention of their calling, should have fellowship, to have unity among themselves, avoiding divisions. Αὐτὸ λέγειν is not to be understood in the sense of uniformity, or absolute similarity of speech, but rather as an

C

acknowledgment of what is most important in doctrine and practice; in fact, it is the expression of κατηρτισμένος εἶναι ἐν τῷ αὐτῷ
νοὶ καὶ ἐν τῇ αὐτῇ γνώμῃ. The νοῦς indicates the theoretical,
γνώμη the practical side of the Christian life, as Billroth has
already justly remarked. (The distinction of later times between
σχίσμα and αἵρεσις, practical and theoretical error, is unknown to
the New Testament. Both expressions were indifferently used
with ἔρις, ver. 11.—The τὸ αὐτὸ λέγειν is the effect of the τὸ αὐτὸ
φρονεῖν, comp. Phil. ii. 2, and shows the natural connexion between mind and speech.—Καταρτίζω, to arrange (in Matt. iv. 21,
it is said of the mending of the nets), thence to perfect or finish, may
illustrate his idea. From this κατηρτισμένοι = τέλειοι. Unquestionably it is not perfection in itself which is here meant, but
perfectness in unity, which, springing from and requiring lowly submissive hearts, may be found where a high degree of intellectual
development does not exist.

Vers. 11, 12. For this admonition, continues Paul, I have
unfortunately reason; for I hear that contentions really exist among
you; and, as the source of his information, he here names οἱ
Χλόης. Of this Chloe nothing further is known; possibly she
was a Corinthian matron, whose slaves alone, as was not unfrequently the case, belonged to the Church. But the expression
would also justify the belief that the intelligence proceeded from
her kindred; however, the want of more precise notice leaves the
subject in doubt. Paul then proceeds to name the four parties,
whose characteristics have already been treated of in the introduction (§ 1). Here the question may occur, are four parties really
specified, or are there not rather only three? and in the words ἐγὼ
δὲ Χριστοῦ, may not Paul have opposed the true position to the
false? so that the meaning of these words is, "Ye say, it is true,
every one of you, I am of Paul, of Apollos, of Peter, but I say, I
am of Christ, that ought ye all also to say." This supposition is
favoured by the passage iii. 22; there three parties only are
named, and all as of Christ. But, were the matter so, every investigation concerning the *Christianer* would be unnecessary; but
such an explanation of the passage appears unwarranted, because
the fourth ἐγὼ δὲ is placed as parallel with the other three. Had
it been intended to place it in opposition, Paul would have written αὐτὸς ἐγὼ or ἐγὼ δὲ Παῦλος. Then 2 Cor. x. 7 distinctly

shows that the *Christianer* really existed in Corinth. (The form λέγω δὲ τοῦτο is to be understood, I consider, I refer to the circumstance.—Ἕκαστος ὑμῶν is not to be urged. Undoubtedly there were some who comprehended the corruption of such adherence to man; in the meantime the great body of the Corinthian church was certainly split into parties.—Κηφᾶς is Peter (John i. 43), and not an unknown man of this name, as some expounders wish to believe; and the conjecture of Κρίσπου for Χριστοῦ need only be historically made known, there being not the slightest critical authority in its favour to justify its reception).

Vers. 13—16. That the apostle in mentioning the four parties considered schism to exist among them, is shown by what follows. He asks whether Christ, that is the church, the body of Christ (1 Cor. xii. 12), that can be but one alone, is divided, and that they thence derive a sanction for dividing themselves into parties. Lachmann has recently seen reason to suppose that this sentence was to be understood as a declaration of Paul's, and not as a question, "then is Christ through you divided." But with this the questions which follow do not well agree. The apostle first speaks of himself as rejoicing that of himself he had not afforded the slightest occasion for these contentions. The first question intentionally involves a contradiction, evidently with a view to make the Corinthians sensible of the absurdity of resting their faith on man, and to point to the crucified Saviour as the sole foundation of their salvation. The second turns upon a fact not impossible, though it could only arise through the grossest misunderstanding. But ignorant persons might suppose that, by baptism, they were placed in particular relation with those who administered the rite, (comp. the remarks on Matt. xxviii. 19 on the form βαπτισθῆναι εἰς τὸ ὄνομα τινος, also on 1 Cor. x. 2); and the manner in which Paul refutes this idea is striking. Instead of opposing to it the nature and intention of baptism, he appeals to the incidental fact that he had baptized very few persons in Corinth. (See further on ver. 17). He names at first only Crispus (the former ruler of the synagogue, mentioned in Acts xviii. 8), and Gaius, in whose house he dwelt (Rom. xvi. 23). Afterwards Stephanas occurs to him, named in 1 Cor. xvi. 15, 17, as a member of the deputation sent to Ephesus; and, in order that the account should be quite correct, he is then also mentioned. (In ver. 15, ἐβαπτίσθην, sometimes ἐβαπτίσθητε, and also ἐβαπτίσθη, is to be found for ἐβάπτισα. Semler therefore thinks that Paul had not used any verb, but had only written ὅτι εἰς τὸ ἐμὸν ὄνομα. Pott, however, more reasonably concludes that the transcriber had made the alteration because of the so frequently recurring ἐβάπτισα. The ἵνα by no means countenances the deduction that "therefore now none may say" is intended by it; for that Paul had intentionally baptized so few, in order that it should not be said he baptized in his own name, is highly improbable; but in the whole passage, viz., in εὐχαριστῶ lies the reflection, "I rejoice that I have so done, as now none can say," &c. In ver. 16 the expression ἐβάπτισα δὲ καὶ τὸν Στεφανᾶ οἶκον is not to be understood as if the family of Stephanas were baptized without him, but that he was included, just as in the well-known form οἱ ἀμφί, the party without the head is not signified. For infant baptism nothing is to be deduced from the word οἶκος, as has been already observed in the Comm. pt. ii. Acts xvi. 17, 18, for the adult members of the family, or the slaves likewise, might be signified by it.

Ver. 17. Paul then proceeds to explain the reason he does not baptize (in Corinth, ought to be supplied at ver. 16, for out of this city he may certainly have baptized many, although still few in proportion to the number converted by him), by saying that he was commissioned by Christ to preach the Gospel, not to baptize. But are the two functions irreconcilable? Is not one necessarily dependent on the other? Many critics, and Pott likewise, say that the sense of this is, that the principal office of the apostle was to preach, not to baptize. But Paul must intend more than this, for he certainly wishes to justify his practice of not usually baptizing as well-founded. Doubtless a trace is here to be recognised of the partition of the various duties among the servants of the ancient church; as is shown in Acts viii., the apostles principally preached and imparted the Holy Spirit by the imposition of hands on the baptized, while the office of baptism was performed by the apostolic assistants themselves. However, we can assign no especial reason for this, and the exercise of this sacrament can, in and for itself, be of no less importance than preaching, for he who preaches may convert, and those converted must be baptized;

under some circumstances, therefore, as the foregoing verses show, this was done by the apostles.  But to Paul, under present circumstances, his abnegation of the custom was of service, by proving that he had given no occasion for undue personal adherence, and what refers to him holds good also of Apollos and Peter.—With the mention of the Gospel he was called upon to preach.  Paul immediately connects a remark upon the manner in which he had delivered it, attacking thereby the most mischievous party in Corinth, the *Christianer*, in the very root of their error, and incidentally condemning the followers of Apollos.  Both of these considered that the simple doctrine of the Gospel might be assisted by the ornament of oratory and the support of human wisdom.  Paul, however, maintains the contrary, asserting that the cross of Christ, $\sigma\tau\alpha\nu\rho\grave{o}\varsigma$ * $\tau o\hat{v}$ $X\rho\iota\sigma\tau o\hat{v}=\lambda\acute{o}\gamma o\varsigma$ $\tau o\hat{v}$ $\sigma\tau\alpha\nu\rho o\hat{v}$ (ver. 18), meaning the doctrine of the crucified Saviour, of the reconciling death of Christ, lost its effect thereby ($\kappa\epsilon\nu\omega\theta\hat{\eta}$, that is, became spiritless, empty, and ineffectual: comp. Rom. iv. 14, 2 Cor. ix. 3).  It may here be asked, what that $\sigma o\phi\acute{\iota}\alpha$ $\lambda\acute{o}\gamma o\nu$ really signified, from which Paul argued so mischievous a consequence?  It might be supposed that $\lambda\acute{o}\gamma o\varsigma$ here meant reason, so that Paul admonishes against the wisdom of reason in contradistinction to the wisdom which is of God. But $\lambda\acute{o}\gamma o\varsigma$ never signifies reason in the New Testament, for which $\nu o\hat{\iota}\varsigma$ is used; it has the sense of word, speech, doctrine, therefore $\sigma o\phi\acute{\iota}\alpha$ $\lambda\acute{o}\gamma o\nu$† is "word wisdom," *i. e.*, a wisdom in appearance, without being so substantially; in ii. 4, therefore $\sigma o\phi\acute{\iota}\alpha$ $\dot{\epsilon}\nu$ $\pi\epsilon\iota\theta o\hat{\iota}\varsigma$ $\lambda\acute{o}\gamma o\iota\varsigma$, or $\dot{\epsilon}\nu$ $\delta\iota\delta\alpha\kappa\tau o\hat{\iota}\varsigma$ $\lambda\acute{o}\gamma o\iota\varsigma$ (ii. 13) stands for this, publishing itself as $\dot{\alpha}\nu\theta\rho\omega\pi\acute{\iota}\nu\eta$, in opposition to the $\sigma o\phi\acute{\iota}\alpha$ $\dot{\alpha}\pi\grave{o}$ $\Theta\epsilon o\hat{v}$ (i. 30).  But consult iv. 20 especially, where $\lambda\acute{o}\gamma o\varsigma$ and $\delta\acute{v}\nu\alpha\mu\iota\varsigma$ may be found in opposition, as in vers. 17, 18.  The words $\dot{\epsilon}\nu$ $\sigma o\phi\acute{\iota}\alpha$ $\lambda\acute{o}\gamma o\nu$, therefore, do not express the true philosophy, which before Christ, was employed in the search after hidden truth, and, after his coming, in striving to understand the truth which was manifested in him, by means of regeneration through the power of God; but they

---

* $\Sigma\tau\alpha\nu\rho\grave{o}\varsigma$ stands first for the death on the cross, and again for the crucified person. (Gal. v. 11, vi. 12, 14; Phil. iii. 18).  The expression is stronger than simply $\theta\acute{\alpha}\nu\alpha\tau o\varsigma$, because it includes in it the pain and disgrace of the death, and in this place it is evident that the cross stands for the doctrine of the cross, since in itself its power could not suffer through human wisdom, but only the doctrine.

† The signification of the form $\lambda\acute{o}\gamma o\varsigma$ $\sigma o\phi\acute{\iota}\alpha\varsigma$ is entirely different; for which see xii. 8.

describe the *false* and *delusive* philosophy (Col. ii. 8), which presented the appearance of this desire without possessing the reality,
and sprung from vain conceit and pride, and not from a thirst after
the knowledge of the Eternal. This philosophy, therefore, truly
makes void the power of the cross of Christ, because the holy
doctrine of the forgiveness of sins through the blood of the Son
of God being inimical thereto, it sought to remove this belief,
instead of acknowledging it as necessary to salvation. It would
be just as erroneous to suppose that under the form ἐν σοφίᾳ
λόγου, simply a well-arranged speech, a close, logical explanation
was meant. The genuine oratory which is the noble expression
of inward conviction is not rejected by the operation of Christ;
although unimportant in preaching, it does not nevertheless
gainsay it; but all false ornament of speech, which is in no respect
the expression of inward life, but purely hypocrisy, seduces the
mind of the hearer from what is so important, and thus injures the
power of preaching. It is almost unnecessary to point out that
the apostle did not refer to oratory as an art, but to the false wisdom which the *Christianer*, not yet fully loosed from the trammels
of heathenism, exceedingly over-prized, and by means of which
the truth of the Gospel was materially altered. The passages ii.
4, 13, show that the apostle had certainly the form of the discourse also in his mind, (if the expression ἐν σοφίᾳ λόγου has no
immediate reference to it, it may be accepted in the sense of
word wisdom), for πειθοὶ λόγοι indicates that which is intended
to *persuade*, not *convince*, and those views only which are directed
to proselytising could consent to make use of persuasion in matters of faith.

Vers. 18, 19. Paul passes somewhat suddenly to what follows; an intermediate thought is evidently wanting, for in itself
the assertion, that the preaching of the cross of Christ is to them
that perish foolishness, affords no ground for the previous declaration (to which the γάρ refers) that it is not to be furthered by
means of human wisdom. The reflection necessary to the connexion of the idea is this: the preaching of the Gospel can never
stand indebted to human wisdom, in fact the latter destroys fundamentally the power of the former, because both (viz., the Gospel
and human wisdom) are antagonistic elements, admitting of no
connexion; one depriving the other of its nature, and each striving

to annihilate the other. Where, therefore, human wisdom rules, the Gospel appears as μωρία, but where the Gospel has manifested itself (*i. e.* as δύναμις Θεοῦ, propagating itself among mankind by the power of God), then the preaching of the cross appears pure wisdom, and that which is human as μωρία. This opposition to the μωρία is indeed not expressed, but is included in the expression δύναμις, for true wisdom is likewise power. Scripture asserts the same concerning the effect of the Holy Spirit upon the fabrications of human school wisdom, (see Isa. xxix. 14), that it destroys the pretended wisdom of the wise man. From ἀπολλύμενοι and σωζόμενοι nothing can be construed favourable to predestination; he to whom the Gospel is foolishness is only so long lost as he persists in the denial of Divinity; let him but abandon his erroneous view, and he may become a σωζόμενοις.— Billroth correctly remarks, that the after-placing of ἡμῖν permits an interpretation, expressing more forbearance than if it had been placed before the rest of the sentence; in the latter situation the rejection of the opponents would have seemed more vigorous, but the words τοῖς δὲ σωζομένοις ἡμῖν may be thus understood, "the saved, among whom we may reckon ourselves."—The quotation from Isa. xxix. 14, follows neither the Hebrew nor the LXX. closely. In the Hebrew, God does not speak in the first person, but the meaning of the words is: Wisdom is fallen, prudence is concealed. The LXX. has the passage on the whole similar, yet read κρύψω instead of ἀθετήσω. The real meaning of the words, as used by the prophets, refers to the wisdom of man, whose opposition to the wisdom of God, though under the most varied forms, always remains the same. The σοφία is the result of the νοῦς, as σύνεσις is of φρόνησις, *i. e.* understanding. In the Old Testament חָכְמָה and בִּינָה have precisely the same relation. See my treatise De Trichotomia Nat. Hum. in the Opusc. Acad. p. 158, sqq.—The σοφοί and συνετοί are evidently those held wise and prudent by men, and by themselves. The seeds of true wisdom and genuine prudence are not, however, destroyed by God where they exist among men who have applied the true test, and hold themselves for no more than they are, but, on the contrary, He lends his aid to perfect the work.

Ver. 20. The fulfilment of this prophecy was beheld by Paul in his own time, in that knowledge of Christ which laid prostrate

all other wisdom. Ἐν Χριστῷ must therefore be added here to
the ἐμώρανε, as ver. 21 shows, in connexion with ver. 23.  In
Christ was manifested the σοφία τοῦ αἰῶνος μέλλοντος, before
whose power the σοφία τοῦ αἰῶνος or κόσμου τούτου was compelled to retire.  The influence of Christ, which, at the time Paul
wrote, first entered upon the conflict with human wisdom, was
viewed by the apostle in a prophetic spirit, as triumphant, a
fulfilment which has so far advanced in our times, since philosophy itself is compelled by the omnipotence of the Gospel to
include its characteristic doctrines in the circle of its inquiries.
" Where is the wise," exclaims the apostle, "since the true wisdom has been revealed?"  At an earlier period, one may suppose
a wisdom was to be found which was considered really such by
him, that which was absolute being yet hidden, but, after the
unveiling of the latter, this belief was no longer possible.  Respecting the agreement of σοφός, γραμματεύς, and συζητητὴς, Billroth adopts the idea entertained by Theophylact, that σοφός
referred to the Hellenes, and γραμματεύς to the Jews, among
whom wisdom was made to consist in an intimate acquaintance
with the sacred writings.  But, in the first place, the import of
συζητητὴς then becomes exceedingly uncertain, for the words of
the Father alluded to, συζητητὰς ὠνόμασε τοὺς λογισμοῖς καὶ
ἐρεύναις τὰ πάντα ἐπιτρέποντας, are just as applicable to the
σοφούς; and further, it cannot be said that the term "false wisdom" is to be applied to the knowledge of the sacred writings of
the Old Testament.  For this reason, others conceive the expression "wise men" to mean the moral philosophers, such as Socrates, γραμματεῖς to signify the grammarians and investigators
of history, and συζητηταὶ τοῦ αἰῶνος τούτου the natural philosophers, such as Empedocles, Anaximenes, and others, styled by
Cicero the *speculatores, venatoresque naturae*.  But τοῦ αἰῶνος
τούτου is just as applicable to all three, as to the latter category,
in addition to which objection neither αἰων nor κόσμος οὗτος signify
nature, as they have a fixed dogmatical meaning in the Greek
language.  We therefore feel obliged to retain the reference of
the term "wise men" to the Greek philosophers, and of the
γραμματεῖς to rabbinnical erudition; but observing, with respect
to the latter, that it is not investigation of the sacred volume
which is condemned, but the manner in which it was conducted

by those who pursued it, the sifting of words, and trifling spirit which, making camels out of gnats, characterised their inquiry, likewise the self-approbation which attended their labours, precisely as described in Matt. xxiii. In short, the συζητηταί may be best distinguished by supposing that the first two expressions describe the learning of the schools, and that skill in classifying, which prevailed among heathens and Jews, but the latter intended that diletanteism in research, then so prevalent, and which propounded itself in a universal spirit of disputation and speculation. To restrict this supposition to the Jewish inquirers of this kind, called דַּרְשָׁן, who amused themselves with the mystical scriptural expositions named מִדְרָשִׁים, as Schleusner and Pott appear to do, is unwarranted; we must rather include both Greek and Jewish lovers of speculative disputation, and observe, that the controversy is directed first against the *Christianer*, and then against the followers of Apollos and Peter.

Ver. 21. The words which follow, according to the usual explanation of the passage, do not show a just connexion with what precedes them. In the expression σοφία τοῦ Θεοῦ, the κήρυγμα of the Gospel is generally understood, which makes the sense "hath not God made foolish the wisdom of this world?" Certainly, for since the world in its (pretended) wisdom, did not receive God in his (true) wisdom by means of the Gospel, it pleased God, by the foolishness of preaching (*i. e.*, deemed such by the world), to save them that believe." To this exposition, however, there is this objection, that the preaching of the cross, which is also the μωρίας τοῦ κηρύγματος, then appears as a consequence of the non-acceptance of godly wisdom on the part of the world, but this is evidently an error. Besides, then, not ἐπειδὴ οὐκ ἔγνω, but γινώσκει would have been used. It may be said that the stress does not justly belong to διὰ τῆς μωρίας τοῦ κηρύγματος, but to the σῶσαι τοὺς πιστεύοντας, which would make the signification, "As the world would not acknowledge God in the wisdom of the Gospel, it pleased God by this (apparently) foolish preaching to save those who believed in it, and thus their pretended wisdom was made foolishness, because they were thereby excluded from salvation." It must be confessed that, by adopting this explanation, the difficulties of the passage are considerably lessened; but, according to our conviction, the position

of the words does not admit of this exposition. Without doubt,
when Paul wished to describe the opposition between the world
and believers, he might have written σῶσαι τοὺς πιστεύοντας διὰ
τῆς μωρίας τοῦ κηρύγματος, meaning, that by means of the μωρίας
τοῦ κηρύγματος itself, he made human wisdom to become folly,
not through the fact, that the faithful accepted the μωρίας τοῦ
κηρύγματος. The consequence then is, that ἐπειδὴ γὰρ ἐν τῇ σοφίᾳ
τοῦ Θεοῦ must be received in a signification different from that
usually adopted, that is to say, that the ἐν τῇ σοφίᾳ τοῦ Θεοῦ must
be understood to refer, not to the Gospel, but to the wisdom of
God, as Billroth has already pointed out; in short, to the circumstances under which, according to Rom. i. 18, 19, any result is
to be expected from human research, viz., that it be conducted
in sincerity with a desire to attain to a knowledge of the true
God. Then the ἐπειδὴ becomes beautifully connected with the εὐδόκησεν, and the apostle says, "Because men made so ill a use of
their power of discovering truth, that they attained only to an apparent wisdom, God, as it were in punishment, has published
salvation by means of the foolish preaching of the cross, which
they have now no power to understand, being blinded by their
own false wisdom." It is true the preaching of the cross has
also its inward and needful foundation, but Paul has here no
occasion to discourse upon it; he merely brings forward the side
which appears to him calculated to show the vanity of confiding in
human wisdom. Rückert has propounded an anomalous view of the
passage; he explains ἐν τῇ σοφίᾳ τοῦ Θεοῦ thus: "by the guid-
ance and disposition of godly wisdom, the world did not comprehend God through its own wisdom." But the thought that the
non-acknowledgment of God on the part of mankind was a con-
trivance of godly wisdom, is entirely contrary to Paul, as Rom.
chaps. i. and ii. show; and besides this, the reception of the ἐν as
grounds for this explanation, is highly questionable, on account of
its connexion with ἔγνω. This verb cannot be separated from
the ἐν τῇ σοφίᾳ, because, in the second part of the verse, it is
stated that the believers recognised the true wisdom in the foolishness of the Gospel. (Billroth finds the expression "hindered
by means of their wisdom, the world knew not God," in the διὰ τῆς
σοφίας; but I rather agree with Winer (Gr. p. 327), who retains
διὰ in its accustomed signification, in the sense of, "by means of

their wisdom they knew not God; *i. e.*, their wisdom was not the fitting means for the perception of truth."—The εὐδόκησεν ὁ Θεὸς stands according to the well-known רָצָה יְהֹוָה, instead of the Greek ἔδοξε τῷ Θεῷ).

Vers. 22—24. Billroth considers that the phrase beginning with the ἐπειδὴ should be a second proposition to the principal point of the sentence εὐδόκησεν ὁ Θεὸς, which latter accordingly must have a double *protasis*, one preceding and the other following it. From this proceeds the explanation of the ἐν τῇ σοφίᾳ τοῦ Θεοῦ (ver. 21), as one to which the learned men mentioned gave the preference. Both the premises introduced with ἐπειδὴ must certainly express a kindred thought, but if σημεῖα and σοφία (ver. 22), as well as σκάνδαλον and μωρίαν (ver. 23), concern the Gospel, σοφία τοῦ Θεοῦ must consequently refer to the same, which, as we have already seen, is not tenable. Therefore ἐπειδὴ does not in this place, as in ver. 21, signify "after," but "for," as in pure Greek ἐπεί is often used, but never ἐπειδὴ (see Passow Lex.) In the New Testament ἐπειδὴ is to be found in the sense of "for," in the passages Matt. xxi. 46; Luke xi. 6; 1 Cor. v. 21, xiv. 16; Phil. ii. 26. It would be better, therefore, to place the second ἐπειδὴ in connexion with what follows, and consider vers. 22—24 as the declaration of the ἐμώρανεν ὁ Θεὸς (ver. 20), which is represented in ver. 21 as well merited. The foolishness into which God permitted them to fall was, that their aims were directed towards false objects, and that the true one, which indeed contained the thing they sought, was mistaken by them. The σημειομανία of the Jews prevented their acknowledging Christ, because, although himself the greatest σημεῖον, and surrounded as it were with a halo of miracles, he nevertheless did not perform them in a manner which accorded with their expectation, neither did he descend from the cross, but died thereon; this was destructive of the glorious picture of the Messiah they had taught themselves to contemplate with exultation, therefore Christ crucified was to them a σκάνδαλον, an unacceptable stumbling-block. The Greeks, on the contrary, required a speculatively founded and well-arranged argument for the Gospel; when this was wanting, the source of all wisdom, and the depths of sound speculation, was to them a μωρία. It was only to those among Jews and Greeks, who from their hearts obeyed the call-

ing of God,* that the crucified Saviour was discernible as a divine
source of power from which the greatest σημεῖα, (but of a spiritual hidden kind), incessantly proceeded, and as the origin of that
wisdom, in comparison with which all human knowledge is folly.
Ver. 25. This effect of the Gospel the apostle deduces from
the fact of the difference between what is divine and that which
is merely human, since the most unapparent divine influence is
more powerful and wise than the mightiest and wisest human
display. The expressions τὸ μωρὸν, τὸ ἀσθενὲς τοῦ Θεοῦ have
something important in them: they are equal to an *Oxymoron*.
Paul certainly did not intend to affix this idea to the Divine
Being, but only to the appearance of certain divine schemes, the
redemption through the death of Christ for example. Even
this might appear to men foolish and weak without being so.
It would therefore be erroneous to refer to τὸ ἀσθενὲς τοῦ Θεοῦ to
the humiliation of Christ, the veiling of his divine power, as Billroth appears to do; this is opposed by the parallel μωρόν. To
the genitive τῶν ἀνθρώπων may σοφίας and δυνάμεως be supplied.

Vers. 26, 27. It appears striking that the apostle should draw
the argument for the wisdom of the μωρὸν τοῦ Θεοῦ, and the
strength of the ἀσθενὲς τοῦ Θεοῦ, from the condition of the faithful. It proceeds, however, from this cause, that both being exhibited
in them, it is clear that it is not the question of the humiliation of
God in Christ that is here to be considered, but the property of
the doctrine of salvation. The ἰδιῶται, or illiterate and ignorant
members of the church, confounded the wisdom of the wise and the
power of the mighty. But how was Paul able to say this at that
period? It might agree with the times subsequent to Constantine,
but not during the rule of Nero. But it was in the existence of the
Christian church itself, and the spiritual power which pervaded
it, that Christianity represented itself triumphant. The Christians

* The repetition of the Χριστὸν in ver. 24 is striking, to which from ver. 23,
κηρύσσομεν must be supplied. At the first glance, the thought will then appear
constructed as if Paul preached two Christs, first the crucified one for the unbelieving, then the glorified, *i. e.* the risen Saviour, for the believing. It is, however,
not to be so understood but that unbelievers, having no faith in Christ's resurrection, make as it were to themselves another, a dead Christ, whom they reject;
while believers, receiving his death only in connexion with his resurrection, possess
in the crucified also a living Saviour.

could effect what neither philosopher, prince, nor potentate were
able to do, create men's hearts anew, and out of sinners and evil-
doers form children of God. (In ver. 26, κλῆσιν stands somewhat
abstract for the *concrete* κλητοί, but it signifies, as in 1 Cor. vii.
20, the external circumstances, the calling. Rückert thinks with
Beza that it should be received in the sense of *ratio quam dominus
in vobis vocandis secutus est*, and with this the opinion possibly
agrees, that ἐξελέξατο ὁ θεὸς forms the principal idea in what follows. But Paul would certainly have expressed this idea differently.—Κατὰ σάρκα, antithesis to κατὰ πνεῦμα, see Rom. ii. 28,
29, signfies here only "in respect to the exterior," for, regarded
inwardly, Christians are in the true sense of the word wise, strong,
noble. Billroth regards σάρξ as κόσμος οὗτος, and this in general
corresponds with the sense, but here it seems not so suitable on account of the words δυνατοὶ and εὐγενεῖς, which in themselves indicate nothing sinful. 'Εὐγενεῖς refers to noble condition ; the greater
proportion of the first Christians were slaves and illiterate men,
and the whole history of the growth of the church is fundamentally
a progressive triumph of the unlearned over the learned, the lowly
over the great, until the emperor himself laid his crown at the
foot of the cross.—In vers. 27 and 28, μωρὰ, ἀσθενῆ, and ἀγενῆ
correspond closely with the three expressions in ver. 26, and the
change of the masculine to the neuter is unimportant, as in ver.
27 τοὺς σοφοὺς comes again between; the masculine is only considered less abstract, the neuter more so. In the ἐξελέξατο is
simply indicated the summoning, distinguishing efficacy of election, without any reference to absolute predestination. According
to God's intention the summons is general, and it is only owing
to the opposition which individuals are free to exercise to his
grace, that it assumes the form of selecting).

Vers. 28, 29. Paul carries the representation yet further, in
the endeavour to realize the striking idea; he adds yet the words
ἐξουθενημένα, certainly μὴ ὄντα, and substitutes for καταισχύνειν
the stronger καταργεῖν. The addition of μέγα τί to the form
μὴ ὄντα is quite wrong. Paul intends to describe believers as not
only not great, but as in effect things that are not, as in Rom. iv.
17, and for this reason, because the natural man has generally no
real being or existence; but as the following τὰ ὄντα means likewise the natural man, it would doubtless be better to reflect upon

the state as such. The natural man indeed has no part in the true life, nevertheless he stands with a certain degree of power, and a perfect consciousness of it. In the transition from the old to the new state, in the repentance and wrestlings with the old nature which ensue, the remnant of the strength of the natural man escapes, and that of the new life not being yet effective, he is indeed a μὴ ὄν, a being now produced by God's creative power. The ἐξ αὐτοῦ ὑμεῖς ἐστε in ver. 30 refers to this new birth in regeneration; the honour and glory being alone of God and of no created being. (In ver. 28, ἀγενής means *ignobili loco natus;* in profane writers it also signifies " childless " or " degenerate," *degener.*—In ver. 29, the πᾶσα σάρξ, like μὴ πᾶς, is formed after the well-known Jewish text כָּל בָּשָׂר and לֹא כָל. For τοῦ Θεοῦ the *text. rec.* reads αὐτοῦ, in favour of which much indeed might be urged, as some one might easily be supposed to have made the alteration on account of the αὐτοῦ immediately following. But the Codd. A.C.D.E.F.G.I. and many *minuscula* read Θεοῦ, so that this text must be retained.—'Ενώπιον=לִפְנֵי, before God, *i. e.*, in his presence, before his face, as if the creature had an individual merit of his own).

Vers. 30, 31. The first of these two verses forms an accessory thought, (for ver. 31 is a continuation of the subject of ver. 29), and places in contrast to their outward debasement the internal gloriousness of Christians. From the Father through the Son (comp. Rom. xi. 36), have believers their existence, not only as regards their creation, but especially referring to their being created anew, *i. e.* their new birth, Christ being the step thereunto. This last idea lies in the ὃς ἐγενήθη ἡμῖν, which words imply not only that Christ by his doctrine and example teaches us wisdom, &c., or that it operates in us through his Spirit, but that he is in fact become (after effectual and suffering obedience), wisdom, righteousness, sanctification, and redemption, and that therefore all these in his followers are only the unfolding of gifts received in him. (Comp. the remarks upon the τετέλεσται in the Comm. Joh. xix. 30). The ἀπὸ Θεοῦ must be connected with the ἐγενήθη, so that Christ himself in his human nature may appear as a gift from God to men, but the idea which expresses the being of Christ stands as a climax, and comprehends the phases of the Christian life from its commencement to its completion. In the σοφία is intimated the real, essential knowledge of God, which is identical with the feeling of one's own nothingness, and, to a certain extent, it is the beginning of a true way of life, the real μετάνοια, for it leads to δικαιοσύνη, and thereby to a perfect enlightenment of the man as a regenerated creature. (See on Rom. iii. 21). The ἁγιασμὸς is furthermore the gradual development of this new life, not the gradual improvement or purifying of the old man, for that must be given up in death ; in short, the ἀπολύτρωσις, which occasionally comprehends in its meaning the commencement of the new life, refers here especially to its end and accomplishment. (See this idea further explained in Comm. on Rom. iii. 25). The perfect inward deliverance from the power of sin, is now expressed together with the ἀπολύτρωσις τοῦ σώματος (Rom. viii. 23), because the mortal body always remains a source of temptation. Paul then again repeats the thought in ver. 29, in conjunction with the scripture from Jerem. ix. 23, signifying that no creature may glory in himself, but only in the Lord; which according to the context would bear this construction, that the Christian is indebted to the Lord alone, and not to himself, for the whole work of his moral perfection, a doctrine destructive of all Pelagianism. Regeneration is entirely God's work, as was the creation, both in the commencement, means, and accomplishment.—(Ver. 31 is an anacoluthon; to the ἵνα, γένηται may be supplied.—Καυχᾶσθαι is generally construed in the New Testament with ἐν, but also with περὶ, ὑπὲρ, κατά).

## § 2. THE WISDOM OF GOD.

### (ii. 1—16).

After exposing to view the vanity of human wisdom, the apostle describes more closely the properties of that which is divine fron ver. 6—16, having beforehand plainly signified to the Corinthians (ver. 1—5), with an allusion to ver. 17, chap. i., that this wisdom, pure and without any admixture of the human element, was what he had faithfully preached to them.

Vers. 1, 2. Paul commences by saying that, upon his appearance among them in Corinth, he preached to them with no human excellency of speech or of wisdom, but that he had simply revealed to them an historical, and, above all, the crucified Christ, exposing to full view the μωρία of divine preaching (ver. 21), instead of veiling it in mystery. This contains the great truth, not sufficiently reflected upon, that the Gospel, in its essence, is neither theoretic, abstract, or reflective, nor even imaginative, *but that it is historical, and the history is divine.* The preaching of the Gospel is a revelation of God's doings, and especially of the one great act of God's love, the gift of his only Son for the sins of the world. When belief is well established, then alone may this act of God become the subject of theory or research among the members of the church; and even then only so far as the whole investigation proceeds from faith. (See on ver. 6, sqq.) Faith could never be a consequence of this inquiry. It has its origin in God's Spirit alone, which ever shows itself most effectual by the simple preaching of the divine history. It is not improbable, from the materialism of the false teachers among the Corinthians, that evidence of supposititious ideas of Christ was to be discerned among them (see on xv. 12), and that the apostle intended to oppose this by holding the historical Christ up to view. (In ver. 1 the ὑπεροχὴν λόγου ἢ σοφίας is an explanation of the rhetorical and speculative elements united in the expression σοφία λόγου (i. 17). This is plainly shown by ii. 4. The substantive ὑπεροχὴ is to be found in 1 Tim. ii. 2. It indicates here the exaggeration arising from vanity, which permits that which is unimportant to usurp the place of that which is valuable.—Upon μαρτύριον τοῦ Θεοῦ see comm. on i. 6. The reading μυστήριον appears to be borrowed from ver. 7.—In ver. 2, ἔκρινά is not to be rendered, as Billroth does, "I determined," but, "I judged in myself, *i. e.*, I had the fullest, most perfect conviction." The εἰδέναι ἐν ὑμῖν is not to be understood as if Paul expressed his conviction that in Corinth only he must have no other knowledge than Christ, while elsewhere, and in himself, he might know many things; but that, *as in Corinth, so everywhere, and also in himself, Christ was all in all;* the εἰδέναι, that is to say, refers to the knowledge of the true and everlasting, and is by no means comprehensive, but is applied to one alone, the revealed God in Christ (Col. i. 16, 17). In this knowledge there are no degrees; it is either possessed in full or is entirely wanting. But it cannot be denied that this sole knowledge of the Eternal is capable

of progression in itself, though it has in no part of its development the character of variety. This latter belongs more especially to the knowledge of what is earthly, and it is from the conjunction of the latter with the more exalted knowledge that a
harmonious whole is formed. Further, it is not to be passed over
that Paul does not say that he knows anything of or concerning
Christ, but that he knows himself, he preaches himself. The
historical Christ is also the living one, who abides by his own
until the last day. He works personally in each believer, and is
begotten again in each. Therefore is Christ himself, the crucified
and the risen, everywhere the object of preaching, and also wisdom
itself (i. 31), for his history repeats itself throughout the church
and in every member of it, not becoming old thereby, for as
what is divine can never decay, it exists in the present day in the
same fulness of power in which it revealed itself at the foundation
of the church.

Vers. 3—5. As the individual has to work out his own salvation
with fear and trembling, God working in him to will and to do,
and inspiring thus a holy sense of God's presence (Phil. ii. 12,
13), so Paul, in perfect consciousness of the divine strength working through him, with fear and trembling, and acknowledging his
own weakness, appeared in Corinth to preach God, without any
admixture of what was human. It must be here observed, however, that it is not slavish fear that is spoken of, but the tender
concern which is in the nature of love, and the holy awe which
accompanies the love of God. It involves no idea of persecution,
mortification, or disorder, because the καὶ directly joins verses 2
and 3, so that the force is, "and therefore," or "in this consciousness." As he therefore preached a Saviour in weakness (viz. as crucified), so he declared himself to be weak. (The idea of his coming
among them is included in the ἐγενόμην πρὸς ὑμᾶς of ver. 3.—In
ver. 4 the first καὶ is to be understood as adversative. Paul lays
down the antithesis in himself weak, but strong in God.—Λόγος
refers to free dissension, κήρυγμα to preaching, properly speaking
as exposition.—Πειθοί is a reproving epithet, which indicates
the peculiar human persuasion, which should find no place in
the promulgation of the Gospel; believers should be converted by
the divine power alone. The form does not occur again; the
Greeks have πιθανός for it, and likewise πειστός, πειστικός, and

D

if some Codd. adopt these forms, or ἐν πειθοῖ, it is clear that these readings originate only in the endeavour to substitute a more usual for the unaccustomed form. The ἀνθρωπίνης is also a spurious addition, borrowed, without doubt, from ver. 13. The correct antithesis to πειθοὶ σοφίας λόγοι is clearly ἐν σοφίᾳ Θεοῦ, instead of which it represents it to be the operation of godly wisdom. Πνεύματος καὶ δυνάμεως is best comprehended as a hendiadyoin. The operation is to be supposed as first internal, because the Gospel has power to reform sinners, then it is external, as displaying itself in the Charismata.—In ver. 5 the ᾗ refers to the rise and lasting existence of faith. It is in the first instance the *creation* of the Spirit, in which the will of man has no part, (although he may obstruct its progress); but he finds a continual support in the divine Spirit, which, as it were, carries on continually the work of his regeneration).

Vers. 6, 7. After this, the apostle commences his important exposition of the characteristics of godly wisdom as manifested in Christ. The connexion with what precedes is this: if the Gospel possesses nothing of what is called wisdom by the world, it is by no means to be considered devoid of this property, having that which is far higher, viz., the wisdom which is from God. But to obtain a correct understanding of the following explanation, an examination of the relation of the πίστις to the σοφία and to the γνῶσις is indispensable.* Paul makes a predominant use of the first expression, but in i. 5 we have already met with γνῶσις, and γνῶναι is to be found in ii. 14; indeed the ideas are so closely linked that it is scarcely possible rightly to comprehend one without the other. The πίστις is, according to the observations upon Rom. iii. 21, the basis of Christian living, to which σοφία and γνῶσις may be advantageous. It is, received as *Christian* πίστις, God's life in man, the influence of Christ's Spirit in his heart, and consequently presupposes the gift of man to Christ. Then faith is next planted in the καρδία, since it certainly is not without knowledge, though it is not original, but proceeds from inward experience. In the progress of the life now regularly

---

* It is scarcely necessary to observe that πίστις, σοφία, γνῶσις are discussed here only as they necessarily belong to the constitution of the internal life of every believer, (one or other prevailing as it may be), and not as Charismata. In the latter quality the reader is referred to the remarks on xii. 7, sqq.

developed, the whole man is swayed more and more by the power of Christ, and consequently his thoughts likewise are sanctified. Thus the γνῶσις is formed as fruit of the πίστις, and the one is ever borne by the other, as the fruit by the branch, for the view which the πίστις alone can elevate is extended beyond the existence on this earth. The church collectively being a repetition of the course of individual life, so likewise then a γνῶσις must arise for it, that is to say, a theology in the true meaning of the word. But the γνῶσις will prove a ψευδώνυμος if not founded upon a life of faith and growing inward experience, but upon elements liable to error, because alien to the faith. In the expressions γνῶσις or ἐπίγνωσις (Eph. i. 17, iv. 13; Rom. i. 28), knowledge, as such, is also distinctly adverted to, not a knowledge apparent and ideal, but a knowledge of the being of God, grounded upon a real possession of him, upon the revelation of his divine nature to men. This knowledge can never be impracticable, since truth beholds with a correct eye outward circumstances, and tempers the energy of the will to work effectually according thereto; in this practical view the γνῶσις becomes σοφία. One side can never exist without the other, the theoretical without the practical, and *vice versa;* therefore, these two expressions might be used indifferently, when a precise distinction was not the object; but Paul here especially and intentionally employs σοφία because the deviations of the Corinthians were in general of a practical kind, and betrayed themselves in practice, though indeed they ultimately rooted themselves, and became as usual dogmatic errors. Paul again opposes the wisdom of God in the abstract, *i. e.,* as proceeding from God, to the wisdom of the world, but its divine properties are only recognised by the perfect, meaning the true believers (the πνευματικοί, iii. 1), who bear the principle of perfectness in themselves, without its being entirely developed (Phil. iii. 12—15). In this view the Gospel has, and ever retains the nature of a mystery, which the Almighty has prepared for men from the beginning of the world, but which should not be discerned of the natural man (ver. 14). In ver. 6, the construction σοφίαν ἐν τοῖς τελείοις is not like the dative "wisdom for the perfect," but equivalent to οὖσαν ἐν τοῖς τελείοις, "which only among the perfect is esteemed what it is in effect." —In that case the σοφία τοῦ αἰῶνος τούτου is = the σοφία τοῦ

κόσμου τούτου of i. 20; and if the ἄρχοντες is separated, it is only
for the purpose of more strongly displaying the triumph of divine
over human wisdom; for the expression does not signify evil
spirits (in which case this form is always in the singular), but
rulers and princes, in the learned, as in the political world, as ver.
8 shows. They had crucified Christ, but were καταργούμενοι,
since he was arisen again, and the church had continually extended itself; and the connexion between influence in the state
and learning proceeds in some degree from the circumstance that
cultivation among the higher classes is in general extended by
means of their learned men.—Ver. 7 has ἐν μυστηρίῳ and ἀποκεκρυμμένη, which is not to be accepted in the sense of an absolute
want of the power of discerning, otherwise no σοφία Θεοῦ could
ever exist among men, but only of the impossibility of its nature
being understood without the peculiar limits of the circle of the
Christian life. (See the remarks upon Rom. xvi. 25).—But the
expressions are not synonymous; the ἐν μυστηρίῳ is more applicable to men, "a wisdom in mysterious form, not discernible of
man in his natural power," but the ἀποκεκρυμμένη to God, "hidden in God and in his being, consequently it is itself of a divine
nature." Ver. 9 pursues the subject of this idea, and Heidenreich supplies γνωρίσαι to προώρισεν. In some passages, as
Eph. iii. 4, 5; Col. i. 26; 2 Tim. i. 9, this idea is prominent
throughout, but here the apostle appears to have intended by the
use of προώρισεν to declare, that God had previously destined to
man the gift of salvation through Christ, because the design of
revelation was sufficiently evident throughout the whole argumentation.—Αἰών has not literally the sense of eternity, it signifies
only a long period; but πρὸ τῶν αἰώνων, i. e., before all ages, indicates the metaphysical notion of eternity.—The δόξα is here not
glory, but glorification, for in i. 29, 31, Paul had completely condemned that which is of men; but the ἡμῶν does not only apply
to the apostles, but to all believers to whom the promises of ages
past were fulfilled).

Vers. 8, 9. That by the ἄρχοντες τοῦ αἰῶνος τούτου the
worldly great in knowledge and tradition were indicated, ver. 8
clearly shows, where they are represented as having crucified the
Lord of Glory. Yet it is by no means to be inferred that this expression referred to the Jews alone: without doubt the apostle

beheld in Pilate the representative of heathen sections, and therefore both Jews and heathens, in their scientific and political representatives, were alike included. The apostle proves the assertion (in agreement with Luke xix. 42, xxiii. 34; Acts iii. 17, xiii. 27), that they had not known the Lord Christ, from the fact that they had crucified him. This they could not *justify*, for had they rightly used the means afforded, they *might* have attained to a knowledge of Christ, as Acts xiii. 27 clearly shows; but it shall intimate and likewise *mitigate* their guilt, that the natural man, as such (ver. 14), ever thus acts, and consequently continually, as it were, crucifies Christ anew. However far the meaning of γινώσκειν might extend, it is restricted and defined by the expression κύριος τῆς δόξης. As a guiltless, and at the same time richly gifted being, *they* knew him well; therefore their guilt must ever remain great, as they delivered him through envy; but they really believed he was not the Son of God, because their notions of God were thoroughly false, and with such notions Christ's conduct by no means agreed. Δόξα is here the entire fulness of the glories of the eternal world, divine power, and glory, just as God is named, Acts vii. 2; Eph. i. 17. Θεὸς, or πατὴρ τῆς δόξης and κύριος τῆς δόξης, marks the divine nature of Christ, the knowledge of whom, indeed, is beyond the power of man, and only to be conferred upon the human race through the gift of God's Spirit, though the operation of this grace may be hindered by man's own resistance. In addition, ἐσταύρωσαν τὸν κύριον τῆς δόξης is one of the passages in the New Testament, in which an exchange of the predicate of the two natures is plain, thereby arguing that a correct principle lies in the doctrine of the *communicatio idiomatum*, although the form of its exemplification may not be suitable.—The quotation which follows (ver. 9) connects itself, as in i. 31, in the form of an anacoluthon. Theophylact considered that the addition of γέγονε would restore the construction; Billroth viewed the whole as an exposition of the σοφία Θεοῦ of ver. 7. But it appears more correct to understand the ἀλλά as introducing the antithesis to the words ἣν οὐδεὶς τῶν ἀρχόντων τοῦ αἰῶνος τούτου ἔγνωκεν (ver. 8). This Paul states impressively, not in his own words, but in those of Scripture; so that the meaning is this, " Which wisdom none of the rulers of this world understood, but it was prepared by God for those who love him, seeing that by human power it can never be attained unto." For ὀφθαλμὸς, οὖς, καρδία indicate the modes by which man, as such, attains either idea or notion; the love so apparent in all God's dealings conducts to a far richer world of knowledge and feeling than earthly means could open to our conception. The quotation therefore refers only to man in his natural state, the following verse representing him under the influence of the divine Spirit, by means of which he perceived essentially the truth of God's things. The ἀλλά alludes to the previously-mentioned οὐδεὶς ἔγνωκε. (See Winer's Gr. p. 421).— In the ἡτοίμασε is intimated the fact forming the subject of the communication, but the second ἃ stands for τοιαῦτα.—Ἀναβαίνειν ἐπὶ καρδίαν=לֵב לַב עַל עָלָה, for the rising of an earnest desire in the heart.—In the Old Testament there is literally no such passage; it is possible that Paul had Isa. lxiv. 3, 4, in his mind, quoting from memory; and something very similar is found in the passages Isa. lii. 15, and lxv. 17. The form καθὼς γέγραπται does not permit us to view the reference as to an apocryphal scripture, for it always signifies the Old Testament. Nevertheless Origen, Chrysostom, and Theodoret imagined that Paul had borrowed these words from an apocrypha of Elias. It is quite possible that these words existed in such a book, now lost to us; but as the book itself was doubtless the work of later times, it appears more probable that the words were quoted from our epistle by the apocrypha in question).

Ver. 10. Paul then derives the σοφία of believers from a similar exercise of God's grace; they knew God through the revelation of his Holy Spirit. Of course this is not to be understood as limited to the twelve apostles, but including all believers, who certainly at Pentecost received the gift of the Holy Spirit at the same time; yet the words strictly refer to the regenerate, and not to all the members of the church community. Concerning the ἀποκαλύπτειν διὰ πνεύματος see Matt. xvi. 17. The question here is not of the one great fact of the appearing of Christ, but of the individual effect which each experiences in himself proceeding from the power of Christ; just as in the same manner the process of seeing is not a consequence of the creation of the sun, but it rather requires that the ray of light reach the eye. (Τὸ ἀπεκάλυψε may be added from ver. 7 σοφίαν ἀποκεκρυμμένην). This revealing effect of the Spirit is deduced by the apostle from his general nature. The Spirit, *i. e.* the Spirit of God, searches likewise the depths of the Godhead, and can thence impart true knowledge concerning God. In consequence of the climax καὶ τὰ βάθη τοῦ Θεοῦ, πάντα must be taken in its widest sense, so that nothing may be excluded from the penetrating knowledge (ἐρευνᾶν) of the Spirit. Besides this, as the Spirit of God is God himself, the βάθη τοῦ Θεοῦ not only intimates the decrees of God, the acts of his will, but must also signify the divine Being itself. The Father is in his everlasting fulness and depth known in the Son and the Spirit, just as a man, (ver. 11), in the spirit of a man, knoweth the things that are in him, and there is also that in God which may be understood of man in his natural power (Rom. i. 19, 20). The τὰ βάθη in connexion with καὶ, "likewise the depths of God," signifies that which is absolutely beyond the limits of human understanding, *e. g.* the Trinity. But from the fact that the Spirit of God knows all, it is not to be inferred that he reveals *all* to men, but that it is only those things which concern Christ, called in ver. 12, τὰ ὑπὸ τοῦ Θεοῦ χαρισθέντα ἡμῖν: and even this, according to the apostle's idea, is *everything*, (see iii. 22). He who knows Christ knows God and all besides; for in Christ lie all the treasures of wisdom and knowledge. (Col. ii. 3). In 1 John ii. 20, 27, it is said of those who have the anointing of the Spirit, οὐ χρείαν ἔχετε, ἵνα τις διδάσκῃ ὑμᾶς, they know all! In this idea is not to be included all the minutiæ of earthly wisdom, but only the knowledge of the Eternal, in which all other is contained. How far the declarations of Paul in 1 Cor. xiii. 9, 12 agree with this, will be further shown in the explanation of that passage.

Ver. 11. Paul illustrates what follows in a remarkable manner by means of a parallel deduced from human knowledge. One would have supposed that the connexion between the divine Spirit and the divine Being was completely incomparable. Paul judges otherwise. Man, as the image of God, bears within himself analogies in certain relations, and similar parallels (see the Comm. on John i. 1) are sanctioned thereby. Upon a due consideration of the thought πνεῦμα ἀνθρώπου οἶδεν τὸ ἐν αὐτῷ. that is to say in the ψυχὴ as the centre of individuality, one might hesitate, because men so seldom truly know themselves, and self-knowledge is

found with few.   But is not the meaning of Paul, that the
spirit of men can know all that is in men, as the divine Spirit knows
all that belongs to God; his idea is rather this: let a man know
much or little as he may, it is ever by means of his own spirit that
he becomes acquainted with what he knows; no stranger can inves-
tigate the depths of another's soul.  Thus understood, the parallel is
equivalent, "as God's Spirit rules over all, so does the spirit of
man bear sway in himself, as in a microcosm."  The construction
which Billroth puts on the words of the apostle in this place is
evidently forced; and we should have thought the difference between the divine and human spirit would have prevented his discovering anything in this passage concerning their *identity*.   At
least the mode of expression chosen by him is easily misunderstood, as πνεῦμα Θεοῦ, or ἐκ Θεοῦ and πνεῦμα τοῦ ἀνθρώπου are
here as expressly separated as in Rom. viii. 16, (compare the explanation to the passage).   It would be more plain to say that
the human spirit is *allied* to the divine; and as originality is
in some degree necessary to a correct understanding, thus is
the human spirit the organ whereby man receives the divine
Spirit, and is enlightened through his influence.   But without
the divine Spirit (ver. 14), and with his natural spirit alone, he
could never know God.—The οὐδεὶς οἶδεν, εἰ μὴ τὸ πνεῦμα τοῦ Θεοῦ,
is, after what precedes, naturally to be received with the addition,
"and he, to whom the Spirit imparts knowledge," precisely as in
Matt. xi. 27, it is said, "No one knows the Father, save the Son,
and he to whom the Son will reveal him."   (See the Comm. on
this passage).   Although εἰδέναι is used in this and the following verse for divine knowledge, it is, as verse 14 shows, completely
synonymous with γνῶναι.

Vers. 12, 13.  By means of the comparison with an earthly
standard, the apostle endeavours to make the condition of the
regenerate mind, really knowing God, more comprehensible.
Over the former the πνεῦμα τοῦ κόσμου rules, whose spirit is so far
identical with that of the kingdom of darkness, as the latter may
be said to govern the world.  (Ephes. vi. 12).   The πνεῦμα ἐκ τοῦ
Θεοῦ is substantially the same as the πνεῦμα mentioned before,
only the ἐκ more strongly expresses the power proceeding from the
divine Spirit, revealing itself in the heart of man, in order that the
πνεῦμα προφορικόν may be in contradistinction to the ἐνδιάθετον.

if we may use the expression. The aim of this communication of the Holy Spirit is theoretical as well as practical, the knowledge of God's mercy in Christ (τὰ χαρισθέντα=χάρις, see i. 5, the gift of the Holy Spirit being falsely understood by some to be included therein) which is proclaimed by preaching, without any admixture of earthly wisdom. (Human should stand in opposition to godly wisdom. Paul, however, expresses it by πνεῦμα, as in ii. 4, the motive of wisdom.—Διδακτοῖς is in both cases derived from the genitive σοφίας and πνεύματος, and indicates the source of the instruction; the expression is also found in John vi. 45, διδακτοὶ Θεοῦ. The reading διδαχῇ would only remove the difficulty which occurs in connexion with the genitive). Some difficulties are to be found in the concluding sentence πνευματικοῖς πνευματικὰ συγκρίνοντες. The verb συγκρίνειν implies to mix, combine, propound something, from thence to bring, as it were, the proper argument in connexion with the individual present. But the dative πνευματικοῖς requires consideration. The translation, "propounding to the spiritual, things spiritual," does not appear suitable, for in iii. 1, Paul says that he could not speak to the Corinthians as with spiritual persons, although he had delivered unto them the Gospel; and certainly the Gospel is commonly preached to those who are yet unbelievers, with a view to their conversion. But the following verses require this explanation, viz., that the Corinthians, being carnal, cannot prevent his labouring spiritually among them, and the Spirit everywhere present may be awakened by spiritual efficacy. Grotius would refer πνευματικά to the Old Testament and πνευματικοῖς to the New, in the sense of explaining things spiritual by that which is spiritual. But the question is not here of the Old Testament; and I should hesitate to adopt, with Beza, the λόγοις, with the πνευματικοῖς, making the idea, "delivering spiritual things in a truly spiritual form," because then the ἐν would be absolutely necessary.

Ver. 14. The mention of the delivery of the Gospel leads the apostle naturally to the condition of man with reference to the same. He indicates accordingly two classes of men, ψυχικοὶ and πνευματικοί, and, taking the former into consideration, declares, first, that they would not receive the operation of the divine Spirit because it was foolishness to them; but, secondly, that they also were not capable of receiving it, since it must be spiritually discerned. The question is, how the idea of the ἄνθρωπος ψυχικός is to be defined, and why in one place it refers to σαρκικός, (iii. 1), and in the other to πνευματικός. First, we must bear in mind that these terms do *not* indicate unchangeably fixed and distinct classes of men, in which it would be impossible for transition from one to the other to take place, but conditions which in themselves men have the power of changing; no one is by birth a πνευματικός, and there are moments in which every one is σαρκικός. If we attempt to define first the extreme, it is clear that with the σαρκικός, the σάρξ *prevails*, and with the πνευματικός the πνεῦμα τοῦ Θεοῦ. The domination of the one principle does not, however, exclude the stirring of the other; on occasion, the Spirit may be perceived working with the σαρκικός, and the flesh with the regenerate; the character of an individual defines itself according as the one or the other of these principles decidedly predominates. But according to the situation of the ψυχή with respect to the σάρξ and the πνεῦμα (see my Treatise de Trichot. Nat. Hum. in the Opusc. Acad. p. 154, sqq.), the ψυχικός is he in whom neither σάρξ nor πνεῦμα decidedly prevail, but the intellectual life presents itself as such. It might be asserted that where this immaterial life predominated, the flesh would certainly ever powerfully exhibit itself as Paul represents, Rom. vii. 14, sqq. This is correct in many respects; nevertheless, even the natural man can maintain a certain δικαιοσύνη, and thus σαρκικός indicates a deep degree of moral depression, called forth by actual sin; but then the two expressions are so distinguished that σαρκικός intimates the *ethical* principle, ψυχικός the *intellectual*. If the natural man is to be designated, without the πνεῦμα τοῦ Θεοῦ, and as the transgressor of the νόμος, he is called σαρκικός; but if, on the contrary, he is to be represented in his incapability to know the Lord, he is named ψυχικός. (See James iii. 15; Jude ver. 19; in the latter passage the ψυχικοί are expressly called πνεῦμα μὴ ἔχοντες). It is precisely so here; as long as the ψυχικός remains what he is, carnal, he *cannot* acknowledge what is divine, for the requisite organ is wanting in him. No man can of his own power arrive at a knowledge of the truth in Christ; it is the work of God whenever accomplished. The knowledge here spoken of is not to be understood as a comprehensive reception of the doctrine of faith, (which might be ac-

quired by natural exertion), but as an insight proceeding from
inward enlightenment and experience. Nevertheless man in his
natural condition is not without the mind, which belongs essentially to his nature, but it slumbers in him, and only the animal
life is awake; yet, when the divine operation of the Gospel excites the human spirit, the ψυχικός ceases, and the πνευματικός, being capable of spiritually discerning, is living. It is true,
it can also be otherwise, and that man, by continued sin, may
sink below the beasts; that even the capacity for spiritual fervour
is lost, and his state is that of hardened obduracy. (See Comm.
on Rom. ix. 18).

Vers. 15, 16. One might now expect that Paul would continue, ὁ δὲ πνευματικὸς δέχεται τὰ τοῦ πνεύματος, as antithesis to
the ψυχικός: but the presence of the Spirit being assumed to
exist in him, (the *transition* between the condition being the
mysterious act of regeneration), Paul only describes the πνευματικός as he who judges all, without being judged of any. The
lofty station which Paul occupies enables him, as it were, to include the lower sphere, through which he had himself passed in
his supervision; but to the ψυχικός as well as the σαρκικός, the
view of the higher sphere is absolutely denied, as the world of
light is withheld from the blind. Paul adduces this fact of the
high comprehensive position as characteristic of the power of a
judgment which includes all in its grasp, because the Corinthians
would not concede it to him, the true πνευματικός, usurping to
themselves, although ψυχικοί, even σαρκικοί (iii. 1) the liberty
of judging Paul, for which they possessed in themselves no standard.* As a proof of the unlawfulness of these proceedings, Paul
appeals to Isa. xl. 13, where the Lord is described as incomprehensible to man. (This passage is also quoted in Rom. xi. 34,
but likewise, as here, concisely, as from memory. The LXX.
read συμβιβᾷ for συμβιβάσει, i. e. the Attic form of the future of
συμβιβάζω, which the LXX. more frequently use for הוֹרָה, " to
teach, to instruct." See Exod. iv. 12, 15; Lev. x. 11; Ps. xxxii. 8.

* It might appear contradictory to this, that Paul judges, nay condemns, Peter
and Barnabas, who must nevertheless be considered πνευματικοί (See Gal. ii.)
But this incident is thus reconcilable with the principle here laid down; that it
is not the spiritually regenerete man who is condemned in the πνευματικός, but
the natural man, who is co-existent in him.

The Attic dialect in this sense prefers the form προσβιβάζειν).
Between νοῦς κυρίου, and νοῦς Χριστοῦ no express difference can
be stated; νοῦς is synonymous with πνεῦμα, only the former expression implies spirit more than ability, as an ingredient in rational knowledge. Paul therefore ascribes to himself, as πνευματικός, the divine incomprehensible νοῦς: and, as mankind can
neither know nor instruct God, neither can the ψυχικός know or
guide the πνευματικός, for God is in him, and is spiritually the
living principle in the regenerate. How decidedly Paul held the
idea of the indwelling of God in believers, is shown in 1 Cor. xiv. 25,
as well as in the present passage, according to which unbelievers
shall acknowledge that God truly was in them. But the apostle
is far from comparing himself with God and Christ; he rather
represents himself as only the organ of God in Christ, in whom
the subjection to sin has been destroyed, though his thought is
often fearfully misused by enthusiasts and fanatics. In spiritual
darkness making themselves like God, as regenerate and true
πνευματικοί, they introduce the most terrible compulsion of conscience in their circle, requiring unconditional obedience to their
dictates, which they publish as operations of the νοῦς Χριστοῦ.
Paul, on the contrary, will admit of no adherence to his person,
but only to the truth which he preaches. (See on iii. 5—7, iv. 1).
Still the decision whether what he preaches is the truth, cannot
be left to men (iv. 3); the divine Spirit must verify it by the
issue, through the ἀπόδειξις δυνάμεως (ii. 4), as it has already
done beyond measure.

## § 3. THE BUILDING OF GOD.

### (iii. 1—22).

Paul proves, from the existing divisions in Corinth (iii. 1—4),
that the Christians there were yet far removed from the true spiritual standard, and displayed themselves rather as carnal-minded.
They had mistaken the instruments in building for the heavenly
Architect himself, and so laid waste God's temple in the church,
which was advancing towards completion, even although the true
foundation, once laid in it, yet remained uninjured, (iii. 5—17).

They might, nevertheless, upon abandoning their false wisdom, and showing themselves to be willing to lose everything for Christ, receive all again (iii. 18—22). Vers. 1, 2. The transition from the 2d to the 3d chapter is incorrectly conceived, when thus understood, "If the spiritual are not to be judged, how can you, Paul, then judge us!" to which the apostle replies, "Because ye are not truly spiritual:" but there exists no trace of the Corinthians desiring to reject the judgment of the apostle, although they, so incompetent, passed judgment on him. Unquestionably the precipitate opinion of the Corinthians was restrained (see iv. 3) by the information that they were not competent to judge in the matter. According to the form the κἀγὼ οὐκ ἠδυνήθην λαλῆσαι is connected in ver. 13 with the πνευματικοῖς πνευματικὰ συγκρίνοντες. Paul intended to say that he was not yet able to submit his discourse to the Corinthians in a form corresponding to the elevation of the subject, but was compelled to present it as they were able to bear it. It is, however, important to observe, that Paul considers the Corinthians as regenerate, as νήπιοι ἐν Χριστῷ, and nevertheless calls them σαρκικοί, which seems contradictory. It is, however, strictly agreeable to the remarks made on ii. 14, that even the πνευματικός can upon occasion be σαρκικός. The Corinthians were upon the whole, according to their standard, believers, regenerate men, Christ the true foundation being laid in them (ver. 11); but they were not faithful as to the gift they had received; for, reverting to their carnal standard, they mingled their old views with the new element of life, and this is what the apostle reproves. That this fact had been the subject of remark at a preceding period is shown by the ἠδυνήθην and ἐπότισα, (in the aorist lies a reference to a second presence of Paul in Corinth, for the first, when the church there was founded, the expression cannot refer; at that period the life of faith was in progress among the Corinthians, and it would not have been made a subject of reproach to them, that it was only in the first stage of development, which however happens here), and that it still continued is plain from the words οὐδὲ ἔτι νῦν δύνασθε. Paul therefore makes use of degrees in describing the progress of the Christian life, as in 1 John ii. 13. Children, young men, and men in Christ, are separately addressed in the passage quoted.

In each of these gradations *salvation* is attainable, but the *degree*
of salvation is measured by the gradation attained unto in sanctification. (See on iii. 15). What is the connexion here between
γάλα and βρώμα ? Some say, that the former expression signifies
the easy, and the latter the more difficult doctrines of the Gospel.
According to this it would be important to observe, that Paul, in
the Epistle to the Corinthians, treats of many subjects which
cannot be included in the former category. In Heb. vi. 3,
the doctrine of the resurrection is reckoned among the fundamental doctrines of the Christian belief; but the discussion
upon the Charismata (1 Cor. xii. 14) does not certainly belong
to the simple doctrines of the Gospel. It may be said that
this doctrine is difficult to be understood by us, because the
power of discerning the gifts is wanting, but I think it would be
better to understand the γάλα and βρῶμα differently. We cannot correctly say that one doctrine, as such, is comprehensible,
and another is difficult; it is rather with all doctrine the purely
positive side which is simple, and the speculative which presents
difficulty. Paul had preached to the Corinthians the crucified
Saviour as their Redeemer, as he himself declares (ii. 2): this
was milk for the babes in spirit, whereby they might grow; but
when he revealed to them in what manner Jesus was the Redeemer of men, the food proved more unpalatable. To this
deeper knowledge men were introduced in the Epistle to the
Hebrews, Paul being yet unable to bring it before the Corinthians, because of the pride of their human wisdom and capacity for deep investigation. (In ver. 1, κἀγώ stands opposed
to what precedes, ἡμεῖς δὲ νοῦν Χρίστοῦ ἔχομεν, in the sense
of, " I have truly the knowledge, but cannot impart it to you."
The *text. rec.* reads σαρκικοῖς, Griesbach and Lachmann have
preferred σαρκινοῖς, and A.B.C.D. have the latter reading.
But as σαρκινός properly signifies " fleshy, of flesh," as is shown
in 2 Cor. iii. 3, and the form σαρκικός on the contrary " fleshly,"
we must suppose an exchange of the two forms to have taken
place in the later Greek, which it was not needful for the
LXX. and the New Testament to demonstrate. I decide therefore in favour of the usual reading, and believe that the variation had its origin in the oversight of the transcriber, and the
little care taken to distinguish the forms which prevailed in later

times; and I the more incline to this opinion, because immediately in what follows, σαρκικοί must be read.—Νήπιοι= παιδία, 1 John ii. 13.—In ver. 2 the connexion of the last word of ver. 1 with ὑμᾶς by means of νηπίους has too slight a critical foundation to claim to be received. Concerning the Zeugma γάλα ὑμᾶς ἐπότισα, οὐ βρῶμα, see Winer's Gr. p. 540).

Vers. 3, 4. As a proof of their slight spiritual progress, the apostle adduces their divisions, in which the excessive appreciation of what was human was displayed in preference to that which was divine, and likewise the blindness of their minds with respect to things eternal. (In ver. 3, ὅπου, "where," takes the meaning of " as far, therefore;" see Viger, 430, sqq.—Ζῆλος is the inward transport of anger, ἔρις the exhibition of it by opposition to others, διχοστασία (Rom. xvi. 17; Galat. v. 20) is the consequence of this expression, the existing dissensions.—Κατὰ ἄνθρωπον περιπατεῖν=κατὰ σάρκα περιπατεῖν, Rom. viii. 4. The antithesis is κατὰ Θεόν or κατὰ πνεῦμα περιπατεῖν.—In ver. 4 and ver. 5, Paul mentions only himself and Apollos, for the reason assigned in iv. 6).

Vers. 5—7. In order to express fully the perversion which exists, in this adherence to what is simply human, the apostle explains by what follows the position of all promulgators of the Gospel, to God the Lord; they are only servants, (iv. 1). He it is who works through them, who is all in all; and on him alone must all depend (iii. 22). (In ver. 5, the τίς οὖν has, like διάκονος, something of under-estimation. Ver. 7 replies to the first question, they are nothing; κύριος is in opposition to servant.— According to critical authority, the reading ἀλλ' ἢ διάκονοι is rejected, although the greater part of minuskela MSS. defend it, and in itself the reading is not objectionable; ἀλλ' ἢ stands for nisi, see Luke xii. 51, Herm. ad Viger, p. 812, who remarks that the supposition of the omission of οὐδέν further explains it. —Ἑκάστῳ ὡς stands for ὡς ὁ κύριος ἑκάστῳ ἔδωκεν. Paul makes this addition, in order to represent the variety of the gifts, and the efficacy arising therefrom, as a disposition of the Lord, and not as arbitrary. Pursuing the simile of the husbandman, with him is found the gift of φυτεύειν, and with Apollos that of ποτίζειν. In the first expression, the faculty of opening the way to a new life, which was so prominent in Paul, is implied. John had it not, nor had Apollos. (See Introd. to Gospel of St John). But these had the gift of advancing the life already kindled, as the expression ποτίζειν seems to signify. But the gifts can effect as little in spiritual, as diligence and expertness in temporal matters, without God's blessing: he it is who gives the increase and sanctification).

Vers. 8, 9. The different gifts stand then equal in the church, as the various members to the body, and certainly, according to their faithful employment, shall every man receive his reward. We labour together for the things of God; ye are his husbandry, his building; every one is therefore rewarded, according as he has laboured in his field. The συνεργοί ἐσμεν and γεώργιόν ἐστε leave no doubt that Paul here distinguishes the teachers from the taught, and that also verse 8 speaks of the reward of faithful teachers; but in the church of Christ, where each may become (1 Pet. ii. 5) a living, self-erected stone of the temple of God (ver. 16), this distinction is merely a current one; and, in ver. 12, we may perceive that Paul proceeds to general observations, and represents every believer as charged to proceed with the building of the temple, whose foundation is laid in him. But, instead of admitting this, if in what follows the foundation is understood like the φυτεύειν, the ἐποικοδομεῖν like the ποτίζειν, the representation which succeeds may form a polemic against Apollos, and a justification of himself, which certainly never formed part of his plan, which was rather in what succeeds to animate the Corinthians to follow after Christ, and in him to attain salvation. (In ver. 8 the ἔν εἰσι declares the impartiality of the standard; no one has any preference before the other, and it is only their faithfulness in the employment of the gifts which places them higher or lower. The parable of the talents (Matt. xxv. 14, sqq.) illustrates at large the idea ἴδιον μισθὸν λήψεται κατὰ τὸν ἴδιον κόπον, (see the explanation of the passage).—In ver. 9 Θεοῦ συνεργοί is not to be understood "labourers with, with God," for he effects all (ver. 7), but, "labourers, who work with each other, for the things of God."—The expression γεώργιον refers to the earlier image, οἰκοδομή to the new one of the temple, (ver. 16) as will sufficiently appear in what follows.

Vers. 10, 11. Leaving the subject of Apollos, Paul now addresses the members of the Corinthian church collectively, upon more enlarged views, (not the teachers alone among them, although ver. 16, sqq. shows that he had them still before his eyes), and declares how he was chosen of God, as master-builder, to lay the foundation, that only may be laid, viz., Christ; and that every one had now to take heed *how* he builded upon this foundation. The question here is, what the apostle intended by the foundation, that as a wise master-builder he had laid,* and which he designates the only one which may be laid? "The doctrine of Jesus, as the Christ?" This doctrine may certainly be the foundation of a theology, but not of a living church; believers themselves are the temple of God (ver. 17). Consequently it is *the living Christ himself* who calls himself the corner-stone, which the builders have rejected, but who nevertheless is appointed by God as the foundation to the whole building of God (see Comm. on Matt. xxi. 42), and is therefore named ὁ κείμενος, meaning, laid by God; for which reason no one can lay any other foundation without resisting him. But if this is the meaning, how can Paul say: According to the grace given unto me I have laid the foundation? The apostle might so far say it, as Jesus Christ, the foundation of the whole church upon earth, must declare himself in his life-inspiring power at the rise of every individual church, nay, in every heart, if it would be sanctified. The state of the great universal temple of God is thus repeated in every church, in every heart; everywhere must the living Christ be the corner-stone, the new man, born in regeneration. Without the evidence of this inward life of Christ in man, it is not possible to imagine either Christian or church, but where it exists in even two or three, there is the germ of a church, (Matt. xviii. 20). This indwelling of Christ is, however, produced by the word of preaching, declared through his messengers, and therefore a continual activity in the church is necessary for this purpose. Paul in this respect was able to say that he had laid the foundation in Corinth, although it was indisputably God who granted the success; but it pleased God to work in Corinth by no

---

* Rückert endeavours, though erroneously, to discover in the epithet "wise" master-builder a reference to the nature of Paul's spiritual labours. But the apostle calls himself so, because in the power of the Spirit he had preached the only true groundwork, Christ; and had not desired, like the false teachers in Corinth, to weaken the power of Christ by human knowledge.

E

other than the apostle; his mouth was, as it were, the door of grace by which the living strength had streamed towards the Corinthians. According to this, it must be clear that, in saying ἕκαστος δὲ βλεπέτω, πῶς ἐποικοδομεῖ, all the Christians in Corinth are intended; not the teachers alone have the Christ at the foundation of the temple in them, but every one who will believe must have this groundwork; it is not the teachers only who construct the building upon the foundation already laid, but it is the task of every individual believer to perfect the work.

Vers. 12, 13. The activity of the faithful in continuing the work upon the imperishable foundation may be exercised upon imperishable materials, but it is also possible to be the reverse of this, and both forms will nevertheless have the appearance of laudable activity. The apostle comprehends both in his representation, because according to the nature of the thing they are connected; they who work for others under a wrong impression will never labour differently for themselves, since outward action must ever flow from the impulse of the whole mental condition. This is the reason for the authority which Paul gives the teachers (whom he ever specially had in view) over believers, which was so much the more necessary, because those who allowed themselves to be falsely persuaded were prevented by their perversion from rightly discriminating between what was true and false; and when we come to ver. 15 we shall perceive with certainty what the apostle intended in the figurative expressions which contained his idea. We shall therefore only now remark, that the single words χρυσὸν, ἄργυρον, λίθους τιμίους, and again ξύλα, χόρτον, καλάμην, imply the materials necessary for costly and durable buildings (see Isa. liv. 11; Rev. iii. 18), and that which is more common and combustible, it being scarcely necessary to add that they are not parallel, as if gold and straw could be equally used in the same house, but that all three of the expressions are antithetical, as if it were called, ἢ ξύλα, χόρτον, καλάμην. The nature of every man's work will certainly be known, continues Paul, for with fire, the element of trial, shall the day of judgment declare it. The μισθὸν λήψεται and ζημιωθήσεται leave us no doubt that ἡμέρα is not to be received in the usual signification of "time" or "light," in opposition to darkness, but that it refers to the day of judgment, as the agent whereby everything, and

being, in its true ποιότης, will be manifest.  We must then only
supply ἡμέρα to ἀποκαλύπτεται, so that πῦρ is the element in
which that decisive day shall reveal itself, in exact conformity
with 2 Thess. i. 8; 2 Peter iii. 10—12.  (The present ἀποκαλύπτεται is quite conformable with the preceding future δηλώσει,
since it is a description of the nature of the day in itself, and
need not therefore to be understood as *futurascens*, as Billroth
asserts.

Vers. 14, 15.  The nature of the building is revealed by fire; that
built with gold, silver, and precious stones stands (μένει) the proof,
while that constructed with wood, hay, and stubble burns; the one
produces advantage, the other injury.  So far the image is simple and comprehensible, and doubtless the whole passage would
have far less occupied annotators if the obscure sentence αὐτὸς δὲ
σωθήσεται, οὕτως δὲ ὡς διὰ πυρός were wanting.  Without these
words one would be able, according to the context, τοῦτον φθερεῖ
ὁ Θεός (ver. 17), to refer· ζημιωθήσεται to condemnation, and
the μισθὸν λήψεται to everlasting happiness; but the words αὐτὸς σωθήσεται forbid this; they manifestly distinguish the
builder from his building.  No proof is necessary to refute the
supposition of the Fathers that σωθήσεται signified preservation
in fire, *i. e.* an everlasting torment in fire, which must be expressed by σωθήσεται ἐν πυρί.*  The question consequently
arises, of which of the capacities for building does the apostle
here speak, the result of which may perish yet the builder be
saved, *i. e.* beatified?  One might suppose that Paul spoke of the
*teachers*, and not of the individual working for salvation on the
part of each believer.  Whoever builds up hay and stubble upon
the real foundation laid in his heart must perish; although we
may suppose that a teacher would not from an evil intention
build falsely upon a good ground the work laid in the church, but
rather from misapprehension, and his work would then, to his
sorrow, perish, although he himself would be saved on account of
his faith.  But it has already been shown (ver. 12) that all believers were included, and that the reference was not only to teachers
as such; in fact the latter were only so far comprehended as they
were likewise believers.  The following account of the temple of

* This unreasonable explanation of Theophylact, is grounded upon the form σώζε-
ται ξύλον ἐν πυρί, one wood is preserved in the fire something longer than another.

God shows that the teachers, together with them, belonged to the one great universal temple, every violation of which Paul would reprove in himself and others. We must therefore confess that although Paul's argument first commenced with the teachers (ver. 5), it nevertheless gradually shaped itself so in its continuance that it acquired a universal character, and that altogether the reference to teachers, as well as learners, is in part simply a current one. Under any circumstances, however, the preceding reference to teachers could not be employed in the explanation of the present passage; for a teacher who could build what was false upon a just groundwork for others, must, in order to be capable of this, have already fallen into the same error as regards himself. But if this nevertheless will not prevent his salvation, though the building in others is destroyed, he may also be saved, if the false building in himself is destroyed by fire; and what is possible for him is practicable for all. Now, as this salvation is the consequence of the true foundation, Jesus Christ, what is the ἐποικοδομεῖν ξύλα, χόρτον, καλάμην?* It has been erroneously supposed that it was a life of crime and transgression of the law, for the absolute rule of sin would again break up the foundation itself and lead to desertion from Christ (see 1 Cor. v. 11). Such persons, in order to be saved, would need a new conversion, i. e. a new foundation of Christ in us. Others have supposed it was the false doctrines, and, when these are corrupt in the fundamental dogmas, it is not inapplicable; for gross and false doctrines are, as it were, intellectual vices, which, having their foundation in the heart, destroy the groundwork of God's building. We may therefore say that to erect wood and stubble upon an everlasting foundation, is indicative of a misplaced labour and false working in the convert, because, being indifferent and slothful in unsubstantial things, he does not proceed more strictly or

---

* Jäger (work already quoted, p. 6) considers that the building thereon with wood, hay, and stubble, does not intimate that which is erroneous, but only a less distinguished activity for the church; the apostle imagines the building shall be constructed out of precious and at the same time humbler materials (which is also the opinion of Grotius), every one aiding it according to his power. But this does not agree well with the burning, whereby the destruction of this is intimated, nor in ver. 17, the εἴ τις ναὸν φθείρει, which Jäger without foundation refers to others than the builders with wood upon the true foundation. The whole comparison is founded on this idea: upon a beautiful firm foundation we do not raise a miserable edifice, but, when Christ is the corner-stone, the building must be continued with suitable materials.

carefully in doctrine, but lays weight upon some things less essential to the practical life, the Charismata for example. (See on xii. 14). Such labour, whether for one's self or others, is ineffectual; if, however, the heart and the inward principle abide in the Lord, the man himself may yet be saved although his work perish. According to this, the important truth is to be found in this passage which the evangelical church has ever decidedly maintained, that *salvation* is alone the condition of the *faith* which is connected with Christ as the foundation; but the *degree* of salvation stands in proportion to the degree of sanctification which the man attains; that is to say, that whosesoever work, together with the foundation in him, shall stand the test in the day of the Lord, will attain unto a higher reward than he who loses his labour and is barely saved himself.* According to this, the subject of this passage cannot be, as Scaliger, Grotius, and others have supposed, a hypothetical salvation, as if the sense of the words was, *if* he should be saved, it can only occur through fire; on the contrary, salvation is assured and certain if the foundation remains, and truly under these circumstances the path to salvation would be a painful one, ὡς διὰ πυρός. The ὡς alludes undeniably to a figurative expression; we have only to inquire what its signification may be. It might relate to that which was *difficult*, or scarcely possible, in the act of saving, what in Jude 23 is called ἐκ τοῦ πυρὸς ἁρπάζειν, and in the analogous passage in Zech. iii. 2, " to pluck one like a brand out of the fire." But it lies not in the strain of the apostle's argumentation, that the saving is hardly practicable; he will rather maintain that salvation is certain, where the groundwork already laid abides. It would therefore be better to lay the stress upon the *pain* which would necessarily arise at the view of the destruction of the building; and as, according to the nature of the thing, there is ever uncertainty as to the foundation being yet firm, the idea of

---

* The objection, that none can be saved who possess the consciousness that they have not made the progress towards grace of which they were capable, proves too much, for then none could be saved, since none have passed through life with a perfect fidelity, and every imperfection obstructs the development of the inward life ; and as the degree of salvation is conditional upon the inward susceptibility for the same, so does the excess of joy that each experiences banish all saddening recollections arising out of the life upon earth—the measure of the former being infinitely greater than that of the latter—nevertheless every one shall receive into his bosom full and overflowing measure.

the uncertainty of being saved is included in the former idea. It may here be asked, if in this conception the Catholic doctrine of *ignis purgatorius* may not be found, to which Zoroaster (in the Zendavesta, Bundehesch, vol. iii. p. 113, 114, Kleuker's ed.)* in his Duzath has an analogy? that purgatory being intended certainly for believers, not for unbelievers, who, as such, according to the Catholic doctrine, are lost; it purifies only the believers from the dross which still adheres, in order to make them fit for the purity of heaven. The Catholic dogmatisers were naturally desirous to find in this passage a foundation for their doctrine of purgatory; but by a closer consideration of Paul's fundamental ideas, which we must maintain to exist also in this passage, we shall perceive that not the slightest similarity exists between the Catholic theory of purgatory and the ideas mentioned, for it refers to the cleansing from the dross of personal sin of believers not sanctified here below; but for purification from sin no other means exist than Christ himself. In one passage the allusion is not to any purifying of persons from sin, but the subject of it is, the test to which their works, and their building must submit, and the works which cannot stand in the day of judgment have their origin in the old man of sin; this, however, can never be purified by the day of judgment and its trial. The apostle Paul never ceases to declare that the original old man must die; a gradual cleansing of the same is as little possible as that an Ethiopian should change his skin (Jer. xiii. 23). The new man, on the contrary, requires no purification, he is, as such, absolutely pure, he has the δικαι-οσύνη Θεοῦ: he may be said to exist in various grades of development, but in each of these degrees he is, and remains, pure, as born of God; therefore throughout Paul cannot be speaking of purification.† The Pelagian Catholic view, however, does not place the old and new man in this rugged opposition as the holy writings do. According to them there is no new birth of the

---

* Every soul, says Zoroaster, must pass through a sea of molten brass; to the holy, this stream is like warm milk, but to the unholy very painful, consuming all the dross in them.

† Passages such as 2 Cor. vii. 1, must, agreeably to Paul's principles, be thus understood: that the gradual extension of the new life which Christ kindles in men also brings by degrees into view the purity of this principle. In this manner the old man gradually dies, and the new man gradually becomes stronger; the individual identity, however, remains the same, *appearing* as if the sinful creature were cleansed, while in fact the new man dispossesses the old.

sanctified creature of God, but the old purifies itself gradually; and they who do not proceed sufficiently far must atone for their neglect in the fire of purgatory for a longer or shorter period. This accordingly appears a painful preparation for perfection, of which the apostle makes no mention; he speaks only of the removal of the useless buildings.

Vers. 16, 17. The apostle here again reverts to the image of the οἰκοδομὴ (ver. 9). Semler says, not inapplicably, that the passage may be understood *hac comparatione commode usus sum.* But what has been said of the building (ver. 9) is heightened by the consideration that this building is pointed out as God's temple. The injury (φθείρειν) of a building (by the addition of worthless materials to it, ver. 12) is enhanced in guilt in proportion to the dignity of the being who should inhabit the edifice; and inasmuch as the faithful constitute the living and holy temple of God (1 Pet. ii. 5), filled by the divine Spirit, any one who presumed to degrade himself, or any other part of this temple, would sorely commit himself. If the reference to teachers alone in this passage is maintained, the οἰκεῖ ἐν ὑμῖν, οἵτινές ἐστε ὑμεῖς must mean the laity without the teachers, which is evidently not the case. Paul addresses all teachers as well as learners, active and passive members of the church, not speaking in his own person, lest the power of the remonstrance should be weakened thereby, although his own authority would stamp a value on it, for through him God's Spirit spoke to the church. But the case of the individual is precisely the same as with the entire temple of God. What is addressed to the latter is also valid for the former. To injure the temple of God stands parallel with building in wood and stubble; and it refers as much externally to mistaken labours for others, as internally to the false working in and for one's self. He who errs in one respect will not fail to do so in the other. In ver. 17 is consequently to be found not only, They who as teachers corrupt you, who are the temple of God, corrupt God also; but also, Whoever corrupts himself, building or permitting what is false to be built upon the real foundation laid in his heart, corrupts God, for to every one is the power given to oppose the labours of others when based upon error.—In itself, as already remarked, the φθερεῖ τοῦτον ὁ Θεός is a strong expression, but the context shows that it does not imply an absolute rejection. It is possible that the apostle only employed it because of the preceding φθείρει, in order to intimate that God requites like with like.

Vers. 18—20. The apostle then returns to the warning against human wisdom (see ii. 4—13) which so many, like wood and stubble, have erected for themselves and others upon the sacred foundation. Instead of the seeming wisdom, the apostle exhorts them to choose the divine true wisdom; because the wisdom of the world, as foolishness before God, will be destroyed in the fire of the divine judgment. (Had Paul, in ver. 18, spoken only of teachers, he could not justly have written μηδεὶς ἑαυτὸν ἐξαπατάτω: the warning is general for all Corinthian Christians. Concerning the form, see Gal. vi. 7.—On σοφὸς ἐν τῷ αἰῶνι τούτῳ, and likewise μωρός, see i. 20, 21.—Ver. 19 is a quotation from Job v. 13. The Hebrew words run לֹכֵד חֲכָמִים בְּעָרְמָם, which the LXX. translate ὁ καταλαμβάνων σοφοὺς ἐν τῇ φρονήσει. Paul seems to have intentionally passed over the strong expression δράσσεσθαι, i. e., grasp with the hand, and to have chosen πανουργία, in order to represent the misapplication of wisdom to evil ends.—Ver. 20 is taken out of Psalm xciv. 11, and quoted literally according to the translation of the LXX.)

Vers. 21, 22. To this is again appended the exhortation not to glory in men, (see i. 31), for all that men have and can have is alone from the Lord. In ver. 21, according to what follows, the ἐν ἀνθρώποις is not to be understood as representing the heads glorying in the numerous followers, but contrariwise, the followers are to be understood as glorying in the head, imagining themselves to acquire lustre from their pre-eminence. For this reason Paul specifies Apollos and Peter, together with himself, as those to whom the Corinthians especially connect themselves, and openly expresses the opinion that they, with all their privileges, belonged to them (the church). Indeed the apostle goes further, and, passing beyond the things of this world, adjudges all to them. It yet appears striking that θάνατος is used, as the sentence refers more especially to advantages; that it should be employed only to complete the antithesis is little probable, it would be better to place ζωή and ἐνεστῶτα (=πάροντα, προκείμενα, Rom. viii. 38; 1 Cor. vii. 26; Gal. i. 4) and θάνατος and μέλλοντα as parallels, so that death signifies all that follows as a consequence, future glorification likewise included; for certainly the death here spoken of is not intended to intimate spiritual death, but rather the natural one, regarding it as a blessing, inasmuch as it conducts to Christ. The world here implies all created things, and its external blessings, without an accessory notion of sinfulness, forming in some degree an antithesis to the other objects named, which are things that represent inward advantages. The idea is the same as that expressed in Mark x. 29, 30. The believer feels himself dependent on Christ alone, and with him the Creator of all things, God himself—all things created are his. Thus understood, the πάντα ὑμῶν ἐστιν is one of the most singularly decided expressions employed by the apostle in reminding his readers how abundantly Christ is the *gnomon* shadowed forth in the contents of the Gospel;* this explicitly states the wondrous nature of the love poured into the hearts of believers through the Spirit, by means of which man spans the world and partakes, with others, of all that is beautiful and excellent therein, as if it were his own. This offers a complete contrast to all envyings and discord which give rise to isolation, as well as to the disposition to view all blessings in others with indifference. The Gospel effects a genuine community of goods, freedom, and equality in a holy sense. It has been sufficiently shown in the Introduction that it is an error to understand this passage as praising the Christians, as Pott, Schott, and others imagine. In the first place they are not mentioned, for the words ὑμεῖς δὲ Χριστοῦ cannot possibly refer to *some* of the Corinthian Christians, but to *all* of them, precisely as the πάντα ὑμῶν ἐστιν includes all. And further, the reason that only Peter, Paul, and Apollos are specified, is to be found in the nature of the name belonging to the fourth party; and another reason that no express mention is made of the *Christianer*, was owing to the form of the discourse, in which the name could not voluntarily be brought in without appearance of constraint. It is true, Paul might have

---

* This saying: "All is yours," is available for the church in all times. May it be heeded now, in the newly awakened strife of creeds, and may the disputants never forget that every creed may possess a value which ought to be made available for the advantage of the whole church!

said, All that is Christ's is yours, or Christ himself is yours; but
under no circumstances could he have placed Christ, through
whom all is, (Col. i. 16, sqq.), in the same category with Paul,
Peter, and Apollos, who only through him are what they are.
(The word Χριστός, which includes also the human nature, in the
person of the Lord (Matt. i. 1) proves, that the concluding words
of the chapter Χριστὸς δὲ Θεοῦ contain no subordinate views favourable to the Trinity, and in reference to his manhood Scripture
everywhere expresses the dependence of the Son upon the Father).

## § 4. HUMAN JUDGMENT.

### (iv. 1—21).

Paul desires to be considered only as a servant of Christ, the
universal Lord; but for this very reason he refuses to permit
himself to be judged of his brethren, referring all to the future
judgment of Christ, (1—5). Bringing forward Apollos and
himself as an example, the apostle exhorts the high-minded
among the Corinthians to humility, and, for this purpose exposes
to them a humiliating view of their despised apostolic life, (6—
13). He then assures them that these warnings proceed from his
paternal love for them, and that he intended shortly to come to
them, in order to punish the haughty if they refused to hear the
words of love (14—-21).

Ver. 1. The transition is by no means assisted by the formula
οὕτως ἡμᾶς λογιζέσθω ἄνθρωπος, ὡς κ. τ. λ., nevertheless a very
strict connexion exists. After Paul had asserted (iii. 22) none
might glory in men, since they all stood in a common dependence
on Christ, he declares that he himself, in this same dependence,
will be recognised and received. But although he thus rejects
all appearance even of being over-estimated by his own party, on
the other side he refuses to submit to the judgment of his adversaries; Christ is rather the judge of all, and, if declared faithful
by him he is content. It is, however, certain that Paul did not
mean by this that an apostle was by no means to be judged of
men, for he himself commented upon the behaviour of Peter,
(Gal. ii.); still less is it to be supposed that all Christians

without exception were intended, as if they were to be exempt
from all judgment, because they were Christians; the meaning is
rather this: that every Christian, and in an especial sense the
teachers and apostles of the church, who, from their office, should
be able to exhibit the Christian character in its purity, shall, *in
as far* as they are truly Christians, not be judged, for they judge
all (1 Cor. vi. 2, 3). But as in all believers, so long as they are
upon earth, a trace of their earthly nature remains, these not
only submit themselves to judgment, but even to punishment,
should the case require its faithful administration; the Corinthians, however, judged the apostle labouring in the truth, without being competent to the task of judging. The question now
arises, whether Paul indicates only the apostles, or all the teachers in the church, or all believers without exception, as the ὑπη-
ρέτας Χριστοῦ καὶ οἰκονόμους μυστηρίων Θεοῦ. The latter is
utterly improbable, because the Corinthians to whom he wrote
were certainly Christians, although he represents himself and Apollos (ver. 6) as differing from them. Of the Christians especially this could only so far be said, as they were thought to oppose
the heathen world (or what is the same, that world which was
absolutely without impulse from the living element of Christ) to
whom every believer, being regenerate, must be opposed, as
stewards of God's mysteries, and of the whole church as a royal
priesthood (1 Pet. ii. 9). In the church itself the words would signify teachers,* but inasmuch as the *external* was not identical with
the true church, they can only refer to the *office*, and not necessarily to the *person* invested with it. The notion, too, that the prerogative due only to the apostle is here intimated is assuredly false;
for God has certainly not again taken back the mysteries from
his church since the apostolic times, and, if they still exist, the

---

* This reference to teachers alone, found in iv. 1, sqq., in connexion with the
paragraph iii. 5—9, affords some colour for the opinion, that what occurs between
these passages is also referable to the same, as decidedly maintained by Rückert.
But I think I have plainly shown, in the observations on vers. 10, 13, 14, 17, 18,
that the paragraph iii. 10—22 must be regarded as an extension of the preceding
subject. From the teachers only Paul passes over to all Christians, who collectively are called to build on the ground-work laid for them, and to whom, in all
important points, what has been said of the instructors is applicable. Nevertheless the apostle has always the latter pre-eminently in view, and they are again
mentioned alone in iv. 1. In iv. 6, the intention is expressed of speaking of and
to all in the names of Paul and of Apollos.

heads of the church (according to the intention of their holy office) must be their stewards. Thus much is however clear, that this passage can only be understood by the admission that Paul wished for the acknowledgment of *an appointed ministerial state*, and does not recommend a *democratic equality of all*. Whilst the expression ὑπηρέται Χριστοῦ (= δοῦλοι Χριστοῦ) warns them against making the servants equal to the Lord; on the other hand, the second name οἰκόνομοι μυστηρίων Θεοῦ exalts the greatness of the office of the Christian ministry; and here evidently the μυστήρια (to which Paul sometimes adds εὐαγγελίου, πίστεως, Χριστοῦ, or Θεοῦ, see Eph. vi. 19; 1 Tim. iii. 9; Col. ii. 2, iv. 3), is to be viewed as a treasure, to be administered, which, according to Matt. xiii. 52, is entrusted to the church. In this treasure, teaching, with its fulness of mysteries, is naturally to be included, but not less so the sacraments, and all utterance of the powers of the Holy Spirit, which only flow within the church, and ought only to be distributed by the appointed servants of the same, in their capacity of instructors. For the preaching of the word, and the administration of the sacraments, Paul regarded himself, and also the teachers generally, as responsible servants, but did not consider that every one indiscriminately should teach (Jam. iii. 1) or distribute the sacraments. (Οὕτως is not to be referred to the foregoing, as if it were, " so let every one then esteem us," but to the ὡς which follows, so that it is equivalent to τοιούτους.— Ἄνθρωπος, according to the Hebrew אָדָם stands for ἕκαστος. See 1 Sam. viii. 22; Prov. xiv. 12; 1 Cor. vi. 18, vii. 1; Gal. i. 12).

Vers. 2, 3. The apostle here as it were discontinues the subject, neither stating the position of the teachers in the church nor what treasures were confided to their care. The further argument with reference to the idea of a steward merely asserts the fact, that substantially he could not be made responsible for the things entrusted to him as steward; he was accountable but to one, his Lord, who alone was capable of judging of the fidelity of his stewards. In ver. 3 they are reminded that the Lord is at the same time omniscient and omnipotent, and that therefore human judgment is of small account. (Ver. 2. Billroth justly explains the ὃ δὲ λοιπόν as an ellipsis of ὃ δὲ λοιπόν ἐστιν, ἐστὶ τοῦτο. Heidenreich conceives the signification of λοιπόν, agreeably to the Hebrew יֶתֶר, to be " most especially;" but in the passages quoted by him, 1 Cor. vii. 29, 2 Cor. xiii. 11, Eph. vi. 10, λοιπόν simply means "*ceterum.*" The reading ὧδε λοιπόν in A.D. has originated solely from the difficulty existing in the usual text.—The ζητεῖται ἐν is best expressed by "it is expected *in* stewards," not "*among* stewards it is expected, *i. e.,* stewards expect." The ζητεῖν expresses in this place the inquiring activity of the κρίνειν. The reading ζητεῖτε must yield both to external and internal evidence; ζητεῖται is defended by A.B.D.F.G.—If in ἵνα of vers. 2 and 3, as Winer and Billroth seek to prove, the main reference is *not entirely* subordinate, we cannot deny that the particle is employed in a weakened signification. The infinitive construction would have undoubtedly approached nearer to the pure Greek form, which is supported by Rückert.—In ver. 3 εἰς ἐλάχιστον, according to the Heb. לִמְעַט Job xv. 11, Isa. vii. 13, Hag. i. 9.    [See Winer's Gr. p. 170].— Ἡμέρα = יוֹם is the judgment-day. With the idea of what is human is connected that of existing liability to error, but every judgment of man is not necessarily human; the apostles had the power to judge as God, so that, what they bound and loosed on earth was also bound or loosed in heaven.    See on Joh. xx. 23).

Ver. 4. With reference to his personal position, the humble-minded apostle does not trust in the least degree to his own opinion of himself, but leaves all judgment to his Lord.    In order, however, not to allow his Corinthian antagonists room for the supposition that he possessed no good conscience, he adds to this that at all events he had a good conscience, although he was not justified thereby; meaning, that his conscience was not yet sufficiently accurate to discover the depths of his own soul, and that the eye of the Omniscient might be capable of discerning what was deserving of reproof in him, although he himself might be unconscious of it.    Billroth thinks erroneously that in the words οὐκ ἐν τούτῳ δεδικαίωμαι exists a reference to justification by faith, as if the sense were, "If I am pure, yet am I not justified by means of this purity, but only through faith in the expiation of Christ;" but this is not properly the subject here.    Of universal remission of sins, and his state of grace, Paul was perfectly certain, and he is rather speaking of the state of sanctification. How far this may have progressed is unknown even to the regenerate, and in this respect he remains also uncertain what the everlasting Judge may discover to condemn in him, how much of his labour will prove to be only perishable wood and stubble. Δικαιοῦσθαι therefore signifies "perfectly holy, to be righteous, and acknowledged as such." The latter exists in the perfect form, otherwise only δίκαιος εἰμί would be used. Chrysostom has already quite correctly expounded the passage. (The γάρ does not refer alone to the οὐδὲν ἐμαυτῷ σύνοιδα, but to the whole phrase as far as δεδικαίωμαι, which affords the ground for the οὐδὲ ἐμαυτὸν ἀνακρίνω).

Ver. 5. The apostle ultimately sets aside rash human judgment, by the assertion of the coming of the Lord, enjoining every one to prepare himself for the judgment of that day in which no deception would be possible, instead of engaging in matters for which he had no calling. The apostle then slightly mentions the praise that Jesus will award, and with this the idea naturally connects itself that his justice will as certainly deal punishment on those whom he cannot commend; it is therefore clearly erroneous to understand ἔπαινος as vox media, or indicating reproof or praise indifferently. (Billroth asserts that there is nothing in the words μὴ πρὸ καιροῦ κρίνετε to imply that hereafter they shall judge. But this may certainly be concluded from vi. 2, 3; and see further on this subject the comm. on Matt. vii. 1.—In the σκότος the idea of what is evil does not exist, but only of what is concealed. See concerning the τὰ κρυπτά Rom. ii. 16, where the same idea is found. Christ is considered as the φῶς (see John i. 4) who in the judgment-day, enlightening the most inward recesses of the soul, will make manifest to men, both in good and evil things, the origin and cause of their endeavours and aspirations, which is frequently concealed even from themselves here below. See Comm. Matt. xxv. 37, sqq.)

Ver. 6. How closely Paul considered himself connected with Apollos is especially shown by this passage. He does not refrain from speaking of him precisely as of himself; and the manner in which the subject is continued from ver. 9, though apparently only referring to Paul, nevertheless admits perfectly of Apollos being included; and that Paul did not avoid this inference is sufficiently corroborative of the degree of confidence which existed between them. The apostle now proceeds again to address his Corinthian readers without distinction, save that, as is shown by what follows, he had his antagonists and their heads especially in view.   To these he points out that all the previous arguments which he had addressed with reference to himself and to Apollos were intended for their instruction, and to abate their pride with respect to themselves.   This has been evidently the object from iii. 5, and to this therefore the ταῦτα applies.   (Μετασχη-μᾰτίζω signifies first to change the form, then generally to change, as in Phil. iii. 21.   From thence—εσθαι, to change oneself, *i. e.* to assume another form, is in 2 Cor. xi. 13—15.   In the con-struction τι εἰς τινά nothing further presents itself; but this combination is evidently to be understood as transferring some-thing to somebody, or bestowing something upon another.   This clearly intimates that Paul was not treating of teachers only, in what precedes, and only chose this form of representation as being more indulgent to the parties.—Concerning the μὴ ὑπὲρ φρονεῖν, see Rom. xii. 3, Phil. ii. 2.—The ὃ γέγραπται is best referred to scriptural passages, as Deut. xvii. 20.   Lachmann prefers the reading ἃ γέγραπται according to A.B.C., which does not contain a reference to the previous subject, for which προέ-γραψα would be employed, but to a passage in the Old Testament. But, under all circumstances, according to A.B.E.F.G. φρονεῖν is to be omitted, though justly supplied in order to secure the con-nexion.   In the εἷς ὑπὲρ τοῦ ἑνός an excess of presumption is signified, wherewith naturally a κατὰ τοῦ ἑτέρου εἶναι is connected. —Φυσιόω, really to swell up, from φυσάω, to swell by blowing; φυσιοῦσθαι, to puff oneself up, *i. e.* to be conceited.   This expres-sion is often found in these Epistles, see iv. 18, 19, v. 2, viii. 1, xiii. 4, and again in Col. ii. 18.—The construction of the ἵνα with the indicative, as occurs again in Gal. iv. 17, is important. Fritzsche takes it in the broad meaning, but against this is the fact, that it does not occur elsewhere in the New Testament in this signification, and likewise that such an explanation would not suit either passage.   The easiest supposition would be that of a solecism; the form φυσιῶσθε might be less familiar to the apostle.

Ver. 7.   Paul proves the foolishness of such arrogance by re-calling to their remembrance the disposition which must form the groundwork of a true Christian life, the consciousness of the worthlessness of all that was their own.   The sentence τί δὲ ἔχεις, ὃ οὐκ ἔλαβες does not include simply all external and internal good or qualities, but all the Christian gifts: faith, love, truth, all is not of man, but of God in man. Augustine employs the passage upon innumerable occasions in his writings. See *e. g. De Spir. et Litt., c.* 9. (In the τίς διακρίνει; who distinguishes thee, who acknowledges higher qualities in thee? is naturally included the negative reply, No one. Christians should all be brethren, and have all in common (iii. 22). The discourse would then advance thus: Even if thou possessed in thyself so much that is valuable, what hast thou that thou didst not receive? This, however, the apostle draws together and says, τί δὲ ἔχεις κ. τ. λ. The ἔλαβες is not applicable to the apostles, who are only the instruments of the divine working, but to God alone).

Ver. 8. Paul ironically reprehends this want of Christian humility; the wish for abundance and riches is too often (Matt. v. 3—6; Rev. iii. 17) the sign of spiritual deadness, of a lack of earnest desire for better things; and where this desire is wanting, proud thoughts find an easy entrance into the human mind. The aorist form ἐβασιλεύσατε compels us to receive the verb in the signification of "to attain unto dominion," but it is important to observe that Paul does not equally reprove the βασιλεύειν for the same reason, but only because they rule χωρὶς ἡμῶν, *i. e.* (not as Rückert supposes, "without our consent, without our co-operation," but) "excluding us;" indeed, he appears in the ὄφελόν γε ἐβασιλεύσατε expressly to approve of their ruling over, as he adds: ἵνα καὶ ἡμεῖς ὑμῖν συμβασιλεύσωμεν, and this is to be explained by the Christian intention of the βασιλεύειν. The Christian *must* govern and desire to govern, because there is in him a higher spirit than that which obtains in the world, and this makes him equal to all things appointed to him, thereby he rules. The Corinthians, who in some degree counteracted the labours of the apostle, were not willing to consider any other spirit than their own as the appointed one; and had it been the spirit in all purity, there had been nothing to admonish them of; but it was an exclusive, illiberal, criticising disposition, *i. e.* they wished to govern without the brethren, neither would they allow the clear Spirit of God to take effect in all the forms of his revelation, but only their prejudiced conception thereof should have any value. They were therefore not rulers, kings in the kingdom of God (Rev. xx. 4), but slaves

FIRST CORINTHIANS IV. 9.

of their self-will and of sin. (Rev. xx. 4). With this idea another likewise mingles itself, viz., that although the spirit already exercised a certain influence, the time of its true dominion was yet far distant, and the Corinthians were anticipating a sway that in the fullest sense of the words was to belong to the next world. For this reason Paul enters upon the following description of his sufferings. ("Ὄφελόν γε = εἴθε is also found in 2 Cor. xi. 1; Gal. v. 12 ; Rev. iii. 15. The LXX. use it for לוּ or אַחֲלֵי. See Winer's Gr. p. 277).

Ver. 9. The revelation of God's kingdom, in which the believers reign, has not yet taken place, continues the apostle with bitter irony, for we have yet daily to suffer; the lightminded Corinthians, on the contrary, believe all to be ready. It has already been remarked on ver. 6 that the subject here refers especially to Paul, for of himself alone could he becomingly use the expression ἐσχάτους, and ver. 12 points alone at him. It is true there is something striking in the use of the plural ἀποστόλους, if this passage has reference to Paul alone; but we signified before, on ver. 6, how this plural was to be explained by the peculiar intimacy which existed between Apollos and himself, in consequence of which Paul employed words which in strict sense could only be said of him, but which admitted the possibility of application to his friend. (Rückert correctly remarks that the choice of the word δοκῶ is ironical: " I presume the matter is thus, ye precede, we follow."—In the ἐσχάτους lies the idea not only of being last summoned, but also of something subservient, *infimae sortis;* just as ἐπιθανάτιος is employed in speaking of gladiators, and such men who, as worthless, were given a prey to death. Indeed the whole passage presents strong evidence of the gladiatorial show having occurred to the apostle's mind while writing it. In this the combatants were led before [ἀπέδειξε] the assembled beholders, in whose presence they afterwards fought. [Θέατρον implies not only the place, but also the *object* of exhibition, otherwise θέαμα would be employed]. In the description of his lowliness, nevertheless, a powerful feeling of the greatness that arises from his office is mingled. As the Lord himself, leaving heaven, and driven out from earth, hung there on the cross between heaven and earth, a touching spectacle to some, and one productive of malicious joy to others, so likewise

F

are his own in the world [1 John iv. 17] a spectacle to the universe [κόσμος] and its inhabitants, as well heavenly as earthly. Angels and men indicate neither the good nor the bad only, but both together. The sight of Christ suffering in his own person awakens both good and bad among angels and men, according to the measure of their different feelings. The following description then proves nothing less than that the Corinthians were wanting in the evident signs of true believers; for Paul by this recital does not intend to express his dissatisfaction with his lot, but rather to exhibit his resemblance to his suffering Lord).

Ver. 10. The expressions μωροί, ἀσθενεῖς, ἄτιμοι indicate the character of the true believer in his connexion with the world; φρόνιμοι, ἰσχυροί, ἔνδοξοι that of the apparent Christian. But we must inquire how the ἐν Χριστῷ is to be understood, which is as applicable to all the latter expressions as διὰ Χριστόν is to the former: certainly it expresses a true prudence, power, and glory in Christ, which the apostle possessed; but according to the whole context, he cannot recognise them in the Corinthians who opposed him. The idea can therefore only be ironically understood, "Ye commend yourselves as prudent, strong, wise in Christ, without being really so; be as I am, (iv. 16, xi. 1), then only will ye gain all this truly, of which ye now possess but the shadow." The explanation of the ἐν Χριστῷ, which Grotius proposes, viz., *in ecclesia Christiana*, as Chrysostom has already expounded ἐν πράγμασι Χριστοῦ, must be rejected as untenable; for all that the Corinthians did in, and with reference to, the church was naturally as Christians.

Vers. 11—13. Paul now enters, by means of a striking picture, upon a description of his earthly distresses, (see 1 Cor. xv. 8, 9), and remarks twice, at the beginning, and also at the conclusion of the representation, that his circumstances were still the same, (ἕως ἄρτι, ἄχρι τῆς ἄρτι ὥρας, viz., from his own conversion, which took place so long since, and which contrasted so greatly with that of the Corinthians which had occurred more recently), it would therefore be wrong to act as if the kingdom of God had already come unto them. (In ver. 11, by the word γυμνητεύω, which only occurs here throughout the New Testament, mean or shabby clothing is to be understood.—Κολαφίζεσθαι, see Matt. xxvi. 67, stands here for ill-treatment of every sort.—Ἀστατέω, to have no certain place of abode, not to have where he could lay his head. The parallel with Christ is obvious throughout. The word is not again to be found in the New Testament.— In ver. 12, concerning the labouring with his own hands, comp ix. 6 sqq., and also Acts xviii. 3, xx. 34; the mention of it in this place is striking, as it was something self-imposed, and consequently no real suffering for Paul. But in so far as he believed himself compelled to exercise it on account of his office, he was able to enumerate it among the sufferings endured for Christ's sake. The sentence λοιδορούμενοι εὐλογοῦμεν κ. τ. λ. presupposes an acquaintance with our Saviour's injunctions. [Matt. v. 44].— In ver. 13, περικάθαρμα [the more usual form is κάθαρμα, whence the origin of the reading ὡσπερεὶ καθάρματα] signifies first a sweeping out that which is rejected or removed as such purifications, *purgamentum;* and then, such persons as at the time of any common calamity, the plague for example, were put to death by way of expiation for the public good. [See the Scholiast in Aristophanes, Plut. v. 454,* Equit. v. 353, Curt. viii. 5, x. 2]. The latter calls them *purgamenta;* περίψημα is also similarly used, which really means [from ψάω to shave] something worn out and thrown away as useless. The true κάθαρμα for the world is none other than Jesus; does Paul then only figuratively call himself so, or does he also ascribe power to his sufferings? There can be no doubt that we must receive the latter supposition. But how is this reconcilable, or how can it be made to agree with the all-sufficiency of Christ's sufferings? The replies to these difficult questions we shall defer until we come to the consideration of Col. i. 24).

Vers. 14—16. After these serious reproaches the apostle returns again to his purpose, and assumes a milder form of reproof. He reminds his readers of the peculiar position in which they were placed with regard to him, he alone being their spiritual father, which conferred upon him an undoubted right thus earnestly to admonish them. (Ver. 14, ἐντρέπω, to cause any one to turn the face away, *i. e.* to make ashamed. Concerning the medium, see Luke xviii. 2. For the οὐ, under the head "Participles," in Winer's Gr. 449 sqq.—In ver. 15, the πατήρ and παιδαγωγὸς

* The words run thus : καθάρματα ἐλέγοντο οἱ ἐπκαθάρσει λοιμοῦ τινὸς ἤ τινὸς ἑτέρας νόσου θυόμενοι τοῖς θεοῖς.

ἐν Χριστῷ relate to each other, as the φυτεύειν and ποτίζειν, see iii. 6.—The Gospel is to be considered the creative power, whereby the new birth is effected.—In ver. 16, the position of father confers a right and title to exact obedience to the command which the apostle lays down, viz., that they should be his followers; the addition καθὼς ἐγὼ Χριστοῦ originated no doubt from such as were scrupulous in allowing an apostle to say that individuals should follow his example. It was adopted from the parallel passage xi. 1, and is therefore, according to the authority of the MSS., an interpolation in this place. It will, however, readily be perceived that Paul's command to all to follow him was to be understood, not of himself, but of Christ living in him. Gal. ii. 20).

Vers. 17, 18. In order to lead the Corinthians in the right way, Paul continued, that he had sent Timotheus to them, who was perfectly acquainted with his manner of proceeding and his doctrine, (Acts xix. 22); but that the blindness and conceit of some of those in Corinth had led them to imagine that he himself dared not to come to them. (Paul could not have long sent Timotheus, whom Erastus accompanied at the time he wrote this epistle, for according to xvi. 10, he was expecting his arrival there.—The τέκνον μου refers to the conversion of Timotheus by Paul. In 2 Tim. i. 1, Paul calls him "beloved son;" 1 Tim. i. 1, "real or own son." The predicate πιστός is not to be translated "believing;" the belief of Timotheus is not disputed, but "faithful" and true in the Lord, i. e., in and through fellowship with him.— In ἀναμνήσει is slightly implied that the Corinthians could also have easily known the way of truth if they had faithfully observed his words. The καθὼς πανταχοῦ ἐν πάσῃ ἐκκλησίᾳ διδάσκω alludes clearly to a certain form of teaching which Paul observed in his apostolic operations, and from which other teachers of the church had departed.—Ver. 18. In the ὡς μὴ ἐρχομένου is to be found the pregnant meaning according to the opinion of the puffed-up Corinthians, "as if I dared not come." See 2 Cor. x. 10, 11).

Vers. 19—21. Although he had sent Timotheus beforehand, he only awaited a sign from God in order to follow also, and then he would see whether a spiritual power, corresponding to their high pretensions, would be displayed by his adversaries; this being ever manifest where the ruling power of God was really present. Whether his appearance among them would be marked by severity

or mildness depended upon the posture they assumed at his coming; and when one considers that the apostle wrote these words
as a poor tentmaker, without the slightest earthly power to lend
force to his words, we can but wonder at his boldness.  But the
consciousness of the divine work which he was labouring to fulfil, elevated him far beyond earthly circumstances, and enabled
him successfully to attack difficulties that were apparently invincible.  (Λόγος and δύναμις form an antithesis, as do μόρφωσις
and δύναμις in 2 Tim. iii. 5.  It signifies here an exhibition of
vain presumption, completely at variance with true inward power.
—The kingdom of God implies here, as it usually does in the language of Paul, the living fellowship excited in the soul of which
Jesus was the author, but manifested in the nature of those belonging to it.  [See Luke xvii. 21; Rom. xiv. 17].—In ver. 21,
ῥάβδος is a symbol of the παιδευτικὴ ἐνέργεια, as Theodorete
justly observes.  See 2 Cor. xiii. 10.—The ἐν in the form ἐν
ῥάβδῳ ἔλθω is to be explained by its analogy to the Heb. בְּ.—
Concerning πνεῦμα πραΰτητος see Gal. vi. 1.  The Codd. A.B.
read here, as in Gal. vi. 1, πραότητος, which, however, Lachmann has not adopted in the present passage, as has been erroneously stated by Rückert).

# II.

# PART SECOND.

(v. 1—xi. 1).

§ 5. OF INCESTUOUS PERSONS.

(v. 1—13).

Vers. 1, 2. With a glance at the presumption of some of the
Corinthian Christians, Paul mentions, with a view to their humiliation, the fact that a member of their church lived in illicit intercourse with his stepmother. It is undoubted that in the most
exalted and best constituted community, an individual may fall
into gross error; but then it is requisite that the said body
should decidedly exhibit its displeasure against the offending
member. This, however, was not the case in Corinth; the universal moral sluggishness displayed itself in the manner in which
this occurrence was viewed, for they still tolerated the sinner in
their community, and thus gave evidence that they were not sensible of the enormity of his offence. Paul therefore justly reproves the church, not as a number of separate individuals, but
in one, all, as a living united body, and, together with directions
for the excommunication of the offender, delivers a serious rebuke
to the whole church. ($\"O\lambda\omega\varsigma$ can only mean "altogether, generally," as in vi. 7. The general idea of unlawful desire, expressed
here by $\pi o \rho \nu \epsilon \iota a$, was more applicable then to the $\kappa a \iota \tau o \iota a \upsilon \tau \eta$
than to a form of this sin of rare occurrence even among heathens.
The reason of its standing first is to be found in what precedes.*
Paul had said: Shall I appear among you as a severe father, or in
the spirit of meekness? He continues: How can I act otherwise

---

* In order to make this observed, Lachmann places the stop at $\delta \upsilon \nu \acute{a} \mu \epsilon \iota$, and
connects iv. 21 immediately to v. 1.

than severely, when fornication commonly prevails among you,
and in such a form as the present one? Billroth's observation
upon this, "that textually these remarks are unsupported, for,
according to unvarying custom, καὶ τοιαύτη implies nothing different to that before-mentioned, but merely gives a closer definition
of it," I cannot understand, as the subject here is certainly the
same offence, only more precisely stated. Calvin considers that
ὅλως refers to the *certainty* of the report; but Rückert would connect it with that which precedes, so that ὅλως=γοῦν would stand
in the signification of *certe quidem;* but in neither acceptation is
it clear. The only explanation of this difficult passage, which it
appears to me can be textually maintained, referring to what has
been already mentioned, is that ὅλως should be received in the
sense of, I briefly say. (See Passow, in his Lex. concerning this
word. Then the connexion would run thus: Shall I come unto
you with the rod or in love? the former will, alas! be certainly
requisite, or, I must alas! inquire into things, for, let me briefly
add, we hear of fornication among you.—The expression ἡ γυνὴ
τοῦ πατρός certainly indicates the stepmother, as אֵשֶׁת אָב. Gen.
xxxvii. 2; Lev. xvii. 7, 8.—῎Εχειν, like *habere* [Suet. Aug. c.
63, Cic. ad div. ix. 26] denotes euphemistically the intercourse of
the sexes.—In ver. 2 πενθεῖν is in some degree opposed to φυσιοῦσθαι, as it expresses the pain of penance, which of necessity excludes presumption. The sincere believer not only exercises a
painful repentance for his own sins, but in brotherly sympathy
also for those of others. The spirit of Christ enlarges confined
individual feeling and consciousness, causing it to extend itself
universally.—For ἀρθῇ ἐκ μέσου, the *text. rec.* has ἐξαρθῇ, but
the *Codd.* have decided for the simplex. The ἐξαρθῇ is possibly
taken up from ver. 13. The phrase αἴρειν ἐκ μέσου can in this
place only signify exclusion from ecclesiastical communion. The
form really means "remove, *i. e.* kill," but the exclusion is to be
understood as a spiritual death, [see Lev. xviii. 29, xx. 11;
Deut. xvii. 7, 12, xix. 15, xxi. 21] as lopping off a member from
the body of Christ. The expression has its origin, without doubt,
in the passages of Deut. quoted, in which the crime here called
to account by the form נִכְרְתָה נֶפֶשׁ הַהִיא is punished with
death. The temporal extirpation has been employed by the
apostle in a spiritual sense. See the observations on ver. 5).

Vers. 3, 4. This indifference and deadness on the part of the Corinthians cognisant of the affair, Paul contrasts with his spiritual participation in the occurrences of their church, although absent in body, and, on this occasion, with the serious displeasure excited in his mind towards the immoral offenders, upon whom he said he had immediately pronounced a decided judgment, which they were yet to expect. By this resolution the apostle aroused the idea in his readers that they, it was true, stood outwardly in connexion with him, but were essentially further removed than many who bore the appearance of being far behind them in zeal. (Lachmann omits the first ὡς that stands before ἀπών, and it certainly appears unseasonable, besides which it is wanting in A.B.C.D. and in many other authorities.—Σῶμα and πνεῦμα stand here, as in Rom. viii. 10, 13, and Eph. iv. 4, only to designate the inward and outward state.—The κέκρικα does not imply that the apostle wishes his opinion to be considered as a command, for that is contradicted by the succeeding συναχθέντων ὑμῶν, but the expression is to be understood thus: "I have already mentally determined, and have not for one moment wavered in the decision.—In ver. 4 the οὕτω may infer that the act was accompanied by aggravating circumstances, but the most simple way would be to refer it to the fact that the man had committed the incest as a member of a Christian body. It may likewise mean, "under these circumstances."—The ἐν τῷ ὀνόματι κ. τ. λ. is to be connected with συναχθέντων κ. τ. λ., but, on the contrary, σὺν τῇ δυνάμει κ. τ. λ. with παραδοῦναι. The mention of power agrees better with the declaration of the sentence, to which it gives impressiveness. The setting forth the name of Christ suits better the gathering together, indicating likewise the Spirit, in whom those assembled are or should be. The words have an evident reference to Matt. xviii. 20, "Where two or three are gathered together in my name, there am I in the midst of them." But Paul speaks of this assembly, at which he professes to be present in spirit, in order to indicate to them in a delicate manner how they ought to conduct themselves in the matter; in the name, i. e. in the mind and spirit of Christ, and, at the same time, in obedience to his commands [Matt. xviii. 18; John xx. 23], they must assemble themselves together and remove the offender from among them. Besides this, the passage may be classed among those in the New Testament in which there exists a reference to all the members of the church upon a democratic equality, for it is exceedingly improbable that in the συναχθέντων ὑμῶν the question is only of presbyters and rulers of the church.

Ver. 5. Here follows then what may be deemed an interpretation of the passage in ver. 2, αἴρειν ἐκ μέσου. Paul desires that they shall παραδοῦναι τῷ σατανᾷ the sinner, and indeed εἰς ὄλεθρον τῆς σαρκὸς, ἵνα τὸ πνεῦμα σωθῇ. It is of course to be understood that any conclusions are censured which deny the existence of Satan,* this being acknowledged by Paul and all the writers of the New Testament. A form of excommunication only, παραδοῦναι τῷ σατανᾷ cannot therefore be considered.† But the form may certainly thus far indicate the exclusion from the religious community, as it may signify a true separation from the blessed participation in light, and a giving up to the unholy principle of darkness. Christ exercises a twofold power; first, in attracting those of a congenial mind; secondly, in rejecting those who differ. But the addition εἰς ὄλεθρον τῆς σαρκὸς, ἵνα τὸ πμεῦμα σωθῇ renders a closer definition of the form παραδοῦναι τῷ σατανᾷ necessary; and, if it is not to be found, it will then be easy to refer it to the total destruction of the man, even to the πνεῦμα. Not that this is Paul's desire, which is rather that the flesh may be delivered a prey to Satan, in order that the spirit may thereby be saved. As the σωτηρία is transferred to the last judgment-day, the ὄλεθρος must be considered as temporal ruin, and the πνεῦμα only received as antithetical to σάρξ, to convey the true idea to the mind, the ἔσω ἄνθροπος, in opposition to the ἔξω ἄνθρωπος. [See Rom. vii. 22]. But σάρξ must not be received in so limited a sense as to suppose only bodily sufferings and diseases; loss of worldly goods and relations, and all external sorrows are to be included, as well as more especially the painful consciousness of being cast out of the community of faith and love, and the earnest desire of being again accepted. The really difficult question is now this: *how can Paul require any*

---

* As Gräfe in three Konigsberg Festprogramme of 1709, 1800, and 1806. By Satan he understood a human accuser before the tribunal.

† The reference to the three descriptions of Jewish excommunication כִּדּוּי (for thirty days), חֵרֶם (for ninety days), and שַׁמַּתָא (for ever), require no interpretation in order to understand the passage.

*one to be given over to Satan for the destruction of the flesh, that the soul may thereby be saved, as this does not seem to depend upon the excommunicating church, but upon the person excommunicated and Satan?* If the person excluded does not obey the admonition, he may be ruined in soul, and what should restrain Satan from attacking only his body, and not his soul likewise? The *first* of these two points is, however, not so difficult, for it manifestly is not to be found in the ἵνα τὸ πνεῦμα σωθῇ, that he *must* be saved, but only that he *may*, in fact that the possibility of salvation shall be left to himself. But then, indeed, the difficulty of the *second* is all the greater, for the whole context sanctions the supposition that the act of exclusion *facilitates* the saving of the soul. The body of the sinner shall be given over to the destruction of Satan, that thereby, where it is to be effected, his soul may be saved, which otherwise were certainly lost. But it seems that the making the saving of the soul to depend on Satan, would in all respects *add to the difficulty,** first, by withdrawing the means of grace from the church, and the power of the Holy Spirit; and then by enhancing the temptation proceeding from the element of darkness, to which he was already sufficiently exposed within the protecting limits of the church. If παραδοῦναι τῷ σατανᾷ only were employed, we must then suppose, as has been already observed, that the offender should be entirely given up, as one that had sinned against the Holy Ghost; but by the addition, the punishment rather appears the means of salvation, for which reason Paul in 2 Cor. ii. 6, himself proposes his re-admission, as the sinner had suffered punishment. In the parallel passage, 1 Tim. i. 20, it is also called οὓς παρέδωκα τῷ σατανᾷ, ἵνα παιδευθῶσι μὴ βλασφημεῖν, consequently the delivering over to Satan has also in this place a pedagogic aim. But how is it supposed that the power of Satan shall be limited to the flesh? We may say that if the God-fearing man pray, the Lord listens to his prayer, and that he restrains the power of Satan, as in Job's case (chap. i.), and the fulfilment of the prayer is presupposed. This is Grotius' opinion. Or we may suppose that the apostle ascribes

---

* Tertullian and Ambrose explain σαρκὸς ὄλεθρος to signify everlasting damnation, and refer the saving of the πνεῦμα to the church, which has the power, by excluding the evil. (*Tert. de Pudic.* c. 13).

to the church itself the power of limiting that of Satan, because God dwells and works in it. I believe that the apostolic representation tends to the latter view.* But if the subject had only referred to prayer to God, it would have been differently expressed; Paul is evidently speaking from a consciousness of the power to bind and loose, that sins may be entirely or partially 1etained. The former was the case with Ananias and Sapphira (Acts v.), while to these Corinthian sinners they were partially retained. In addition to this it may be supposed that with this resolution of the church, to deliver him over to the power of Satan,† to the destruction of the flesh, to which also all the sufferings of the ψυχή may be added, but to the saving of the soul, continual prayer would be made by the church for the offender, and thus his spiritual connexion with the church would be maintained, and he could likewise be brought back into the way of salvation. (Chrysostom discriminates between παραδοῦναι and ἐκδοῦναι, the latter signifying a perfect giving up, while the former retains the hope of his restoration. Paul chose the words; he says: ἀνοίγων αὐτῷ τῆς μετανοίας τὰς θύρας καὶ ὥσπερ παιδαγωγῷ τὸν τοιοῦτον παραδιδούς. In the hand of God, even Satan can become an instructor for believers).

Vers. 6—8.‡ Under such circumstances of the Corinthian church, continued the apostle, their glorifying (in their wisdom and spiritual gifts) seemed singular. It is evident that Paul really meant to say, this occurrence, and their behaviour on the occasion, proved how much true spiritual life was wanting, to permit so great a pollution to occur among them. He, however, expresses it with forbearance, as if it *might be* the consequence of such deficiency. The whole admonition is clothed in symbolic

---

* Chrysostom, Augustine, Lightfoot, Vitringa, Wolf, and others, have already expressed the same opinion. Only that they erroneously conceive this to be an especial Charisma, while it rather arose only from the divine Spirit filling the church. The same were just as possible in the present day, if those who laboured in the church possessed the same intensity which manifested itself in the apostolic times.

† Billroth adopts Grotius' explanation of the passage, but treats the whole as a Jewish representation. He says, "It is presupposed of Satan that he desired to inflict pain upon him;" this inference he appears to wish to prove false. But as in Christ is necessarily the σωτηρία, out of him is ὄλεθρος, and indeed of the *whole* man, if the powers of darkness are not expressly confined to the lesser powers of the σάρξ.

‡ That the words ὅτι μικρὰ κ. τ. λ. can be read as an iambic trimeter, is only to be considered accidental. (See Winer's Gr. p. 562).

language, based upon the typical signification of the Passover, and the ordination respecting it in the Old Testament. The leaven is to be understood as the image of sin; and in the command to purify the house from it, at the dawning of the Passover, (Ex. xiii. 3—7), the moral commandment to walk purely and inoffensively is implied. The image is not, however, equally carried through, as often happens with the apostle, e. g. 2 Cor. iii. 7, sqq. In ver. 7 the image is so applied, that the Corinthians collectively constitute the φύραμα νέον, from which all leaven is to be banished; in ver. 8, on the contrary, they are represented as keeping the festival, but tasting no leaven. However, these are free applications of the idea, which by no means obscure the principal thought. The fundamental principles of the apostle, as well as the sentence καὶ γὰρ τὸ πάσχα ἡμῶν ὑπὲρ ἡμῶν ἐτύθη, Χριστός, afford sufficient evidence that the apostle will by no means allow the reference to the authority of the Old Testament to be considered as *accidental*, but as an *explanation* agreeing in all respects with his own opinion. The words quoted show clearly that Paul attaches the very highest importance to the *whole idea of the feast of the Passover*. Christians likewise have their paschal lamb (τὸ πάσχα=פֶּסַח signifies the paschal lamb, and Passover, see Matt. xxvi. 17), of which they receive the benefit in the holy communion, and they also avoid the leaven (sin), bearing themselves as true ἄζυμοι, and walking in purity and truth. It is possible that this passage originated in the design to exhibit to the followers of Peter that the Christians possessed the essentials of the old leaven, though without the Jewish form. It is also possible that the period of the Easter festival gave occasion to the apostle to make use of this explanation. But we are not to deduce from the words καθώς ἐστε ἄζυμοι any meaning like the following: "As ye even now abstain from leavened bread, by reason of the feast of the Passover;" for it is not probable, that in the uncorrupt church as founded by Paul, the Jewish form of celebration would find place. The words can only be translated: "As ye then are certainly determined to keep yourselves free from the leaven of sin." (Grotius defends the other acceptation of ἄζυμος, and considers ἄσιτος and ἄοινος parallel.) The passage therefore cannot be employed as a stringent *proof* that already an annual Passover or Easter festival was celebrated;

for the typical meaning of Paul agrees more with the exhortation to keep the Passover always in the Gospel.  But it is highly probable that, from an early period, the weekly celebration on Friday and Sunday as πάσχα σταυρώσιμον and ἀναστάσιμον* was distinguished by increased solemnity at the time of the Jewish Passover, and therein lay the idea of the festival.  (In ver. 6, φύραμα is the church, ζύμη the member that can infect the former.  See on Matt. xiii. 33, where the leaven is employed in a good sense.— In ver. 7, the word ἐκκαθάρατε refers to the custom among the Jews of thoroughly cleansing their dwellings, in order that no leaven may remain, which is an image of moral strictness and fidelity in purifying from sin.  The terms *new* and *old* refer to the new and old covenant.  The ὑπὲρ ἡμῶν has very weighty authorities against it, for which reason Lachmann has not retained it.  When we, however, consider how easily the preceding ἡμῶν might lead to the omission of the second, but that there existed little motive for the addition, it would nevertheless appear to be genuine.  For ἐτύθη the *text. rec.* has ἐθύθη.  As this is the more unusual form, it may be asked if it be not the more preferable.— In ver. 8, ἑορτάζειν contains the idea of dedication, and especially consecrated to God.—Κακία appears to correspond to εἰλικρινεία, and πονηρία to ἀλήθεια : the two former words point out the negative, the latter the positive side of good and evil).

Vers. 9—11.  The apostle now at once corrects a misunderstanding of the Corinthians, with reference to a passage in his earlier letter, which is lost.  The warning which it contained to avoid association with dissolute persons and gross sinners, had been applied by them to all men, instead of restricting its reference, as Paul intended they should, to those persons only who gave themselves out as believers.  Probably this was done by Paul's adversaries, in order to represent his commands as impracticable.  (Συναναμίγνυσθαι is again to be found in the New Testament in 2 Thess. iii. 14.  In the LXX. it stands for יִתְבַּלְלָל, *e. g.* Hos. vii. 8, " to have fellowship, intercourse," which must always imply the interchange or communication of spiritual properties, on one side or the other.—In verse 10, I understand the καὶ οὐ πάντως, as does Winer (Gr. p. 457), thus: " And indeed [as is apparent] I do not mean that ye should altogether avoid

* See Suiceri Thes. s. v. πάσχα, page 621.

intercourse with the carnal of this world." Billroth, however, supposes it to mean, "not certainly with the fornicators of this world, but only not with carnal members of the church," which appears to me rather difficult; πάντως according to this must be inserted in a parenthesis, and mean, "as may be supposed." It is true that it is included in the idea, nevertheless it is not found in the single expression πάντως.—Κόσμος οὗτος, according to the analogy of αἰὼν οὗτος, is really pleonastic ; κόσμος alone were sufficient, but as subsequently κόσμος is employed in another signification=οἰκουμένη, οὗτος is added by Paul in order to mark the difference.—For ὀφείλετε Lachmann reads ὠφείλετε. According to the sense, either might be used ; ye *must* go out of the world, or, ye *must* go out from it. Critical authorities, however, incline more to the use of ὀφείλετε.—In ver. 11 νυνί does not refer to the time, in contradistinction to ver. 9, but it indicates the conclusion, "but I have rather written unto you." See vii. 14, xii. 8, xv. 20.—The words which follow are not to be regarded as a quotation from the earlier epistle, they only recapitulate more precisely the substance of the subject contained therein.— Ὀνομαζόμενος signifies here " call themselves only without being so :" τοιοῦτος is likewise to be understood reprovingly.—Μηδὲ συνεσθίειν, which connects itself somewhat as an anacoluthon to the preceding, heightens the μὴ συναναμίγνυσθαι, it indicates the entire renunciation of familiar intercourse. [See Matt. xviii. 18]. The severe ecclesiastical religious penance of the ancient church is here defined by the apostle himself,* and we can only observe therein a sign of the church's decline, for this charge *is* not only now neglected, but *cannot* be carried into execution).

Vers. 12, 13. Paul proves conclusively from his own position, and that of all Christians with respect to him, that he was not alluding to those without the church. From the complete difference which existed in their course of life, the Christians had only to judge themselves, not others, and could thence only exclude the profligate from their community. (The passage, vi. 2, by no means contradicts the assertion, that God alone judgeth them that are without the church, for the latter is spoken of judgment in this life, while in the former passage the last judg-

* Theodorete says in this place εἰ δὲ κοινῆς τροφῆς τοῖς τοιούτοις οὐ δεῖ κοινωνεῖν, ἤπου γε μυστικῆς τε καὶ θείας, i. e. the holy Communion.

ment is alluded to, which the Lord will accomplish in and through his faithful followers. In ver. 12, καί is probably an erroneous addition; it is wanting in A.B.C.F.G.; Lachmann also omits it; but, on the other hand, κρινεῖ is decidedly preferable to the usual κρίνει. It would be best to point it with Lachmann thus: οὐχὶ τοὺς ἔσω ὑμεῖς κρίνετε, τοὺς δὲ ἔξω ὁ Θεὸς κρινεῖ.— Concerning οἱ ἔξω and οἱ ἔσω see Col. iv. 5; 1 Thess. iv. 12; the representations in which are based upon the idea that the church encloses the faithful like a temple, within whose hallowed precincts strangers may not set a foot.—For ἐξάρατε is to be found ἐξαρεῖτε, ἐξαιρεῖτε, ἐξαίρετε, ἐξάρετε. But only the first two forms can, from critical considerations, and with respect to ver. 2, come under notice. Of these ἐξαρεῖτε is the usual text, while ἐξάρατε has the authority of the codices A.B.C.D.F.G., as well as of others in its favour, and therefore doubtless deserves the preference.—The conjecture of πόρνον for πονηρόν is very plausible, because the devil is commonly designated by the appellation ὁ πονηρός. But the supposition is unsupported by critical authority).

## § 6. LAW-SUITS.

### (vi. 1—20).

Ver. 1. The mention just made of the judging of unbelievers leads the apostle to speak of another unbecoming custom of the Corinthian Christians, which must be reproved; they appealed to the heathen authorities upon any difference which arose among themselves. This is severely condemned by the apostle. The Christians were not to erect themselves into judges over the heathen, but it was yet more inconsistent that they, who were *some day* to judge the world with Christ, should set the heathen over themselves, as judges.* This discussion, like many others

---

* In consequence of the apostolic decision, it followed that the bishops obtained a jurisdiction. (See Euseb. vita Const. iv. 27). How this was exercised by worthy bishops is shown by the example of Ambrose (August. conf. vi. 3). But the right of jurisdiction was from an early period restricted to civil causes, criminal cases were referred to ordinary tribunals, as is proved by the Rescript of Arcadius and Honorius in the Cod. Justin. lib. 1. tit. iv. lex 7.

of the apostle in the Epistles under consideration, was peculiarly adapted to moderate the exaggerated representations respecting the moral condition of the Corinthian church. Although so short a period had intervened since the Christian church had sprung into life in Jerusalem on the day of Pentecost, where the believers were of one heart and one soul; neither said any, of his possessions, that they were his own (Acts iv. 32), the power of the Spirit filling the church had lost so much in intensity, that in Corinth they openly disputed before heathen rulers concerning mine and then (ver. 7). And yet in this church the Charismata ruled so powerfully! But so much the bolder appeared the faith of Paul, which, in a community where so much was to be desired, could nevertheless distinguish the germ of the destined new creation, which was appointed to give the world another form. —Besides, it is well to observe, that this practice of the Corinthians, so much condemned by the apostle, of bringing their differences before heathen judges, instead of Christian arbitrators, was occasioned by their internal dissensions. Love and confidence had vanished, and this is especially blamed by the apostle (ver. 7); no such disputes among Christians should exist. (Πρᾶγμα is here lawsuit, otherwise λόγος, causa.—Concerning ἐπί, coram, see Mark xiii. 9, Acts xxiii. 30, xxiv. 19.—For ἀδίκων in ver. 6, stands ἀπίστων. The expression is not intended to apply an idea of individual blame to heathen rulers, as if they were intentionally unjust, but only of their general character, the absence of Christian δικαιοσύνη, precisely as the designation ἅγιοι indicates nothing individual among the Christians. See on Rom. i. 7).

Vers. 2, 3. The argument for the unlawfulness of such proceedings is carried out by Paul, so as to direct attention to the higher destiny of believers, to judge the world, nay angels: but while conscious of this, they should yet be competent to adjust inferior differences. The form ἢ οὐκ οἴδατε, and likewise the οὐκ οἴδατε of ver. 3, show that the apostle supposes the Corinthians already acquainted with their lofty calling; the words may be rendered, ye know certainly right well! Whatever this judging by the believers may lead to, we have no foundation for unhesitatingly receiving κρίνειν for κατακρίνειν. As in speaking of angels,

good as well as bad* must be included, the κόσμος likewise,
although opposed to the church as under the practical dominion
of the saints, contains not only those upon whom eternal condemnation must fall, but also such as, not having yet received the
spirit of Christ, live nevertheless in a condition relatively faithful. (See the remarks on Matt. xxv. 31, 37; Rom. ii. 1).
However, this idea, in its simple form as propounded by the
apostle, appears doubtful to most interpreters. They consider
that it would elevate the Christians too highly to make them
judges over the human and spiritual world; while on the other
side, the scriptural doctrine of sin appears to many to degrade
man too low. But it is precisely in this that the sublimity of the
doctrines contained in the Bible consists, by extending in every
direction, and passing far beyond the narrow limits of the human
standard. Let us more closely consider this idea in connexion
with the Scripture doctrines generally. As the future is employed
upon both occasions (κρινοῦσι, κρινοῦμεν), there can be no reference to a present operation of the faithful; the intermediate
present (κρίνεται) is determined by means of the futures. In
the ἡμέρα κρίσεως the universal judgment of the world is of course
to be understood as the future judgment, and this is commonly
ascribed to Christ, (see on Acts xvii. 31; Rom. ii. 16), which
agrees perfectly with the subject of our passage, inasmuch as
believers do not judge men and angels without Christ, but with
him, indeed he in them, for the judging power in the faithful is
Christ in us. They come not into judgment, because whoever
believes in him is judged already (John iii. 18), and the Lord
himself says, agreeably to this unity of Christ with his faithful;
in the regeneration, when the Son of Man shall sit on the throne
of his glory, ye also shall sit upon twelve thrones *judging* the
twelve tribes of Isarel. (See on Matt. xix. 28; Luke xxii. 30).
Those whom the Lord here terms the twelve, as representatives
of the church, he calls in another passage, all the believers (see
on John xvii. 22). All the prerogatives of Christ belong also to
the church, which both is and is called the true Christ. (See on
1 Cor. xii. 12). It must be allowed that this vast thought,
which indeed elevates man to a height hardly to be contemplated,

---

* Bad angels likewise are called only ἄγγελοι, although seldom, as in 2 Peter
ii. 4; Rev. ix. 15. Also in 1 Cor. iv. 9 the expression implies good and bad angels.

becomes in some degree inadmissible when one would apply it to every member of the external church. But in the apostolic times the members of Christ's visible church agreed better with its principles than at present; Paul could therefore introduce the thought objectively, without marking the difference of form and of nature. But the Saviour himself (Matt. xiii. 47) found both good and bad fish in the net of the kingdom of God, and the evidence of our senses must have informed us that in the visible church itself, a κόσμος exists, even unto the present day; yes, that in the true members of the invisible church, in those born again of water and of the Spirit, there nevertheless still abides in their old man the principle of the κόσμος, which it requires their continual exertions to subdue. The full force of the assertion, therefore, that the saints shall judge the world of men and angels, can only apply to the spirits of the perfectly righteous (Heb. xii. 23), *i. e.*, to the members of the invisible church in their perfect state. In this mankind attains its true ideal, and to it applies then in its fullest sense Ps. viii. 7, (according to the explanation in Heb. ii. 6, sqq.) "*all things* hast thou put under his feet." Angels themselves stand lower in the order of their being than those in whose hearts is Christ's image. (See further on Heb. i. 14, xii. 23). The only manner to remove the obstacles which the interpretation of our passage presents to many by the assertion that believers shall judge with Christ, is this, to urge, as Chrysostom and Theodorete have done, the ἐν ὑμῖν κρίνεται. This preposition signifies, (in which Billroth coincides), that, according to the real idea,* the judgment by the believers is simply the effect produced by the operation in them of a higher standard of living, upon the world, and upon angels, according to the analogy in Matt. xii. 42, where it says: βασίλισσα νότου ἀναστήσεται καὶ κατακρινεῖ τὴν γενεὰν ταύτην, καὶ ἄνδρες Νινευῖται ἀναστήσονται καὶ κατακρινοῦσι τὴν γενεὰν ταύτην. But Billroth is sufficiently unprejudiced to allow that this negative kind of judgment does not agree with the course of the argument, as Raphelius has

---

* According to the form of the idea, Billroth admits that following the direction of בְּ, ἐν signifies "through," but according to the true sense "in;" the meaning therefore may be, "your faith is the measure applied in judging the world." In a similar measure the form of every view of the apostle might be changed at pleasure.

already ably proved the capability of actively judging in inferior
matters, is connected with the capacity for more refined discrimi-
nation; the latter must therefore, according to Paul's views, have
been an essentially active quality. But it is impossible to consider
this as all that is included in the idea, but we should rather conceive
the just meaning to be, that if we hold steadfastly the doctrine of
the real communication of the divine nature to those who believe
(2 Pet. i. 4), there can be no hesitation in admitting them to be
rulers and judges with Christ (Matt. xxv. 40; 2 Tim. ii. 12;
Rev. xx. 4), and him the firstborn among brethren. (See on
Rom. viii. 29). In ver. 2, ἤ is justified by the most weighty
authorities, viz., A.C.D.F.G. Then, according to the analogy
with μήτι γε βιωτικά, the sentence καὶ εἰ κ. τ. λ. must be understood as a question; without an interrogation, the sense would
be: "And if by you the world is to be judged, it is unworthy of
you to appear before such inferior judgment-seats." It is certain
that κριτήριον signifies first, tribunal [Jam. ii. 6], but in this
place, according to ver. 4, public proceedings at law, = κρίματα
in ver. 7. It would be best to understand the interrogatory in
the same sense with Billroth, viz., to leave it depending on ὅτι,
and erase the note of interrogation after κρινοῦσι accordingly.—
The epithet ἐλάχιστα places controversies concerning earthly
things in contrast with those of a spiritual nature.—In ver. 3
βίος has, like the Latin *seculum* in the language of the church,
an accessory idea of something sinful; in a higher sense ζωή is
used. The adjective form is found again in the New Testament,
Luke xxi. 34.—Μήτι γε, *nedum*, does not again occur in the New
Testament).

Vers. 4—6. The apostle in continuation reprehends the Corinthians for addressing themselves to strangers, in contentions
arising out of the affairs of ordinary life, and also because that
they, who would be so wise, could not find among themselves
one wise man, who could arrange such differences as an arbitrator. (In ver. 4, the ἐξουθενημένοι ἐν τῇ ἐκκλησίᾳ are the heathen
rulers. See on ii. 6. The expression is difficult, and may not be
referred to the office, for Paul by no means despised the heathen
authorities [see on Rom. xiii. 1], certainly not to the *person*, for
the church of Christ despises none of God's creatures, but is applied only to the *element* in which they stand, to the κόσμος.

The τούτους, as in ver. 6 and ver. 8, serves only to indicate more pointedly the error of applying to *these* judges. The reception of καθίζετε as imperative, although defended by Chrysostom, Theodorete, Grotius, Calvin, and Bengel, is less probable than the supposition that it is in the indicative, for this reason ; in the former case the ἐξουθενημένοι must refer to the Christians, which evidently cannot be maintained on account of what follows.— In ver. 5, ἐντροπή, which occurs again at xv. 34, signifies "a shaming," see on iv. 14.—The οὕτως and οὐδὲ εἷς heightens the idea considerably, " Is wisdom so entirely wanting among you, that not so much as one wise man is to be found?"—In the διακρί- νειν is signified the function of arbitrator, which presents the particular κρίνεσθαι, i. e. bringing a lawsuit before the judge.— The form ἀνὰ μέσον τοῦ ἀδελφοῦ αὐτοῦ presents some diffi- culty; it is easy to imagine that on account of the αὐτοῦ, καὶ τοῦ ἀδελφοῦ has been interpolated, as it is a reading by no means sufficiently authorised. It would be best to take ἀδελ- φός = ἀδελφότης (1 Pet. ii. 17), for only in this manner can ἀνὰ μέσον,* and αὐτοῦ agree. Billroth considers that the reason one only of the two parties is mentioned is, that they were both Christians, but I do not see how this explanation diminishes the difficulty).

Vers. 7, 8. After this description Paul proceeds a step further, and shows that, leaving the subject of disputes before the heathen magistrates, lawsuits were unbecoming amongst Christians. The principle among them should be, rather to suffer wrong than to do it. The consideration of this subject leads us to inquire, whether the precepts laid down by the apostle in this chapter were only avail- able for the circumstances *then existing*, or whether they would admit of application to those of the *present day*. One might suppose that all magistrates and judges being now Christian, the present condition of the church rendered the apostle's directions singularly inapplicable to us. But that is not conclusive, for the entire character of the judicial experience of the present day presents all the prominent features of that in ancient times. When Paul requires that the matters in question should be sub- mitted to a brother, he intended by it, that forsaking the path of

* For this form is also to be found κατὰ μέσον or ἐν μέσῳ. See Matt. x. 16, xiii. 25; Acts xxvii. 27.

the strict law, which may often prove highly unjust, they should consult only, and yield to the decision of the love and forbearance which dwells in the hearts of brethren. Such a measure, however, cannot be applied to the large masses of men contained within the limits of the visible church of the present day, for these the public law institutions are necessary. If it may therefore be asserted that in the apostolic times, the contrast was greater between the heathen world and the church, than between the law establishments of the present day and the regenerate; we reply that it is still essentially the same, and must accordingly declare, that the admonitions of the apostle, as well as the analogous commands pronounced by Christ in the Sermon on the Mount, possess a significance for the sincere Christian in all ages; Christian brethren ought not to carry their disputes with each other concerning their rights before the authorities; should any difference of the kind unfortunately arise, let them at least settle it by way of composition, to avoid giving subject for public offence. (Concerning ὅλως see on v. 1.—Ἥττημα, or ἥσσημα, is properly overthrow, injury, but here want of morality, like ἐλάττωμα, see Rom. xi. 12.—That the subject before us is contentions regarding earthly possessions, is especially shown by ἀποστερεῖσθε and by ἀποστερεῖτε. The whole passage is enlarged upon and proved in Matt. v. 39, sqq. See the observations on the passage in the Comm.)

Vers. 9—11. The remonstrance is strengthened by reminding them of the character of the kingdom of God, which, as a kingdom of righteousness and purity, rejects all unrighteousness; adding that being purified from all uncleanness by the power of Christ, they would be doubly guilty in yielding themselves again to the power of sin. In the enumeration of the many forms of sin which exclude from the kingdom of God, he passes beyond a strict connexion with the subject before him; this would only have given him occasion to name the κλέπται, πλεονέκται, ἅρπαγες. But referring to much that precedes, as well as what follows, he mentions all descriptions of immoral excesses. (In ver. 9 ἄδικοι is to be understood of transgressors of positive commands, a different sense to that occurring in ver. 1; and the βασιλεία Θεοῦ refers here to its external appearance, such as will be triumphantly manifested at a future period, for internally it was

already to be found in the hearts of believers, which were under
its dominion, but the kingdom of God was not yet inherited by
them. See on Matt. iii. 2.—The form μὴ πλανᾶσθε, as pressing
exhortation, is to be found again in xv. 33; Gal. vi. 7; and also
Jam. i. 16.—In the Greek speech πόρνος is properly synonymous
with μαλακός, qui muliebria patitur: in this place it stands together with μοιχός for the lowest kind of debauchery, and signifies those persons who allowed themselves licentious freedom
with unmarried persons: it bears the same signification in v.
10, 11.—The expression εἰδωλολάτραι has here without doubt
especial reference to the voluptuousness connected with idolatrous services, more particularly in Corinth.—The passage v.
10, 11, shows that nothing may be argued from the series
of individual forms of sin which are there enumerated; it
would be trifling to seek for the grounds upon which they are
mentioned in a different or very particular order.—The οὐ before κληρονομήσουσι is properly omitted by Lachmann.—Billroth has certainly correctly explained the ταῦτά τινες ἦτε of
ver. 11: the τινες expresses no degree of qualification, as if it
signified only some, not all; for if all have not actually sinned
in every possible form, it is nevertheless certain that they have
offended against God's laws in some degree, and especially against
the Christian meaning of the law. The ταῦτά τινες is rather to
be understood = τοιοῦτοι: "such people were also ye." We
must allow that this connecting of two genders presents a difficulty, but it is possibly to be explained by an accessory notion of
something contemptible [see Winer's Gr. p. 152], which would
make the sense: "Ye were such people, practising these things,
beware that ye fall not back!"—The three words ἀπελούσασθε,
ἡγιάσθητε, ἐδικαιώθητε comprehend in the form of a climax,
progressive Christian generation, the thrice repeated ἀλλά adding strength to the expression. The ἀπελούσασθε must, as well
as the two other verbs, be considered passive [see Winer's
Gr. p. 232, where, however, this passage is omitted]; because the negative operation of grace, forgiveness of sins, by
means of baptism, is understood by it; but the latter is not to be
supposed a self-baptism, for the person bears himself entirely
passive in the celebration. The medial signification is only so
far maintained when translated, "Ye have permitted yourselves

to be washed."—The ἁγιάζεσθαι cannot here, as in i. 30, be received as Christian sanctification, else it must stand after ἐδικαιώθητε. It signifies here only separated, to be reckoned among the ἅγιοι. See on Rom. i. 7.—In the δικαιωθῆναι, then, the positive side is defined, the portion with the δικαιοσύνη Θεοῦ. [See on Rom. iii. 21].—The ἐν τῷ ὀνόματι without doubt refers to all three particulars, and the name Jesus again points to his essence, and being communicated to man by him in the δικαιοσύνη. —The addition καὶ ἐν τῷ πνεύματι τοῦ Θεοῦ ἡμῶν cannot be understood of the universal power of God, as it would never be secondary to the operation of Christ Jesus, but of the Holy Spirit, which is also only called πνεῦμα Θεοῦ, as in 1 Cor. vii. 40. The effect of the latter commences where the working of Christ has made a place. In Matt. x. 20 the Holy Spirit is called τὸ πνεῦμα τοῦ πατρὸς ὑμῶν τὸ λαλοῦν ἐν ὑμῖν, and in Luke xii. 12 is found πνεῦμα ἅγιον in reference to the same).

Ver. 12. The whole section which follows this verse, as far as ver. 20, is uncommonly difficult when considered with reference to the context. Without proceeding further with the subject of lawsuits, the apostle lays down in ver. 12 a universal principle for certain other relations, which are again brought under consideration in x. 23, and then proceeds in ver. 13 to the mention of meats, and from 14—20 exhorts against fornication. As subsequently (chap. x.) the subject of meats is amply enlarged upon, the verses 12, 13, in the present chapter appear in some degree foreign to the subject, and as little suitable as the admonition against fornication, which agrees better with the contents of chapter v. It may be asserted that the warning is occasioned by the mention which is made in verse 9 of certain vicious practices, and introduces the remarks presently to be made upon marriage, commencing vii. 2. But then, so much the more striking are verses 12 and 13, and their entire contents. Billroth does not appear to have found the difficulty of so much importance, and thus explains himself concerning it: "The connexion with what precedes is this. Some one may have alleged Christian liberty as an excuse for these crimes, but therein he would certainly err; this may not be misused, even in Adiaphora, e. g. in meats, how much less in things immoral in themselves, such as fornication." Nevertheless the supposition of the learned man mentioned is too remarkable, that there really existed in Corinth Christians who justified fornication on the principle, πάντα μοι ἔξεστιν. He asserts in opposition to Neander, who with reason declares this inconceivable, (Apost. Zeitalt. vol. i. p. 307), that it is not necessary to admit that this offence was general. Throughout the Epistles Paul always addresses those alone whom the subject concerned;* but if only one of the parties which existed in Corinth, e. g. the Gnostic Christians, had defended such a principle, Paul would have as unconditionally commanded their exclusion from any connexion with the church as he had done with the incestuous member. But if we cannot consent to this acceptation of the passage, the question arises, whether in any other way some direction as to its contents may be discovered. Neander thinks that Paul intended to enter upon the subject of meats offered to idols, of which mention is first made in x. 23, but that, diverted by an idea which occurred on the mention of κοιλία, he changed the subject of exhortation. Perhaps, in order to guard his words concerning the perishableness of meats, and of the organs of digestion, from misconstruction, on the part of those who denied the doctrine of the resurrection, he distinguished the form of the body, from its nature, which led to the digression upon the πορνεία. But although the declarations concerning the resurrection, which immediately follow, agree well with this supposition. we cannot but think that by accepting Neander's views, the apostle's procedure is made to appear. unmethodical. First, the mention of fornication leads him to discuss the relation of the sexes to each other; then, at the commencement of the eighth chapter, he returns from another subject to the theme of eating meats offered in sacrifice to idols; and after numerous digressions, easy to explain by the subordinate connexion of ideas, reaches at last in x. 23, a discussion commenced in vi. 12. As this supposition has little to recommend it, we must assume as a foundation, that Paul did not intend in vi. 12, 13, to discourse concerning meats offered in sacri-

---

* As sins of another character are named in vi. 9, Billroth must likewise suppose that individuals among the Christians in Corinth had defended the commission of them by the principle πάντα μοι ἔξεστιν. But is it conceivable that Paul would have permitted persons capable of such enormities to continue in the church? Such Bileamites or Nicolaitans would have been immediately expelled by his directions.

fice; but that the words in ver. 13 only serve to make clear the difference of the Adiaphora, from positive prohibition. According to my own conviction, therefore, the transitions in the various passages are to be thus understood: The apostle having the intention to enter upon the question of sensual vices, from vi. 9, mentions in that place not only such offences as regard property, but also those of the former kind. The discussion upon the πορνεία serves as an introduction to the remarks upon marriage, in which, according to God's ordinance, the passions are brought under restraint, and are sanctified. Now although certainly among the Christians in Corinth there was none sufficiently hardy to assert that licentious connexions were allowable, there nevertheless reigned in that place a gross laxity in this respect. This position of affairs, which *considerably* tended to gross abuse of Christian liberty, prompted Paul to publish the inapplicability of the Christian principle of liberty to the circumstances of the sexes. We thus accept what is correct in the views both of Neander and Billroth, and cast aside what is untenable in both. Rückert's supposition, that the apostle was interrupted at vi. 11, and upon reading again what he had so far written down, felt himself induced to make the supplementary remarks which follow, hardly commends itself to our attention; without doubt, an introduction to chap. vii. may be recognised.—If we examine ver 12 more closely, the question presents itself: did Paul acknowledge the principle πάντα μοι ἔξεστιν, or, as it is written in x. 23, πάντα ἔξεστιν, as his own, and consequently as true or not? We must certainly allow that Paul acknowledged it. The sentence introduced with ἀλλά says, the principle is correct, but due caution is required in the application. But is the principle really just? Paul proves, immediately in what follows, that fornication is not under any circumstances allowable, that πάντα therefore seems limited to the πολλά. But under this exposition the sentence is but meagre. "Much is lawful" has also the converse of the proposition, which is just as true, "much is unlawful." We therefore believe that the sentence may be thus understood: "All the laws that we find in the Old Testament, with reference to the prohibition of various meats, are no longer binding." The passage is thus explained by Flatt, but upon what ground do we add so much to the original text, thereby depriving the πάντα of all its force? We must rather receive the idea in its most extensive and likewise profound sense, as in iii. 22. Precisely as we may say: to God and Christ, to the Son of the living God, all is free, because it is an impossibility that he should will what is sinful, so to him born of God, in whom Christ lives, is all lawful, for God's seed is in him, he cannot commit sin (1 John iii. 9). The πάντα ἔξεστιν, then, is only another expression for the state of true *libertas*, the ἐλευθερία τῆς δόξης τῶν τέκνων τ. Θ. (Rom. viii. 21), of which the *impossibilitas peccandi* is the characteristic; and if this condition were even fully displayed in the believer here on earth, the sentence πάντα ἔξεστιν would require no restriction, but this is not the case. First, even among the regenerate backsliding is possible, and when this occurs, it is the antithetical principle which must be quoted to the apostate: οὐδὲν ἔξεστιν, for there being among the perfect no possibility of sin, there is as little probability of what is good among the entirely fallen. Therefore, even in the regenerate, as long as he dwells upon earth, the old man is co-existent with the new, and for this reason a limited application only can be made of the latter principle in the Praxis. In the first place, it is utterly inapplicable beyond the sphere of the βασιλεία τ. Θ., that is to say, within the dominion of sins positively prohibited by the divine laws; because the becoming subject to this dominion leads to apostacy from Christ, and even within the sphere of God's kingdom the principle of liberty can only be applied here below in a restricted sense. Secondly, the believer must act with consideration for others, sparing the weak, and therefore for their sake he cannot do all that would otherwise be permitted to him. The sentence ἀλλ᾽ οὐ πάντα συμφέρει expresses this, likewise in x. 23, ἀλλ᾽ οὐ πάντα οἰκοδομεῖ sc. ἀδελφούς.* And besides this, he must ever keep the old man in mind, even while enjoying what is lawful, lest by means of his lusts he again become his prey; that is to say, the righteous sway of Christian principle may be subverted, and the new man driven from its position, for sin once more to assert its power. The other sentence cautions against this: ἀλλ᾽ οὐκ ἐγὼ ἐξουσιασθήσομαι ὑπό τινος.

Ver. 13. The principle of Christian liberty may be applied in

* In this sentence the reference to himself is not to be disregarded, thus ἐμοί might be added to συμφέρει.

behalf of believers to the rules for meats, but this could not be
asserted with reference to any proceeding so clearly sinful as that
of πορνεία. This opinion is clear and perfectly intelligible; not so
the argument which the apostle adduces to corroborate it. The
βρώματα, and the κοιλία appointed for the same (i. e. the digestive
organs especially), will be destroyed by God; being perishable, they
will decay, like all things perishable (vii. 31); then comes the antithesis, that the body itself (apart from the form) is, however, imperishable, and that God will raise it up. But can the perishable
nature of the organ become a reason for its being subjected to the
principle of liberty, or for that member being made Adiaphoron?
Are not gluttony and immoderate drinking (distinctly named by
Paul in vi. 10), referable to the perishable body? And may we
not say, that other organs necessary to the human species may
likewise be wanting in the glorified body (see on Luke xx. 36)
as well as those of digestion? How then can we comprehend the
apostle's argument? Possibly the sentence ὁ δὲ Θεὸς—καταργήσει does not refer to πάντα ἔξεστιν, but only to ἀλλ᾽ οὐκ ἐγὼ
ἐξουσιασθήσομαι ὑπό τινος? So that the sense would be, that
we are not to allow ourselves to be brought under the power
of anything, least of all of that which is so perishable as meat.
This construction would not, however, aid the elucidation; for
there the antithesis between καταργήσει of ver. 13, and the
ἐξεγερεῖ of ver. 14, would be lost; likewise we should not be
under the dominion of the body, even of the glorified, but the
body is rather to be subject to the spirit under all its forms and
appearances. We must prefer looking to the antithesis, τὰ
βρώματα τῇ κοιλίᾳ—τὸ δὲ σῶμα οὐ τῇ πορνείᾳ. The organs
destined for the nourishment of the body, having their precise and
appointed office, it would be unnatural were the entire powers of
men to be engaged in eating and drinking; for the whole soul
being thereby absorbed, gluttony and excess would be the result,
and that not only as to quantity, which may be relative. It is
quite otherwise with the sexual impulse; this by no means affects
merely the organs through which it operates, any more than the
speech affects merely the tongue. The mere corporeal indulgence
of this impulse is rather sinful; in its true form, as the highest expression of conjugal love, it concerns the whole man. The sexual
impulse therefore has its origin in a far profounder law of na-

ture than eating and drinking, consequently offences against the former are also evil deeds of the inward man, to which absolutely no application of Christian liberty can be allowed. Thus $\Theta\epsilon\grave{o}\varsigma$ $\kappa\alpha\tau\alpha\rho\gamma\acute{\eta}\sigma\epsilon\iota$ $\tau\grave{\eta}\nu$ $\kappa o\iota\lambda\acute{\iota}\alpha\nu$ must be understood as expressing the mean unimportant position, $\sigma\hat{\omega}\mu\alpha$ on the contrary the sign of perfect individuality, the body in its necessary union with the individual, the $\psi\upsilon\chi\acute{\eta}$.

Ver. 14. The resurrection of our body is proved as usual by Paul, from the resurrection of our Lord. Our body belongs to Christ, it must therefore be deemed holy, and employed accordingly, nor is this inconsistent with the marriage state, which is sanctified by God, and endowed with blessing. The introduction here of $\acute{o}$ $\kappa\acute{\upsilon}\rho\iota o\varsigma$ $\tau\hat{\wp}$ $\sigma\acute{\omega}\mu\alpha\tau\iota$ is difficult to understand. The supposition that the Lord ministers to the body, provides for it (as is said in Ephes. v. 29), does not precisely and sufficiently state the change of idea; and, without doubt, the only correct view to be taken of this passage, which also renders intelligible that which follows, of all bodies being *members* of Christ, is this: "the Lord is appointed for the body," *i. e.* he himself is flesh (John i. 14), endeavours to corporify himself in the body. By this act of God, the body first obtains its true dedication; it becomes an abode of God, a temple of the Holy Spirit. (Lachmann has decided in favour of $\dot{\epsilon}\xi\acute{\eta}\gamma\epsilon\iota\rho\epsilon\nu$ and $\dot{\epsilon}\xi\epsilon\gamma\epsilon\acute{\iota}\rho\epsilon\iota$, but for evident as well as internal reasons *the reading* $\dot{\epsilon}\xi\epsilon\gamma\epsilon\rho\epsilon\hat{\iota}$ is preferable.)

Vers. 15—17. The apostle's warning against fornication (to which all offences against morality, either of a gross or more refined nature, must be appended) acquires unusual force from the profound idea just mentioned. The bodies of believers are Christ's members, he alone shall have dominion over them, therefore the impure deprive him of his own, making Christ's members members of fornication! This Paul proves by the connexion with Christ in spiritual unity, which is perfected through faith: as the Son is one with the Father, so are believers one with him in the Spirit (John xvii. 22); and, precisely as the body and soul of men are dependent, is the body consecrated to Christ, through the union of the spirit with him; to him belongs the whole man, spirit, soul, and body. It is, however, important to observe that the apostle does not rest here, but that he also pursues the subject under another view. The apostle says, that as with Christ a holy spiritual union takes place, so with the harlot one of a contrary character; and he then quotes Gen. ii. 24, which is a passage that might be considered referable to marriage, and not to fornication.  The specific character of marriage is ordained and sanctified by God's command, but in the immoral relation alluded to it is desecrated, and thereby becomes a curse; in the former state, the reciprocation of pure and deep feeling becomes hallowed, while in the latter every exalted attribute disappears, and nothing remains but what is fleshly and sinful.  The whole passage is evidently grounded upon the comparison which is instituted between Christ and his church (Ephes. v. 23, sqq.), and the relations of the married state; and therefore it is not improbable that, when the apostle said that he which is joined to an harlot is one body with her, he had in view the great whore that sitteth upon many waters (Rev. xvii. 1).  The sacred fellowship of Christ with the church, which corresponds with God's ordinance of marriage, stands then in direct opposition to the unholy association of the carnal, which, drawing into its circle all who approach, imprints upon them ineffaceable marks of its evil nature, while those who draw nigh unto Christ are adorned with his likeness.  (Ver. 15 is perfectly intelligible, as out of $\mathring{a}\rho\alpha\varsigma$, $\mathring{a}\rho\alpha$ can be formed, it appears pleonastic from the $\pi o\iota\eta\sigma\omega$ which follows.  It is used in analogy with the Hebrew לָקַח.—Upon $\mu\eta$ $\gamma\acute{e}\nu o\iota\tau o$, see on Rom. iii. 4.—In ver. 16, the earthly connexion is implied, but grounded upon agreement of sentiment; the offenders must stand equal under one point of view, or, so far as this is not the case, one party endeavours to effect the necessary analogy in the other.  With the sinful this bias assumes the form of temptation to profligacy, but in the good that of urging regeneration.— In the quotation to $\phi\eta\sigma\iota$ is to be added $\mathring{\eta}$ $\gamma\rho\alpha\phi\eta$.  The Hebrew וְהָיוּ לְבָשָׂר אֶחָד refers to the preceding בָּשָׂר מִבְּשָׂרִי.  Eve was taken from Adam to be again restored to him as his helpmate.  The $o\mathring{\iota}$ $\delta\acute{v}o$ is supplied by the LXX., and the words are quoted according to their rendering in the passages Matt. xix. 5, 6; Mark x. 7, 8; and Ephes. v. 31.  Doubtless they are intended to comprehend a declaration against polygamy; nevertheless we must confess that the occurrence of passages speaking more decidedly against the practice is to be desired,

as there is no direct mention made in the New Testament of
polygamy being contrary to the principle of marriage).
Vers. 18, 19. The apostle, in conclusion, draws attention to
the specific nature of the sin under consideration, as being
directed against the offender's own body, against a portion of
that which is identified with himself. Nay more, as the believer
is no longer his own, but God's, so is also the body the Lord's.
Fornication is therefore a higher degree of sacrilege, or a mixture of sins against himself, his neighbour, and his God. The
beneficent influence of the Bible realism here strongly displays
itself; spiritualism inculcates an indifference towards the body,
and even its pollution, but the Gospel teaches that the body is
to be honoured as an existing organ of the soul, glorified with it
through the Holy Spirit. (In ver. 18 ἐάν stands for ἄν, as is
likewise found in profane writers. See Winer's Gr. p. 285.—
In ver. 19 the ἢ οὐκ οἴδατε is to be thus understood: The peculiarity of this kind of wickedness cannot offend you, for ye certainly understand the importance of the body.—The body is truly
the sanctuary, the temple of the soul, but both coming under the
influence of the Holy Ghost are not only purified in their nature,
but the Holy Spirit thenceforward dwells in a human body, as in
a temple.—The οὗ ἔχετε ἀπὸ Θεοῦ forms the antithesis with οὐκ
ἐστὲ ἑαυτῶν, "Ye belong no more to yourselves, that ye may
govern yourselves by your own wills, for God is your Lord, and
ye must be led by his Spirit."

Ver. 20. The relation of believers with God, Paul thinks, is
this: being by Christ, who has paid the λύτρον, who is it himself, ransomed from the slavery of sin (Matt. xx. 28; 1 Pet. i. 18,
19), he has become the servant of God (Rom. vi. 17, 22). For
through this reason the believer praises not himself for his pure and
moral life, but him who gave him power to lead it. (The ἠγοράσθητε τιμῆς is again found in vii. 23. The τιμῆς is by no means
only pleonastic: "ye are bought for a price," but emphatic, for
a *great* price.—Ἐν τῷ σώματι is here perfectly suitable, because
the subject of what precedes is the body and its sanctification.
The additional sentence καὶ ἐν τῷ πνεύματι ὑμῶν, ἅτινά ἐστι τοῦ
Θεοῦ, is wanting in the oldest and best Codd., and can therefore
only be regarded as a gloss, to which very possibly the passage
vii. 34 gave occasion).

## § 7. MARRIAGE.

### (vii. 1—40).

With the exception of the detailed laws respecting marriage in the Old Testament, this section is the most important treatise in the Holy Scriptures on that highest institution in the social relations, the type as well of the state as of the church. St Paul was led by the direct questions of the Corinthians in their epistle to the apostle (ver. 1), to treat of this subject, and the question first arises, to what the inquiries of the Christians in Corinth referred? what was the nature of their doubts on the marriage tie? from what did their scruples emanate? There are several points of which the apostle treats. First, he speaks of marriage in itself (vers. 1—9), and represents that it serves to prevent fornication, and consequently that married people ought not to abstain from the conjugal duty. In the second place (vers. 10—16), he speaks against divorce, declaring it to be inadmissible even if one party remain heathen, should this heathen party desire to continue in the married state. This leads the apostle (vers. 17—24) to the digression, that the Gospel in general does not interfere with the outward position of Christians, and that every one is at liberty to remain in the vocation which he held previous to his conversion. Paul next treats of the unmarried (vers. 25—38), and, on account of the existing difficult relations of the church, he counsels them to remain in the single state. Finally (vers. 39, 40), he briefly alludes to the second marriage of women. This last point, however, appears rather as a supplementary remark, than as an answer to any question seriously proposed: there remain, therefore, only three points for consideration. Of these, it must be admitted that the question respecting divorce is of a nature to be raised from a general Christian point of view. Whether it was admissible to remain with a heathen in so close a relation as that of marriage, was a question which might readily occur under any circumstances. But it is different with the first and third points. Whether marriage was allowable in itself, how married people had to conduct themselves in that state, whether the unmarried, especially of the female sex, were to engage in marriage,—these

were questions which could not arise from a general Christian
point of view.   Christianity indeed admitted no question as to
the allowability of marriage, and neither Jews nor heathens entertained any doubts on this . point.   It may be said that the
Corinthians had no cause to entertain a doubt or scruple respecting
marriage in itself upon Christian principles; they could only have
been uncertain as to *whether it was advisable to marry under
existing circumstances;* or, in other words, they might have entertained the same view which Paul himself advocates,—that in the
difficult relations of the church at that period it was better to remain single,—and they might have questioned the apostle in their
letter upon this expression of his opinion.   In fact I should see
no decisive reason against adopting this view, were it not for the
striking passage, vii. 3—5, in which Paul recommends the conjugal duty not to be forborne, except during a short time for
prayer.   Paul must have been led to remind the Corinthians thus
expressly, and in so special a manner, by peculiar circumstances:
doubtless there were ascetic views prevalent in Corinth, in accordance with which many persons even in the married state believed
themselves obliged to abstain from sexual intercourse.   But if
such was the case, it is more than probable that this ascetic
tendency occasioned the apostle's also treating of other points
relating to marriage.   In this view chap. vii. acquires a marked
contrast with chaps. v. and vi.   Whilst at first a caution was held
out against false freedom, there is here likewise a warning against
self-imposed severity.   But which of the parties in Corinth could
have fallen into this ascetic tendency?   Neander (Ueber Das
Apost. Zeitalt. Part I. p. 308, &c.) is of opinion that no ascetic
tendency was spread among the Judaizing Christians, but amongst
the followers of Paul.   The addition: "The followers of St Paul
thought themselves in this respect likewise obliged to follow the
example of their apostle," appears to indicate Neander's opinion
that the single state of Paul was the cause of his disciples over-
estimating this condition.   But this seems to me highly improbable.   Paul explains his unmarried state so distinctly as being
merely individual, and combats the mistrust of marriage so
emphatically (1 Tim. iv. 3),—indeed we find no traces in the
later period that the followers of Paul rejected marriage (for
the opposition to marriage amongst the Marcionites, who may

H

be considered as ultra-Pauline, proceeded from their Gnostic views of the nature of matter),—that we must seek some other explanation. The most probable one is that the *Christianer* also fostered this error. Their idealistic tendency, as we find it developed among the later Gnostics, might lead either to moral indifference (as if the pollution of the perishable flesh were a trifling consideration), or to false asceticism, and the two tendencies might have co-existed in the germ, and not have been distinctly separated until a later period. Before, however, taking a special view of the subject, we must glance at a general point, on the correct conception of which depends the comprehension of the whole section. We find (vii. 6, 10, 12, 25, 40) that the apostle distinguishes between what *he* says and what *the Lord* says; between a decided command (ἐπιταγή) of Christ, and his subjective opinion (γνώμη). Paul refers the whole contents of this section, up to vers. 10, 11, merely to his own opinion, not to the command of Christ. Billroth remarks upon this, following Usteri, that the apostle does not distinguish between *his own* commands and those received through *inspiration*, but between *his own* commands and those preserved by *tradition*. In fact St Paul speaks, xi. 2, 23, expressly of traditions, and the passage, vii. 10, refers to a command of Christ preserved to us. From vii. 40 it is also clear that the γνώμη is not intentionally opposed in any way to inspiration, for it has its origin in the Divine Spirit; but this distinction is insufficient for the explanation of our section. St Paul manifestly adduces the distinction to show that the command of Christ, but not his γνώμη, required an unreserved fulfilment. *His advice too could not be followed without thereby sinning* (vii. 36). Let us suppose that Paul had received no traditional command of Christ upon any particular subject, we must consider that his inspired conviction was equivalent to such a command, since Christ created it within him by his Spirit! In the passage, xiv. 37, he openly lays claim to this right. It is there said: εἴ τις δοκεῖ προφήτης εἶναι, ἢ πνευματικὸς, ἐπιγινωσκέτω ἃ γράφω ὑμῖν, ὅτι κυρίου εἰσὶν ἐντολαί. No traditional commands of Christ can be here intended, for a person required to be no prophet to perceive them; but the judgments of Paul are called commands of Christ in so far as Christ worked them in him by his Spirit. Billroth's explanation (on xiv. 37) of the ἐντολαὶ

*κυρίου* as referring to commands of God in the Old Testament,
is in the highest degree forced, nor can we on closer reflection
agree with Billroth (although we have advanced a similar view on
Acts xv. 1), on the opinion that this passage is important for a
comprehension of Paul's doctrine of the agency of the Divine
Spirit in man; as we here see that Paul explains the *γνώμη*
raised in him by the Divine Spirit as not absolutely binding, and
consequently as not absolutely true. The difficulty must rather
be explained by the distinction of positive commands and the
Adiaphora. Where dogmas or express commands are treated of,
St Paul continually lays claim to his apostolic authority; his
*γνώμη* is therefore here decisive, since it is enlightened by the
Divine Spirit. But in the Adiaphora it is true wisdom to avoid
decided commands, partly because the position of individuals to
them alters, and partly also because in the progress of development the whole period takes an altered position with reference
to them. Fixed commands would therefore be only obstructive,
instead of furthering their object in Adiaphora, and we may say
that the wisdom of the holy Scriptures is manifested no less in
what they have *not* forbidden than in what they forbid. The
only objection that might suggest itself against this view, is, that
St Paul would in that case have said: "*I* forbid it not, I merely
give good advice under existing circumstances;" but he says in
ver. 25, *ἐπιταγὴν κυρίου οὐκ ἔχω*, yet this formula appears to
refer to the possibility that the Lord might have given objective
commands also respecting these relations. But those words may
equally well be understood to mean, "I have no command of the
Lord upon this point, because he has not seen good to give any;"
his precepts are never purposely defective,—where Christ has
given no law, he intended there should be none. According to
this it is clear, that the advice given by the apostle in this section is not intended by himself as objective rules applicable to all
times, and consequently that we are not at liberty to give to them
this extended application, unless they change their nature.

Ver. 1. According to what has been said, therefore, no absolute
validity can be ascribed to the words, *καλὸν ἀνθρώπῳ γυναικὸς
μὴ ἅπτεσθαι* according to the apostle's view, as a false asceticism
pretends. The word of the apostle receives its comment in vers.
26, 29. The circumstances of the period rendered an unmarried

life relatively desirable, yet several of the apostles (ix. 5) were married. (Καλόν has here no moral meaning; it merely signifies "salutary."—Ἅπτεσθαι = נָגַע, Gen. xx. 6, xxi. 11. Prov. vi. 29 stands euphemistically for "to have conjugal intercourse." The formula only occurs here in the New Testament, but elsewhere frequently. The answer is directly connected with the statement of the question,—οἴδατε may be supplied.

Ver. 2. The apostle here apparently starts from a very low view of marriage; it is represented as a prevention of harlotry. But the reason of this is clearly that Paul was induced by circumstances to dwell only upon the *negative* side. Recent investigators* rightly attach weight to the *positive* side, namely, the spiritual union, on which the bodily union, and the consequent procreation of children, rest as on their basis. The apostolic view involves an indirect exhortation to the haughty *Christianer* not to sink deep in the mire of sin by affected sanctity in contemning marriage.

Vers. 3, 4. Probably married men had already forgone conjugal intercourse with their wives, and hence this admonition, which would otherwise be entirely superfluous. The manner in which the apostle treats this point shows clearly that he finds the specific of marriage in the sexual union, which must also be adhered to in every high ideal conception of the relation. "They shall be *one flesh*," not merely one *spirit* (which all believers are), and one *soul* (which all friends likewise are). Moreover, not only does the wife appear here dependent on her husband, but the husband likewise dependent on his wife. (For ὀφειλήν the received text reads ὀφειλομένην εὔνοιαν, by which the special meaning is extended to the more general one, "due kindness." But the more general sense does not suit the connexion. The best Codd. from A. to G. are for ὀφειλήν).

Vers. 5, 6. St Paul does not desire the conjugal intercourse to be discontinued, except in lengthened spiritual exercises. The apostle therefore discountenances the opinion that such intercourse was only allowable for the express purpose of begetting

---

* Compare especially the instructive writings on marriage by Liebetrut (Hamburg, 1834) and Märklin (in the "Studien der Würtembergischen Geistlichkeit)." On the Catholic side, the clever work, "Adam und Christus, oder über die Ehe," by Papst, (Vienna, 1835), is particularly remarkable. Compare the criticism of Göschel in the Berlin Jahrbuch, 1836, number 8, &c.

children.  He sees in it only the outward expression of true inward affection.   This passage, however, gives the impression that
conjugal intercourse is a hinderance to the serious exercise of
prayer; but the Christian should lead a life of prayer, consequently this act must always be considered as a hinderance, although a *necessary* one in the present state of sinfulness.   If
indeed the Christian's life were presented in an absolutely pure
form, man would not require a time thus set apart for prayer,
but it never does appear on earth in this pure form.  The Saviour
himself passed whole nights in solitary prayer, although his holy
soul was continually engaged in prayer.   But man has need of
such periods to suspend or to restrict the ordinary occupations
of life, and so it is also with conjugal intercourse.   From these
words, therefore, no conclusion can rightly be drawn prejudicial
to the apostle's view respecting sexual intercourse and its injurious effect on the spiritual life.   The expression σχολάζειν τῇ
προσευχῇ, moreover, contains an indication of the requirement of
stated festivals in the ordinary course of life.   Probably it was
an early custom, previous to the festivals, especially before Easter,
for people to devote themselves some time (for this is indicated
in the expression) to solitary prayer, in which beautiful custom
originated Lent.   St Paul, however, does not regard all this
(τοῦτο is not to be referred merely to verse 5, but also to the preceding verses) as a command, but as good advice, for it is all
continually modified according to different relations and individuals.   (In ver. 5, with ἀποστερεῖτε is to be supplied τῆς
ὀφειλῆς.—The ἄν stands, which is rarely the case, without a verb
[comp. Winer's Gr. p. 279]; γένηται may be supplied.—'Εκ συμ-
φώνου stands opposed to the isolated conclusion of the one part.
In the Septuagint σύμφωνον occurs adverbially; compare Eccles.
vii. 15.   In the New Testament it only occurs here.—The expression πρὸς καιρόν naturally conveys the idea, " for a short
time;" but the idea of the shortness is again determined by the
nature of the relation.—The reading σχολάσητε, and the omission
of τῇ νηστείᾳ καί before τῇ προσευχῇ, are fully confirmed by the
great majority of critical authorities.   The mention of the fasting
is quite in accordance with the meaning; but it is also, after the
ancient Christian custom, necessarily comprised in the idea of
prayer, as a lengthened exercise of prayer.—The readings συνέρ-

χεσθε and συνέρχησθε are to be regarded as mere interpretations of ἦτε.—The expression πειράζειν διὰ τὴν ἀκρασίαν refers back to διὰ δὲ τὰς πορνείας in ver. 2, and the above remarks likewise apply to it: St Paul dwells only on the negative side of marriage, but without intending to deny a higher positive one.—In ver. 6, 40, συγγνώμη is here to be distinguished from γνώμη in ver. 25, only so that the subjective opinion of the apostle, his good advice, comprises at the same time the accessory notion of a concession).

Vers. 7—9. This thought, that he was far from giving objective commands in the name of the Lord (comp. ver. 35) on such relations, is more closely explained by St Paul's saying that the gifts in reference to this are differently distributed. In the case of unmarried people, he wishes (on their own account, as is further explained in ver. 26, sqq.) that they should remain single on account of the impending troubles of the church; but for him who has not the gift of continency, it is better that he should enter the ordinance of marriage, which is founded by God. The apostle moreover here states the theme—especially in the words λέγω δὲ τοῖς ἀγάμοις καὶ ταῖς χήραις—which he pursues further in ver. 25, sqq., and 38, sqq. (In ver. 7. θέλω contains only the idea of wishing, which St Paul, however, himself acknowledges to be impracticable. The words πάντας ἀνθρώπους are of course only to be referred to the members of the church, for they alone were at that time called upon to suffer persecution.—Χάρισμα has here, but nowhere else, the meaning of a natural gift, which the mercy of God imparts, not an extraordinary spiritual gift. [Compare the particulars in 1 Cor. xii. 4]. In Matt. xix. 12, the Lord expresses the same thought.—In ver. 8 ἄγαμος is only fully determined by the connexion with χήραις: they are those persons not yet married. The opinion that widowers were hereby referred to is untenable; they are rather to be classed with the χήραις, but are not particularly named, because widowers are mostly compelled by circumstances to marry again, but not so widows.—In ver. 9 πυροῦσθαι, for which the Greeks also use καίεσθαι and φλέγεσθαι, is like the Latin uri, referring to the sufferings from the force of sexual impulse).

Vers. 10, 11. The apostle next turns to believers living in a state of marriage, and reminds them shortly of the Word of the Lord (Matt. v. 31, sqq., xix. 9; Mark x. 9, 12), that among

Christians no divorce should take place either on the man's side or on the woman's side, either from ascetic (1 Tim. iv. 3) or other reasons. He makes no mention of adultery as a valid cause of divorce, since this constitutes the divorce itself. (Compare remarks on the Comm. on Matt. v. 32, and Tholuck's Sermon on the Mount, p. 258). The remarkable addition, ἐὰν δὲ καὶ χωρισθῇ, shows the impossibility of absolutely carrying out this principle, valid as it was for the true Christians, in the early and zealous state of the church at that time. The conviction is therein expressed that, in the case of many persons belonging to the church, but not sufficiently penetrated with its spirit, matrimonial differences would not be overcome by affection, and that separation would ensue; in this case St Paul desires that no fresh marriage should be contracted, or still better, that reconciliation should be effected. This last thought, ἢ τῷ ἀνδρὶ καταλλαγήτω, shows that St Paul had in his mind separations not only arising from ascetic motives, but from dissension, and he regards these among the Christians of that time as by no means impossible. But the second marriage of those persons who have been divorced appears to be here absolutely forbidden, and thus the *separatio* is here also reduced to a mere separation from bed and board; a *separatio quoad vinculum* involved the admissibility of marrying again. But from the more exact determinations in the words of the Lord (Matt. v. and xix.), it follows, that the second marriage of divorced persons is not to be considered as absolutely forbidden for the dead members of the outward church. This passage is to be explained from the former, as St Paul himself grounds it upon them, but not the former from this one. At all events the passage before us affords no argument to prove that *malitiosa desertio* is a valid reason for divorce, for the μενέτω ἄγαμος forbids marrying again. (The expressions χωρισθῆναι of the wife, and ἀφιέναι of the husband, are carefully chosen. The wife is continually dependent on the husband; she cannot therefore dismiss him, she can only withdraw from him; the husband, on the contrary, can ἀφιέναι her, a milder expression for ἐκβάλλειν. Comp. remarks on ver. 13).

Vers. 12, 13. In the peculiar circumstances, undoubtedly of frequent occurrence in the first age of the church, when a por-

tion was still heathen, St Paul does not venture to enforce the
command not to divorce,—an important hint to us, in our half-
heathen church relations, how we should moderate the importance
attached to the prohibition of divorce.   St Paul rests the decision
on the consent of the heathen party; on the side of the believing party, he presupposes willingness from the greater love which
is to animate the latter.   A marriage with a heathen is to be considered binding on a believer, so long as the heathen party sepa-
rating him or herself does not contract another marriage.   These
precepts have in modern times acquired a new importance in reference to the labours of religious missions.   Marriages, in which
one party remains heathen, are never to be dissolved; it is indeed a difficult question, what course should be pursued, when
a converted heathen has several wives.   Since in the Old Testament God permitted polygamy to the holy patriarchs, it seems
proper not to compel those who are in this position to put away
their wives and children; but, on the other hand, in the case of
new marriages, strictly to introduce monogamy.   (In ver. 12, the
words τοῖς λοιποῖς are to be explained from the apostle's view,
according to which he resolves the γεγαμηκότες into certain
classes.   He of course does not speak particularly of those in
whose marriage state there was no interruption of harmony, for
where dissension existed, he *commands* the parties not to separate; the rest, that is to say the remaining class of married
persons, in which one party was heathen, he *allows* under certain circumstances to separate, but counsels them to keep fast the
marriage tie wherever possible.*   In ver. 13, ἀφιέναι is used of
the wife, in so far as in a mixed marriage the Christian party is
considered the ruling one).

Ver. 14.  In order to give importance to the admissibility of
such a union between a Christian and a heathen, the apostle expresses a thought, which, especially in connexion with the following, where the children are also called holy for the sake of their
Christian parents, must have presented no ordinary difficulty to
the ancient commentators, with their notions respecting infant

* As the apostle here expressly remarks, that in what follows he gives merely
*good advice*, it is clear that the subsequent passage can only be applied as the
basis of the Christian law of marriage, in so far as its precepts are confirmed by
the express law of Christ.

baptism. Some critics have therefore arbitrarily understood ἡγίασται to refer to baptism, and the conversion effected by the
Christian party. But in verse 16 this is only represented as *possible;* here, on the other hand, the continuation of the marriage
union is meant to be justified by the previous holiness in the heathen state. Others, who endeavour to maintain the claims of infant baptism, allege that Christian children may be baptized, but
not heathen children, because the former only can be supposed
destined to this privilege. Here then is indicated the destination
of the heathen party for Christianity by union with a Christian.
This view is held by Calov, Vitringa, and others; nor is it unsuitable; according to it the word ἁγιάζεσθαι might be taken in
its proper fundamental signification, " to be set apart for a sacred
purpose, to be dedicated," (compare remarks in the commentary on
John xiii. 31, 32). But the following contrast of ἀκάθαρτα and
ἅγια shows, that in the word ἡγίασται the *real influence* of the
Christian principle on the heathen party is rather to be considered,
than the *mere destination* for this. At all events, the reference of ἡγίασται to marriage, and the following word ἀκάθαρτα to bastards, is decidedly to be rejected; for the apostles
never denied the reality of heathen marriages; the validity of a
marriage, and the legitimacy of the children, could not therefore
have been first determined by the circumstance that one party
became Christian. This idea, however, is highly important, that
a relative sanctification (for the word ἁγιάζεσθαι can only be understood here to refer to a slight infusion of the Christian principle) can be effected merely by contact with those who possess
it. That is to say, in those who are closely united with believers,
without allowing themselves to be overcome by the power in them,
a certain resistance is always to be conceived; and yet the mighty
power of Christ unites itself with the better part in them, and
elevates it to a certain grade. According to this view we may
conceive, that Judaism existing among Christians for cen-
turies, was imperceptibly operated on by the power of Christ,
the consequences of which will one day be gloriously revealed.
Nor is the second half of the verse less important, treating
of the sanctification of children by their parents. Ἐπεὶ ἄρα
(comp. v. 10) presupposes the thought expressed in the following words as one generally recognised: "for else were

your children unclean; but now they are, *as ye all know and acknowledge*, holy)."\*   The ὑμῶν of course cannot refer merely to the half-heathen marriages (for what was valid in them must have been still more so in purely Christian marriages), nor merely to the latter, as this would not suit the line of argument; it refers to *all* Christian children.† The ancient Christians therefore considered these as *holy*, on account of their descent from Christians. But this expression cannot possibly, according to the contrast (ἀκάθαρτα), be merely rendered " dear, valued," as some interpreters maintain; it must rather be explained, according to the analogy of ἡγίασται, "relatively sanctified by the influence of the parents, touched by nobler influences." It is self-evident that it is not intended here to deny the peccability of the children, any more than in the case of the sanctified heathen party, who, according to ver. 16, has yet to be converted; but a destination for conversion, and a means of facilitating this, is unquestionably included. This is the blessing of pious ancestors, (2 Tim. i. 5). It is moreover clear that St Paul would not have chosen this line of argument had infant baptism been at that time practised; but it is certain that in the thought which the apostle here expresses lies the full authorization of the church to institute this rite. What pertains to the children of Christians in virtue of their birth is affirmed to them in baptism, and is really and fully imparted to them at their confirmation or spiritual baptism. It cannot be a matter of indifference to the child in what spiritual state its parents were when he was begotten. But the child of Christian parents always requires a personal regeneration.

Vers. 15, 16. In these verses the apostle brings forward the other side, which, in a mixed marriage of heathen and Christian, must raise a question. A case might occur in which the heathen party, on religious grounds (for we are here only speaking of such) did not wish to remain in the married state, or, in other words, required the Christian to forsake his or her faith. In such

---

\* According to the passages here cited by Wetstein and Schöttgen, the same view holds good with the Jews. Children who are descended from a half-Jewish marriage were treated as true Jews. The good is rightly considered stronger than evil.

† De Wette (Stud. 1830, part iii. p. 669, sqq.) is quite right in considering the reference as not merely to the children of mixed marriages, nor only to those of purely Christian marriages; the Christian principle operates strongly from one of the parties.

a case the apostle declares that the Christian party shall consent to a separation from the heathen; that the Christian party,
(brother or sister) is, in such a case, not bound, (οὐ δεδούλωται
ἐν τοῖς τοιούτοις). But God has called believers to peace; it is
therefore the duty of the believing party to maintain peace as
long as possible, and to bear with the heathen party; nor can
he indeed know, but that perhaps this very gentleness may win
over the unbelieving party, and bring him or her to salvation.
Viewed in this light, the passage appears to be quite simple, and
yet it has presented very grave difficulties to interpreters. Some
have imagined they detected in it a second ground for divorce, the
*malitiosa desertio*, whilst in Matt. v. 32, xix. 9, adultery is
stated to be the only sufficient ground; here then appears to
arise a discrepancy between our Lord's words and the apostle's.
In this explanation the undetermined οὐ δεδούλωται ἐν τοῖς τοιούτοις scil. πράγμασι* was understood to mean that the permission is herein conveyed for the Christian party, not only to dismiss the heathen party, who wishes to separate, *but also to
marry another*. But this is evidently not conveyed in the
words.† Ver. 15 forms a contrast to ver. 12 ; the heathen
party who wishes to remain, says St Paul, shall not be allowed;
but he who desires to go, he adds in ver. 15, shall not be
detained. That at the same time the permission to marry
again was granted by the apostle, is the less probable, since in
ver. 16 the possibility of the conversion of the heathen party is
dwelt upon. This passage indeed does not refer to the state
which is inferred by χωρίζεσθαι, for the words ἐν δὲ εἰρήνῃ
κέκληκεν ἡμᾶς ὁ Θεός κ. τ. λ. evidently contain a limitation of
the preceding thought: " The unbeliever may separate, *but* the
main principle always remains to the Christian, that he is called
to peace, and therefore a peaceful disposition must always prevail, in order not to give cause on his or her side for separation."
The possibility, however, cannot and must not be denied, that the
mind of the heathen party may also change *after* the separation.
It cannot, from this very possibility, be the apostle's meaning,

---

* It is of course also possible, that τοιοῦτοι was used in the masculine, but it does
not seem to me probable on account of the ἐν.—Olshausen Commentar., 2nd edit. iii.

† Comp. the article in the Evangelische Kirchenzeitung, for March 1829, p.
180, sqq.

that the Christian party is at liberty to marry again when the
heathen has left him or her (the re-marrying of the Christian
party would always be according to Matt. v. 32, μοιχεία); the
Christian is only relieved from the obligation of living with a
heathen party, and this alone is intended to be enforced by the
words οὐ δεδούλωται. That this passage has been understood to
imply that St Paul considered the *malitiosa desertio* as a valid
ground of divorce to Christians, may be explained by the feeling
of necessity in the existing state of the outward church, not to
limit divorces to the single case where adultery has been actually committed. It was felt that malicious desertion and im-
placable hatred might also form valid grounds for divorce, and
biblical sanction was sought for this opinion. But we have before
remarked on Matt. v. 32, that the New Testament absolutely
forbids divorce as well as oaths; adultery forms only an apparent
exception; this is not so much a *ground* of divorce as the divorce
itself. Although nevertheless it is clear from experience that
this absolute prohibition is no blessing for the numerous heathens
in the net of the kingdom of God, yet we must say, that the New
Testament does not intend to apply this command to the heathens likewise. It is moreover self-evident that the legislation
of Christian states must continually strive to approach the
exalted goal.

Ver. 17. The mention of the divine vocation, which is in the
first instance only cited in reference to marriage, leads the apostle
to its general consideration, which extends to ver. 24. He proceeds to observe, how in all congregations he acted on the principle, to leave every one in the outward vocation in which he was
before conversion. Among these outward vocations St Paul
reckons marriage. The mighty spirit of the Gospel produced an
immense excitement in the minds of all; the glance at a higher
world which it opened, excited in many an indifference to the
outward world; many Christians forsook their earthly vocation,
and would only live and work in the spirit (comp. remarks on
2 Thess. iii. 6, sqq.) Similar misunderstandings probably existed
at Corinth, especially among the *Christianer*, who were inclined to
a false conception of freedom, and led St Paul to this diatribe.
The apostle's wisdom opposed, by word and act, this proceeding, which must have brought ruin on the church, by not him-

self relinquishing his handicraft on assuming his apostolic vocation. To this fanatical and revolutionary movement he opposed calm discretion. He rightly conceived that the Gospel does not seek to overthrow all that is ancient in a sudden and tumultuous manner, but brings about a change by a slow process, penetrating into all the relations of life. (The εἰ μή is intended to render prominent again the other side, namely, that it is better for every one to remain in the relations which God has allotted to him, and consequently also in marriage, even when one party has remained heathen. Billroth correctly explains εἰ μή = πλήν. The course of thought may be thus understood: "But if the heathen party wishes to separate, let him not be compelled to remain, his conversion is always uncertain ; *only* it is a fixed general principle, that every one should remain in the vocation which God has allotted to him." In idea Rückert's conception of the εἰ μή is the same; he takes it for εἰ δὲ καὶ μή, "but even if not," namely what precedes is the case, *i. e.* at all events. The reading ἢ μή is a simple correction, arising from the difficulty which was conceived to exist in the expression εἰ μή.—With respect to the attraction in ἑκάστῳ, compare Winer's Gr. p. 482, sqq.—The passage already cited, 2 Thess. iii. 6, throws light on the words οὕτως ἐν ταῖς ἐκκλησίαις πάσαις διατάσσομαι, compare the explanation).

Vers. 18, 19. St Paul first touches on the great difference between Jews and heathens. The apostle is not in favour of abolishing the outward means of recognition on entrance into the Christian church, since in the New Testament this contract has lost its meaning. The τήρησις ἐντολῶν Θεοῦ is here alone valid,* in which is embraced the belief in Christ and his redemption, since he also is an ἐντολὴ Θεοῦ. (The abominable custom, to which the words μὴ ἐπισπάσθω refer, namely, the renewal of a foreskin in an artificial manner, is mentioned again in 1 Macc. i. 15. According to Buxtorf [Lex. Talm. p. 1274] those Jews who had abolished the token of their election from shame toward

---

* The conception of the words, which Billroth proposes, seems to me erroneous. "Circumcision and foreskin are nothing in themselves, they only acquire signification when men believe that in them they keep the commands of God." But the strict Judaists, believing circumcision to be a command of God, would have done quite right to attribute importance to it, which, however, the apostle cannot have intended.

the heathens were called מְשׁוּכִים, in Latin *recutiti* [compare Martial. Epigr. vii. 30]. Joseph. Ant. xii. 6 also speaks of such a custom. According to Celsus [de Medic. vii. 25] a peculiar instrument was employed for this purpose called the ἐπισπα- στήρ. For more particulars compare an article in the Stud. 1835, pt. 3, p. 657, sqq.—In ver. 19, in the expression ἀλλὰ τήρησις ἐντολῶν Θεοῦ, is to be supplied ἐστί τι. as it is called in iii. 7).

Vers. 20—24. The general principle (ver. 20, 24) is here also applied to the relation of slavery, which prevailed throughout the whole ancient world. This is certainly opposed to the spirit of the Gospel, which makes men free, and Paul advises also the converted slaves to seek freedom if they can obtain it (of course in a lawful and proper manner), and the free men in no manner to trifle away their freedom. At the same time, if this is not possible, he exhorts them not to vex themselves about it, since the free man is also the servant of Christ.—This conception of the passage differs from that which the Fathers of the church have maintained since the time of Chrysostom, and in fact at first sight the connexion seems rather to favour their explanation. They supply in ver. 21, with μᾶλλον χρῆσαι, not ἐλευθερίᾳ, but δουλείᾳ, so that the sense is: "If thou art called as a slave, care nothing, much more although thou (εἰ καί = *quanquam*) canst become free, yet serve rather; for the believing slave is yet free in the Lord, and the free man a slave of Christ." The connexion appears, according to the other and now usual explanation, not to be rendered by any means so clear, and especially εἰ καί (ver. 21) and γάρ (ver. 22) appear to be inappropriate. But the words, μὴ γίνεσθε δοῦλοι ἀνθρώπων (ver. 23), militate against the opinion of the church Fathers; beside which, we may observe, that the apostle cannot possibly have expressed the idea, that a slave should remain in a state of slavery, even when he can obtain freedom. The point therefore is, to obtain from the εἰ καί and the following γάρ an appropriate reference in accordance with our view. But this presents itself in a very natural manner, if we only give to the δοῦλος ἐκλήθης the proper emphasis. According to the meaning of the apostle, spiritual freedom is included in καλεῖσθαι: from this idea he proceeds: "But if thou canst *also* obtain bodily beside spiritual freedom, do it rather, *for* the slave called in the Lord is by the Lord made free from all outward power, therefore it is befitting also that he should be *quite free.*" Then the emphatic ἀπελεύθερος suits very well, as also the μᾶλλον χρῆσαι, which last, even with δουλείᾳ supplied, has still a great hardness. With respect to the other half of ver. 22, namely the words ὁμοίως καὶ ὁ ἐλεύθερος κληθεὶς δοῦλός ἐστι Χριστοῦ, they in the first place express, that no one here on earth can be otherwise than in a state of dependence; and they are in so far consolatory for servants—the most free are also servants of Christ. But these words also contain a warning to the free to preserve their freedom, not to become the servants of men by dependence on human opinions—for to be a servant of Christ is itself the true freedom; every life spent out of his service is in a measure like slavery. (If κλῆσις is referred to the outward vocation, and ἐκλήθη in ver. 20 to the inward calling, the ᾗ strikes us—it should be ἐν ᾗ. But if the expression, ἐν τῇ κλήσει ᾗ ἐκλήθη is conceived as an idea, ἐκλήθη must be understood of the outward vocation. This is certainly uncommon, according to the usage of language in the New Testament, but not unfitting; it is far more completely in accordance with the Pauline circle of ideas, that the almighty will of God is believed to condition the outward position of man, however apparently free he may be to choose it. We therefore prefer this last conception to the difficulty of supplying the ἐν.—In ver. 22, comp. on the notion of true freedom, the remarks on John viii. 36.—The formula τιμῆς ἠγοράσθητε is found in vi. 20.—In ver. 24, the παρὰ Θεῷ is derived from every human mode of conception of the relations; the most inward condition of the soul is of importance in the sight of God,—by it slavery or freedom is first sanctified).

Vers. 25, 26. These following verses contain advice for the unmarried. Under the existing difficult relations of the church, the apostle, as he again assures us, considers it better that they should not enter upon marriage. (Compare vii. 1). At the same time he again expressly observes, that he does not give this as a command of the Lord (that is to say, in order not to impose a burden upon any one), but as his own opinion. Nevertheless he makes his opinion (as in ver. 40) very striking and worthy of consideration by adding: ὡς ἠλεημένος ὑπὸ κυρίου πιστὸς εἶναι. This πιστὸς εἶναι, which St Paul refers, not to himself, but to the pity of God, cannot mean, as Billroth is of opinion "to be a true servant of the Lord," nor, as Augustine thinks, "to be faithful in my vocation:" neither sense has any direct reference to the context. It can only mean, as Flatt correctly remarks, "to be worthy of belief, *i. e.* of confidence." This is peculiarly referred to in the mention of his γνώμη. But he was worthy of confidence because he had the Spirit of God, which judges correctly all circumstances, and this is alluded to in ver. 40. But if the apostle here expresses thus generally the thought, καλὸν ἀνθρώπῳ τὸ οὕτως εἶναι, it is at the same time apart from the consideration of the persecutions, especially to be remembered, that St Paul believed the return of the Lord to be near at hand. The ἐνεστῶσα ἀνάγκη are to him the חֶבְלֵי הַמָּשִׁיחַ, with which is connected the revelation of the kingdom of God. (Comp. on x. 11). But as this hope subsequently receded, when he no longer believed himself to be "clothed upon," 2 Cor. v.), but when he hoped to depart (Phil. i. 23; 2 Tim. iv. 6), his view of marriage must also have become modified. (In ver. 25 the expression παρθένος refers, as it frequently does, to both sexes, it is = ἄγαμος. Rückert is of opinion that it only refers to virgins, but this is completely contradicted by the δέδεσαι γυναικί (ver. 27).—In ver. 26, the ὅτι καλόν merely takes up τοῦτο καλόν again to strengthen the thought.—On ἐνεστώς compare remarks on iii. 22, and Rom. viii. 38. Ἀνάγκη refers not merely to the persecutions, but also to the great events in nature expected at the last day [compare on Matt. xxiv. 20, 21, 29], in short to the θλίψεις of the last period of time in the widest compass).

Vers. 27, 28. In the clearest manner St Paul guards against being misunderstood, to represent a marriage as a sin (which was probably taught in Corinth); but he openly declares that the unmarried would at that time lead an easier life, and his advice may accordingly be considered as intended to save them from trouble. (In verse 27 λέλυσαι must not be referred to the death of the wife; it merely means "to be unmarried."—In verse 28, the addition of τῇ σαρκί transfers the whole consequences of marriage to a lower sphere; it prepares the way for want, anxiety, care, in outward circumstances, but no θλίψις τῷ πνεύματι).

Vers. 29—31. The apostle enforces this good advice in the following verses by a detailed description of the state of mind which the character of the times required. The heart must not be wholly given up to any earthly possession or affection; it must rather always belong to God and the imperishable world, and a love of the future state. Without doubt St Paul wrote these words in expectation of a near approaching transformation of the σχῆμα τοῦ κόσμου τούτου, and the introduction of the αἰὼν μέλλων with the βασιλεία τ. Θ. If, however, this hope is not realised, the meaning of these words is by no means destroyed. (Compare the remarks on Matt. xxiv. 1). The whole development of the church on earth is such as to lead to the continual expectation of the coming of Christ, and the state of mind of believers is to be such as is here described. The period of expectation is only extended by the mercy of God (2 Pet. iii. 9), but its character is not altered. (In ver. 29 the explanation of the words ὁ καιρὸς κ. τ. λ. is not without difficulty. With respect first to the punctuation, the division after συνεσταλμένος, when ἐστί must be supplied, is not suitable, because, according to this, τὸ λοιπόν, which must then be taken adverbially, becomes somewhat laboured. The same objection applies to the division which Lachmann proposes, placing ἐστί before τὸ λοιπόν, besides which this transposition has not critically sufficient authority. The thought only becomes concise by placing the point, as Griesbach and others do, after ἐστί, and taking τὸ λοιπόν as subject, in the sense "the [of this cycle still] rest is the heavy time." The article before καιρὸς thus acquires its full force, whilst it points to the great period of suffering before the Parousia known to all Christians. With respect then to the explanation, we had the word συστέλλω, Acts v. 6, in the signification "to bury a dead man." Here it is to be taken in the simplest meaning of the word, "to contract." The participle therefore might signify, "short, of brief duration." But the meaning, "anxious, heavy," must be considered more appropriate. There is no well-authenticated passage to justify the use of συνεσταλμένος for "short." On the contrary, in the classics, συστολή means simply "anxiety, contraction of the heart." [Cic. Quæst. Tusc. i. 37; Læl. c. 13]. In the same sense συστέλλεσθαι occurs in Ps. lxxii. 13, according to the translation of Symmachus.—The ἵνα is to be understood τελικῶς: this want has the *purpose*, according to the intention of God, of freeing the soul from dependence on perishable

things.—The words ὡς μὴ ἔχοντες γυναῖκας are of course merely
to be understood inwardly, keeping the spirit so free in the love
of the creature as not to be impeded by this in the fulfilment
of the highest duty, the relation to the kingdom of God.—
Ver. 30. Not joy merely, but sorrow likewise is not to have dominion over the servant of God; in God's power he rules over all.—
Κατέχοντες is emphatic, as in a subsequent passage καταχρώ-
μενοι: the κατά is meant to indicate the false tendency of the spirit
abandoning itself altogether.—In ver. 31 σχῆμα is *facies externa;*
the world itself does not perish at the dawning of the kingdom
of God, but only its *form.*   Not until after the kingdom of God
follows the new heaven and the new earth.   [Rev. xxi. 1].
What perishes in the world is the sinful; compare 1 John ii. 8 and
17.—Lachmann very appropriately connects with the preceding the
θέλω δέ κ. τ. λ., so that between the two sentences lies this
supplying thought, " You would therefore prepare for yourselves
much want if you should give yourselves up to the perishable
things of this world)."

Vers. 32—34. The following words are so strong, as in fact to
incline to the belief that the apostle gives an objective preference
to celibacy, as the (Roman) Catholic church maintains.*   But on
this very account, that the words are so strongly expressed, the defenders of celibacy are themselves obliged to limit their meaning.   If
the expression, ὁ γαμήσας μεριμνᾷ τὰ τοῦ κόσμου, πῶς ἀρέσει τῇ
γυναικί is intended to refer to marriage, this could be no sacrament, it would directly destroy the idea of a life devoted to God.
The passage can therefore only be understood to mean that the
apostle is describing the ordinary state of things, from the influence of which even the believer is frequently not exempt; but by
no means that a description of marriage, or of Christian marriage,
is here given.   (In ver. 32 μεριμνᾶν is used in a good sense, " to
do zealously, to manage."—Semler thinks falsely here only of
deacons, as if τὰ τοῦ κυρίου were an allusion to their office.   The
general tenor of the command plainly contradicts this view.—
There are various different readings and punctuations of ver. 34,
which are probably only occasioned by μεμέρισται.   This word
might be connected with the preceding one with the addition of

---

* Compare the clever treatise by Papst on the theory of marriage, in the Journal for Philosophy and Catholic Theology, in the fifteenth and earlier numbers.
Cologne, 1835.

καί, so that the sense would be "and is divided;" that is, serves two masters, God and the world; or it might be referred to the following, with the meaning, "there is a difference between a wife and a virgin." This last usual conception of the passage may deserve the preference. Lachmann, however, decides for the first, and reads, καὶ ἡ γυνὴ ἡ ἄγαμος καὶ ἡ παρθένος ἡ ἄγαμος, instead of the usual reading, ἡ γυνὴ καὶ ἡ παρθένος· ἡ ἄγαμός).

Ver. 35. St Paul again declares that his intention is not to lay down any law, but only to impart profitable advice, for the more easy attachment to the Lord and honesty. On account of the following ἀσχημονεῖν, the expression τὸ εὔσχημον can only be understood in the sense of honesty, honestas. But this appears to stigmatize marriage as inhonestum. The difficulty might be avoided, by referring τοῦτο not merely to the last-mentioned object, but to the contents of the whole chapter; then τὸ εὔσχη-μον would refer to an honourable marriage, which was spoken of in the beginning of the chapter, in contrast to the πορνεία. But in the first place ταῦτα would in this case have been used, because more than one object is treated of; again, the expression εὐπάρε-δρον τῷ κυρίῳ refers too decidedly to what has been just said; and lastly, there is here no conclusion,—the question concerning unmarried persons is still continued. We must therefore say, that, to be an ἄγαμος is not in itself an εὔσχημον, any more than to be married is in itself an ἄσχημον, but only in so far as, under the peculiar existing circumstances, the service of the Lord re-quired this. Billroth understands βρόχος to mean a snare, but this does not agree with the verb ἐπιβάλλειν. A snare, more-over, would imply something secret, whereas everything here is open; it alludes only to something difficult. It is therefore better conceived as = ζῦγος.—Instead of εὐπάρεδρον the received text reads εὐπρόσεδρον; but the former reading, which Lachmann also adopts, has the authority of the Codd. in its favour. It is the neuter form of the adjective transferred to the substantive, and the expression therefore carries the dative. It denotes "attach-ment, fast adherence."—The ἀπερισπάστως only strengthens the idea of the εὐ. It means, "without being drawn away by any relation." This form is only found here in the New Testament).

Vers. 36—38. The reader will thus far have understood the apostle's representation as relating in the question of marriage to

the decision of the persons themselves interested; but St Paul, at
the conclusion of the inquiry, speaks of the father as deciding
the marriage of his daughter. This is perhaps not to be understood as if the apostle by way of example wished to cite merely
a form, how a marriage is brought about or prevented; but, after
the ancient mode of conception, he considers the question of marriage as entirely placed in the hands of the father, or of his representative. We must confess that this state is a subordinate
one, and the free self-decision of the betrothed parties, recognised
by the parents, although rightly subjected to certain conditions,
appears to be more befitting a mature age; but St Paul, in his
wisdom, does not convert the form, which was adapted to the
relations of that period, into a rule for all ages. (In ver. 36,
ἀσχημονεῖν is to be taken in an active sense; "he who thinks
that he behaveth uncomely toward his daughter." The thought
is to be explained from the point of view of the Jewish Christians,
who regarded childlessness as the greatest earthly misfortune and
the greatest disgrace to the wife.—Ver. 37. Compare on ἑδραῖος
1 Cor. xv. 58, Col. i. 23. The apostle here refers to the steadfast
conviction, that it is better to remain unmarried. Διακρινόμενος,
Rom. xiv. 23, forms the contrast.—In the words μὴ ἔχων ἀνάγ-
κην, κ. τ. λ., there appears to be an intimation that the father
may also be in a certain measure bound by the will of the daughter. But outward circumstances are undoubtedly first to be considered. The view entertained generally by the ancients, as still
at the present day in the East, recognised no independence of
the wife; this first resulted from the Christian-Germanic civiliza-
tion.—In ver. 38, we need not suppose with Billroth, that Paul
intended first to oppose to the expression ὁ ἐκγαμίζων καλῶς
ποιεῖ merely καὶ ὁ μὴ ἐκγαμίζων, but then corrected himself.
The principle expressed here lay in the whole connexion. But
κρεῖσσον ποιεῖ can only be referred to peculiar relations of the
time, or certain persons.—For γαμίζω we find in Mark xii. 25, the
form γαμίσκω, as also in Luke xx. 34, ἐκγαμίσκω stands for
ἐκγαμίζω, which again occurs in Matt. xxiv. 38, Luke xvii. 27).

Vers. 39, 40. In the last place, touching the second marriage
of the *woman*,* St Paul remarks, that in marrying a believer

* There seems to be no doubt entertained respecting the second marriage of the
man, probably because in the case of widowers a new marriage was generally of

she need have no scruple; but in the apostle's opinion, she had
better remain unmarried.    The addition of the words δοκῶ δὲ
κᾀγὼ πνεῦμα Θεοῦ ἔχειν, to the expression κατὰ τὴν ἐμὴν γνώ-
μην, plainly indicates a contrast to those who, as it were, appropriated to themselves the Spirit, which naturally calls to mind
the *Christianer*.    Since, however, the observation stands at the
conclusion of the whole exposition, its allusion cannot be restricted to the last remark, but it must be considered as applying
to the entire subject.    In later times, moreover, a certain odium
was attached in the church to a second marriage, traces of which
occur as early as in 1 Tim. iii. 2, v. 9.    Ministers of religion,
therefore, could not be δίγαμοι.    (Comp. Binghami Origg. vol. ii.
p. 153).    From the last-mentioned work indeed (vol. vi. p. 423),
we see that, under certain circumstances, *digami* were excluded
from the communion-table.    (The whole passage has a detailed
parallel in Rom. vii. 1, sqq.    From this passage also in some
Codd. νόμῳ is added to δέδεται.—Billroth, following Calvin, is of
opinion that by ἐν κυρίῳ more is intended than that the widow
should merely marry a believer, namely, that she should make her
choice and enter upon the marriage in a truly Christian spirit.
But as ᾧ θέλει precedes, ἐν κυρίῳ can only first refer to the
person marrying.    It is self-evident, however, that if the faith of
the chosen person is investigated, there must also be faith, for
only belief recognises belief.—In ver. 40 μακαριωτέρα cannot refer to eternal blessedness, but to the συμφέρον [ver. 35] of this
life, whilst the unmarried woman will be better off in the καιρὸς
συνεσταλμένος [ver. 29] than the married woman).

## § 8. CHRISTIAN LIBERTY.

### (viii. 1—xi. 1).

In this large section the apostle treats of the use of meats
offered in sacrifice, participation in idolatrous festivities, and es-

---

pressing importance, on account of the motherless children; therefore, the question here is only touching the woman.    The μόνον ἐν κυρίῳ, moreover, must be
regarded as referring also to the man (2 Cor. vi. 14, 15).

pecially of Christian liberty, and the manner of its exercise.* It
appears that several members of the Corinthian church had proceeded to such lengths as not only to eat meat which had been
offered in sacrifice to idols, but actually to take part in some
sacrificial festivities held in the heathen temple itself (viii. 10).
It is possible that some of the immediate followers of Paul, or of
Apollos, had fallen into this extreme, but it appears especially
to have been the *Christianer*, whose Gnostic prejudices (viii.
1—3), leading them to suppose themselves elevated above all sin,
rendered them thus perfectly regardless of the weaker brethren.
It was doubtless the Judaising followers of Peter, who received
from such proceedings just and great offence. The apostle having first, in viii. 1—13, adverted to the general use of meats
that had been offered in sacrifice to idols, and directed attention to the offence likely to arise to the weaker brother
by the exercise of false liberty therein, proceeds to expatiate
(ix. 1—27) upon the high degree of self-restraint with respect
to the liberty permitted him, which is exercised by the true
Christian on his brother's account, and then shows (x. 1—13)
from the sacred writings of the Old Testament, how severely God
punishes the misuse of liberty. He then returns to the circumstances of the Christian with respect to the heathen festivals,
declaring that the believer cannot celebrate alike heathen and
Christian sacrifice. But in order to avoid introducing Jewish
formality into the church, he permits the use of meats offered to
idols, if purchased in the market, and likewise sanctions the participation in repasts given by the heathen in their own dwellings,
and the free use of all meats served up on such occasions, provided it was not expressly declared that such had formed part of
an idol sacrifice (x. 14—xi. 1). The apostle thus decides between
the claims of the party advocating freedom on such points, and
also on that which inculcated a stricter observance, with a high
degree of impartiality and wisdom.

Ver. 1—3. Verse 1 is evidently resumed in verse 4, so that the
subject occurring between may be considered parenthetical, and
it would be better to consider the parenthesis as beginning at the

* The passage Rom. xiv. 15 bears so close an affinity to the one before us, that
we desire that the exposition thereof may be compared with that under present
consideration.

words ὅτι πάντες γνῶσιν ἔχομεν, instead of ἡ γνῶσις, as many others suppose. The words with which the apostle commences his discussion, and which are more fully carried out in verse 4, evidently convey an impression to the mind that they refer to some disclosures regarding the Corinthians; there is accordingly to be found in the οἴδαμεν the assertion of their unimportance, but also a slight reproof of their presumption. The words are capable of being understood thus: "we know as well as you," &c., and received thus, the context ὅτι πάντες γνῶσιν ἔχομεν agrees well. It is impossible that this πάντες can be understood to apply to many or several individuals, or as Billroth thinks, only to one party, viz., that indicated by the passage in connexion, but it is rather *all Christians as such* who are included therein. To this exposition the words of verse 7, ἀλλ' οὐκ ἐν πᾶσιν ἡ γνῶσις is apparently opposed; for a certain defined knowledge is there spoken of, for which reason the article is made use of, but here knowledge in general, and therefore the words of verse 1 must be translated so as to express, "for all men have a certain degree of knowledge,"* that is to say, every Christian must certainly know that only one true God exists, from its having been laid down as a fundamental doctrine in the Old Testament. In order to repress immediately the over estimation of the γνῶσις, to which the Christians were so prone, the apostle contrasts it with love, upon which the 13th chapter affords such a copious commentary; self-denying love has nothing dazzling in its character to allure its followers, for which reason even the spiritually inclined Corinthians had not striven to acquire it themselves, as they had knowledge and other gifts of the Spirit; nevertheless love is the most elevating divine element which exists in man's nature. The further consideration of the nature of the γνῶσις is deferred to xii. 8; the remark here is sufficient, that when separated and distinct from love, as in this case understood, it indicates the partial direction of the reflective faculties towards divine things, whilst the characteristic of love is the perfect subservience of the will. (Concerning the remarkable psychological appearance that may present itself in the man in whom it is evident, comp. the Comm. on xiii. 1, and sqq.) As long as knowledge is selfish, it

---

* In Bengel's Gnomon, it is correctly stated : *non addit articulum, non nimi-num concedens.*

likewise dwells with pride, but love expands towards its neighbour to edification,* (presupposing of course that the knowledge
is a right knowledge, while the wisdom that is unaccompanied
by love is often only *apparent*, attained by means of false paths,
through speculations, the motive for which may be blindness or
curiosity; then is it naturally pernicious in the highest degree;
but love, on the contrary, is from its very nature ever accompanied by a knowledge often undeveloped it is true, but nevertheless
genuine, substantial; knowledge may exist without love, but the
latter never entirely without the former.   The expression δοκεῖ
εἰδέναι τι sufficiently indicates wisdom which is only imaginary,
the purport of the form οὐδὲν ἔγνωκε καθὼς δεῖ γνῶναι, however,
is rather uncertain.   The vanity of knowledge might be thereby
signified, but in this case the sentence appears somewhat tautological.   It would be better to refer the words to the erroneous
means by which the apparent wisdom is attained, and the antithesis οὕτως ἔγνωσται ὑπ᾽ αὐτοῦ agrees with this arrangement,
as it intimates the way to obtain the true divine knowledge.  God
is a φῶς ἀπρόσιτον: no created soul can by his own power pene-
trate to him, or become possessed of his mysteries; every attempt
of the kind is utterly vain.   Nevertheless God can certainly manifest himself in the soul of him who longs after the true wisdom,
and so passively create the true γνῶσις.   The knowledge of God,
therefore, presupposes the being known of him, as Bengel observes in the Gnomon, the *cognitio activa* presupposes a *cognitio
passiva;* the soul will not vivify with life from above, until God
has drawn nigh.   It cannot be doubted that, in expressing the
connexion of the soul with God, the image of a bride passed
through the apostle's mind, so that the γινώσκειν = יָדַע is significant both of knowledge and union.    Billroth is of this opinion
in the passages, xiii. 12, and Gal. iv. 9, which may likewise correctly bear this construction.   Other expositions of the passage
by previous interpreters, defended by Usteri, and according
to which ἔγνωσται signifies " he is lovingly acknowledged by
God, accepted as a child of God," are sanctioned neither by the
connexion, nor grammatically.    Beza, Heidenreich, Pott, and
Flatt, would call γινώσκεσθαι " to be instructed," but this cannot

* Bengel is worthy of notice with respect to x. 23: scientia *tantum dicit*,
*omnia mihi licent*, amor *addit, sed non omnia ædificant.*

be philologically proved. (In ver. 2 the reading ἐγνωκέναι instead of εἰδέναι has only originated from the circumstance that it was deemed necessary to have a word in the text corresponding with γνῶσις. Lachmann has, however, received the reading ἐγνωκέναι. This learned man reads for οὐδέπω οὐδὲν ἔγνωκε only οὔπω ἔγνω. It is nevertheless difficult to perceive how the usual reading should have arisen out of this, to which Griesbach justly gives the preference, and which is defended by A.B.D.E).

Vers. 4—6. After this parenthesis the thread of the discourse is resumed from ver. 1, and the former and more general περὶ τῶν εἰδωλοθύτων is better defined by the περὶ τῆς βρώσεως. As that which is universal is first held forth to view, it must be generally acknowledged in all Christian minds that there is no εἴδωλον in the world, no other God but one. (See Jerem. ii. 11; 1 Sam. xii. 21, כִּי תֹהוּ.) But it is striking that this sentence appears to be nullified by what immediately follows, by the εἴπερ εἰσὶ λεγόμενοι Θεοί and ὥσπερ εἰσὶ Θεοὶ πολλοί, with which the expressive ἀλλ' ἡμῖν εἰς Θεός is connected. Paul cannot intend to say that for believers there exists one God, but for unbelievers many, when he had just before declared οὐδὲν εἴδωλον ἐν κόσμῳ. It therefore follows that in x. 20, the sacrificial festivals are represented as establishing a fellowship with dæmons, and this also plainly shows, that in the apostle's opinion the idols were by no means unproductive of evil. It has been attempted to remove this difficulty by substituting λέγονται εἶναι Θεοί for εἰσὶ λεγόμενοι Θεοί: but besides being entirely ungrammatical, were these words received, the ὥσπερ εἰσί in which Paul, with reference to such passages as Ps. cxxxvi. 2, 3, acknowledges the truth, that there are many gods and many lords, is decidedly opposed to it. The λεγόμενοι certainly signifies that they are falsely so called, and the ἐν οὐρανῷ and ἐπὶ γῆς, which refer to the higher and inferior orders of mythological deities (viz. the celestial deities and their representative stars, likewise the strong ones of the earth, deified heroes, and kings), form an antithesis with the τὰ πάντα (ver. 6), but their reality is not questioned; they are, it is true, no real gods, i. e. not uncreated, everlasting, self-existent beings; they are created powers, creatures of the only true God whom Christians honour, and whose power and mighty hand created all things, including the gods and lords themselves mentioned, but they are not to be regarded as fabulous. Billroth's interpretation of the passage cannot therefore be deemed perfectly satisfactory; for although he correctly acknowledges that the apostle views the heathen gods in the light of dæmons (see further on x. 20), he does not solve the apparent contradiction between οὐδὲν εἴδωλον ἐν κόσμῳ and εἰσὶ Θεοὶ πολλοί, the difficulty being increased by the τί οὖν φημι; ὅτι εἴδωλον τί ἐστι; of x. 19. But this contradiction is perfectly removed, if we strictly distinguish between εἴδωλον and Θεός or κύριος.* The first expression indicates the creations of fancy, as devised by the mythographers and propagated among the people. The existence of such beings as Jupiter, Mars, Venus, under recognised forms, and with certain attributes, and decided characteristics, was really not to be found *in rerum natura,* but only in the human imagination, from whence the representation was transferred to stone, brass, or wood. Nevertheless these creations were *founded upon a real potency* which excited the senses,† and was prejudicial to the development of a nobler life in man. This is signified by the apostle in the passage ὥσπερ εἰσὶ Θεοὶ πολλοί. Paul thus fully expresses both sides of this important position, it being necessary to confute the reality of the mythological beings in order to set free the heathen from their erroneous ideas; but it was likewise as important to prove that in the worship of idols the powers of sin were propitiated, lest indifference and erroneous ideas in connexion with the subject should be strengthened.—Ver. 6 demands a closer investigation, Usteri and Billroth having already correctly discerned in it the element of the doctrine of the Trinity. It is evident that the εἷς Θεὸς ὁ πατήρ, and εἷς κύριος Ἰησοῦς Χριστός, form a parallel with the before-mentioned Θεοὶ πολλοί, κύριοι

* Nitzsch (Stud. Jahrg. 1828, Part iv. note) endeavours to reconcile the apparent contradiction by reading " as hopeful helpers," and ἀλεξίκακοι, they are nothing; but to the help expected from idols there is positively no allusion.

† Notwithstanding the abundant declarations in the Old Testament that idols are nothing (Is. xl. 19, xli. 6, xliv. 6, xlvi. 6; Jer. ii. 11, 26, sqq., x. 8, sqq.), passages are nevertheless to be found acknowledging their reality. See especially the remarkable passage Deut. iv. 19, where it says, God has assigned certain stars to all nations as leading potencies, and also Deut. xxxii. 8 according to the LXX.— In the New Testament the apostle's thought is best expressed in Acts xvii. 29, οὐκ ὀφείλομεν νομίζειν χρυσῷ ἢ ἀργύρῳ ἢ λίθῳ χαράγματι τέχνης καὶ ἐνθυμήσεως ἀνθρώπου, τό θεῖον εἶναι ὅμοιον, which it will be perceived contains nothing from which we would infer that the θεῖον is nothing.

πολλοί, and the Θεοῖς ἐν οὐρανῷ καὶ ἐπὶ γῆς. The heathen possessed but vague notions of the divine Being, and dominion which is only realized in absolute perfection in God and Christ, to whom the Father hath delivered all things, (1 Cor. xv. 25). The true God hath also alone the prerogative to create. The inferior powers may certainly change that which is created, but can produce nothing save in the power of God. The signification of the prepositions ἐξ, διά, εἰς, in such a connexion has already been considered in the Comm. on Rom. xi. 36. The Father is here represented as the origin and end of all things; in the εἰς the operation of the Holy Spirit is indicated which conducts all to its source. It may excite attention that it is here only styled ἡμεῖς εἰς αὐτόν, while in Rom. xi. 36, τὰ πάντα is found; but the difference is immaterial, for, if the church be appointed to receive all men to herself, and a restorative principle proceeds from her even towards the κτίσις (see on Rom. viii. 19, sqq.), then are believers immediately a community. At the conclusion of the verse καὶ ἡμεῖς δι αὐτοῦ is cited after the δι οὗ τὰ πάντα, in the activity of the Son. It will be readily comprehended that transcribers might imagine that δι αὐτόν would be preferable, since the ἡμεῖς was already subordinate to the πάντα. But this originates in pure misconception of the words, for the δι οὗ τὰ πάντα refers especially to the creation (see on John i. 3), but καὶ ἡμεῖς δι αὐτοῦ to the new birth, which is represented as a second creation. Some Codices of a later date have also here made mention of the Holy Spirit and its attributes, and according to this the shorter reading must be viewed as the original one.

Ver. 7. This definite perception, however, (see on ver. 1), that the authority of both form and power were involved in idol-worship, was not yet imparted to all the individuals composing the then existing church (which may be said to signify that, under progressive development, this knowledge would extend itself universally); for which reason the weaker brethren were to be considered, because, upon the principle that "whatsoever is not of faith is sin," they would pollute their consciences by a proceeding which another might pursue without detriment. (See on Rom. xiv. 23). Very authentic Codices read συνηθείᾳ for συνειδήσει, and I might agree with Lachmann in preferring this

reading, since the use of the same word in two significations in
our sentence always presents a difficulty, if it did not create a
possibility that the συνείδησις once expressed might be changed
into a word apparently more suitable.

Vers. 8, 9. As it has been stated that eating, or abstaining
from so doing, can possess no meaning as regards spiritual life,
or in relation to the Almighty, the exercise of Christian liberty
in such things must be connected with consideration towards the
weak. (In ver. 8 it would be very easy to substitute the more
usual συνίστησι for παρίστησι, but for that very reason is the
latter preferable. Lachmann has accepted the reading παραστήσει. Παρίστημί τινά τινι really signifies "I present some
person, e. g. to a prince," including of course the idea of recommendation.—The context shows that περισσεύειν, like ὑστερεῖν,
refers only to spiritual circumstances, to grow or to decline in the
new life. Probably these words have reference to some appearances among the Corinthians intimating the wish to defend their
liberty.—In ver. 9 Lachmann has preferred ἀσθενέσιν to the general reading ἀσθενοῦσιν, but the adjective form is probably
chosen because it occurs in ver. 10).

Vers. 10, 11. Paul intentionally selects a very conspicuous
misuse of Christian freedom, viz., participation in sacrificial festivals in the temple itself, in order to exhibit the evil consequences which must arise from such proceedings; and such circumstances must have really taken place, otherwise the argument
would lose its force. If in this passage it should appear that
Paul did not reprove such participation in itself, but only on
account of the consequences in regard to the weak, it will be
seen in x. 14, sqq., that the apostle declares such participation in and for itself entirely unlawful. (In verse 10, εἰδω-
λεῖον is a sanctuary which would possess an image of its
deity, in contradistinction to lesser sanctuaries without images,
or simply sacred enclosures. To individual deities the forms
Βακχεῖον, Σεραπεῖον are also applied.—The use of οἰκοδομεῖν in this passage has, as Wetstein and Semler have already
correctly stated, something ironical. The conscience of the
weak is strained to a higher pitch, not through the power of
the Holy Spirit, but by human means, through respect for person-
alities; for in the apposition τὸν ἔχοντα γνῶσιν exists the

signification, that the weak Christian brother, acknowledging the brother who claims liberty as more advanced than himself, is thereby misled by imitating what he does.—In ver. 11 Lachmann reads ἀπόλλυται ἐν for ἀπολεῖται ἐπὶ: but the future is more applicable, signifying that not one isolated deed, such as related, occasions the loss of salvation, though it *may* ultimately be its consequence if the weak brother by *perseverance* in such conduct gradually loses ground in his faith. [Compare the parallel passage Rom. xiv. 15]. Properly speaking, it is not knowledge itself which exercises an injurious effect upon the brother, but the wrong use of it; but Paul chose the more energetic expression in order to draw the Corinthians from their over-estimation of worldly wisdom.—See Winer's Gr. p. 374 concerning the ἐπὶ used here.—The phrase δι᾽ ὃν Χριστὸς ἀπέθανε expresses the value which even the weakest soul possesses in the sight of God. Διά seldom stands as found here; ὑπέρ or ἀντί is more general. See on Matt. xx. 28; Rom. v. 15).

Vers. 12, 13. Under such circumstances it is plainly the duty of those in a higher position to act with reference to the weaker brethren in order to avoid offence; and in placing limits to their freedom it is better that they restrain too much than too little. This idea is also expressed by Paul in Rom. xiv. 21. (In verse 12 τύπτειν is to be understood in the sense of "to wound." Sins against the brethren are sins against Christ himself, because they are his members. [See vi. 15].—The οὐ μὴ φάγω κρέα εἰς τὸν αἰῶνα of ver. 13 is a hyperbolical expression, intended for the highest degree of self-denial in such things. It ought not therefore to be rendered by "for life," although, from the nature of the thing, nothing more can be said. That there were in Corinth, as in Rome [see on Rom. xiv. 1], persons who deemed the eating of meat an especial sin, is not to be inferred from this passage).

Chap. ix. 1. In order to present to and at the same time to animate the Corinthians to a self-denial of freedom lawful in itself, from Christian love, the apostle offers himself and his proceedings as a pattern and example. We must nevertheless confess that if this alone had been Paul's intention, first, the passage might have been considerably curtailed, and next, the subject would have continued uninterruptedly (viii. 1) from this point, instead of having much that was irrelevant interwoven with it.

This can only be explained by perceiving that Paul, without letting fall the principal theme to which he returns in x. 14, takes occasion in describing his proceedings as an example for all (xi. 1) to enter upon a defence of those points which had been made objects of attack by the adverse parties in Corinth. The conclusion which the apostle seems to have aimed at was, that the liberal *Christianer* party asserted as a duty that they were exempt from law. In this view they might have affirmed that meat offered to idols might be eaten, perhaps even in the temple, in order to prove the nothingness of the idols. To this extreme the apostle opposes the true liberty which upon necessary occasions can refrain from the use of what in itself is permitted. This liberty Paul claims for himself, and defends at the same time his apostolic dignity, which the antagonist party appear to have attacked, upon the ground that he had not dared to lay claim, as the other apostles had done, to a subsistence from the church. But as it is more likely that such imputations and suspicions circulated secretly than that they were openly spoken, the apostle justifies himself only in an indirect manner. At the time the second epistle was written his opponents had proceeded to far greater lengths, and for this reason Paul opposes them in it without disguise. (2 Cor. x.)

Ver. 1. The reading of the *text. rec.*, according to which οὐκ εἰμὶ ἀπόστολος stands first, could only originate in the view that Paul was passing to something perfectly different. The sentence οὐκ εἰμὶ ἐλεύθερος, which connects itself immediately with the preceding subject, comes first in order, as Griesbach and also Lachmann have acknowledged. The meaning of the words would then be this, "But should I, who observe such self-denying conduct, not be free?" The glance at his opponents, who might have made such an observation, brings immediately to his mind the chief idea, "Am I not a real apostle? have I not seen the Lord?" and, in order to apply directly the refutation, he adds what his enemies themselves could not deny, "Are ye not as it were my work in the Lord? have I not likewise founded the church in Corinth?" It will be seen that by means of these questions the representations had already acquired a more general direction, which Paul could prosecute at his pleasure, leaving him likewise at liberty to return to the subject upon which he had already treated, the use of meat which had been offered to idols. Concerning the ἑώρακα Ἰησοῦν Χριστόν, Neander and Billroth have long since made it clear that the subject can neither be an acquaintance with Christ during his earthly sojourn, nor simply knowledge of his doctrine, nor any other appearance of Christ, but can decidedly only refer to the circumstance which took place at Damascus (Acts ix. 1; 1 Cor. xv. 8), for this fact alone stands in that direct connexion with the apostolic dignity of Paul to which this sentence is to direct attention. But it is highly probable that these words arose from the accusation of the Corinthian antagonists that Paul was no real apostle, he had certainly not seen the Lord. In the mouth of his adversaries this really meant that he had not sojourned three years with Christ as the Twelve had, and of this Paul himself could offer no evidence, even though he might (see on 2 Cor. v. 16) have seen Jesus again and again ; but his vision of the glorified Redeemer richly compensated for this deficiency.

Vers. 2, 3. In full consciousness of the divine power through which he had laid the foundation of the Corinthian church, he names the Corinthians themselves a seal, a solemn confirmation of his apostolic office, yes, his written defence against all opponents. (The εἰ ἄλλοις κ. τ. λ. of ver. 2 is to be understood, "If I am not esteemed such to others, am no apostle unto others, I am, nevertheless, to you." See Winer's Gr., p. 453, concerning the εἰ οὐ.—For σφραγίς, see Rom. iv. 11. In ver. 3, ἀπολογία as well as ἀνακρίνειν are borrowed from the language of the law).

Vers. 4—6. Three separate subjects now form the theme of the apostle's consideration, and his intention is to make the prudent use of the freedom which was his of right perceptible in them; first in the use of meats, next in reference to marriage, and lastly, on the subject of his acceptance or non-acceptance of support from the church. It is precisely on the latter point that he enlarges most amply, because, as has been already stated, the adversaries employed it in order to represent Paul as uncertain with reference to his apostolic prerogative. The φαγεῖν καὶ πιεῖν certainly refers back to chap. viii., so that the sense is, "Have I not surely also the freedom which ye claim for yourselves?" at the same time the contrary is also to be found expressed in it, "Am I not also at liberty to eat, if I will?" Billroth, however, justly remarks, that the general expression went much further, and referred not *only* to the before-mentioned discussion concerning meats offered to idols, but especially to the Jewish laws relating to food. See ix. 20.—What gave occasion to the apostle then to mention marriage? The remonstrance is surely not without occasion, for Paul quotes the example of the apostles. As Κηφᾶς is particularly named, and mention is made of the brethren of the Lord, including James of course, we might suppose the occasion to be furnished by the followers of Peter. The Judaising Christians had, as is shown by the Clementine homilies, and Epiphanius' account of the Ebionites (see Neander, bk. i., p. 309), the idea, that it was the *duty* of every one to marry; we may therefore suppose that the apostle had been reproached for his celibacy, and was desirous of defending it. On this supposition the hypothesis of Storr, who would consider the mention of our Lord's brethren as a proof that the Christian followers of James were connected with those of Peter, may demand attention. (On this, see the Introd. § 1). But in this case the words must run otherwise! The μὴ οὐκ ἔχομεν ἐξουσίαν ἀδελφὴν γυναῖκα περιάγειν can only be translated, "May I not likewise as the other apostles take with me a sister, *i. e.* a Christian woman, as my wife?" or, in other words, *must* I then continue unmarried? May I not be so from free choice? Even his liberty in this particular must have been contested! It was a sign of notions carried to excess as to the efficacy of celibacy, and perfectly consistent with the idea which seems, from vii. 3 sqq., to have been current in Corinth, that marriage was objectionable (1 Tim. iv. 3). The possibility of a thing of this sort must by no means be considered confined to the Gentile Christians; the mention of Peter and James points sufficiently clearly to the Jewish Christians, among whom ascetic principles were not unusual, as Rom. xiv. 15 shows, and the example of the Essenes and Therapeutics. (In ver. 5 λοιποὶ ἀπόστολοι is said to intimate clearly that he, Paul, is himself also an apostle.— Concerning ἀδελφοὶ τοῦ κυρίου, see the Comm. on Matt. xiii. 55. As they are mentioned here distinct from the apostles, and no passage speaks of two kinds of brethren of our Lord [brothers really such, *and* cousins], it is evident that none of them were among the Twelve. [See on John vii. 5; Acts i. 14; 1 Cor. xv. 7].

But as two of the cousins bore the same names as the brethren
of Jesus, quoted Matt. xiii. 55, it is most probable that the four
ἀδελφοί, the cousins of our Saviour, are sons of Cleopas and
Maria, the sister of Mary. See further the Introd. to the Epistle
of James.—Concerning the marriage of *Peter* the reader is referred
to the observations on Matt. viii. 14.*—Ver. 6 shows that *Barnabas*, in a similar manner to the apostle Paul, must have maintained himself by the labour of his hands, and have been attacked
upon the self-same grounds; and from the notice which is here
taken of this early fellow-labourer of Paul, a fresh engagement
would appear to have taken place on the part of the apostle with
him. See the remarks on Acts xv. 39.—The form of expression,
ἢ μόνος ἐγὼ καὶ Βαρνάβας οὐκ ἔχομεν ἐξουσίαν τοῦ μὴ ἐργάζεσθαι, is rather ironical, and means, labour is not commended to
us alone! This refers to the fact that the antagonists had asserted
that he possessed no right to be maintained by the church, not
being a legitimate apostle. At another time they reversed the
accusation, and required that Paul should not distinguish himself
by anything exclusive, but should allow himself to receive support
from the church community, as did all the other teachers of the
Gospel. [See ver. 15, and 2 Cor. xi. 7, sqq.] The apostle nevertheless on this head defends his individual liberty, while he
pressed it upon no one as law. In the same degree he reserves
to the teacher the right to demand a subsistence if necessary).

Vers. 7, 8. Paul, in what follows, discusses at length the right
of preachers of the Gospel to receive from the community a provision for their bodily wants, but states in ver. 12, and sqq., that
he has not judged it expedient to avail himself of this privilege,
disclaiming any inference affecting his apostolic calling as the
consequence of this forbearance. This proceeding of the apostle
has been already brought under notice in Acts xviii. 2, when,
upon the occasion of his residing in Corinth (to which the accusations of his adversaries refer), he worked with Aquila and Priscilla. To this passage we must accord some further degree of

* It is remarkable that Tertullian (*de Monog.* c. 8) will not allow this passage
to refer to the wives of the apostles, but to women who accompanied them mi.iis-
tering unto them of their substance, as our Lord is described to have been attended in Luke viii. 3. This explanation has been adopted by the (Roman)
Catholic Church in defence of celibacy.

notice, as the pertinacity is remarkable with which Paul insists
upon carrying out his principle of maintaining himself by the
labour of his own hands. According to Acts xx. 33, sqq.,
at first he might have felt some solicitude lest any should believe
that he availed himself of the preaching of the Gospel to enrich
himself; but, on the other hand, when this course was made the
precise subject of accusation against him as in Corinth, one might
think it had been better for the apostle simply to accept the support, as the other apostles had done. He must necessarily have
expended much time in labour which had been better employed
in his spiritual calling. It has been already well remarked on
Acts xviii. 2, *that a self-exercise was aimed at in it;* Paul
wished thereby to mortify the flesh; it belonged to the ὑπωπιά-
ζειν τὸ σῶμα that, according to ix. 27 he considered necessary
for himself. 2 Thess. iii. 6, sqq. is very instructive on this head.
Paul there warns his readers against idleness, and continues to
say that he has employed his hands in gaining his own livelihood
in order to give them an example. In the passage under consideration, this last point is not stated.—It is then proved from
soldiers, vine-dressers, and shepherds, who all live by their occupation, that the preacher of the Gospel also may and should live by
his calling. (In verse 7, Lachmann has preferred the reading τὸν
καρπόν to ἐκ τοῦ καρποῦ, and there appears internal evidence in
its favour, for the ἐκ is very likely to be derived from the ἐκ τοῦ
γάλακτος following, and would make both members agree.—In
ver. 8, Lachmann and Billroth have decided that only a comma
should stand after λαλῶ, and certainly the reading οὐ λέγει cannot be the correct one. For this Griesbach has already substituted ἢ οὐχί, and οὐχί even might be omitted, as in verse 10, for
μή governs the whole sentence. The law forms so far an opposition with κατὰ ἄνθρωπον, as it includes the divine will).

Ver. 9—11. It appears striking that to prove the acknowledgment of the principle under consideration, so remote a passage as Deut. xxv. 4 should be quoted, as the apostle in verse 13
refers to something admitting closer application. Paul seems,
however intentionally, to have chosen this proof in order to
afford more stress to his argument. The sense is this: if the
holy Scriptures adjudge even to the beast the requisite food in
return for his labour, how much more shall this be observed in

relation to the human race. In the μὴ τῶν βοῶν μέλει τῷ Θεῷ
κ. τ. λ. by no means lies the idea that God does not provide
for the beasts; but, as the δὶ ἡμᾶς ἐγράφη which follows shows,
it only asserts that the ordinances of the law relating to animals
have also a reference to man, and were written for his good, and
that consequently what is valid as regards animals admits of application in increased potency to the human race.    The passage
1 Tim. v. 18 is treated in the same manner.  (In verse 9 φιμόω=
κημόω, from φιμός, capistrum, to close the mouth with a muzzle.
As a trope it occurs in Matt. xxii. 12,—᾿Αλοάω, properly to beat,
stamp, thence beat out the corn, i. e., thresh, which, as is well-
known, is performed in the East either by means of oxen or thresh-
ing-carts.—In ver. 10 the interpunctuation must be so restored, as
Lachmann supposes, that after Θεῷ only one comma stands, consequently the whole only forms one question.    With πάντως λέγει,
ἡ γραφή must be borne in mind as subject.—Concerning the her-
meneutic principle δὶ ἡμᾶς ἐγράφη, see the observations on Rom.
iv. 23.—Lachmann has decided in favour of the reading received
by Griesbach, in opposition to the *text. rec.* of τῆς ἐλπίδος αὐτοῦ
μετέχειν ἐπ᾽ ἐλπίδι.  To plough and to thresh constitute a portion of husbandry, and it is taken for granted the whole exercise
of activity in this direction has for impulse and likewise aim, the
hope of participating in the produce; this hope, therefore, may
not be deceived.  The τοῦ μετέχειν belongs indifferently to both
parallel divisions of the verse.  The spiritual activity of sowing
and reaping is paralleled, and in such a manner that it is again
argued *a minori ad majus*, " If we impart to you that which
is great, we may certainly lay claim to that which is of less value,
and especially we, through whom the faith has been planted
among you."  The expression σαρκικά has here at all events the
signification " that which is necessary to the support of life,"
although with it is connected the accessory idea of the subordinate.    The ἄλλοι naturally takes a retrospective glance at vers. 5,
6.—The 12th verse should properly commence with ἀλλά: it then
goes on to say for what reason Paul does not lay claim to this his
acknowledged right).

Vers. 12—14. To the observation, that he abstained from the
exercise of the right belonging to him, Paul adds that he wished
to give no offence to the Gospel of Christ.  This can, in agree-

ment with Acts xx. 33, sqq., only be understood that he did not
wish the Gospel to be regarded as a means of worldly gain.   Yet
unwilling for a moment to sanction the supposition that this was
wrongly done by the other teachers who made use of their lawful
claim on the community, he adduces in addition the parallel of
the priesthood of the Old Testament, as a proof that the acceptance of maintenance by the preachers of the Gospel was not unbecoming, and observes that ζῆν ἐκ τοῦ εὐαγγελίου was appointed
to his followers in the words of our Lord himself.   (Matt. x. 10;
Luke x. 8).   It is quite apparent that the apostle speaks on this
subject so as to bear general application in all times, so that
there is nothing opposed to the Gospel in the payment of the
clergy (by the end of the second century appointed salaries and
fees appear [*divisiones mensurnæ Cypr. epist.* 39, (34), *fratres
sportulantes Tert. apol.* c. 39, Bingham origg. vol. ii., p. 261,
sqq.]); indeed, the mention of ἱερά and of θυσιαστήριον might
be employed in the defence of confessors' fees, which in recent times appear almost generally offensive.   However, we must
certainly say, that if Paul was referring especially to the oblations at the communion, an offering which from circumstances
very early became customary, he was supposing the condition
of the church to be such in which the spirit of love united both
rulers and congregation.   But when this spirit is wanting,
and the gifts are bestowed reluctantly, then come they truly of
evil.   (In ver. 12 the τῆς ὑμῶν ἐξουσίας is to be understood,
of the right in you, and not the right which ye possess.   The
alteration in ἡμῶν, which Rückert himself approves, is quite
unnecessary.   Besides this, we may perceive in the πάντα στέ-
γομεν that the apostle, as might have been expected, found it
very difficult to carry out his principle, and indeed with his numerous employments [2 Cor. xi. 28] it is difficult to imagine how
he could reduce it to practice at all.   However, as he (at least in
Corinth) worked with his intimate friend Aquila, it is possible
that in the literal sense Paul did not earn his entire livelihood.—
Upon the ἐσθίειν ἐκ τοῦ ἱεροῦ, see Lev. vii. 7, 14; Deut. xviii. 1,
sqq.   The priests received a portion of certain sacrifices.   To eat
without the temple was styled, receiving subsistence from the
temple.—In verse 13, Lachmann has preferred παρεδρεύοντες to
προσεδρεύοντες: the signification of both forms is the same.

Hesychius explains it by σχολάζειν, to have leisure for something, *i. e.* to pursue some occupation, to labour at something.
In 3 Macc. iv. 15, the substantive προσεδρία is found.—Συμ-
μερίζεσθαι is also only to be found in this passage; it means "to
divide among themselves," so that the distributors themselves
obtain a portion.    Thus in the Old Testament the sacrifice was
divided between the altar and the priests; the priests also ate
the shew-bread after it had been offered before the Lord, and in
the ancient church, according to the same principle, a portion of
the oblations fell to the priesthood).

Vers. 15—17. Paul, however, by this representation, by no
means desires that for the future his subsistence should be provided for him; his own labour is to him a glory which he will not
suffer to be taken from him.    The announcement of the Gospel,
he says, is a duty imposed on him, but the reward thereof was
conditional on the manner of this, the ready self-sacrificing application to it.    In this lies the expression of a high moral feeling.    Man can do whatever he perceives it is the will of God he
should perform, but with inward reluctance and contrary heart,
he has his reward accordingly.    But he who in cheerful mind does
more than is needful, secures to himself an especial gain.    The
following passage, which describes what he hoped for as a reward,
proves how remote the apostle's idea was from justification by
works, or desire of gain.    It will therefore be easily understood
that the "doing more" than was necessary cannot be construed
that man is capable of *opera supererogatoria*.    In the command
to love God above all things is of course comprehended the injunction to do all that we acknowledge to be God's will ἑκών, not
ἄκων.    Yet a command may be perfectly or partially fulfilled according to human acceptation of it, and it therefore follows that
an imperfect fulfilment in the sight of God is equivalent to an
omission altogether.    In reading this passage, an impression
of exaggeration always remains.    The καλὸν γάρ μοι μᾶλλον
ἀποθανεῖν seems to be hyperbolical, for were this glorying in not
being chargeable so significant, Paul should never have accepted
the slightest assistance, which, according to Phil. iv. 15, 16, he
appears to have done; and then the other apostles might justly
have followed the same course, for there is no foundation for
believing that Paul alone had such a dispensation.    To this

may be added, that true humility requires what is offered in love to be accepted; the reproof in this place seems directed against self-justifying presumption. Something similar is found in the history of Abraham, Gen. xiv. 22, 23. But all such doubts and suppositions vanish if we consider that the καύχημά μου, which Paul so highly exalts, is not a glorying before men, but in the sight of God: these words therefore only express the apostle's sincere love to God, he would rather die than in the slightest degree offend his eye. (In ver. 15, οὕτω γένηται is an indication of support from the community. In the sentence ἢ τὸ καύχημά μου ἵνα τις κενώσῃ is somewhat in the nature of an anacoluthon. First it is probable an infinitive should follow, but in the earnestness of discourse Paul continues with ἵνα, in which may be found the threat, I will not suffer that, &c. Ἵνα has evidently here, as in the following verse, a feebler meaning. The reading received by Lachmann, and sanctioned by Billroth, καλὸν γάρ μοι μᾶλλον ἀποθανεῖν, ἢ τὸ καύχημά μου· οὐδεὶς κενώσει, by no means removes the difficulty, for something must necessarily be supplied to καύχημά μου, as it were "to let myself be defamed." Further, it has only B and D in its favour, and the original reading in D was departed from. Seeing then that other Codd. differ again in these words, this reading must decidedly yield to that in general acceptation.—Ver. 16 refers to Christ's commission [see Acts xxii. 21, xxvi. 16] in the ἀνάγκη, signifying likewise a moral necessity.—Ver. 17 resumes the subject from the γὰρ in ver. 15, so that ver. 16 takes the nature of a parenthesis.—Upon the meaning of μισθὸν ἔχω, see further on ver. 23, and on οἰκονομία what is written on iv. 1. The same is found in Col. i. 25. In other respects οἰκονομία signified the institution of salvation, Ephes. i. 10, iii. 2, 9.—Upon the well-known construction of the passive with the accusative consult Winer's Gram. p. 205).

Vers. 18—23. Rich as Paul's epistles are in passages expressing the purest love, there is scarcely one in which the apostle's sincerity of intention shines so pre-eminently as in this one. In perfect *amour disinteressé* he claims for reward the permission only to live in the hardest self-denial as a servant. He adapts himself in self-forgetting love to the peculiarities of each, in order to win them to their salvation. This incomparable passage possesses the beneficial properties of Rom. ix. 3 without the hyper-

bolic form in which the latter is expressed. It is easy to understand how this proceeding of the apostle's, to be a Jew to the
Jew, &c., would be very difficult of application in lesser matters.
Its exercise required in fact entire sincerity of purpose, otherwise it would be easy to exchange simply Adiaphora for important objects, and to be betrayed into a false indulgence. It is
of course unnecessary to explain that the compliance which the
apostle here so earnestly recommends has no reference to positive
errors, but only concerns Adiaphora. According to the same
principle of freedom we see the Redeemer himself acting. In
the Ἰουδαίοις ὡς Ἰουδαῖος, ἵνα Ἰουδαίους κερδήσω, exists no contradiction to the convention which Gal. ii. 9 treats of; for this
does not affirm that Paul would convert no Jew, the other
apostles no Gentile, but that they desired to settle the theatre of
their labours among Gentiles or Jews; and even this was subsequently modified, since Peter visited Rome, and John, Ephesus.
(On ver. 18 consult Winer's Gram. p. 265, concerning the use
of the future with ἵνα.—Ἀδάπανος, without reward, with reference to Christ's command, Matt. x. 8. In the New Testament
it does not again occur. According to the before-mentioned
deduction of the apostle, the εἰς τὸ μὴ καταχρήσασθαι signifies
only that it would be an error in him, because the Spirit had revealed this knowledge to him, but not in all preachers.—In ver. 19
ἐκ πάντων must be considered masculine, independent of any one,
answerable only to Christ. The article before πλείονας points to
those called to salvation, appointed him of God. Rückert erroneously takes it as synonymous with πλεῖστοι. In ver. 20—23
the distinction between the four classes there enumerated is not
easy. It would be best to regard the Jews and the ἄνομοι, i. e.
Gentiles, as the chief heads of opposition, and the οἱ ὑπὸ νόμον
as a modification of the Gentile. It cannot be intended to say
of the ἄνομος that he acknowledged no other law, such a one
would have been designated ἀσεβής, but merely that the
Mosaic ceremonial was unknown to him. But in order to avoid
any misunderstanding of this expression, Paul adds μὴ ὢν
ἄνομος Θεῷ, ἀλλ' ἔννομος Χριστῷ [where Lachmann has substituted the genitive for the dative, which appears preferable to me,
because here ἄνομος and ἔννομος are used substantively]; to be
loosed from the law of the Old Testament, is to be bound by the law

of Christ.    Now if, according to the principle laid down by the ἀσθενεῖς, Gentiles are indicated who manifested a certain degree of
strictness in their lives, as in Rom. xiv. 1, sqq., such Christians are
described among the Gentiles; the οἱ ὑπὸ νόμον must be the same,
who, without being actually Ἰουδαῖοι, have nevertheless taken
upon themselves the yoke of the law, are consequently proselytes.
Between proselytes of the gate and those of right no distinction is here made.    But Billroth thinks Jewish Christians cannot
here be meant, they having first to be gained over, and he considers also that κερδήσω might signify the passing from Judaizing
Christianity to that preached by Paul; but in opposition to this
is the analogy in the three other passages and the σώσω in ver.
22.    Paul means to say that to those scarcely admitted into the
pale of Christianity, he yielded in matters of secondary importance,
but after their conversion he naturally sought to render them in
all things consistent with their profession; but of any connexion
with the principle of Judaism or heathenism not a word can be
inferred, as the epistle to the Galatians proves.—In ver. 22 the
article before πάντα is certainly genuine, and refers to what precedes, " all this have I been to all;" and πάντας is evidently an
alteration of the genuine πάντως τινάς, i. e. out of every category,
to save some, which the power of Christ could certainly effect.
Paul does not contemplate gaining all, without exception, but only
those ordained to everlasting life.    In ver. 23 the most critical
authorities decidedly prefer πάντα to τοῦτο.—The signification
of συγκοινωνὸς αὐτοῦ is not alone participation in the extension
of the Gospel, as Billroth thinks, but in all the blessings declared.    Paul would participate in the publication, if he preached
ἄκων, but he includes within it an earnest self-denial in his
course of proceeding, in order not to be an ἀδόκιμος [ver. 27].
It is only by following this conception that the following gains
connexion with that which precedes.    This by no means comes
into collision with the doctrine of justification by faith, for all
that Paul here enumerates are likewise fruits of faith.    The
apostle simply contrasts a state of devotedness in self-denial, a
building with gold, silver, and precious stones, with the negligence of the indifferent; and only to the former is the promise
made of perfect participation in the Gospel, i. e. the kingdom of
God.    See on Matt. xxv. 1, sqq., 14, sqq.)

Vers. 24, 25. The apostle then recommends the exercise of this principle. Every believer according to his position ought to conduct himself with caution, not permitting to himself the practice of every privilege conceded to him, without regard to those entertaining different opinions, but denying himself. This endeavour is represented under the image of a race, from which in the Scriptures, and especially in the early ages of Christianity, so many comparisons were taken. It is, however, not only the act of running in itself which forms the point of comparison, but it is also the ἐγκράτεια, the numerous renunciations which the champions undergo, in order to prepare themselves to win the victory on the day of contest.* In a similar manner the Christian must crucify his flesh in the struggle for salvation, if he hopes to win the crown. Referring to the passage iii. 15, we cannot consider the βραβεῖον λαμβάνειν to imply salvation generally, for this, if no complete backsliding follow, is even possible where wood, straw, and stubble have been built up; but that it intends the highest degree of bliss, conditional upon faith and the step in sanctification. Therefore the τρέχοντες are the faithful without exception, but the εἶς who receives the βραβεῖον indicates the body of the true elect, not only those who can be saved, with the loss of their whole building, but also they who have externally and internally built with gold; to these therefore their works, because they are imperishable, shall follow them. Rev. xiv. 13. (Βραβεῖον or ἔπαθλον is the technical term for the crown decreed to the victor by the judges of the combat. The *etymol. magn.* explains the expression: Βραβεῖον λέγεται ὁ παρὰ βραβευτῶν διδόμενος στέφανος τῷ νικῶντι. It occurs again Phil. iii. 14.—Upon the ἄφθαρτος στέφανος, 1 Pet. i. 3, v. 4, may be consulted).

Vers. 26, 27. This salutary self-denial the apostle represents in conclusion, as the reason (although it may not be considered the only one) for the abandonment of his lawful claims in the particulars before mentioned. Besides the race, he now draws his simile from personal contest, in order more strongly to excite the idea of an adversary, which the first image did not present. He mentions his body as this adversary. Of a false *Askesis* not a

* See Œlian. Var. Hist. iii. 30, x. 2. Horat. de Arte Poët. v. 142, sq.

word is here said, that he himself blames (Phil. ii. 23), but he desires to restrain the liberty of the flesh, and to admonish the Corinthians in a right Christian mind, to crucify the flesh with its affections and lusts (Gal. v. 13—24). We may also unhesitatingly suppose, that Paul apprehended it would not be entirely beneficial for him to abandon altogether his handicraft, and live solely by his spiritual calling, though without in the least degree proposing to make his proceeding in this particular a rule for the conduct of others. This view shows an unusually refined conscientiousness and strictness on his part, coupled with the tenderest indulgence towards others. (Ver. 26, ἀδήλως = εἰς ἄδηλον, 2 Macc. vii. 34, uncertainly, without aim. Ἀέρα δέρειν is to be understood as a parallel to the ἀδήλως, "without real antagonists, in imaginary contest;" its other acceptation "to make a false stroke," presupposes also an opponent.—In ver. 27, the readings ὑποπιάζω and ὑποπιέζω yield to the more usual. The expression is borrowed from pugilists [πύκτης, pugil], "to strike under the eye," means to hit hard, to render incapable of continuing the combat. The δουλαγωγεῖν stands in opposition to the false carnal liberty into which so many Corinthians were in danger of falling.—The conjecture ἄλλους receives the κηρύσσειν, as the herald's proclamation of the conqueror; but then Paul must leave the image of the combatants, in order to pass to that of the herald. It is more probable that, now abandoning figurative speech altogether, he mentions his calling with the usual expressions, and declares that he will not teach the way of salvation to others, but himself remain behind as one deficient in divine wisdom, who therefore in the day of judgment will be found incapable of standing the highest proof).

Chap. x. 1, 2. A representation of the dangerous consequences which may arise from the misuse of Christian liberty, even in those upon whom grace has been bestowed, very appositely follows the above description of his proceedings in Adiaphoris. The apostle by no means contents himself with a dry exhortation on the subject, but strengthens his argument by the addition of eloquent and animated examples drawn from sacred history. (See ver. 6, sqq.) This passage, besides, is the first instance which occurs in Paul's Epistles of that peculiar biblical conception of the Old Testament which may be regarded as allied to allegorical interpretation, and which has been usually considered in the authors of the New Testament as invincible remains of their Judaism. We shall advert to this subject *in extenso* in the Introduction to the Epistle to the Hebrews,\* and with reference to earlier writers, content ourselves with the remark here, that the mode in which the writers of the New Testament employ this interpretation, viz., as foundation for the most important assertions, by no means sanctions the assumption that such interpretation was simply to be viewed as the customary one of that day, but we must rather ascribe objective truth to this description of exposition. It was ordained by God that not only the ceremonial prescribed in the Old Testament for the worship of the Almighty, but also the narratives relating to the people of God, were to form types of a higher spiritual condition, viz., the institution of Christianity, its doctrine, and history. Thus in this passage the history of Israel is typically received as referring to the sacramental rites of baptism and the Lord's Supper, which contain like a holy vessel all the blessings of the Gospel, and thus in this very passage lies indirectly a powerful argument for these two sacraments.—Ver. 1, 2 treat of the subject of baptism,† that is to say, ver. 2 contains the apostolic interpretation of the facts related in verse 1. The passage through the Red Sea, and the cloudy and fiery pillar, are the objects held up to our view. When it is said ὑπὸ τὴν νεφέλην ἦσαν, as in ver. 2, ἐβαπτίσαντο ἐν τῇ νεφέλῃ, reference is made to the relation in Exod. xiv. 19, 20, according to which the pillar of cloud concealed the Israelites from the view of the Egyptians, surrounding them as it were with a veil. In the ὑπὸ then lies the existence of a benevolent protecting power signified, and the typical signs in this case are generally supposed to point to baptism. But it is undeniable that the mention of the cloud and the sea in ver. 2 is by no means casual, but on the contrary it presents the most important allusions to baptism. Just as in John iii. 5, baptism is represented as the new birth out of water and spirit, so

---

\* Ein Wort über tiefern Schriftsinn. Koenigsberg 1842.—Die biblische Schrifttauslegung. Hamburg, 1825.

† Upon comparison of 1 Pet. iii. 21, it will be seen that the Flood is in a similar manner received as a type of baptism. Perishing human nature is the old man, buried in baptism (Rom. vi. 3, 4), Noah with his family the new born creature, the new birth. In the passage of the Red Sea, the Egyptians signify the death-doomed old man, while Israel typifies the heir of God born to a new and spiritual life.

here the cloud (symbol of the Divine Presence) is to be understood
as the type of the Spirit.   Not that the apostle intended by any
means to assert that the passage through the Red Sea under the
conduct of the pillar of cloud exercised a similar power to that
possessed by baptism, the former was simply an *image* of the
latter.   Yet this passage, as the actual means of release from
their former rulers, was introductory to the future relation of Israel to Moses, the leader appointed to them by God; hence the
additional phrase εἰς τὸν Μωϋσῆν, by which is signified the connexion of the people with the economy of the Old Testament, represented by Moses.   It appears unnecessary to add that all
attempts to render the type more perfect by means of trifling
suppositions, such as, that drops from the clouds fell on the Israelites, or that they were sprinkled by the sea, must be utterly
discarded.   (Verse 1 οὐ θέλω ὑμᾶς ἀγνοεῖν = οὐκ ἀγνοητέον
of Rom. i. 13, xi. 25; 1 Thess. iv. 13, is a form whereby the
following thought gains great expression.—In verse 2, ἐβαπτίσαντο is not to be considered strictly passive, but may be translated "They allowed themselves to be baptized."   Lachmann
and Rückert have preferred ἐβαπτίσθησαν from external authority; but the passive is without doubt only to be regarded as a
correction of the transcriber with a view to facility).

Vers. 3, 4.  In what follows relative to the Lord's Supper, the
interpretation of the manna (Exod. xvi. 15, which had already in
Ps. lxxviii. 24, 25; Wisd. xvi. 20, 21; and John vi., been understood typically), and of the water which miraculously sprung forth
from the rock (Exod. xvii. 6), is immediately supplied by the addition of πνευματικόν.   The same epithet is also applied to the
origin of the water, to the rock, and immediately afterwards
Christ is indicated as the Rock.   But we should greatly err if
our deduction from the expressions βρῶμα, πόμα πνευματικόν
was, that Paul had in view only a spiritual participation of the
Lord's Supper.   The πνευματικόν stands only in opposition to the
σαρκικόν, in the same degree that the temporal manna and
water *represented* something higher, namely Jesus' glorified
flesh and blood, and in so far also is the Rock, Christ, as it
in one respect prefigures Him.   As the water streamed from
the rock, so flow from Christ streams of living water (John vii.
38), He is the ζωή for the entire human race (John vi.)   A

difficulty is created only by the phrase ἀκολουθούσης. Rabbins dreamed strangely enough of the rock really following (see Wetstein on this passage); others considered that, because the Israelites took water with them in pitchers, or because the miracle was repeated (Num. xx. 10), the rock, *as it were*, moved with them; but these and similar conceptions need no refutation. Calvin's view on the subject is more deserving of attention, and in it Billroth agrees, that the rock here signifies the water which streamed from the rock; and inasmuch as water never failed the Israelites in the wilderness, it may be said the rock followed them. But in this construction it is overlooked, that it is certainly not said of the rock itself, but of the spiritual rock, *i. e.* of the rock in a spiritual sense, that it followed the Israelites, and it therefore appears to correspond better with the meaning of the apostle, to receive it as signifying that the divine presence of Christ, the Son of God, the bestower of all things, was ever present with them, his blessing likewise accompanying them.

Ver. 5. These gifts of mercy *all* received without exception, in this respect no individual Israelite had less than another; as one family they ate one food, and drank one drink. (Comp. vers. 3, 4, πάντες τὸ αὐτὸ βρῶμα, τὸ αὐτὸ πόμα, where the equality of all in the enjoyment of God's blessings is expressed, certainly with reference to the Lord's Supper, as described in verse 17). Nevertheless the greater number displeased God, he had delight but in few, and their punishment deprived them of their inheritance of the sight of the promised land; so likewise the untrue in the Israel of the New Testament will never see the kingdom of God. (In Heb. iii. 17 this occurrence [Num. xxvi. 64, 65] is treated exactly in this manner, only here the more expressive κατεστρώθησαν stands for the milder ἔπεσον which occurs there).

Ver. 6 These events in the Old Testament form the subject of an earnest exhortation from the apostle to his reader. He regards the ἐπιθυμία as the origin of all evil, adducing individual examples as he proceeds. As concerning the form ταῦτα δὲ τύποι ἡμῶν ἐγενήθησαν, it may literally be understood that the examples quoted from the Old Testament were only warnings intended for Christians, such instances of the manifest punishment attending sin being capable of beneficial self-application. But the explanation of the events recorded in vers. 1—4, argues a de-

cided parallel which the apostle wishes to draw, and this is confirmed in verse 11, in which the idea is repeated, and where the
sentence εἰς οὓς τὰ τέλη τῶν αἰώνων κατήντησεν only gains a reference to the context by bringing it in juxtaposition with the
preceding ταῦτα δὲ πάντα τύποι συνέβαινον ἐκείνοις. So that
the sense is: this all happened unto them as prefigurations intended by God, having reference to those coming afterwards.
Paul viewed the types as tangible prophecies, real images of subsequent occurrences, just as in the first germ or leaf formation of
a tree, the future blossom is represented and shadowed forth.
Besides this, in the εἰς τὸ μὴ εἶναι, κ. τ. λ. is comprehended
the idea that the intention of these prefigurations was also ethical;
history should present a living mirror for present times, ἐγράφη
πρὸς νουθεσίαν ἡμῶν, verse 11. Without this retrospective view
of the building, all type is rendered valueless. (See the remarks
on ix. 10).

Vers. 7—10. Paul adduces from the history of Israel four
forms of sin, as manifestations of the one sinful basis; the ἐπιθυμία: idolatry, fornication, temptation, and murmuring against
the Lord. It admits of no doubt that the Corinthian community approached in some degree these forms of sin, even
if none had so deeply fallen as to have proceeded actually
to the commission of one or other of these sins. From the
mention of idolatry again in verse 14, we may perceive how necessary Paul considered it to warn against relapse into sin. In a
city like Corinth, in which the worship of Venus so universally
prevailed, it was not to be supposed that a participation in the
sacrificial festivals of the temple itself could take place unpun-
ished. Undoubtedly also the grosser and more refined forms of
idolatry were to be distinguished, every turning away from the
Lord to the creature constituted idolatry. We must accordingly
say that the proceeding of the Corinthian Christians was a pure
πειράζειν τὸν Θεόν, a temptation to πορνεία. The temptation
to γογγύζειν is in short experienced by all who do not stand firm
in self-denial. To any special occasion of murmuring, such as the
unequal distribution of the gifts of grace (certainly not yet alluded
to), or the command to abstain from participation in meats offered
to idols, it is not my intention here to advert; it is better to
leave to the expression its general signification. (Verse 7 refers to

Exodus xxxii. 6. The words literally are more applicable to
fleshly enjoyment than to idolatry, but they are spoken of the
Israelites upon occasion of their worship of the golden calf, and
describe properly the moral consequences of this lapse.—Ver. 8
refers to Numb. xxv. 1, sqq., only in that passage, ver. 9, 24,000
is mentioned. The supposition that, in the smaller number mentioned by the apostle [see ver. 4], those put to death by the express command of Moses were not reckoned, appears unsupported.
Either Paul erred in the numbers, or the abbreviation εἰκοσιτρς
was falsely read by the transcriber.—Josephus (Arch. iv. 6) for
similar reasons only gives 14,000.—Ver. 9. The reading Θεόν is
certainly false; one might with some reason hesitate between
κύριον and Χριστόν, for κύριος may also indicate Christ, who, manifested as God, is also acknowledged in the Old Testament efficacious [1 Peter i. 11; Heb. xi. 26]. The apostle's words besides
refer to Num. xxi. 5, 6, wherein thus far an ἐκπειράζειν = נִסָּה
may be said to lie, as by their discontent they put God's long-suf-
fering to the proof. Such discontent, it is true, is not exactly
attributed to the Corinthians, but they nevertheless tempted
God in the same degree, when they, by their misuse of Christian
liberty, exposed themselves to unnecessary hazard.—Ver. 10 refers to Num. xiv. 2, sqq., 36, sqq. It is true that the punishment
is not there represented as immediately following the murmuring,
but that God forgives the people at the entreaty of Moses [see ver.
20]; immediately, however, the threat that all shall die in the
wilderness is added; and in ver. 36, sqq., attention is especially
drawn to the fulfilment of this threat. The ὀλοθρευτής [Exod.
xii. 23 = מַשְׁחִית) is accordingly only mentioned as the fulfiller
of the divine intentions; and it is by no means necessary to understand a bad angel thus employed, good angels likewise appear
as executors of the divine judgments).

Ver. 11. The connexion in this verse has already been adverted
to in ver. 6. (The reading τυπικῶς, preferred by Lachmann, is
nothing more than a correction of the more obscure τύποι), and
therefore it is only the sentence εἰς οὓς τὰ τέλη τῶν αἰώνων κατήντησεν which requires elucidation. In the principal passage concerning the *Parousia* (Matt. xxiv. 1, sqq., to the Comm. upon
which the reader is referred), and frequently in the apostolic
epistles it is described as near at hand, consequently the aposto-

lic was considered the latter age (Gal. iv. 3; 1 Pet. i. 20, iv. 7; 2 Pet. iii. 8; Heb. ix. 26; 1 John ii. 18). This mode of expression leads us to infer that the apostle was not acquainted with the precise period, and was not to know it (Acts i. 7), yet that he earnestly desired the coming of our Lord. But the time of the New with reference to the Old Testament, may be regarded as the latter time (inasmuch as it was borne though hidden within it), whose manifestation in the Parousia appears in some degree conditional upon human faith (2 Pet. iii. 9); for which reason, without any untruth, all the pious of all ages may represent the coming of the Lord as at hand. The history of the world is a continual coming of the Lord, though an invisible one, but in the end it shall be visible. (The expression $\tau \grave{a}$ $\tau \acute{e} \lambda \eta$ $\tau \hat{\omega} \nu$ $a \grave{\iota} \acute{\omega} \nu \omega \nu$ is only to be found here. $A \grave{\iota} \hat{\omega} \nu \epsilon \varsigma =$ עוֹלָמִים indicates as well the greater epoch in which all history is fulfilled, as that also in which created things themselves are developed. [Heb. i. 2, xi. 3]. The plural $\tau \acute{e} \lambda \eta$ refers to the merging of isolated epochs in and with one another, as well physically as in the history of mankind. The expression stands accordingly $= \pi \lambda \acute{\eta} - \rho \omega \mu a$ $\tau \hat{\omega} \nu$ $\kappa a \iota \rho \hat{\omega} \nu$, Ephes. i. 10.—$K a \tau a \nu \tau \acute{a} \omega$, to attain unto, to come, is frequently found in the language of Paul. See 1 Cor. xiv. 36; Ephes. iv. 13; Phil. iii. 11).

Vers. 12—15. The apostle then proceeds to say that the circumstances of that period demand great watchfulness and faith, for the $\tau \acute{e} \lambda \eta$ $\tau \hat{\omega} \nu$ $a \grave{\iota} \acute{\omega} \nu \omega \nu$ being the חֶבְלֵי הַמָּשִׁיחַ (see on vii. 26, 29) with it, in which the hardest temptations of believers are to be found. Hitherto no other than human temptations had overtaken them (i. e. such as, founded on and arising out of human circumstances, were from that cause easily overcome); God who had called them, was faithful, and in future also would only allow them to fall into such circumstances of difficulty as were proportioned to their strength; but so much the more was it their (the Corinthians') task not to prepare temptations for themselves, and by gradually weakening their spiritual strength, incapacitate themselves for resistance in the day of trial.—They must therefore show themselves to be prudent, and avoid every approach to idolatrous services which could only have sinful results, because issuing in evil (ver. 20) powers.—This is evidently the construction of this passage, which has been misunderstood by most

commentators, and even by Billroth.    That is to say, he remarks
that πειρασμός in ver. 13 cannot imply suffering and disappointment, that it rather contains an allusion to the temptation to
participate in idolatrous sacrifices, or (should this construction be
deemed too narrow) to all the sins inclusively named in ver.
6—10.  But temptations are certainly not sins! The apostle
admonishes all unconditionally to keep from sin, but from temptations none can secure himself, they occur to all without exception, and to be well armed with a view to their successful resistance is the only course to be taken.  To this shall the ὁ δοκῶν
ἑστάναι, βλεπέτω μὴ πέσῃ animate, and the observation in ver. 13
inspire courage.*  Accordingly it is impossible that the meaning
refers to the temptations to which the Corinthians exposed themselves, for these were even the ἐκπειράζειν τὸν κύριον which were
so expressly rebuked as sins, but rather to such temptations as
occurred to them without their own instrumentality.  Whatsoever temptations of the kind they have hitherto experienced,
says Paul, have been moderate, so that they have been able to
conquer; but should severer trials occur, God, who is faithful,
would not refuse his assistance; he nevertheless requires earnestness and watchfulness from believers.  Opposed to the πειρασμός ἀνθρώπινος there exists in the opinion of Paul a higher
and more dangerous (Gen. xxii. 1; Exod. xv. 25, xvi. 4, xx. 20;
Deut. xiii. 3), for which the Christian must reserve his weapons,
consequently not endanger them by entering into voluntary conflict.  (In ver. 12 the words ἑστάναι and πίπτειν, stantes, lapsi,
are borrowed from the language of combat.—Ver. 13, πιστός,
faithful in his promises; but the promise to defend believers in
their warfare is manifested in their calling.—Ποιήσει is to be
combined with τὴν ἔκβασιν; he permits the exigency to arrive,
and provides the help for it.—In ver. 15 the κρίνατε ὑμεῖς ὅ
φημι refers certainly to what precedes, but more especially to
what follows, for Paul now returns to the principal question under
consideration, viz., idolatrous repasts).

Ver. 16. The words which now follow concerning the Lord's
Supper (ver. 16, 17), and which are a continuation of vers. 3, 4,
*teach nothing upon the subject of this sacrament.*  The apostle's

---

* From this mode of expression in Scripture proceeded the names employed
later in the church, *stantes, lapsi.*

purpose is rather to obtain the admission of the questions introduced with οὐχί, represented as internally allowed by the faith of his readers; and the object of the passage is, after pointing to the analogy of the Christian communion and the Jewish sacrifice, to add, that even if idols have no existence, and an evil power were not substantially inherent in the meats offered in sacrifice to idols, nevertheless participation in such things was fellowship with the kingdom of darkness (ver. 20—22). These parallels are, however, hardly adapted to convey to us any important elucidation of the dogma of the holy communion, for neither in the sacrifices of the Jews, nor in those of the heathen, is it possible to recognise such a connexion as that existing in the Lord's Supper between the elements and Christ's body and blood. Paul's argument can only thus be understood: "As it is acknowledged that the receiving the holy communion is a means of fellowship with Christ, and that the Jewish sacrifice establishes a fellowship with the altar, and with him to whom the altar is dedicated, that is God, so likewise by means of their sacrifices do the heathen form a fellowship with devils." The passage before us contains nothing more as to the precise definition of the connexion between Christ's body and blood and the bread and wine. Only so far is clear, first, that the Lord's Supper is not represented here as a sacrifice, as Roman Catholic interpreters maintain, but only as a sacrificial repast, as is clearly shown by the parallel drawn of analogous usages among Jews and Gentiles; next, that the expressions κοινωνία τοῦ αἵματος and τοῦ σώματος τοῦ Χριστοῦ by no means sanction Zwinglius' view of an empty commemorative repast; but grounds for the Catholic as well as the Lutheran and Calvinistic doctrines might be found in these words, did none other appear for the Lutheran; at the most it may be said that the expression ἄρτος applied to the consecrated bread (ver. 17) is in no degree favourable to the theory of transubstantiation. Did no other fellowship with Christ exist in the communion than a spiritual one,* it would have been called κοινωνία τοῦ Χριστοῦ, not τοῦ αἵματος, τοῦ σώ-

---

* Of the κοινωνία τοῦ πνεύματος τοῦ Χριστοῦ such passages as 1 John i. 3 are to be understood. This must precede, in order that the more elevated degree of community with the glorified corporeality of Christ may follow; without baptism, *i. e.* without being born of the spirit, no communion!

μ α τ ο ς τοῦ Χριστοῦ. (See xi. 27). But as the ascended
Christ is naturally the subject, his glorified flesh and blood is
also spoken of; and this in the holy communion coming into a
certain relation with those admitted to its mysteries, consequently
effects a fellowship. This is evidently the fundamental idea in
our passage, which perfectly agrees with the declaration of our
Lord in John vi. (Billroth would receive κοινωνία as a partaking, the participation, but it is impossible that the cup can
signify the *action of partaking*. It is also not the *action*
of *communication*, but the means whereby the fellowship is
effected. Cup and bread stand, however, for the repast celebrated with cup and bread). In the contents of ver. 16 the
following sentence only demands consideration: τῆς εὐλογίας ὃ
εὐλογοῦμεν. Wine which we drink should stand over against
ἄρτον ὃν κλῶμεν. Ποτήριον stands truly *continens pro con-
tento* for the wine in the cup, but τῆς εὐλογίας ὃ εὐλογοῦμεν has
something striking; it seems not to correspond with the ὃν κλῶμεν.
But the κλᾷν is even "*with blessing to break and eat*,"* as it is
mentioned in Matt. xxvi. 26, and εὐλογεῖν is likewise "with
blessing to administer and drink," so that some degree of tautology appears to exist in the phrase τῆς εὐλογίας. The reading
εὐχαριστίας does not remove this, for there is no important difference between this expression and εὐλογία. (See xi. 24). But
it vanishes if we do not accept ποτήριον τῆς εὐλογίας in the passive sense, " cup, that is blessed," but the active, " cup, which
confers blessing, the cup of blessing." In these words the idea
is then expressed that in the church itself rests the positive
power of consecration by means of the Spirit of the Lord, and
that those receiving the consecrated elements are thereby advanced in inward life, and in fellowship with the Lord. The
officiating minister represents the active principle in the
church, the communicants the passive. For the εὐλογεῖν or
εὐχαριστεῖν indicates not only the praise of God which is offered
with the prayers in the Lord's Supper, but has a reference to

---

* It can require no further proof that the conception of the κλᾷν by which it
should stand metonymically, *antecedens pro consequenti*, and received as synonymous with to eat, cannot be maintained. The passage xi. 24 shows very plainly
that the breaking had a symbolic reference. It is therefore perfectly in order to
retain this symbol when celebrating this holy rite.

bread and wine. *Εὐλογεῖν ποτήριον, ἄρτον describes the effect of prayer, whereby the elements cease to be common bread and common wine,* the attainment of the verbum ad elementum, ut fiat sacramentum.* Yet this effect may not be regarded as transforming the substance, nor as remaining identified with the elements, as the [Roman] Catholic church erroneously supposes, but as present at the moment of receiving.

Ver. 17. The notion of the κοινωνία is yet further explained, that the fellowship with Christ produces likewise fellowship among all those celebrating the sacred feast. All who constitute the church (οἱ πάντες) eat of one and the same bread (administered with and through the body and blood of Christ), so the common participation of the several elements (οἱ πολλοί) becomes a higher unity, a σῶμα Χριστοῦ in a comprehensive sense, and thus the church itself may be called Christ (xii. 12). This thought is evidently based upon the fundamental idea that the nature of the consecrated elements is communicated to the recipients. These elements are here changed into the body and blood of Christ, so that the saying (Ephes. v. 30), we are flesh of his flesh and bone of his bone, is literally fulfilled. The holy communion imparts to the body the ἀφθαρσία of Christ's body, that he may be able to raise him up at the last day. (See my observations in the Comm. on John vi. 39, 54, 58). The εὐχαριστία in the sacrament is therefore the antithesis to the curse that was pronounced upon the κτίσις after the fall. But it is peculiar that in this place the unity of the faithful is represented not only as σῶμα, but as ἄρτος also; as the individual grains yield their separate existence in order to form bread, and are absorbed in the unity of the φύραμα, so likewise the sinful laxity of the individual shall vanish before the unity of the Spirit replenishing the church. In the same manner as Christ calls himself the bread that came down from heaven (John vi. 35), so is the church collectively the representation of Christ, the bread of life for the whole world. (Re-

* Compare thereon the words of Justinus, M. Opp. 93 sq., edit. Paris, printed in my Mon. Hist. Eccl., P. ii., p. 167, sqq.: εὐχαριστήσαντος δὲ τοῦ προεστῶτος καὶ ἐπευφημήσαντος πάντος τοῦ λαοῦ, οἱ καλούμενοι παρ' ἡμῖν διάκονοι διδόασιν ἑκάστῳ τῶν παρόντων μεταλαβεῖν ἀπὸ τοῦ εὐχαριστηθέντος ἄρτου καὶ οἴνου καὶ ὕδατος, καὶ τοῖς οὐ παροῦσιν ἀποφέρουσι· καὶ ἡ τροφὴ αὕτη καλεῖται παρ' ἡμῖν εὐχαριστία.—Οὐ γὰρ ὡς κοινὸν ἄρτον, οὐδὲ κοινὸν πόμα ταῦτα λαμβάνομεν.

garding the grammatical connexion of verse 17 with verse 16, ὅτι cannot, as Rückert supposes, signify "because," this is decidedly negatived by the γὰρ following. But it is rather to be taken in the meaning of "for," serving in connexion with the following γὰρ, which again furnishes the argument for the first portion of the verse, for the basis of verse 16).

Ver. 18. The following parallel of the Jewish sacrificial festivals (see Lev. viii. 31; Deut. xii. 18, xvi. 11) removes any doubt of the apostle's regarding the holy sacrament as a sacrificial banquet, *i. e.*, he considers it not only a commemoration of the sacrifice of Christ on the cross, but also as a smybolic representation of the same (though not an actual repetition, see Heb. x. 14), and an appropriation of its blessings. But as has been already observed, this parallel must not be carried so far, that we suppose the apostle to have ascribed a higher power to the flesh of the earlier sacrifice; the *tertium comparationis* is only the κοινωνία, which in the Old Testament stood in relation to the altar. The θυσιαστήριον, however, is used as a synecdoche, implying the entire institution of the Old Testament, and this by analogy for the God operating in it;* but in the same degree as the Old Testament dispensation is an inferior form of revelation to that of the New Testament, the κοινωνία also in the former is more outward. (Concerning Ἰσραὴλ κατὰ σάρκα, antithesis to Ἰσραὴλ κατὰ πνεῦμα, see Rom. ii. 28, 29; Gal. vi. 16).

Ver. 19, 20. In order in the meantime to remove the apprehensions of his readers (who saw the tendency of the argument), that the apostle participated in the opinions of many materialistic Jews, respecting the reality of idols, and the evil power pervading the flesh of their sacrifices, Paul declares that these were by no means his sentiments, there were no such idols, and the idolatrous sacrifices were attended by no power. These words clearly explain the passage, viii. 4, sqq., as we then observed. The imaginary creations of gods had no existence, it is true, but heathenism was nevertheless based upon an agency, against the influence of which it behoved all to guard. From thence the warning against taking part in the festivals held in the temple (viii. 10), although the use of such meats in private circles (ver. 25, sqq.)

---

* Bengel strikingly and justly remarks on this passage: *Is cui offertur, ea quæ offeruntur, altare, super quo offeruntur, communionem habent.*

was allowed by the apostle in wise moderation, to discountenance
the strict Jewish spirit.  Concerning the *nature* of the power
governing the heathen world, Paul here gives a closer definition;
he says the sacrifices of the Gentiles are offered to *dæmons*, and
they thereby effected a fellowship with them.  They attempt to
vindicate the meaning of the expression δαιμονία to signify "false
imaginary gods," has been already justly rejected by Billroth.
The expression is continually employed in the New Testament in
the sense of "evil spirits," πνεύματα ἀκάθαρτα, and to accept it
in the former meaning would be to destroy the significance of
the whole argument.  As the heathen gods were always considered in the light of dæmons in the ancient church, a clear historical conception of the passage can ascribe no other idea than this
to Paul; and acknowledging the truth of the biblical doctrine relative to the kingdom of darkness, no doubt of their continual
nothingness can exist.  By means of sin man becomes a prey to
the evil powers, and their sway is unopposed in heathenism.  The
worship of idols is one form in which sinful human nature exhibits itself, the potency of evil consequently cannot be excluded
therefrom, nay, it must therein proclaim itself in an especial
manner, as it diverts the noblest aspirations of man into a wrong
direction, and invests crime itself with apparent sanctity.  It
may not be imagined, as some Jews, and the unlearned among
the Christians were prone to do, that to every god a corresponding
dæmon was appointed,—those gods were only creations of fancy.
It was the power of darkness entirely, and in its fullest extent,
and the natural faculties influenced by it (especially those which
were sexual), which constituted the governing principle of heathenism and its worship.  It would be difficult for any one to be
present at the worship of Venus, so much in vogue in Corinth
especially, without feeling the dominion of sin in his heart; his
presence at such rites is therefore called tempting the Lord.  (In
ver. 20 the words δαιμονίοις θύει καὶ οὐ Θεῷ are found, a quotation
from Deut. xxxii. 17, according to the LXX.—In Ps. xcvi. 5, following the same authority, and Baruch iv. 7, the same idea occurs.
—For the passages in the Fathers referring to this subject,* consult Usteri's Paulin. Lehrbegr. p. 421, sqq.)

* Justin Mar. employs dæmons in conveying a representation of the supper in the
worship of Mithras: ὅπερ καὶ ἐν τοῖς τοῦ Μίθρα μυστηρίοις παρέδωκαν γίνεσθαι

Vers. 21, 22. Such an intermixture of entirely dissimilar elements the apostle justly declares to be perfectly inadmissible, upon which more will be said, 2 Cor. vi. 14, sqq. No man can serve two masters, if he adheres truly to one, he must despise the other! It is not necessary to understand by the expressions ποτήριον δαιμονίων, τράπεζα δαιμονίων that Paul had some particular heathen festival in mind, the service of Mithras for example, (Kreuzer's Symb. i. 728, sqq., iii. 364, sqq.), in which not only the sacrifice was eaten, but also a cup passed around; for it being customary to drink on all such occasions, ποτήριον and τράπεζα, which by a figure stand here for βρῶμα, together signify the repast. To sharpen the admonition, Paul alludes briefly to the jealousy of the Lord, and his power to punish the disobedient. (In ver. 22, the παραζηλόω is probably chosen from Deut. xxxii. 21. It indicates the jealousy of Jehovah on account of the deviation of his people from hearty love towards him. It corresponds to the Hebrew הִקְנִיא, and is rendered παροξύνειν, παροργίζειν, by the LXX.—Regarding the use of the indicative in the direct question, see Winer's Gr. p. 260. The παραζηλοῦμεν may be also understood as not signifying what shall happen, but what has taken place, " or is it the meaning by our way of proceeding to provoke the Lord?")

Vers. 23, 24. Paul then again proceeds to assert the principle which he had already laid down in vi. 12, in order to apply it not only in Adiaphoris to individual liberty, but with reference to the brethren. It might appear exaggeration for the apostle to say μηδεὶς τὸ ἑαυτοῦ ζητείτω, ἀλλὰ τὸ τοῦ ἑτέρου (ἕκαστος is only added to facilitate the sense), but it should be ἀλλὰ καὶ τὸ τοῦ ἑτέρου. But this principle ought certainly to be taken in its most extensive signification, and we must say, were it generally carried out, every one would be better cared for, than if each thought only of himself. But so long as this is not the case, the exercise of a pure love in earthly things can only bring disappointment, but in heavenly he will in the κόσμος οὗτος gain.

Vers. 25, 26. It was not unusual for portions of the beasts offered in sacrifice to be exposed for public sale in the markets, so that it was possible to purchase such meat. The Judaizing

μιμησάμενοι οἱ πονη ροὶ δαίμονες, ὅτι γὰρ ἄρτος καὶ ποτήριον ὕδατος τίθεται ἐν ταῖς τοῦ μυσομένου τελεταῖς μετ᾽ ἐπιλόγων τινῶν, ἢ ἐπίστασθε ἢ μαθεῖν δύνασθε.

Christians took offence at this, but Paul counselled them to make no difference, and for conscience sake not to inquire. Here follows a quotation from Ps. xxiv. 1, acknowledging the dependence of all created things on Jehovah, but it is not his intention to deny the disturbances among the κτίσις, and to subvert the biblical injunctions regarding food; we must rather take it for granted, both here and in the parallel passage 1 Tim. iv. 4, that the apostle conceived all created things sanctified in Christ, as Peter was given in a vision (Acts x. 11, sqq.) to understand. This is further explained in my Comm. upon the Epist. Rom. p. 426.* (Ver. 25, μάκελλον belongs to the Latin words adopted by the later Greeks; the particular Greek expression is κρεωπώλιον.—Ἀνακρίνειν is here =ἐξετάζειν, ἀναπυνθάνεσθαι, as Phavorin correctly asserts; and the διὰ τὴν συνείδησιν, like that of ver. 27, refers to the individual conscience of him who buys or is invited.—Lachmann reasonably omits the comma before and after μηδὲν ἀνακρίνοντες, likewise in ver. 27 it belongs with διὰ τὴν συνιίδησιν to ἐσθίτε).

Vers. 27, 28. Then follows the counsel, that if believers are invited as guests by the heathen, only to refrain from eating, if a distinct declaration is made of the nature of the food served up. Neander and Billroth have both decided that the words ἐὰν δέ τις ὑμῖν εἴπῃ apply not to the host, but some one among the guests, whose scruples were aroused, and this supposition alone gives significance to the explanation of διὰ τὴν συνείδησιν. Such a remark could never have been made by a heathen, either in mockery or designedly, to prove the Christian, therefore this view is not practicable. But these words require some addition, having been already twice applied in speaking of the conscience of the claimant for liberty. The μηνύσας must accordingly be distinguished from the interrogator, and might be presumed to represent the host, who alone would know for certainty, if the meat placed before them had formed a portion of a sacrifice or not. But to this the ἐκεῖνος presents a difficulty; and as besides δια is not repeated before συνείδησιν, it seems better to refer them both to the same person, for μηνύω implies not so much the positive information, as the opportunity of becoming acquainted that it was meat that had been sacrificed. The words εἰ θέλετε πορεύεσ-

---

* See pp. 387, 8, of the translation, F. T. Lib.

θαι (ver. 27) indicate, as Pott correctly observes, that the apostle considered it advisable to accept such invitations from heathen acquaintance with the greatest caution, for heathen customs were in use at all their festivals, and the Christian who took part in them ran the risk of denying his faith by his practice. Nevertheless the circumstances did not warrant a formal prohibition. (Lachmann has preferred the reading ἱερόθυτον in ver. 28, and indeed it is more easy to account for the change of this expression into the general εἰδωλόθυτον, than on the other hand the admitted form into the more unusual one. But the additional τοῦ γὰρ κυρίου κ. τ. λ. here is decidedly not genuine, and only borrowed from ver. 26, from the preceding word συνείδησιν being the same).

Ver. 29—31. In an interrogating form, and likewise in the first person, the current idea is repeated, in order more vividly to present it to the mind. "For why should I allow my liberty to be judged of another man's conscience," meaning, "why should I, by my exercise of freedom, afford a pretence to others for judging me?" "If I (the meat) partake with thanks to God (consequently in a right mind), why am I evil spoken of, for partaking of meat received with thanksgiving? i. e. wherefore shall I give occasion (in appearance) for evil to be spoken of me. Is it then not better that I should have the necessary regard to the weak and avoid all offence?" Let all be done therefore to the glory of God. Govern yourselves entirely according to circumstances. Be not only heathen to the heathen (to which inclination urges you), but be not ashamed to be Jewish to the Jew. (See ix. 20, sqq.) Pott has attributed another and apparently easier construction to these words, viz., as an objection proceeding from one of the liberal party: "What have I to do with another's conscience? and why should I allow my liberty to be judged of them? If I have eaten with thanks, why should I be evil spoken of?" But this exposition of the verse, although the words are by no means inconsistent with it, is opposed by the subject of the foregoing one, according to which even the conscience of the stranger is to be respected, and also by ver. 31. It is only by adopting the above explanation that the εἴτε οὖν κ. τ. λ. becomes connected. In reference to the πάντα εἰς δόξαν Θεοῦ ποιεῖτε, we cannot truly weaken the force of the πάντα, as if it signified only something. In the

Christian life things great and small should stand in harmonious agreement! However, the εἰς δόξαν Θεοῦ is not to be thought to imply attention to every trifle. The inward living principle must exhibit itself in things of every degree as the generator of a pure life displaying itself in love towards all, manifesting the δόξα Θεοῦ thereby in the most glorious manner. (In ver. 29, ἐλευθερίας may not, as Heidenreich supposes, be supplied to the χάριτι μετέχω, but the verb stands rather for "to taste meat," as the ὑπὲρ οὗ ἐγὼ εὐχαριστῶ which follows plainly proves. The expression χάρις is in this passage the *gratiarum actio* in eating.)

Ver. 32.—Chap. xi. 1. Then follows the admonition to accommodate themselves in Adiaphora charitably, not to one party alone, but to all without exception (according to the enumeration ix. 20, sqq.), as he, the apostle, was accustomed to do in the whole sphere of his labours. Nevertheless Paul will not be the pattern by which they (the Corinthians) were to regulate their conduct, and therefore he adds: I am a follower of Christ. I have not devised my course of proceeding, but have learned it from the holy prototype of mankind! (The ἀπρόσκοπος of ver. 32 has appeared in Acts xxiv. 16; it also occurs in Phil. i. 10. Hesychius and Suidas explain it by ἀσκανδάλιστος. But here it is employed actively the same as ὁ προσκοπὴν μὴ διδούς.—The mention of Jews and Gentiles with the church of God, which makes a difficulty with Billroth, is entirely unimpeachable if we glance at ix. 20, sqq., where Jews and Gentiles are also mentioned. Consideration is to be had for them, in order if possible to win them to the truth, as is expressly declared in ver. 33. [See on Rom. xv. 1].—The rule of their conduct is to be only the benefit of others and not their own advantage. The Christian should rather be prepared to purchase the former even at the expense of personal self-denial and discomfort. The division of the chapters is evidently not well arranged in this place. Ver. 1 of the 11th chapter belongs essentially to the preceding deduction. Paul was unwilling to afford his adversaries the most remote occasion to accuse him of pride, and he therefore, while holding forth his own example, represents it as a following after the great example which was offered to the whole human race).

# III.

## PART THIRD.

(xi. 2—xiv. 40).

### § 9. THE SUITABLE APPAREL.

———————

As we have already remarked in reviewing the contents of these epistles in the Introduction, the *second Part* treated chiefly of private circumstances, and now in the *third* the public assemblies, and occurences in connexion with them, are brought under consideration. In entering upon the subject the apostle commences with externals, viz., the apparel and appearance suitable to believers, and it seems probable that this was because he was able to award praise in this particular, for in this respect the better spirit appears to have influenced the Corinthian Church, and led them to observe the strict apostolic injunction (ver. 2). The argument which follows these is more by way of enforcing a due observation of the customs enjoined, and reproving those who had attempted innovation (ver. 16), but had not succeeded in carrying it out. The θέλω δὲ ὑμᾶς εἰδέναι is not to be regarded as antithesis, but a corroboration of the foregoing. This is decidedly proved by the τοῦτο δὲ οὐκ ἐπαινῶ of verses 17 and 22, but the apostle prefaces with this observation, because it connects itself perfectly with the subject of chap. viii.—x., which was likewise an abuse of liberty, prejudicial to the morality of the members of the church. This paragraph also shows, that the παραδόσεις referred not only to such important doctrines as the holy communion (see ver. 23), but likewise to such lesser injunctions as are here brought under consideration. The 2 Thess. ii. 15 proves that Paul included therein his verbal and *written* directions

concerning Christian doctrine and living.* From the nature of
the thing, it was natural to suppose that an early attempt would
be made to collect such precepts, and as the rapid growth of the
church elicited new circumstances rendering new directions imperative, these collections increase and come down to us in this
form, without our being always able to discriminate between what
is really apostolic and the later additions. (The πάντα might
create a difficulty, for vers. 17, 22, certainly show that Paul by
no means commends all, and that the Corinthians had not remembered everything. It is best, therefore, to receive it = πάντως,
which is quite reconcilable, as it stands before in the same manner
as πάντως usually does. See Luke iv. 23; Acts xviii. 21, xxi.
22, xxviii. 4).

Ver. 3. The apostle then leaves the subject of the connexion
of husband and wife, and enters upon that referring to the veiling
of women, which was then agitated in Corinth. The preachers
of unlimited liberty might have attempted to remove this ancient
custom (Gen. xx. 16), but the firm principle of the followers of
Peter maintained it, which Paul justified. This custom possessed once a symbolical signification, the veil expressed the
authority of the husband over her, and the idea of the seclusion
and reserve becoming the woman; it had likewise a moral aim,
for all unlawful excitement was avoided in the assemblies, and
the attention was withdrawn from the women. The apostle's
argument is not applicable to married women alone, but includes
the whole female sex as such: in a profound allegory he views
the women's long hair as a veil lent to her by nature herself
(verse 15). According to this he must intend that the young
women also should come to the assembly veiled. But under
all circumstances we must remember that, according to the remarks on chapter vii., we are not to regard this in the light
of a command, but as good counsel justified by the period,
and it would be unnecessarily precise to require that the representations here laid down by the apostle should be liter-

* Neander in his Church History (Kirchengeschichte), vol. i. part iii. p. 1105,
sqq., and Krabbe upon the Apos. Constit. p. 50, appear unwilling to admit any
written apostolic regulations. The pastoral letters are, however, evidently nothing
more than small collections of apostolic rules; that besides these many of their
directions were written down during the life-time of the apostle, is certainly not
improbable; our collection of so called apostolic institutions are without doubt of
a much later origin.

ally followed in all ages.   But although the German custom
concedes a freer position to the female sex than the eastern
Greek allowed,* the apostle's fundamental idea in this paragraph
preserves a significance for all times.   The Holy Scriptures
recognise nothing of the emancipation of women, and the noblest
adornment of the woman must ever remain a modest decency,
the expression of which must be a becoming dress.—That the opposite custom should ever have found currency in Corinth, viz.,
the *veiling of the men*, appears to me very unlikely.   The passages which appear rather to favour the supposition (ver. 4, 7),
are there only by way of antithesis; had such a custom really
required to be formally attacked, it would have been brought
under more signal notice.   The custom of the heathen to cover
themselves at sacrifices, and in the presence of the aruspices,† may
indeed be appealed to, but it is thoroughly improbable that the
Christians should have transplanted anything of heathen rites
into ecclesiastical usage.   There is likewise not a trace of this
to be found elsewhere, while the subject of the veiling of women
came under consideration at a later period, as the work of Tertullian *de virginibus velandis* proves.   It is more reasonable to
suppose that it was the well-known custom of the synagogue which
was implied, the covering the head with a cloth during the hours
of prayer.   But as we said before, there is no sufficient foundation for supposing that such a custom ever existed among men.
—The argument in ver. 3 has in addition something peculiar.   The
comparison between the relation of Christ to the church is based
upon matrimony (Eph. v. 20, sqq.)   But in spiritual marriage,
Christ is not alone the head of the man, but of the woman also,
without regard to distinction of sex.   Yet is it here said, παντὸς
ἀνδρὸς ἡ κεφαλὴ ὁ Χριστός.   However, that cannot be urged, for
in all such parallels discrepancies must exist.   But wherefore
the addition κεφαλὴ δὲ Χριστοῦ ὁ Θεός?   To the general context it bears no reference; it only completes the accessory idea

* The unbridled customs of the age prove how necessary such severe regulations
were in the times we are speaking of.   The Fathers of the Church, *e. g.* Clemens
Alex., Cyprian, &c., were obliged to express their displeasure at certain Christian
women, who bathed with men without the decency of dress.   (See Krabbe on the
Apost. Constit. Hamburg, 1829, p. 125, sqq.)

† Servius in Virg. Aen. iii. 407, writes: *Sciendum sacrificantes diis omnibus
capita relare consuetos ob hoc, ne se inter religionem aliquid vagis offerret obtutibus.*

of the gradual advancement, as in iii. 22. The remarks already made on this passage, upon the question how far in such passages a subordination of Christ to the Father may be traced, are likewise valid here. (In the idea κεφαλή, according to the context, dominion is especially expressed. As in the human organization, the exercise of dominion over all the members proceeds from the head; so in the family, from the men; in the church, from Christ; in the universe, from God).

Vers. 4, 5. The first verse is only *per contrarium* to elucidate the meaning of the second, concerning which it really treats. In a spiritual fashion, the apostle views the bearing of men and women as of importance to their being. The man represents the governing principle in mankind, the woman the ministering; in the former, therefore, the free open appearance was becoming; to the latter, the reserved, symbolically expressed by the veil. The expressions προσεύχεσθαι and προφητεύειν, refer, however, as xiv. 13, shows, to the Charismata of tongues and prophecy. We learn from this passage that this was also conferred upon women, though at a later period the *public exercise* of these gifts (see xiv. 34, and 1 Tim. ii. 12) was entirely prohibited by the apostle. That this prohibition is not alluded to here is by no means important. Calvin has justly replied *apostolus unum improbando alterum non probat;* he desired here first to continue the discussion already commenced. (In ver. 4 τί is to be supplied to κατὰ κεφαλῆς ἔχων, some wearing and covering for the head. —Billroth with propriety recognises a double meaning in the twofold καταισχύνει τὴν κεφαλήν. It signifies first, it dishonoureth his head, *i. e.*, the part of the body which declares dishonour, and next of the man, that he dishonoureth Christ. Of the woman, that she dishonours her husband, by omitting the sign of her subjection to him.—Shaving the woman's head was a punishment for adulteresses, the expression also bears application to want of discipline and shamelessness).

Vers. 6—9. The necessity for adherence to strict morality is yet further enforced by the apostle from the relation of man to woman, shown in the Mosaic account of the creation. The man is God's εἰκὼν καὶ δόξα, the woman only man's δόξα. This refers back to Gen. i. 27, where man is styled צֶלֶם and דְּמוּת of God. But Calvin has justly reminded us that this argument, and like-

wise that arising out of the κεφαλή in verse 3, must be adopted
with the necessary restriction, and that the conclusion arrived at
by numerous schismatics is perfectly unsupported as to the man
alone being the image of God, and not the woman. In the passage of Genesis alluded to (i. 27) dominion is declared to be the
chief characteristic of the divine image; this was manifested more
in the man than in the woman, and only for that reason, and so
far Paul ascribes to him the image, and not to the woman. This
latter has a dependent position assigned to her, and all her faculties should be applied to the one purpose of serving the man,
and elevating him in his higher and more important condition.
This is signified by the expression δόξα ἀνδρός, wherewith the
apostle drops the parallel with the εἰκών. In order to place the
subjection of the woman to man more clearly in view, the
apostle borrows an argument from the 2d chapter of Genesis. The
fact that the woman was formed out of the rib of the man (ἐξ
ἀνδρός) and was destined to be his helper (διὰ τὸν ἄνδρα ἐκ-
τίσθη), is employed by Paul for this purpose. This sort of argument would appear singular in these days, but evidently only because we have not accustomed ourselves to read the Holy Scriptures, especially the Old Testament, so literally. Paul, however,
proceeds upon the unrestricted divinity of the Old Testament, and
the more this is generally recognised the more shall we be enabled
to perceive the admissibility of such proofs. (In ver. 6, ξυρᾶσθαι
is to be understood as the increased κείρασθαι).

Ver. 10. This passage has received more trouble and labour
than its meaning appears to deserve. Ἐξουσία is evidently
nothing more than an indication of the covering for the female head, and therefore of the veil, which is thus the symbol of the man's power over the woman.* The conjectures
ἐξουβίαν, ἐξιοῦσα are quite unnecessary and untenable.† The

---

* Hagenbach (Stud. 1828, pt. 2, p. 401, sqq.) would derive ἐξουσία from ἐξεῖναι
in the sense of " descent, extraction." But Lücke (pt. 3, p. 568, sqq.) has lexico-
logically and exegetically proved this unsound. Lücke himself admits a *brachylogy*
in the passage, viz., the omission of the definite genitive relation, which may
be understood in a twofold reference, first to the man as an exercise of the ἐξουσία, and then to the women and the object thereof.

† The reading ἐξιοῦσα has certainly something in its favour, and is therefore put
forth by Junius, Valckenaer, and others. (See the Scholia of the latter, vol. ii.
p. 279).

supposition that ἐξουσία is precisely the name of a head-dress, admits of no proof. The Hebrew רָדִיד, a large upper garment, capable also of covering the head, is not derived from רָדָה, to rule, but from רָדַד, to spread. In the middle ages *imperium* certainly signified a woman's head-dress (see Du Fresne Glossar. Med. Ævi. s. v.); and others have desired to receive ἐξου-σία in an active sense, "symbol of the protecting power of the man over the woman," with a reference to Ps. lx. 9, מָעוֹז רֹאשִׁי, guard of my head, *i. e.*, protecting helmet. But this turn of the expression by no means agrees with the context. The apostle is engaged in proving, not that the man has to protect the woman, but that the latter has to obey him. The difficulty in the phrase διὰ τοὺς ἀγγέλους is much more important. The conjectures ἀγέλης (on account of the flock), ἀγελαίους (by reason of unedu-cated men), ἄνδρας ὄχλους, are collectively without authority; the Codd. give no variations, but the supposition that ἄγγελοι intimates human messengers, suitors, or heathen spies, even mar-ried men, or overseer of the church, requires no serious refutation. The view of Heidenreich, that διὰ τοὺς ἀγγέλους is a *formula obsecrandi*, as *per omnes sanctos*, cannot be maintained, for the New Testament acknowledges no invocation of angels. We may certainly hesitate as to good or bad angels being here meant, and it appears not unlikely that a reference exists to the narrative of Gen. vi. 2, where it is stated that the sons of God (Elohim) found the daughters of men fair, and united themselves to them. But we cannot admit the reference in this place, because ἄγγελοι never implies bad angels alone. In the iv. 9 we understand by ἀγγέλοις all the higher orders of beings, good and bad together, but the connexion here does not sanction this supposition; for if it were proposed to express the temptation of man by means of the sight of unveiled women, at the evil instigation of bad angels, as Mosheim among others thinks, and also the sorrow experienced by the good angels for sin, it must have been more precisely stated. *Good* angels alone are therefore referred to. Theodo-rete, and following him other expositors, have had the *guardian angels* (Matt. xviii. 10) specially in mind, so that the sense were, " in order to avoid afflicting your holy guardian angel by an im-moral behaviour." But whether the angels mentioned in Matt.

xviii. 10 (see Comm. on this passage) are to be regarded as a distinct class, is too uncertain for us to venture to derive our explanation therefrom; we can then only in a general way think of all the good angels. But on what grounds shall the women cover themselves on their account? Bengel replies, because (Isa. vi. 2), the angels veil themselves before the Almighty. But that would prove too much, for by a similar reasoning he might conclude that the men also should veil themselves before Christ, their Head. We can only admit the general reference, on account of the joy which the angels have in all that is holy and good (see Luke xv. 10); and as the subject has a particular reference to veiling in the assemblies, we may entertain the idea that the angels, being themselves likewise engaged in the praise of God the Father, must be considered actively participating in the worship of God.* Thus, according to the LXX., Ps. cxxxviii. 1 says ἐναντίον ἀγγέλων ψαλῶ σοί, although verse 2 shows the subject to be the hymns in the temple.

Vers. 11, 12. In order, however, to furnish no pretence for pride in man, Paul now brings forward the other side of the position, that is to say, that by the command of God the man came of woman, being born of her; then again occurs the observation, that all comes from God, men as well as women. (In ver. 11 the ἐν κυρίῳ is to be understood, " According to the command and appointment of the Lord." The *text. rec.* has transposed the phrase in ver. 11, but critical authority is so unanimously opposed to the usual reading that no doubt can prevail concerning its rejection).

Vers. 13—16. The apostle concludes, that every one must be sensible of the propriety of women being covered, especially in religious assemblies; nature itself indicates this by the long hair which she bestows upon the woman as a covering and veil. This universal custom in all God's churches cannot therefore be departed from, in accordance with the views of certain who were contentious. In the latter remark (verse 16), is as it were contained the threat, " to whomsoever this is not agreeable, let him withdraw from the church, the custom cannot be changed." (In

---

* This has been already propounded by the fathers of the church. See Tertull. de Orat. c. 12, Orig. c. Cels. v. p. 233, Constit. Apost. viii. 4.

M

ver. 14 the expression ἡ φύσις διδάσκει must not be overlooked, for this mode of expression occurs but rarely in the holy Scriptures, since nature is commonly conceived as being in absolute dependence upon God, and therefore whenever it expresses purely physical subjects, is styled God. Passages like these show that the present prevalent practice of referring all to nature, is not in itself objectionable, but the circumspection with which the name of God is avoided is evidently the fruit of unbelief; nature is considered without any relation to God. Κομάω is = comam alere, to permit the hair to grow long.—In ver. 15, περιβόλαιον is really a wide-flowing garment [Heb. i. 12], consequently veil. See Gen. xxiv. 65, xxxviii. 14.—In ver. 16, Hesychius explains φιλόνεικος by μάχιμος, φίλερις; it does not occur again in the New Testament. This concluding verse decidedly points to a certain party in Corinth who wished to assert a greater degree of liberty. The extremes to which this tendency gave occasion in later times, is shown in church history, by the accounts of the antinomian sects of the Karpokratians, &c.

## § 10. THE HOLY COMMUNION.

### (xi. 17—34).

Far more important is the second subject upon which the apostle now enters, the conduct of the Corinthian Christians at the holy communion. With reference to this, the example of the better disposed appears either to have effected nothing, or they themselves were carried away by party spirit. At all events the apostle blames their conduct unconditionally, stigmatising it as calculated to change the blessing upon the assembly into a curse. (The τοῦτο παραγγέλλων of verse 17 refers to the subject already mentioned in verse 16, and the maintaining a better principle of order upon appearing in the assembly; and with the commendation contained in verse 16, a degree of reproach is connected in what follows.—The συνέρχεσθαι alludes especially to the assembling together, at which, according to the custom among early Christians, it was usual to celebrate the holy communion daily, and also the love-feast. Billroth refers κρεῖττον and ἧττον to the assembly itself, making the sense "these are not better, but rather worse," but this is not favoured by the εἰς τό : it would be more correct to regard it as expressive of the ethical end of all congregation, prejudiced by the unsanctified state of mind in which the Corinthians were accustomed to meet together.   In verse 34, εἰς κρίμα συνέρχεσθαι expresses this).

Vers. 18, 19.  Paul does not now enter at once upon the main argument, but mentions first the dissensions among the Corinthians, by employing πρῶτον μέν, to which no δεύτερον δέ succeeds, the οὖν of verse 20 rather supplying its place.  From this somewhat undivided form, we are by no means to conclude that Paul proposed to treat first of the divisions, and afterwards of the abuses in the Lord's Supper, or that he considered these same errors as σχίσματα, but that he intended to expose the relation of these corruptions to existing dissensions (see on chap. i.), and how the corrupt practices on occasion of celebrating the holy communion which Paul bewails, arose from the want of unity in the church (through the four αἱρέσεις), and further exhibited themselves in the assembly by σχίσματα, when the greatness of their purpose in assembling together should rather have restrained any disposition to cavil.  The sentence καὶ μέρος τι πιστεύω is also to be thus explained.  For it refers not to the σχίσματα as such (the information concerning it being credited entirely, and not in part, by Paul), but to its influence upon the forms of the congregations.  Concerning this latter point exaggerated reports might have arisen which the apostle perceived to be such, but that they were not entirely without foundation Paul's acquaintance with God's dealings enabled him to see.  He continually passes his winnowing fan over a community, in order to separate the impure from it, and make manifest the approved. (In verse 18 ἐκκλησία is not to be understood as the place of meeting, but the congregation: "If ye come together, so that ye form an ἐκκλησία, that faithful believers are present."  That is to say, smaller circles of persons closely connected might be formed who would yet represent no real ἐκκλησία.  It would be advisable to omit, with Lachmann, the comma after γάρ and ἐκκλησία, thus extending the current idea as far as ὑπάρχειν.—The difference between the σχίσματα and αἱρέσεις in this place is, that the latter expression, as the stronger, contains the ground

of the former, to which the καὶ points. The αἱρέσεις are also the
chief points of division mentioned in chap. i., a consequence
whereof was that the parties held themselves separate, even at the
celebration of the holy supper, i. e., occasioned σχίσματα.—Billroth correctly observes that here the ἵνα is to be understood properly of the object: God's *purpose* in these very lamentable
divisions is to discover those who are firm in the faith. The
good principle displays itself in moderation; the bad in the separation of the impure. 1 John ii. 19).

Vers. 20—22. The apostle now proceeds to that which is the
real object of reproof. (In verse 22 οὐκ ἐπαινῶ is to be received
only as Meiosis). According to custom among the ancient Christians, the celebration of the love-feast was regularly connected
with that of the holy communion, so that the whole ceremony
formed a strict commemoration of our Lord's passover feast.
Together they were viewed as one operation, and called δεῖπνον
κυριακόν.* All believers, as members of a single God's family,
ate and drank together earthly and divine food, in witness of
their inward unity for time and eternity. Each individual, according to his ability, brought provision for this festival, which
was then consumed in common, and this custom continued to
exist down to the end of the fourth century, when, in consequence
of the congregations becoming so numerous, it was found necessary to separate the love-feasts from the Lord's Supper. Now,
in Corinth, where the spirit of love had lost considerable ground,
these festivals were so conducted that each partook only of what
he had provided, the rich enjoying fully while the poor lacked.
The Lord's Supper, the supper of love, thereby sank into an ἴδιον
δεῖπνον, and was a proceeding without meaning or significance,
which each might have performed at home, and that which was
intended as a bond of union became of none effect and was dis-
honoured. However well calculated this account may be to dis-
turb the pleasing illusions we are prone to form concerning the
state of perfection existing in the ancient church, much may be

* Catholic interpreters desire to understand here only the Agape without the
Lord's Supper. This is decidedly an error; the apostolic church never celebrated
an Agape alone, without the holy communion. But at all events we may infer
from what is stated, that the errors here reproved found only partial acceptance
in the δεῖπνον κυριακόν, which, when at a subsequent period separated from the
Lord's Supper, formed the feasts styled Agape.

found to operate in tempering our judgment. First, the proceedings of the Corinthians did not spring from disrespect towards the sacred rite, and in no degree from covetousness or a selfish appetite, but from the divisions among themselves, which was the fundamental cause of the isolation of individuals. Every one shared only with the members of their own party without regard to the wants of the other. Such a course of proceeding, which would arise from attaching too great importance to slight points of difference, was in no way incompatible with a nature capable of more enlarged views, and it does not appear that this fault as thus explained was general. Had each applied himself seriously to the duty of self-examination, he would not have rated his brother's sin higher than his own, and this the apostle endeavours earnestly to impress upon them in what follows. (In ver. 20 the emphasis is to be laid on ὑμῶν, "when *ye* come together it is no true Lord's Supper that ye celebrate in so wrong a manner."—Concerning ἐπὶ τὸ αὐτό, consult Acts i. 15, ii. 1.— Δεῖπνον κυριακόν only occurs here. In the Acts of the Apostles the expression used is κλάσις ἄρτου [see Acts ii. 42], signifying love-feast and Lord's Supper together. Tertullian employs also the term *convivium dominicum, convivium Dei* [Ad Uxor. ii. 4, 8]. But the name is not to be explained as Heidenreich supposes, *coena in honorem domini instituta*, but "feast, given by the Lord, to which he invites believers."—In ver. 21 προλαμβάνειν means the consuming of the food supplied for themselves and those belonging to them, without sharing the same with their poorer brethren.—In ver. 22 Heidenreich erroneously places the expression ἐκκλησία Θεοῦ in opposition to οἰκία, and concludes that it signifies church buildings. But the acceptance of this view is forbidden by the Θεοῦ, which is inapplicable to a building, and moreover by the καταφρονεῖν and παταισχύνειν τοὺς μὴ ἔχοντας, which are parallel. The circumstances of the apostolic church were not yet of a nature that Christians could possess buildings which were exclusively churches).

Vers. 23—25. To this reproof on the part of the apostle follows a communication concerning the tradition relative to the celebration of the Lord's Supper, which by the γὰρ would appear to be elicited by circumstances similar to those which had called for the former; although it was not the Lord's Supper itself, but only the love-feasts preceding it, which had been profaned by the Corinthians; from this we may understand that Paul, holding forth the exalted nature of this sacrament, and its intimate and important connexion with the love-feast, desired to make the Corinthians fully sensible of their guilt in introducing their differences into the solemn rite. The passage from ver. 27 especially refers to this. Paul brings before their view what the Lord's Supper is, in order more strongly to impress upon them the necessity for self-examination. That dogmatic errors in the doctrine of the Lord's Supper were propagated is not expressly stated, but, according to 1 Cor. xv. 12, it is extremely probable that such were ready prepared to find entrance upon the slightest deviation from the pure faith. If the resurrection of the body were denied, the presence of the glorified body of our Lord was easily made the subject of error. In order, therefore, to remove all pretext for the adoption of these errors, the apostle furnishes them textually with the entire doctrine which he had himself already preached to them.—Concerning the Pauline form of institution it has already been fully entered upon in Comm. vol. ii. 440, sqq., third edit., to which the reader is referred. In the life of the apostle (Exposition of the Epist. to the Romans, p. 8) it has already been stated that we could not reasonably conclude that every individual historical fact in the life of the Lord had been immediately imparted to the apostle by Christ, but with the holy communion it was an especial case. The dogmatic principle contained therein was so closely bound up with historical foundation that it was not possible to separate the one from the other; in this particular, therefore, an immediate revelation from the Lord is correctly inferred. Exegetically the ἀπὸ τοῦ κυρίου cannot be otherwise received than with the antithesis οὐκ ἀπ᾽ ἀνθρώπων, as expressly stated by Paul in Gal. i. 12. Accordingly we have here *an authentic declaration of the risen Saviour himself concerning his sacrament*, and the church has ever regarded this as the most important passage in the New Testament respecting the holy communion. It has been alleged in opposition to this, that ἀπὸ only signifies the receiving through an agent, and that, consequently, the apostle only here lays claim to having received from the apostles as eye-witnesses. But then Paul would stand upon a level with all other Christians who likewise received the sacrament from the apostles, while here something especial is attributed. It therefore follows that in the New Testament it is not always strictly indispensable to observe the distinction between ἀπὸ and παρὰ, as is further shown in the remarks upon Gal. i. 1. In fact it may be supposed that Paul here employs ἀπὸ, because he desired to discriminate between the personal appearance of our Lord (see Acts ix.) and his revelation by means of his Spirit. The reading παρὰ in some of the Codd. is therefore only correction.

Ver. 26. Christ's own words are only contained in vers. 24, 25; ver. 26 is added by Paul himself as an illustration of the εἰς τὴν ἐμὴν ἀνάμνησιν. The announcement of the Saviour's death shall not only take place as often as the Lord's Supper is celebrated; but this celebration, and the announcement bound up in it, shall continue until the second coming of the Lord, consequently through the entire αἰὼν οὗτος, until the supper of the Lamb in God's kingdom. (Rev. xix. 9). The idea of making known the death naturally includes, as Œcumenius appositely remarks, the remembrance contained therein, πᾶσαν τὴν δωρεὰν καὶ πᾶσαν τὴν φιλανθρωπίαν καὶ πᾶσαν τὴν σωτηρίαν, only that we may be uncertain whether καταγγέλλετε is to be received as indicative or imperative. The γὰρ, connecting verses 25 and 26, agrees with both; for ye certainly make known, would call to mind the custom in the celebration of the communion, thanking God for creation and also redemption through the death of Christ. But Heidenreich has correctly observed that the phrase ἄχρις οὗ ἔλθῃ must be taken imperatively, for it was impossible Paul should say, ye do it until the coming of the Lord.

Ver. 27. Of the highest importance to the dogma of the Lord's Supper are the words of exhortation from the apostle which here follow. He says one may partake of the sacred feast ἀναξίως, and thereby make himself worthy of punishment. The question arises, what is to be understood by ἀναξίως? In connexion with the subject before us, the judging others instead of ourselves, and uncharitableness towards others, is intended. This may be found to include the idea admitting of universal and especial application to all times and circumstances, *the impenitent are unworthy guests at the Lord's Supper*, not from the sinfulness abstractedly, but the sinning without repenting, the hardy persistence in sin. It is the more important to uphold this view, because individuals of tender consciences feeling the operation of sin in themselves, often deem themselves unworthy, and so refrain from the strengthening influence to be derived from the holy sacrament. It is the impenitent participation which constitutes ἔνοχος τοῦ σώματος καὶ τοῦ αἵματος τοῦ κυρίου. The expression ἔνοχος (from ἐνέχεσθαι, *adstrictus teneri*) signifies *reus*, to incur a penalty, ὑπεύθυνος, as Hesychius explains it. It is usually connected with κρίσις or θάνατος (Matt. v. 21, sqq., xxvi. 66; Mark iii. 29), here it is placed together with the object to which the guilt has reference. But it is obviously consistent neither with the connexion or Paul's meaning to understand the idea thus, "Whoever partakes unworthily of bread and wine, is so wicked that he would have joined in condemning Christ to death." The thought of the apostle tends not to the distant Saviour crucified on Golgotha, but considers him as present in the last supper which he instituted, which he continued as a memorial of himself. Therefore not only Χριστοῦ is used, but σώματος καὶ ἅματος Χριστοῦ, which would be irreconcilable with the former acceptation. The sense is rather, " Whoever unworthily partakes of the bread and wine, is guilty of an offence against the most Holy One." As the greatness of the offence is determined by the elevation of the object against whom the deed is directed, as likewise he who affronts a prince finds it more difficult to excuse himself than he who mocks a beggar, or he who robs a church, than the man who steals from a private house, so is the unworthy receiving of the Lord's Supper the more heinous, because the holiness of Christ present therein is so great. Indeed we must say, that a mighty argument against Zwinglius' views of the Lord's Supper lies in this passage; the apostle treats it as a high mystery, which bears within itself a power to bless and likewise to destroy. Christ is present in the Lord's Supper in his human nature, so that he who receives the elements unworthily, is guilty of sin towards Christ himself. The fact that the consecrated elements are here denominated bread and wine, proves sufficiently that the Catholic doctrine of transubstantiation is entirely unscriptural. But it is just as certain that *concerning the manner of Christ's presence in the holy communion*, nothing further can be drawn from this passage. That the Calvinistic

acceptation of this doctrine must yield in the chief points to the
Lutheran can only be inferred by a strict analogy of the general
points of doctrine, especially as they refer to the person of Christ
and to the relationship of the divine and human nature in him.
In that case we may here find a certain guide.—Verse 27 is employed by the Roman Catholics as a defence of the *communio
sub una*, because it says, ὃς ἂν ἐσθίῃ τὸν ἄρτον τοῦτον, ἢ πίνῃ τὸ
ποτήριον τοῦ κυρίου. It is true that several good MSS. read καὶ,
but without doubt ἢ is preferable to the more unusual form.
Winer (Gr. p. 413) has therefore with reason remarked that this
certainly permits us to suppose that some may devoutly receive
the bread without the wine; and in addition to this, if, according
to the Roman Catholic view, the cup ought never to be received,
the ἢ can in no manner apply. Paul, in that case, must have
written ὃς ἂν ἐσθίῃ τὸν ἄρτον τοῦτον.

Vers. 28, 39. To this the exhortation to serious self-examination before receiving the holy Sacrament naturally connects itself. The δοκιμάζειν is, as may be readily comprehended, to be
considered in conjunction with the result of this exercise of self-
investigation and repentance. As perfectly conformable to this
passage, confession was instituted by the church, and it were
much to be desired that the practice of real private confession
were still retained, instead of a general admonition being substituted in its place. At the same time, the former idea is again
taken up here (ver. 29), and the form ἔνοχος σώματος καὶ αἵματος κυρίου elucidated by μὴ διακρίνων τὸ σῶμα τοῦ κυρίου. These
words, however, only confirm the view before taken of the ἔνοχος
κ. τ. λ., for διακρίνειν signifies likewise in this place "to separate
as holy from unholy, consequently, to treat the Lord's Supper as
if it were an ordinary matter, and as if he were not present."
The question then occurs, whether these words justify Luther's
supposition that the unbelieving do also receive the body of the
Lord?* Had the great Reformer declared, with reference to this,
that those who received unworthily not only did not receive

---

* The strict Lutherans of the 16th century went so far as to assert: *Nihilo plus
recepisse in prima coena Petrum quam Judam.* Calvin, on the xi. 27, expresses
himself thus: *Ego hoc axioma teneo, neque mihi usquam excuti patiar, Christum
non posse a suo spiritu divelli. Unde constituto, non recipi mortuum eius corpus,
neque disjunctum a spiritus sui virtute. Jam qui viva fide et poenitentia vacuus est,
quum nihil habeat spiritus Christi, ipsum Christum quomodo reciperet? Sicut ergo*

the blessing, but thereby suffered positive evil consequences
(a κρίμα), this would have been perfectly compatible with
the sense.   The words κρίμα ἑαυτῷ ἐσθίει evidently bind the
curse to the action of unworthy participation.   But that the
unbelieving communicant *receives* the body and blood of Christ in
itself is not sanctioned by the words ; we may suppose the pernicious effect of his unholy act to be, that the power of the body
and blood repels him.   As he who sins against the Holy Ghost
does not receive the Spirit, but is rejected of it, so likewise the
unbelieving recipient of the Lord's Supper does not receive Christ,
but is rejected by Him.   It is well to distinguish between the
*unbelieving* and the *unworthy* receiving of the Sacrament.   Even
believers may receive the Sacrament unworthily, and this possibility is here stated by Paul; inasmuch as the person so sinning is
still faithful, he can receive Christ; in so far as he sins, however, he can have no blessing, but a curse.   But the thorough unbeliever, in whom no regeneration is found, can in no sense whatever be said to receive the body and blood of Christ, because the
faith is wanting which would enable him to do so.   The degree
of offence in such a case depends upon the measure of consciousness with which he, wanting faith, approached the table of the
Lord: he who drew near in voluntary ignorance will also be
judged according to this circumstance.   Luther arrived at his
decision from the attempt to maintain the union of the greater
and lesser objects in the Sacrament, which also led him to suppose that not only bread and wine, but also Christ's flesh and
blood, were received with the physical mouth, although not again
after a Capernaitish manner.   But these extreme opinions were
not necessary to Luther's object: Christ's glorified flesh and
blood can only be received by regenerate man (without the baptism of regeneration there is no Lord's Supper)! for such, the
Divine presence is in and with the elements; the unregenerate,
on the contrary, has no faculty to appropriate the Divine presence to himself, and consequently receives only the external sym-
bols.   Brenz says very appositely, although a good Lutheran
(Luther's works, vol. xvii. 2482), " The mouth of faith receives the
body of Christ, the carnal mouth bread and wine."   Because the

*fateor, quosdam esse qui vere simul in cœna et tamen indigne Christum recipiant,*
*quales sunt multi infirmi, ita non admitto, eos qui fidem historicam tantum sine vivo*
*pœnitentiæ et fidei sensu afferunt, aliud quam signum recipere.*

bread and wine are not changed, the physical mouth receives them alone, the spiritual food being reserved for, and perceptible only to the mouth of faith, or, yet more closely, the mouth of the believing and inwardly renewed man, who already, though yet below, bears within himself the germ of the glorified body.

Vers. 30—32. The condition of the Corinthian church, which in many points of view appears to have been unsatisfactory, is clearly attributed by Paul to their disrespect towards the holy communion. Only the strictest self-examination could save them from the Divine judgment; and if this were wanting, the judgments of the Lord must take effect (as they had already experienced); but in his mercy he would chastise the faithful, in order to save them from condemnation with the world.— This passage is important, as more precisely fixing the sense of the $\kappa\rho\iota\mu\alpha$ (ver. 29). Without the subsequent advance of the $\kappa\rho\iota\nu\epsilon\sigma\theta\alpha\iota$ ($=\pi\alpha\iota\delta\epsilon\upsilon\epsilon\sigma\theta\alpha\iota$) to the $\kappa\alpha\tau\alpha\kappa\rho\iota\nu\epsilon\sigma\theta\alpha\iota$, we should have already concluded in ver. 29 $\kappa\rho\iota\mu\alpha$ to signify eternal condemnation. But the omission of the article intimates that it is not the last judgment which is meant, but an admonishing reproof calculated to impress the mind, and at the same time prove of advantage to the faithful.* The Corinthians had partaken of Christ's flesh and blood unworthily, but they were not for that reason eternally condemned,† they had thereby materially prejudiced their inward living, they were on the way to condemnation, from which the Almighty sought to recover them by chastisement, the apostle by reproof.‡ The only difficulty in these verses is to deter-

* Thus Wolf and Bengel decide. The latter also correctly observes on this passage: $\kappa\rho\iota\mu\alpha$, sine articulo, indicium aliquod, morbum, mortemve corporis, ut qui Domini corpus non discernunt, suo corpore luant. Non dicit τὸ κατάκριμα, condemnationem. Nevertheless Billroth himself considers it refers to eternal condemnation.

† The supposition that the unworthily participating in the Lord's Supper, in itself, can lead to everlasting condemnation, or stand equal in guilt to sin committed against the Holy Ghost, may prove hurtful, by deterring individuals from approaching the sacred rite. The confession of Goethe is remarkable on this point. He was first led by this fear to avoid both church and altar. (See his works, last edit., vol. xxv., p. 125). The ancient church possessed a far clearer view respecting the supper instituted by Divine love!

‡ The remarks of Rosenkranz (Encycl. p. 52), mentioned by Billroth, in this place, and which I shall likewise quote, are much to the point : "As the baptismal confession requires the acknowledgment of sin, so likewise the celebration of the Lord's Supper demands the knowledge of one's self. It assists to the extreme in fortifying the will and desire to lead a life agreeable to the same, because it immediately

mine, whether in verse 30 the ἀσθενεῖς and ἄρρωςτοι, as well as
the κοιμᾶσθαι, are of inward or outward application, or to be received in both senses together. My own views incline to the
latter belief; the nature of the thing appears to forbid the supposition, that only outward sufferings are intended without internal
likewise. The consequence of an act, such as the unworthy participation in the holy Sacrament, must be, in the first place, a
mental disturbance. The only question, therefore, that could
arise is, whether such inward detriment is not alone to be understood, without any reference to outward suffering? But the supposition of suffering endured by the Corinthians, being sent by
the Lord as a means of chastisement and profit to them, does not
allow the outward sufferings to be omitted. These, such as sickness, &c., are rather the means in God's hand of awakening the
slumbering conscience to the condition of the inward life. This
passage may be regarded as parallel with v. 5, in which the apostle
commands the body of the sinner to be given over to Satan, in
order to save his soul in the day of the Lord. The expressions
(verse 30) may consequently be regarded as a climax: ἀσθενεῖς
and ἄρρωστοι express the lesser and higher degree of laxity in
the inward life, and analogous physical sorrows, but κοιμᾶσθαι,
the highest degree of inward deadness, indicating likewise the
physical death. According to 2 Cor. v., it cannot be doubted,
that at the time the apostle wrote these epistles, he regarded the
second coming of the Lord as near at hand. Death, in a frame of
mind verging towards apostacy, consequently appeared to him to
preclude all participation in Christ's kingdom ; while this forfeit,
being the precise penalty inflicted by God, might in effect prove
the means of awakening fallen sinners for eternal life. (In
verse 30, διὰ τοῦτο = because this has happened among you.—
Ἱκανός, the custom of many, is found also in Luke vii. 11, 12,
viii. 32.—In verse 31, the ἑαυτοὺς διεκρίνομεν is indulgently expressed. Διακρίνω appears to be selected with reference to verse
29 ; as the Lord's Supper should be perfectly distinguished from
an ordinary repast, so likewise the unworthy guest at the same

gives to the individual the consciousness, that the task he has to discharge is in
itself (through Christ) already effected, and that consequently the reality of a
godly life, such as he desires to lead, is not impossible. But he who lightly receives the holy communion without repentance, and without the desire to live con-
formably to the principle in the same, eats and drinks to himself a condemnation.

should be distinct from the worthy, and out of this distinction a
voluntary separation followed).

Vers. 33, 34. In conclusion, Paul recommends brotherly love,
and devout, respectful behaviour in celebrating the sacred rite.
Other points touching the right celebration of the holy Sacrament
appear to require mention, but as this might involve an explanation of his own personal views on the subject, he promises to make
it the object of further communication upon his arrival among
them. (Ver. 33. Ἐκδέχεσθαι generally signifies in the New Testament "to wait," like ἀπεκδέχεσθαι. The idea, "wait for one
another," would convey the erroneous impression, that some had
partaken earlier, before the others came. But it has here the
signification of "excipere convivio," the sense being, share with
one another what ye have, that the feast may be a real festival of
love).

## § 11. THE GIFT OF TONGUES.

### (xii. 1—xiv. 40).

The following section belongs unquestionably to those in the
New Testament which are best calculated to convey a lively impression of the most remarkable times in the history of the world,
viz., the early days of the disciples, and the period when wings of
the infant church were gradually extending over mankind, which
was marked by the most important appearances ever revealed.
The stream of life which, like a sacred living flame, was poured
on the first disciples of the Lord at Pentecost, extended itself
over the newly arisen churches, and awakened in all those who
yielded themselves to its influence a depth of purpose, a power of
action, a sentiment of heavenly joy hitherto unfelt by mankind,
and which only beamed all the clearer amid the dark shadows of
the heathen world which surrounded the apostolic churches. But
the spiritual gifts were manifested in the first instance, that is to
say, in their first striking potency, and in the contest with a prevailing world of evil, in a miraculous manner (i. e., one contrary to
the laws of nature), and their further development by appearances

which were inexplicable.* The miraculous power of Christ appeared extended to the whole church! Down to the end of the third century, and consequently until the period of the church's dominion over heathenism, these miraculous gifts of the infant church were continued, although gradually diminishing. (See the passages of the K.V.V., referring thereto, with learned research, in Dodwelli Dissert. in Iren. Oxoniæ, 1689, 2nd treatise). Among the excitable Greeks, particularly in Corinth, the spiritual gifts displayed themselves in the most forcible manner. All forms and appearances under which they became known seem to have been here prominent, and to have operated with a powerful fermentation. As in the meantime the men upon whom these gifts, sacred in themselves, descended, were not yet perfectly sanctified, since in them the old man yet retained his power, and many of them likewise permitted their human weaknesses to interfere with the exercise of the spiritual power which filled them, it was possible that the *employment* of the gifts gave occasion to numerous abuses. This happened especially with the gift of the tongues, the striking and dazzling display of which led the Corinthians to overrate its value, and the whole of the following observations arose from the existence of this error, which the apostle was determined to reprove. In order to make the Corinthians aware of the right position of the gift of tongues, with regard to the other phenomena, Paul takes a retrospect of the gifts in general, with a view to prove from the analogy of the various members of the corporeal organism that the members of the spiritual organism also, although differing among themselves, must yet all serve the same end, and have their origin in the selfsame spirit (xii. 1—31), stating that love must be the ruler of all the other gifts, because by that their first real value is obtained (xiii. 1—13); and he then finally proceeds to enlarge upon the special application of the gifts of speech in Christian assemblies (xiv. 1—40). However attractive the whole section may be, it is nevertheless an extremely difficult one.

* See among recent works on the subject, Die Geistesgaben der ersten Christen, insbesondere die sogenannte Sprachengabe, by David Schulz, Breslau, 1836. In connexion with it may be mentioned Baur's Neue Abh. ueber die Sprachengabe (Stud. 1838, part 3), which contains a criticism on Schulz's work. Koester's work, Die Propheten des alten and neuen Testaments (Leipzig, 1838), also deserves attention.

and principally for this reason, that the Charismatic form of operation of the Holy Ghost ceased with the third century, and
we have, therefore, now no means of taking a right view of the
apostolic condition.   It cannot be surprising that we must
feel this regret, when we see that Chrysostom, who lived nearly
fifteen hundred years nearer to the apostolic age, expressed
himself in just the same manner, because he likewise could
gain no precise views as to the spiritual operation of the Charismata.   His 29th homily upon our Epistles begins with the words:
τοῦτο ἅπαν τὸ χωρίον σφόδρα ἐστὶν ἀσαφὲς, τὴν δὲ ἀσάφειαν ἡ
τῶν πραγμάτων ἄγνοιά τε καὶ ἔλλειψις ποιεῖ, τῶν τότε μὲν συμ-
βαινόντων, νῦν δὲ οὐ γινομένων.

Vers. 1—3.  The 12th chapter is so clearly a continuation of the
preceding one, that Paul observes, had he time before his appearing among them to prolong his remarks upon the Lord's Supper
he must nevertheless immediately explain himself concerning the
πνευματικά, in order that his admonitions may act as an immediate
prohibition of the abuse.   Billroth has with Heidenreich considered the περὶ δὲ τῶν πνευματικῶν masculine, and received it in
the special signification " of those speaking with the tongues."
But the passages xiv. 1, 37 do not confirm this explanation of
the words: for in xii. 1, τὰ πνευματικά sc. χαρίσματα, as in
this place, is especially to be understood of the spiritual gifts,
and in xiv. 37 the πνευματικός is every possessor of a Charisma,
not only the gift of tongues.   Starting from the most general point
of view, Paul next reminds the Corinthians of their heathen condition, in which no quickening power could be conferred by their lifeless idols; while all those who acknowledged Christ were conscious
of receiving a spiritual strength from him, whereby they were enabled to call Jesus their Lord, that is to say, to pronounce in word
and truth the acknowledgment of the circumstances of their dependence on him, and endowment by him.   The universality of the
working of the Holy Spirit in the church is thus established, with
which the following description of the variety of its operations perfectly agrees.   This could only be objected to in so far as it might
be urged that a supernatural power was also evident in heathenism.
The worship of Bacchus and of Cybele inspired its followers, although with an unholy spirit.   But Bauer (work already quoted,
p. 649, note) remarks with reason, that it could not be replied

to this, that Paul was not considering such isolated appearances of Gentilism, but rather regarding it in its whole and comprehensive working; for in the oracles as well as other orgiastic appearances, much existed that was analogous to the gift of tongues. The emphasis is rather to be laid upon the expression εἴδωλα: the lifeless idols were contrasted with the living, efficient Christ, who as the λόγος created the λαλεῖν ἐν πνεύματι in the faithful. It is evident besides, that this expression does not strictly and singly apply to the gift of the γλωσσαις λαλεῖν, but to the active operation of the Spirit especially, by which confession of faith is incited. (In verse 2 some hesitation may occur between the choice of the readings ὅτι and ὅτε. Billroth decides for the latter, Lachmann has adopted the former, placing, however, the ὅτε near within brackets. I prefer the ὅτι, because then the expression, "ye know that ye were Gentiles," includes in it the presupposition of the Gentile condition. The change into ὅτε arose, in my opinion, from supposing that Paul intended to say, "Ye know, that, as ye were Gentiles," as in that case ὅτι ὅτε is read together. Valckenaer conjectures it should be ὅτι, ὅτε ἔθνη ἦτε, ἦτε.—See concerning ἀνάθεμα in verse 3 on Rom. ix. 3, 1 Cor. xvi. 22.—Billroth correctly observes that Jesus is used and not Christ, in order to mark more distinctly the historical individuality of the Redeemer. —The two related sentences are by no means the same; οὐδεὶς λέγει ἀνάθεμα Ἰησοῦν and οὐδεὶς δύναται εἰπεῖν κύριον Ἰησοῦν, are not identical in meaning. The former sentence stands opposed to the Satanic evil spirit, the latter to the natural human spirit. Even the unenlightened man may take pleasure in Jesus, when the beam of divine light reaches his heart, and he can first call him his Lord; it is only the devilish impulse that is capable of cursing Jesus. It is, therefore, probable that ἐν πνεύματι Θεοῦ may indicate a more general working of the Spirit, ἐν πνεύματι ἁγίῳ the specifically Christian; so that the sense would be, "No one, even he who only speaks in a general way in the Spirit of God, can curse Jesus, but none also, except he in whom the holy Spirit speaks, can call him Lord."—Lachmann has accepted the reading according to which ἀνάθεμα Ἰησοῦς, κύριος Ἰησοῦς, are regarded as explanations; but this has something so constrained, that I am induced to prefer the more usual connexion).

Vers. 4—6. The unity of the divine Spirit present in all believers appears manifested under various forms as διαιρέσεις, in
different individuals.     But this by no means signifies that the
various gifts, freeing themselves from their source, incorporate
themselves as it were with the soul in which they are to appear;
it rather supposes the division of the gifts (see Acts ii. 3), as the
lights in colours are divided by the prism.   The unity of the
Spirit is thereby not annulled, but the same Spirit is only re-
fracted into various gifts, according to the capacity of the soul
with which it comes into contact.     But when in the passage
under consideration the unity of the spiritual principle is indicated by various expressions, πνεῦμα, κύριος, Θεός, it can certainly not arise from accident.   The substantiality of the Divine
Being, the Spirit in itself, is the principle of unity, the condition of the Trinity, which manifests itself everywhere, but speaks
also in the gifts; and thus the gifts are of the Father, of the Son,
and of the Holy Ghost.    But holding this view, it cannot be denied
that *all* gifts are in an especial manner gifts of the Holy Ghost;
and ver. 7, sqq., plainly show that Paul refers them all to the
Spirit.    As, however, the Father and the Spirit is in Christ, so
also the Spirit is one with the Father and the Son, and certain gifts correspond equally with the Father or the Son.    In
placing together the three divine persons, the Holy Ghost always appears as the manifestation of the inmost depths of the
Godhead, and therefore in this place the three positions may be
viewed as an anticlimax.    The expression χαρίσματα, which in
a more extended sense includes all gifts without exception (xii.
31, xiv. 1), refers here to the spiritual gifts as enumerated, in
ver. 8, to the σοφία, γνῶσις, πίστις.   The διακονίαι indicate the
more external ecclesiastical gifts of government and lending aid
to the necessitous (ver. 28): and finally, the ἐνεργήματα, those
gifts in which power was revealed, such as the healing disease
under all its various forms (ver. 9, 30).    The *most general* and
comprehensive class of gifts is quite correctly referred to the
Father and the *omnipotence* revealed in him; the more *limited*
class, manifesting itself within the precincts of the Church, to the
Son, as the principle of compassionate *love;* while the third and
*smallest* class, restricted to the circle of the enlightened members
in the church, is referred to the Holy Spirit as the principle of

N

*sanctification* and *knowledge.* (1 Cor. ii. 10). It would be interesting to have the power of arranging the nine gifts which follow, under one or other of these rubrics; but in the Scripture, as in nature, there is a kind of vast irregularity often apparent amidst accuracy and order, and this is precisely the case here.* Of the second class there appears no especial forms mentioned until ver. 28; the προφητεία belongs rather to the first than the last division, and various other deviations occur. Just as little does the account agree (ver. 28—30), with the corresponding passage in Isa. xi. 2, sqq.; a free course must be acknowledged in such passages.

Ver. 7—11. The main object of the enumeration of the single Charismata which follows, as shown by the frequent repetition of the πνεῦμα, is evidently to keep in view the identity of origin, and destination of the same, notwithstanding any internal diversity. The one and the same Spirit of God (ver. 11) works all these φανερώσεις (ver. 7) to one end, and divides them as he will. It is easily understood that this καθὼς βούλεται (ver. 11 and ver. 18) certainly refers to the personality of the Spirit, and is not to be received of absolute free will, but of a conditional will, which, according to the nature of man, is also from God. Regeneration does not absolutely create other qualities in men, it predominates over them, sanctifying and glorifying those already present. No individual, however, possessed the power of gaining at any time, or appropriating to himself the Charismata, by exercising them (as according to Acts viii. Simon Magus intended); it was only the will of the Spirit which conferred it ἰδίᾳ ἑκάστῳ *i. e., singulis singulatim.* This does not infer, however, that the individual could possess but one single gift; several were frequently in operation in one subject, and the apostles each exercised the greater part, if not all. All gifts are appointed πρὸς τὸ συμφέρον (ver. 7) of the possessors of the gift and of the community,†

---

* By the exchange of ἕτερος and ἄλλος, nothing would be gained for the order of the gifts, as Billroth has correctly observed. For if we should say that ᾧ μέν, with both the ἑτέρῳ δέ, mark the three principal rubrics, whilst the gifts subordinate to those were expressed by the ἄλλῳ δέ, these three classes do not agree with those named in vers. 4—6. The apostle binds himself to no rule in the recapitulation, save that he descends from the higher to the lower.

† Billroth here erroneously supposes πρός to signify *secundum*, according to measure, which (see Winer's Gr. p. 343, d.) is not an impossible meaning, *only* that in this case it is clearly intended to say, that the gifts were not to be trifled with, but to have a *use*, for which reason πρός here signifies *ad.*

single and collectively.—It has been already remarked that all
the gifts are not here enumerated, since ver. 28, sqq. serves as a
continuation of the passage under consideration, the subject of
which commences with ver. 4; there exists, however, absolutely
no ground for supposing that there were other gifts besides those
mentioned in this chapter; it is, at the same time, not unreasonable to suppose that some of them might be under slight regulation. Some degree of importance may also be attributed to the
fact that the first three gifts are not miraculous, while the succeeding are of miraculous order; wisdom, knowledge, faith may
be always in a certain degree present in the church, but not the
gifts of healing and of tongues, &c. Certainly this distinction is
by no means unimportant, yet wisdom, knowledge, and faith, as
Charismata, must be distinguished from the analogous appearances not being such which belong chiefly to the essence of
the Christian life, as we have taken occasion to observe in
the Commentary on ii. 6, 7. No Christian is without faith,
yet all do not possess the Charisma of faith, which is something
more than a simple increase of general belief, for then there
might also be Charismata of love, hope, and prayer. We cannot
therefore employ this distinction in classifying the Charismata,
for all without exception are miraculous and extraordinary in
their operation through the Holy Ghost. We are not speaking
of a wisdom or knowledge attained gradually by practice and
faith, but of a condition proceeding from higher illumination,
and must of ourselves perceive and allow that as Charismata,
wisdom, knowledge, and faith, are no longer existent in the
present church, but are only to be found in agreement with
their general idea, exhibiting themselves in some individuals
in a greater degree than in others; but Charismatically, the
Holy Ghost has ceased to work in the church since the time
of the apostles; all, even wisdom and knowledge, must now be
gained by gradual exercise, whilst in the apostolic times* it was

---

* Baur (Stud. Jahrg. 1838, part 3, p. 683) thinks this goes so far as to deny that
the Holy Spirit yet operates in the church. This is evidently an error. The
assertion that the revelation and inspiration of the apostles was not imparted to
the whole church, but was confided entirely to themselves, is as little justifiable
as the supposition that the Spirit no longer works by means of miraculous gifts
in the established condition of the church; these gifts being only requisite to the
foundation of the church would seem to infer that the Holy Spirit had ceased to

an immediate consequence of divine operation in the soul.  Just
as little can we discern between the spiritual powers in which
the enlightening property of the Holy Ghost manifested itself;
for, as we shall see, however the difference of reason, understanding, the will, may be brought under discussion, it can furnish no
certain ground of decision in our inquiry, because other objects
than these powers must be considered in the Charismata. Without
doubt Neander (Apost. Zeitalt. vol. i., p. 174, sqq.) has written
most to the point on this subject; and, with a few exceptions, such
for example, as his view regarding the gift of tongues, I cannot
withhold my agreement from what he has advanced.  According
to this, *two principal classes* of gifts are to be considered, the
*first* comprehending all those verbally, the *second* those actively
manifested.  But both classes may be subdivided into two other
divisions, according as the condition of mind of the possessor of
the gift is more or less passive, since what is divine manifests
itself directly without being wrought upon by any concurring
capacity for judging.  The first form may be considered especially operating where early mental discipline had increased self-
knowledge and exercised reflection, and to have been found
among the more learned in the church, of whom, for example,
Apollos appears to have been one.  A third might be added to

work therein; it reveals itself now, however, in another manner.  It may be consequently asked if *some Charismata* may not now and ever remain, as possessed by
the apostolic church.  This applies particularly to wisdom, knowledge, spiritual
discernment.  But if we reflect upon the manner in which such Charismata were
displayed in the apostles and such members of the ancient church as we may assume were possessed of these gifts, we must allow that, in this form also, the
Spirit reveals itself no longer.  The story of Ananias and Sapphira is an instance
of the gift of spiritually discerning (Acts v.); where shall we now find anything
similar?  The Charismatic knowledge was likewise deeper, more intuitive, than
is now even perceptible in the most enlightened individual.  The Spirit certainly
is now, as then, in the church, but it works in a different manner.  Formerly
the Holy Spirit operated as an immediate, efficacious, suddenly inspiring power,
but now it acts slowly, presupposing the employment of all natural means of aid.
These views concerning the Charismata were early laid down by our dogmatizers in
opposition to the Catholic doctrine of the continuance of the miraculous gifts.
(See Gerhard Loci Theol. vol. xii. p. 104, sqq., ex. edit. Cottae).  And even the
later Fathers confess that there was no more revelation of the Holy Ghost's Cha-
rismatical manner of operation.  (See the passage in Chrysostom quoted at the
commencement of this chapter.  The passage Rom. xii. 6, sqq., may also be consulted; one might there suppose that a Charisma not mentioned here was quoted
by the apostle, that of the παρακλῆσις.  But according to the intention of the
correct reading, and the right explanation of the passage, it is not the fact.  (See
on this passage the explanation in the new edition of my Comm. upon the Romans).

the two subdivisions of the gifts operating by speech, which possessed a *criticising* power, and which might therefore have especial reference to the understanding.  By this arrangement the
two first mentioned λόγος σοφίας and λόγος γνώσεως belong to
the first subdivision of the first class.  Whilst *wisdom* signifies
the *practical,* and *knowledge* the *theoretical* side in views we
have made our own of things divine and human, they have this
common quality that they do not proceed from an immediate outpouring of what is divine, but rather from peaceful gradual study.*
This especially applies to the γνῶσις of ver. 28, which corresponds
with the διδάσκαλοι (see also on Rom. xii. 7).  These call forth
by their operation not so much the new life, as they advance that
which has commenced.  Therefore in vers. 28 and 29, and Ephes.
iv. 11, they stand with ποιμένες, in contrast to the apostles, prophets, and evangelists.  The λόγος, which is added, places both
Charismata in immediate connexion with the office of teacher,†
so that the ἀπόστολοι (vers. 28, 29) appear the real possessors
of the gift of σοφία, whilst the διδάσκαλοι or ποιμένες may be regarded as the holders of the Charisma of the γνῶσις.  The Charismata of the σοφία and γνῶσις are, however, very distinct from
the wisdom and knowledge which every true regenerate Christian
attains, not only in the degree of increase or security (for, according to John xvii. 3, we must consider the knowledge of every believer thoroughly certain), but rather in the perfected form in
which they appear.  The believer acknowledges God and Christ,
and has in him all treasures of wisdom and knowledge (Col. ii. 3),
but he possesses this knowledge implicitly, not explicitly.  The
Charisma of the γνῶσις (and so likewise of the σοφία), moreover supposes the development of matters of individual purport.  It grants
in a supernatural way what the science of theology now offers by the
usual course of learning, both practically and theoretically, from
which the universal operation of the Holy Spirit is not excluded,
but must be presupposed.  To admit a Charismatic operation of
the Spirit among the Theosophs, as is done by Jacob Boehme, is

---

* Concerning this reference may be made to Comm. on ii. 6, 7.

† In the passage of the Epistle to the Ephesians i. 17, in which mention is
made of the Charisma of σοφία, πνεῦμα σοφίας is used, but this πνεῦμα is not
to be regarded as identical with λόγος, it only points out the Spirit as the principle of wisdom.  Here it is styled λόγος σοφίας, a wisdom which is connected
with the faculty of being communicated by words.  In the same Ephes. i. 17, the
Charisma of προφητεία is expressed by the use of πνεῦμα ἀποκαλύψεως.

for this reason doubtful; since error and truth are usually too much mixed in them for their knowledge to be considered the pure working of the Spirit. (See Comm. thereon on xiii. 9, sqq.) In the *second* subdivision of the first class of gifts (revealed through words) stand the προφητεύειν and γλώσσαις λαλεῖν, of which further on 1 Cor. xiv. and Acts ii. In both the divine efficacy predominated over the human, but so that the prophet's consciousness of facts which might have reference to the circumstances and hearers, remained undisturbed, while, on the contrary, in those speaking with tongues all worldly knowledge was subject to the consciousness of God, they held, as it were, converse with God. The προφητεία is, therefore, the real gift of awakening the soul, the principal Charisma for the *arising* church, while the διδασκαλία, the gift of γνῶσις, appears to be the chief Charisma for the church firmly established, but ever *increasing in itself.* Finally, the *third* subdivision is constituted by the criticising powers of the διακρίσεις πνευμάτων and of the ἑρμηνεία γλωσσῶν. Concerning this latter Charisma, and its connexion with the γένη γλωσσῶν, more will be said on 1 Cor. xiv. The gift of discerning spirits does not simply refer to the power of distinguishing between good and false prophets, but also to the language of the prophets themselves, who were filled with the Holy Ghost (see on xiv. 29, and 1 Thess. v. 19, 20). The *second* class contains gifts manifested by deeds, and to the *first* subdivision belong those acts of government not named in this place, but mentioned in ver. 28, the κυβερνήσεις and ἀντιλήψεις. The former expression indicates the gift of church government and administration, the latter the numerous duties comprehended in the office of deacon, viz., the care of the poor and sick. (Concerning ἀντιλαμβάνεσθαι in the signification of "to support, to help," see Acts xx. 35). But the *second* subdivision, in which again the sense of the immediate presence of divine power prevailed, contained the ἰάματα and the ἐνεργήματα δυνάμεων, under which latter expression were included, besides healing the sick, all those in a·special sense miraculous gifts mentioned in Mark xvi. 18, Acts v. 1, sqq., xiii. 6, xxviii. 3, sqq. The apostle in this passage again names the πίστις as Charisma, whereby, as Neander justly remarks, we are not to understand the general foundation of a Christian life, for then we might also speak of a χάρισμα τῆς ἀγάπης, τῆς ἐλπίδος,* but that peculiar operation of what is

---

* The entire want of clearness in Baur's views concerning the nature of the Cha-

divine on man, whereby the energy of the will is increased in no ordinary degree.* (See Matt. xvii. 20; 1 Cor. xiii. 2). The πίστις is consequently here only the more general, out of which the χαρίσματα ἰαμάτων and the ἐνεργήματα δυνάμεων are developed, or, in other words, both this Charismata are φανερώσεις of the wondrous power of faith. In conclusion, it is easy to understand that one individual might enjoy at the same time several gifts, and that the principal apostles especially possessed many Charismata. However, according to their opportunity, sometimes one, sometimes another, predominated with an apostle, thus John had pre-eminently the gift of γνῶσις, Paul that of προφητεία and σοφία.

Vers. 12, 13. But in order to render evident the perfect unity of all these gifts, notwithstanding their internal difference, the apostle in what follows exposes the perfect agreement of all the members constituting the unity of the organismus. (See Rom. xii. 5). Their multitude is no impediment to their unity; on the contrary, the latter may be rather said to be constituted by it. From the context, it might be expected that the holders of

rismatic operation of the Holy Spirit, is especially shown by his seriously considering that Neander (work quoted, 685, note) agreed with him, while precisely the passages quoted from the writings of this theologian argue from my opinions, which are likewise those of the Protestant church. Baur considers these were Charismata of faith, especially love and hope, and that it was only accidental that they are not named. This representation of the matter in question, has doubtless its foundation in Baur's opposition to the miracle as such; therefore the gifts of healing are viewed by him among other Charismata of love, or probably prayer, since Baur considers the prayer pronounced over the sick as the principal thing. That this is a thoroughly inadmissible view, requires no proof. Chap. xiii. clearly shows that love is no Charisma, it is contrasted with all the other gifts; but the whole passage is of such a nature that we must assume Paul was enumerating the Charismata, for which reason they are regularly arrayed according to certain rubrics (vers. 4—6). All these gifts, as extraordinary forms of divine operation, are to be strictly distinguished from the regular forms of the same; the latter always and necessarily belong to every Christian, but the Charismata may altogether be wanting without injury to the Christian character; for although no Christian can positively be without wisdom or knowledge in comparison with the Gentile world, the wisdom or knowledge he has is of a general character, and not a Charisma: in the former sense all Christians profess both, in the latter Charismatic acceptation only some. For this reason alone could Paul say of the Charismata, ᾧ μὲν δίδοται λόγος σοφίας, ἄλλῳ δὲ λόγος γνώσεως (ver. 8). Concerning the difference between γνῶσις as Charisma, and as the general prædicate of every Christian, see the remarks on 1 Cor. xiii. 9—12.

† Theodorete is of this opinion, and says: πίστιν ἐνταῦθα οὐ τὴν κοινὴν ταύτην λέγει, ἀλλ᾽ ἐκείνην, περὶ ἧς μετὰ βραχέα φησί · καὶ ἐὰν ἔχω πᾶσαν τὴν πίστιν, ὥστε ὄρη μεθιστάνειν (xiii. 2).

the various Cnarismata should now be named, in order to point
out their manifold nature; instead of this Paul mentions other
distinctions, Jews, Greeks, servants, free; but probably this is
so far coherent as differences of nation or education may have
had an influence upon the* capacity for receiving this or the
other gift. The Greeks appear to have had a particular susceptibility for the gift of tongues, the Romans for the practical gifts of the church, and the Jews for spiritual gifts. The
unity which these gifts as members form, is, however, styled ὁ
Χριστός, or, ver. 27, σῶμα Χριστοῦ, not only because Christ is
the head of the church, but also because his life and nature pervade it, because he has newly created it, through regeneration,
flesh of his flesh and bone of his bone. (See on Eph. v. 30).
This new creation out of Christ is pronounced in *baptism*, which
in its idea and original appearance was the λοῦτρον παλιγγενε-
σίας itself.   In this all old earthly distinctions were removed, and
mankind were refined to an elevated union through the Spirit.
The reading εἰς ἐν πνεῦμα is very embarrassing to this passage;
Lachmann correctly reads ἐν πνεῦμα.   The εἰς is introduced by
transcribers, who thought the second sentence must be made
parallel with the first, εἰς ἐν σῶμα.   But it is not the contrast
between σῶμα and πνεῦμα which is here the subject; σῶμα signifies in this place only " organic unity," spiritual bodies.   In
order to exalt this conception of the spiritual nature of the
church, the Spirit is described as the element of the new birth,
and the abiding principle of the same in all its members.*   (Concerning the connexion of the ποτίζω with the accusative, see iii.
2).   It is impossible to mistake an allusion in this passage to x.
1, sqq., so that we may say the ἐποτίσθημεν applies to the Communion.   The reading πόμα for πνεῦμα would seem to make this
yet more evident, but must be rejected as a correction on the part
of the transcriber.   The attempt to deduce anything relative to
the nature of the Sacrament from the πνεῦμα is entirely useless.
Rückert has brought forward the aorist ἐποτίσθημεν against the
reference to the Lord's Supper; he considers the holy commu-

---

* The aorist ἐποτίσθημεν may make us rather doubtful as to the correctness of
this acceptation, as the maintenance is not so definite as the new birth.   But, as
Billroth has rightly remarked, Paul considers it so, because he desires to state the
objects which decide the Christian life as entirely of an objective nature.

nion was thenceforward always celebrated, and therefore the present should be employed. But Paul understands the condition of the church, as the body of Christ, perfectly accomplished, and for that reason he has made use of the aorist.

Vers. 14—21. The apostle now expatiates at large upon the image of the limbs, as in the fable of Menenius Agrippa (Liv. ii. 32). As the so-styled faculties of the mind, agents of the intellectual soul, form a whole, supporting, extending, and bearing each other, so likewise in the great spiritual unity of the church all the gifts should support each other, not contend. This representation shows us that in Corinth the possessors overprized some gifts and undervalued others. The fourteenth chapter acquaints us that they particularly exalted the value of the gift of tongues, requiring that it alone should govern, and that it should be exercised by all; thence the turn in ver. 17, εἰ ὅλον τὸ σῶμα ὀφθαλμός, ποῦ ἡ ἀκοή; The power to discern the various gifts is a necessary consequence of the subjection to God's will; he has so ordained it (ver. 18), therefore none can change his decree. (In ver. 15, 16, the ὅτι in ὅτι οὐκ εἰμί χεὶρ, ὀφθαλμός, is not an introduction to the direct subject, but must be taken in the sense of "because." The freedom of the whole body is likewise grounded upon the distinction of its members. The form οὐ παρὰ τοῦτο οὐκ ἔστιν ἐκ τοῦ σώματος has been erroneously considered interrogatory by Griesbach, from which the contrary sense arises. Lachmann has received it correctly without interrogation. The meaning of the words is, he is not for that reason not of the body, i. e. such an explanation does not prove that he is no longer a member of the body, the human will is powerless in opposition to God's will. The two negations destroy one another. See Winer's Gr. p. 466).

Vers. 22—26. The apostle continues the image of the human body, but employing it to another purpose. That is to say, from the general point of view, he distinguishes the several sorts of members; first, such as appearing weak, are nevertheless necessary to the whole organism, then those which are honoured (εὐσχήμονα), but which seeming less honourable (ἀσχήμονα), human vanity seeks to advance by ornament (e. g. ear-rings, bracelets, &c.) But God in his wisdom has so ordained all in the human organism, that the pleasure or pain of a portion affects the con-

dition of the whole.  This assertion has evidently strict reference
to circumstances in Corinth, where such a false and human estimation of the gifts was entertained : the meaner to which God
had lent a lustre, for this very reason (ver. 24), *e. g.*, the gifts
of tongues, were over-valued beyond measure for their brilliant
effects, while they despised important gifts (ver. 22) for their
plainness.  The absurdity of such conduct must have been brought
before the Corinthians in a striking manner by the present representations.

Vers. 27—30.  The application of the comparison now follows.  The church of Christ is one body, filled by his Spirit ;
the individual believers, with their various gifts, are the members,
whose difference was yet to be ascertained, in order that all
should be employed together to the same end.  The two accounts
of the gifts, as we have already taken occasion to observe on ver.
7, do not exactly agree.  The ἀντιλήψεις and κυβερνήσεις in the
first group are wanting in the second, and the διερμηνευειν of
the second are wanting in the first.  The terms which are here employed have already for the most part been explained in the Comm.
on ver. 7, sqq.  I shall therefore only make a few remarks upon the
difference of apostle, prophet, and teacher.  That besides the difference, a *gradation* is also here perceptible, is not only shown by
the terms πρῶτον, δεύτερον, τρίτον,* but also by similar passages
in Rom. xii. 6, sqq.; Ephes. iv. 11, sqq.  In the first passage
the apostles are not mentioned, but then the Abstracta come in
the following order : προφητεία, διακονία, διδασκαλία, παράκλησις, so that the προφητεία stands before the διδασκαλία.  But in
Ephes. iv. 11, the expressions stand thus : ἀπόστολοι, προφῆται,
εὐαγγελισταί, ποιμένες, διδάσκαλοι, the διδάσκαλοι again succeeding the prophets.  According to the explanation given of
verse 7, sqq., the διδάσκαλοι, as possessors of the Charisma of
γνῶσις, ought rather to precede the prophets.  But the 14th
chap. shows that the apostles affixed a very high value to the gift
of προφητεύειν : at first it is true only in relation to the gift
of tongues, but the nature of the apostolic church was such that,
considered in and for itself alone, the προφητεύειν must be of the
greatest importance.  It was the awakening power, necessary

---

* The circumstances and order observed among the teachers of the apostolic
church, are entered upon in the explanation of the pastoral epistles.

to the extension of the infant church, and for that reason always commanded especial respect. The διδάσκαλοι were more adapted for the Church, when improving in faith and knowledge; their office therefore first became significant when the church was consolidated, and its internal advance in science and life began. Concerning the offices not here named, consult on Ephes. iv. 11; and this reminds me, that in that passage the *offices* are not enumerated before the *gifts*.\* In the church the prophet was not a distinct office, but the apostles† were at the same time prophets, although every prophet was not necessarily an apostle; the so-called evangelists were likewise travelling teachers, who preached where as yet no church had arisen. The διδάσκαλοι, however, were properly both διδάσκοντες and κυβερνῶντες, their official appellation was πρεσβύτεροι or ἐπίσκοποι. Concerning this difference, more will be said, when we take occasion to remark on the pastoral epistles. The name of the Charisma of the gift of tongues which occurs here, and likewise xii. 10, γένη γλωσσῶν, is rarely used; see further the observations on 1 Cor. xiv. 10. (In ver. 27, the difficult ἐκ μέρους is changed in some Codd. to ἐκ μέλους: the former is decidedly the correct reading, because a change of μέλους cannot be supposed. Luther translates the ἐκ μέρους distributively, " each according to his part;" but that might be expressed by κατὰ μέρος. It would be more correct to render ἐκ μέρους, " according to a part," *i. e.* no part is the whole, or can be considered as such. —In ver. 28, οὓς μέν κ. τ. λ. has something of an anacoluthon; οὓς δέ should follow, which is wanting from the altered turn of construction, rendered necessary by the πρῶτον, δεύτερον).

Ver. 31. The concluding verse has its commentary in xiv. 1. The χαρίσματα τὰ κρείττονα cannot be, as Billroth supposes, the fruits arising from love, but the higher gifts in contrast to

\* Rothe (von der Kirche, vol. i., p. 256) thinks that the subject here is *by no means* of offices, but that it is evidently assuming too much, for the apostolate was undoubtedly an office, and no gift. But at all events it is certain that nothing can be gathered from this passage or Ephes. iv. 11, 12, concerning the various ecclesiastical offices in the apostolic church, as the subject treated of is the gifts.

† The name apostle indicates here only the twelve, so that we may plainly see from their relation to the other classes of teachers, how the twelve were regarded as possessing an especial, and indeed the highest, rank among all the teachers of the church. The body of the twelve apostles was only calculated for the earliest times in the church, it was not to be continually supplied. We hear of no new apostle being elected on the death of James the elder. (Acts xii. 1).

those only attractive from their brilliancy, especially the προφητεύειν. However, there is certainly a difficulty in this idea. The
principle laid down in what precedes is decidedly that every one
should be contented with the gifts imparted to him. The ζηλοῦτε
appears to negative this, because it presupposes discontent with
what one has. The difficulty is relieved by remembering that in
these spiritual gifts the higher degree could also exercise the
lesser in conjunction; consequently, he who strove to attain the
better gifts, did not despise those he already possessed; he sought
only to advance in spirit, to grow in the new birth. Love towards God would also imply the endeavour to obtain his good
gifts.    But before the apostle lays down how the προφητεύειν
ranks higher than the γλώσσαις λαλεῖν (xiv. 1, sqq.), he draws
the attention of the reader to the nature of love as the power
which first gives an aim and direction to all gifts. As all the
members of the corporeal organism are held together and maintained according to their design by the general vivifying power,
so is love, which, according to its nature, is God itself (1 John iv.
16), the power which confers life and unity to the body of Christ,
nay, the principle of eternity in its temporal appearance.    To
follow after this is, therefore, far more important than to seek
gifts, because without the latter all gifts are nothing.    In conclusion, the ζηλοῦτε does not gainsay the above assertion of Paul,
that the Spirit imparts the gifts as he will (ver. 11), for the striving after which Paul here counsels, is a wrestling in prayer with
God, the bestower of the gifts.    (Καθ' ὑπερβολήν ὁδόν is to combine *viam eminentiorem*, namely, as the seeking after the gifts.
The connexion with the verb as proposed by Billroth is, it appears to me, not advisable, for the ὑπερβολή does not lie in the
indicating, but in the ὁδός: or we must connect it with ἔτι, as
Grotius intimates, in the sense of "yet to excess."    It must, however, be carefully inquired if the expression may be so construed,
for in the New Testament at least it is never so employed.    Καθ'
ὑπερβολήν always *precedes* the substantive, rendering its signification more forcible.

Chap. xiii. 1, 2.    The following triumphal song of pure love:*

---

* Heathenism has not passed beyond the ἔρως, and is unacquainted with the Christian ἀγάπη. In the Old Testament it is only the strict δίκη which rules. *Eros*,
even in the purest noblest form, is the result of a defect, the desire for love which

is doubly beautiful in the mouth of the apostle Paul. It is John the evangelist whose theme is ever of *love*, while Paul may be more regarded as the preacher of *faith*. This paragraph is an evidence of his new nature; in his old man Paul was quite un-acquainted with the force of this love. His speech even changes itself; he exchanges its dialectic form for a simplicity, smoothness, and transparent depth which approaches that of John. The ἀγάπη here described is not simply feeling or perception, but a tendency and direction of the inward personality, of the real self, towards God and his will. The most exalted exhibitions of *natural* love, such as that of the mother towards her infant and the child's love towards its parent, are but weak reflections of the *heavenly* love, which the consciousness of the redemption awakens in the human heart. This lights up in the heart of the apostle a flame of grateful love, unextinguishable even to the last sigh. This love removes the sinful condition of isolation, substituting for it in man unity with God and God with him. The love of God be-comes his, for he lives no more, but Christ lives in him. (Gal. ii. 20). According to this notion of the ἀγάπη it seems incredible that any one could possess such gifts as προφητεία, γνῶσις, πίστις, without their being all in the highest degree of potency (πᾶσαν γνῶσιν, πᾶσαν πίστιν). If we should say that the apostle desired to express something unimaginable, the sense being this, Even supposing such a division of what is inseparable could possibly take place, would man, having all the gifts, without love, be no-thing? But this would not agree with ἐάν, which always refers to an objective possibility. (See Winer's Gr. p. 269). We should rather say, such a separation has in it something unnatural, yet through the ruinous effect of sin in human nature, it may happen that head and heart may so entirely disagree that the divine power may be felt and acknowledged while the inward desire of the heart towards God, and the wish to yield one's-self to him, may have fallen off. This sad, but too true possibility is repre-sented by the apostle in the strongest colours, in order to place the nature of love in its true light, which first imparts to all reli-

the consciousness that we have not what is lovely gives birth to. But the Chris-tian ἀγάπη is the positive outpouring love, God himself dwelling in the believer, so that streams of living water flow from him. (John iv. 14). See concerning Plato's description of the Eros in the Symposion, Fortlage's striking remarks in his Philosophical Meditations. (Heidelberg, 1835).

gious appearances truth and connexion with the highest aims
of mankind. In Matt. vii. 21, sqq., the Redeemer shows that
even evil persons may be in possession of the gifts. Natural
talents or disposition may qualify many for more readily receiving such gifts than others; but if this is unsupported by sincerity of mind, even the gifts afford no security for the salvation
of the possessor. With reference to the form γλώσσαις τῶν ἀνθρώπων καὶ τῶν ἀγγέλων λαλεῖν, Billroth explains it as hyperbolical. But if we reflect that the Jews admitted a language of
angels, that Paul himself in the angelic world (2 Cor. xii. 4) heard
unutterable words, it would be easier to suppose that by the
tongues of angels a higher degree of Charisma is meant, an especial γένος γλωσσῶν,* displaying itself in high ecstatic excitement
and the employment of entirely uncommon and elevated expressions. At all events, we must admit that the expression does not
justify the supposition of an original language. The human
tongues could only be the various languages which prevailed
among men; these must, therefore, as it appears, have been introduced into the Charisma, whether in discourses in foreign languages, as I suppose according to Acts ii., or in the use of glosses
from various languages, as Bleek thinks, and in which opinion Baur
(see work already quoted, p. 695, sqq.), now coincides. But if
Baur attaches so much weight to the article in this passage that
he considers an ideal conception of the γλώσσαις λαλεῖν might
be expressed in it, leading to the mythic idea of one discourse in
various languages, on the contrary the form γλώσσαις λαλεῖν, without the article, indicates only the employment of unusual
expressions in the ecstacy; there is nothing to justify this supposition. The article points out simply *all* human languages, in
contradistinction to the use of this or that one in particular, as
Rückert correctly explains. But Paul particularly intends to express an extreme in the gift of tongues, not in opposition to the
use of a gloss, but to that of a language real, not ideal. Still
less applicable is Weiseler's explanation of this passage. (See
Stud. 1838, Part iii. page 734, note). He considers that γλώσ-
σαι signifies glosses; that to speak with glosses of men means
to interpret them at the same time; but to speak with glosses of
angels means not to interpret them. This supposition, however, is

† The various sorts of γλώσσαις λαλεῖν are more fully entered upon in xiv. 15.

bound up with his whole theory, which will be further adverted to in the Comm. on chapter xiv. At all events, it is undeniable that γλῶσσαι signifies *languages*, and not *tongues*, in the form in question. (The employment of the first person throughout the whole section is only, as may be readily perceived, a form, used in order to give to the whole idea the most comprehensive and general application. Every reader ought so to think of himself as one that could utter the words, and appropriate to himself the idea. In verse 1 the expressions χαλκὸς ἠχῶν, κύμβαλον ἀλαλάζον are highly descriptive. The speaking with tongues exercised vaingloriously might occasion as much disturbance as would proceed from all sorts of sounding instruments. [See the description in chapter xiv., especially in verses 7, sqq., and 23]. This comparison alone speaks in the most decided manner against Weiseler's theory, according to which the gift of tongues declared itself in whispers.—Χαλκός, brass, signifies brazen instruments, such as trumpets and drums. Κύμβαλον stands in 2 Sam. vi. 5 for מְצַלְתַּיִם, a hollow basin, which being struck emitted a loud noise.—In verse 2, Flatt considers the καὶ εἰδῶ τὰ μυστήρια πάντα as indicating wisdom, so that five Charismata were named, but it would be better to view it only as an exposition of the γνῶσις. In conclusion, this passage shows that, in accordance with the apostle's view, the μυστήρια are not things absolutely not to be known, but such as could not be known by the natural powers.—Πίστις is here, as in xii. 9, applied in a special sense, the increased energy of the will which is proved by the addition ὥστε ὄρη μεθιστάνειν. See on this the Comm. on Matt. xvii. 20).

Ver. 3. Labours of love so called, and self-denial of the most difficult kind, if not sincerely flowing from love, are of no avail towards salvation. The οὐδὲν ὠφελοῦμαι depicts the condition of mind in Paul's thought when he mentioned this state. He describes a self-righteous person, who desires to gain renown for himself by his works and self-denyings; but a blessing only accompanies that which springs from pure unselfish love. (Ψωμίζειν, sometimes to give a crumb, here to distribute, to give away in crumbs.* [See Isa. lviii. 14; Ecclesiasticus xv. 3].—Lach-

* This is very strikingly rendered by Meyer by bestowing, *i.e.*, by gently bestowing to distribute everything.

mann has substituted for κανθήσωμαι the reading καυχήσωμαι, and certainly according to the sense it appears to deserve the preference.  But even on account of the difficulty, and the verbal form, since κανθήσωμαι is conjunctive of the future [see Winer's Gr. p. 72], Griesbach, Knapp, and Rückert prefer this reading, and with reason.  The permitting one's-self to be burned is then another expression for the " submitting to the most acute pains.")

Vers. 4—7.  Paul now describes the characteristics of love in a series of fifteen expressions.  The two first indicate its nature in general; then succeeds a course of negative signs, whereby the conduct of the Corinthians is shown to be entirely at issue with real love; and then certain positive characteristics follow, presenting a true picture of the same.  The subject is love in the abstract, not the individual exercising it, because the former never presents itself in a perfectly developed form, even the best can only be supposed to make some approach to its absolute nature.  (Ver. 4. The form χρηστεύεσθαι, περπερεύεσθαι, occurs only in this place in the New Testament.  The latter word especially is seldom used.  It is doubtless derived fron the Latin *perperam sc. agere,* and certainly originally signified " to conduct themselves perversely," the manner of which is to be discovered from the context.  In this place, with φυσιοῦσθαι, it is = ἐπαίρεσθαι, as Hesychius explains it.  Suidas expresses it by προπετεῖν, precipitate, to proceed rashly.  Cicero [ad Attic. i. 11] employs ἐμπερπερεύεσθαι = κολακεύεσθαι.—In verse 5 the ἀσχημονεῖν seems to refer to unbecoming freedom in dress, which the Corinthians were guilty of.  See on xi. 3. sqq.—Λογίζεσθαι τὸ κακόν, חָשַׁב דָּעָה, is our " to cherish resentment," μνησικακεῖν, to think incessantly of the evil that some one has done.—In verse 7 the στέγει bears close affinity to the ὑπομένει, the former also signifying to bear, to suffer.  [See 1 Thess. iii. 1].  It would perhaps be better to accept it in its original signification of " to cover, to conceal," the sin, that is to say, of the brother.—The two phrases πάντα πιστεύει, ἐλπίζει, imply that love bears in itself, from its nature, both hope and faith, but on the other side we cannot necessarily say the same of hope or faith.  For that reason, in verse 13, we find μείζων δὲ τούτων ἡ ἀγάπη).

Ver. 8. A new property in which love displays itself as a καθ'

ὑπερβολὴν ὁδός (xii. 31), is its imperishable nature.   It continues
in all time and eternity, while even the best gifts cease.   The subject of how far the προφητεία and γνῶσις cease, is pursued by the
apostle from verse 9, the gift of tongues is not further mentioned.
But it is evident that it would be difficult to state how these
could cease, when they themselves signify the spiritual origin, the
capacity for communicating the Spirit.   The choice of the expression γλῶσσαι in describing the Charisma evidently shows that Paul
was thinking of the human languages (xiii. 1), i. e., of the various
forms of speech employed among men, which commenced in sin,
and will cease with the same.   These various languages must therefore in some manner have appeared in the γλώσσαις λαλεῖν.
(Ἐκπίπτω = לבּנ, Joshua xxi. 45, xxiii. 14, implies to lose its
significance, to cease, to become powerless.—Concerning καταργεῖν,
see Luke xiii. 7; Rom. iii. 3, 31).

Vers. 9—12.   The assertion that the gifts of προφητεία and
γνῶσις shall cease, requires some further examination, for we might
have supposed, that like the objects to which they refer, they were
imperishable.   Of the difference between these two gifts themselves,
the apostle takes no further notice; as they are both gifts of
knowledge, and the προφητεία only takes the more inspired form,
while the γνῶσις appears in that of reflection, the argumentation
is equally applicable.   The argument itself is this: here on earth
knowledge is only partial (ἐκ μέρους), but when a state of perfectness arrives, in which knowledge also possesses a character of
completeness, the former ceases.   Two comparisons throw light on
the reasoning.   First, (ver. 11), the relation of childhood to manhood
is employed; in the latter, the partial knowledge of the former
ceases, then (verse 12) we have the imperfectly reflected image,
and the direct view face to face; the former corresponding to
the γινώσκειν· ἐκ μέρους, the latter, to the ἐπιγινώσκειν καθὼς καὶ
ἐπεγνώσθην.   Knowledge, therefore, according to the apostle,
ceases, because here on earth it always continues imperfect and
partial; we know διὰ πίστεως, not διὰ εἴδους = πρόσωπον πρὸς
πρώσωπον (2 Cor. v. 7).   Here, it might be said, that love being
also imperfect on earth, we may just as well assume that it will
cease, as that the γνῶσις may.   But the difference is this.   The
love is certainly capable of being enhanced, but the love of
the faithful, even in its imperfectly developed form, is not a

o

divided love, provided it is of the right kind; it is no ἀγάπη ἐκ μέρους, but the perfection of that love is in heaven, and from thence it will descend upon earth (ver. 10), and the form is not specifically different from that here. *But the manner of discerning will be entirely different;* the basis of the inward life of faith will remain the same, in its increased development, but the view will be reserved for the next world. The state here is not precisely the same there. Certainly there is much to be found which appears to contradict this assertion, which renders this passage one of the most difficult in the New Testament. At the same time, if other interpretations are examined, it will appear that believers are in them promised a γνῶσις, which must be more than a simple γινώσκειν ἐκ νέρους. In John xvii. 3, the knowledge of God and Christ is directly called everlasting life, which could not possibly be said of a *partial knowledge.* In 1 John iv. 7, 8, we read, whoever loves, knows God, and whoso loveth not, knows him not. Now, as Paul represents love as unchangeable, we must conclude that it is conditional on a knowledge of God. not ἐκ μέρους. Further, John, in his first Epist. ii. 20—27, ascribes the knowledge of all things to those who have received the Spirit, so that none can teach them; and agreeing with this, we read in 1 Cor. ii. 10, "The Spirit searcheth the deep things of God," and this Spirit God has given to believers, revealing himself to them by the same. In 1 Cor. viii. 3, Paul speaks likewise of a knowledge of God as the true source of real love towards God, and the knowledge of him which here (ver. 12) appears deferred to the future. How is this to be reconciled with the express declaration ἐκ μέρους γινώσκειν in our passage ? The attempt to effect this has failed in two particulars. First, some whose bias of mind made them interested in placing human knowledge at the lowest possible point, maintain from this passage, that the declarations laid down in the New Testament concerning the γνῶσις entitle us to regard it as only an approximate knowledge, and not a thorough real knowledge of its nature. *The everlasting as such* can never be known by man; he can at the utmost only comprehend some of its *workings*, he can only understand the doctrine of God and Christ, not the divine being itself. Others, on the contrary, whose interest it was to advance human knowledge to the utmost, place the chief importance on the former passages, and assert that the Bible enforces the necessity of an absolute knowledge of God. It has been endeavoured by Billroth so to connect these suppositions with the passage before us, that we may say, " This representation is based upon the fact, partly that the knowledge of the individual, as such, can only be of a partially limited nature, and that he only extends it to the more perfect kind in proportion as he presses into the kingdom of God, there yielding up his own individuality; and it is also in a degree founded upon the truth, that this temporal life is not final, but that after the same, the knowledge of the spirit will become more abundant and deep." But these words are evidently concessions forced from Billroth by the power of the text, for, according to his view, perfect knowledge in the individual in this world would be very improperly styled a γινώσκειν ἐκ μέρους, it being central and comprehensive in its character. The truth lies in the mean between these two extremes. The sacred Scriptures make known man's need of a true knowledge of God's nature. Regeneration through Christ and the Spirit imparts to man this *very knowledge*, and by it alone he attains everlasting life. In the death of the natural man, Christ, the source of life itself, is born again, and with him, Christ in us, the believer gains the true ἐπί-γνωσις τ. Θ., which can be no knowing in part, for he knows the whole Christ, with him he knows all (1 John ii. 20), for in Christ is all (Col. ii. 3).

This knowledge, however, although true and real (a γνῶσις ἀληθινή), is nevertheless one which rests upon the general ground of faith, for this life, we are told, is not the time for beholding (2 Cor. v. 7). The veil is removed in the αἰὼν μέλλων, and the believer first beholds that which he has perceived here in faith. The holy Scriptures know nothing of the supposition that the γνῶσις here below does not differ from the εἶδος of the future. But in truth *universal Christian knowledge* cannot be a γινώσκειν ἐκ μέρους : this is said only by the apostle of the *Charisma of the* γνῶσις, which is so far distinguished from universal Christian knowledge that, as mentioned in the remarks on xii. 7, sqq., the former possesses the *implicit* special characteristics, the latter the *explicit*. This implies an advancement, and for that reason this developed form of knowledge is a Charisma, but this advancement necessarily makes apparent the bounds of things human.

What is special can only be known ἐκ μέρους. This gift, like all the others, will consequently end, when the διαιρέσεις πνεύματος cease, and the powers of the Spirit can be imparted in full perfection to mankind. As therefore the blind when his eyes are opened regards the light and the world surrounding him, so man, truly regenerate by the grace of God, beholds Him in all his gloriousness; but as the blind on the first actual view of the world can neither comprehend all the individual circumstances surrounding him, or the optical law which enables him to perceive everything; just as little can the believer understand heavenly things, the object of his present view, in all their special relations: even in the Charisma of knowledge it only amounts to a γινώσκειν ἐκ μέρους. (Ver. 9. Whether the ὅταν ἔλθῃ τὸ τέλειον refers to eternity or the kingdom of God, beginning with Christ's coming, is essentially unimportant, for the latter is available for the arisen and glorified as well as eternity for them; the coverings of this mortal life are shaken off.—In ver. 11 νήπιος and ἀνήρ are placed in opposition, as in xiv. 20, Ephes. iv. 13. The climax λαλεῖν, φρονεῖν, λογίζεσθαι, corresponds to the three gifts of tongues, to the προφητεία and γνῶσις.—In ver. 12 the δι᾽ ἐσόπτρου is to be explained by the mental impression, because it is as if one looked beyond through a glass. The phrase ἐν αἰνίγματι indicates only the nature of the reflection; it is enigmatical, i. e. dark, undecided, general. We must here keep in mind the imperfect mirrors of the ancients. It is from the apostolic representation of seeing the image through the glass, that doubtless Rückert and likewise Schoettgen, Elsner, and others, have explained the δι᾽ ἐσόπτρου to signify a window made of isinglass instead of a looking-glass. — Πρόσωπον πρὸς πρόσωπον is = פָּנִים אֶל פִּים Gen. xxxii. 31; Num. xii. 8.—The form ἐπιγνώσομαι καθὼς καὶ ἐπεγνώσθην means particularly here, I shall as perfectly know, as God knows me. But we must not overlook that the γινώσκειν is always based upon the idea of penetration, as we have already remarked in viii. 3. It corresponds with John's phrase, "He in us, and we in him." [John xvii. 21]. Here God reigns in us, but in the perfected world we shall also be entirely in him, and then first behold him as he is [1 John iii. 2], whilst we here see him only as he is in us).

Ver. 13. Finally, the perishable Charismata, calculated only

for the earthly condition of the church, are represented as the
pillars of all Christian life, and among this love is again declared
the greatest, because (see ver. 7) it contains faith and hope, but
contrariwise these do not comprehend love within themselves, the
ἀγάπη is therefore placed last, so that the sentence has the arrangement of a climax. When the intention to exalt love does
not predominate, Paul places hope last. (See Col. i. 4, 5 ; 1
Thess. i. 3). It will of course be perceived that πίστις is not any
longer here employed in the special sense as a Charisma, but in the
more general sense. It has already been strikingly remarked by
Billroth how the three objects faith, hope, and love, should form the
antithesis with the Charismata, so that the μένει stands opposed
to the ἐκπίπτει (ver. 8). But we are not to suppose with Rückert
that the νυνί refers to time (= ἄρτι as opposed to τότε, ver. 12),
for Paul has certainly proved that love extends beyond time (ver.
8), but much rather accept it as a consecutive particle, so that the
succeeding verse 13 concludes the whole discussion. The only
thing to object to in this supposition is, that faith and hope also
seem to cease, since the former is to behold and the latter to be
perfected. But Billroth correctly remarks that beholding and
perfecting do not so much remove faith and hope as fulfil them,
and entirely authenticate their object in the spiritual world.
Nevertheless they may both be so far concluded in an inferior
degree to love as the *passive* principle predominates in them ;
whilst God himself, the absolute power of love, powerfully and positively reveals himself in love. For this reason, the apostle
has already said in ver. 7, ἡ ἀγάπη πάντα πιστεύει, πάντα ἐλπίζει, in order to signify that love is the root, contents, and fruit
of the whole.

Chap. xiv. 1. After this information respecting the order of
the gifts, the apostle resumes his discourse from the conclusion of
chap. xii., commending love before all things, but representing
the gifts as worthy objects of attainment,* especially the προ-

---

* The expression πνευματικά not only indicates the tongues, but all the spiritual Charismata. But as the gift of tongues had given rise to more evil in Corinth
than all the other gifts, and had drawn down the whole of this remonstrance, Paul
proceeds at once, with especial reference to this gift, and had it principally in mind,
although employing the more general expression. This explains the μᾶλλον,
which must otherwise be considered superlative.—Between διώκειν and ζηλοῦν

φητεία, while the Corinthians had shown themselves more ready to appreciate the gifts of tongues. We must first proceed to examine the nature of this Charisma, which only received brief mention in xii. 7, sqq. In ancient language,* those who were inspired by a deity to utter divine oracles were called μάντις (from μαίνεσθαι, to be placed in a state of inspiration), while those who explained or simplified the often unintelligible speech of the Mantis were styled προφήτης or ὑποφήτης. The γλώσσαις λαλῶν of the present passage, in whom the inspiration was manifested, appear before us under precisely similar circumstances, the διερμηνεύων signifying likewise those who conveyed to others in general and intelligible language the inspired but obscure expressions of the former. It appears from the Old Testament that the μάντις and προφήτης were frequently united in the same person. Although their perception was not so far advanced that they themselves comprehended the full meaning of their oracular enunciations (1 Pet. i. 10, 11), they were nevertheless far from any Montanist senselessness. According to the whole aim of the Old Testament, the prophetic capacity was especially directed to the revelation of the future. Everything in the fundamental institutions of the Old Testament, as well as the inward desire for the better, tends to what was to come. In the New Testament, on the contrary, the other view must be received, it being founded upon the actual enjoyment of the fulfilment of the promises. It is true the mention of the gift, with reference to the future, occurs in Acts xi. 27, and also eminently in the Apocalypse of John, but in no other place, it may rather be said to retire before any other. In the New Testament the προφητεία appears the spiritual gift, which is more particularly the awakening power for the minds of unbelievers. Its *characteristic sign*, therefore, was likewise inspiration, but, together with the knowledge of God which was conferred, existed also a perfect knowledge of the world and of self, which enabled

we must observe this distinction, admitted by Rückert, that the former signifies the personal activity of the will included, the latter the entreaty by prayer.

* See Bardili de notione vocis προφήτης ex Platone, Gott. 1786. The principal passage in Plato is to be found in the Timæus, p. 1074, ed. Ficin. Plato ascribed to the prophets a capacity for judging over the harangues of the μάντις, for which reason the Charisma of διάκρισις πνευμάτων is in a certain degree allied to it. (See on xii. 10). He says, therefore, (see work above quoted), ὅθεν δὴ καὶ τὸ τῶν προφητῶν γένος ἐπὶ τοῖς ἐνθέοις μαντείαις κριτὰς ἐπικαθιστάναι νόμος.

them to speak with the necessary reference to circumstances and existing matters ;* this the γλώσσαις λαλῶν, in whom self-knowledge was destroyed, or at least much obscured, did not possess. On the other side, again, the προφητεία was distinguished from the γνῶσις (see on xii. 7, sqq.), inasmuch as the latter was not so well calculated to call forth faith as to assist its progress when awakened. Paul, therefore, appears in iii. 6 as the possessor of the προφητεία, and the γνῶσις as residing in Apollos. The apostle correctly assigns a lower position to the γλώσσαις λαλεῖν than to the προφητεύειν (and if he seems to rank it before the γνῶσις, it is to be accounted for by the then existing circumstances, which made those gifts which conduced to the extension of the church more important than those which aided the progress of the already believing), for the speaking with tongues might operate very beneficially, but as soon as it came to be over-estimated and exercised too frequently, it would become prejudicial to the peace and order of a community. It was precisely so in Corinth! Many had spoken at the same time, and thereby caused confusion without profit. They had despised other gifts less dazzling in comparison with their gift of tongues, and this with other abuses is now condemned by Paul. We should certainly not err in considering the proceedings in the Corinthian church similar in a degree to the proceedings in a Methodist community, and earlier to the appearances among the Montanists.† Had this course been followed, the church would

---

* Chrysostom correctly affirms this on 1 Cor. xii. 2 : τοῦτο τὸ μάντεως ἴδιον τὸ ἐξεστηκέναι, τὸ σύρεσθαι ὥσπερ μαινόμενον· ὁ δὲ προφήτης οὐχ οὕτως,ἀλλὰ μετὰ διανοίας νηφούσης καὶ σωφρονούσης καταστάσεως καὶ εἰδὼς ἃ φθέγγεται φησὶν ἅπαντα.

† The Montanist Tertullian (De Anima, c. 9) speaks of a woman whose cir- cumstances betray at the least a great affinity with the γλώσσαις λαλεῖν. I quote the passage because I consider it very instructive ; to the understanding of the following relation we must, however, bear in mind that among the strict sects of the Montanists women might not speak in their *assemblies*, the woman therefore imparted her vision to the presbyter Tertullian alone. His words are as follows : *est hodie soror apud nos, revelationum charismata sortita, quas in ecclesia inter dominica solennia per ecstasin in spiritu patitur conversatur cum angelis, ali- quando etiam cum domino, et videt et audit sacramenta* (i.e. ἄῤῥητα ῥήματα, 2 Cor. xii. 4) *et quorundam corda dignoscit et medicinas desiderantibus subministrat. Jam vero prout scripturæ leguntur, aut psalmi canuntur, aut adlocutiones* (παρακλήσεις) *proferuntur, aut petitiones delegantur, ita inde materiæ visionibus subministrantur. Forte nescio quid de anima disserucramus, cum ea soror in spiritu esset. Post trans-*

inevitably have been lost in fanaticism ; the wisdom of the
apostle was therefore directed to control undue individual and
partial feeling as a sure means of restoring the equilibrium of the
church. By taking the representation which follows upon this
ground, all appears evident and free from obscurity. We must
certainly admit, as already observed on Acts ii., that this passage
affords no grounds for ascribing a speech in a foreign language to
the γλώσσαις λαλεῖν. It is only in the relation of the miracle
at Pentecost that we find the account ; but this is so decided
that, if we will not suppose two kinds of gifts of tongues (a supposition negatived by the whole series of facts), or regard, as
does Baur, the whole relation in the Acts of the Apostles as a
mystic transformation of a general form of speech (see Baur's
work already quoted, p. 656, sqq.), we shall be compelled to admit the idea of a foreign tongue, at least at times, with the idea
of the Charisma. This was my opinion in the investigation of
the Acts of the Apostles, and I see not any present reason to
change it. The view that in the γλώσσαις λαλεῖν the use of original language was again introduced is extremely ingenious. I
have already compared it with my own opinions, but as can be
shown, the apostle's account does not justify this acceptation.
According to my own conviction, the following is stated ; it
pleased God to convey in the gift of tongues an *allusion* to the re-
establishing unity of a common medium of speech, exercised in the
harmonizing power of the Spirit. The new hypothesis of Wieseler
concerning the nature of the spiritual gifts is certainly laid down
with much ability (Stud. 1838, Part iii.), but it appears to me to
labour under an unconquerable difficulty. This learned man considers that the γλώσσαις λαλῶν had become quite internal, and
may only have moved the lips, speaking so softly that none were
able to understand him. The sighing of the Spirit (Rom. viii.
26) is with him the γλώσσαις λαλεῖν ! But in such a case every
one must have been his own interpreter, for another perceiving
nothing could have interpreted nothing. In Acts ii. Wieseler

---

*acta solennia, dimissa plebe, quo usu solet nobis renuntiare quæ viderit—nam et dili-
gentissime digeruntur, ut etiam probentur—inter cetera, inquit, ostensa est mihi anima
corporaliter, et spiritus videbatur, sed non inanis et vacuæ qualitatis, imo quæ etiam
teneri repromitteret; tenera et lucida et aërei coloris et forma per omnia humana.*
The condition here described undeniably bears close affinity to somnambulism.

considers it implied that the speaking with tongues took place
before the entrance of the crowd, upon which succeeded the interpretation; this was delivered in various languages, acquired by the
speakers in a natural manner. No proof can, however, be necessary that such a dumb Charisma was not very probably a λαλεῖν, or that Paul could compare it with trumpets and sounding instruments (xiii. 1) when it displayed itself in gentle whispers.
Schulz's idea of its exhibiting itself in loud cries of joy (see this
learned man's work already quoted on the gifts of grace) corresponds far better in this respect to the description given of this
Charisma; the character of lively excitement decidedly belongs to it.

Vers. 2—4. The apostle begins his proof of the assertion that the
gift of the προφητεία stands higher than that of tongues, by showing how the former edifies the church, since the prophet can ever
speak according to the necessities of the community or individual,
while the latter is only an enjoyment, or at the most a means of
advancement to those speaking with the tongues themselves (verse
4, ἑαυτὸν οἰκοδομεῖ), not to others. According to this representation, we cannot consider the γλώσσαις λαλῶν otherwise than as
subdued and overpowered by the operating power of God, so that,
as it were, he converses aloud with God (τῷ Θεῷ λαλεῖ, ver. 2).
This discourse must, however, be unintelligible to others (οὐδεὶς
ἀκούει, verse 2); and not because the speaker introduces into
it a provincial gloss (as Bleek thinks), but as Paul adds πνεύματι (i. e., ecstacy proceeding from the impulse of the Holy
Spirit, not, as Wieseler considers, simply inward inspiration
without outward expression), μυστήρια λαλεῖ. As Paul also
says of himself (2 Cor. xii. 4) that he was caught up into
heaven and heard there ἄῤῥητα ῥήματα, those also speaking
with tongues, received impressions from the upper world which
he uttered, as he received them without reference to established media, and were therefore unintelligible. The οὐδεὶς
ἀκούει evidently contains no allusion to employment of foreign
languages, for this must have implied an acquaintance with them
on the part of those so using them; and to imagine that they were
uttered when no one was present who used the same, is highly
improbable. According to Wieseler (work already quoted, p. 719,
sqq.), the οὐδεὶς ἀκούει bears reference not to the understanding,
but to the hearing; those who spoke with the tongues, though

not altogether without uttering sound, spoke nevertheless so softly
that none could hear them; for this reason every one who exercised the Charisma could only himself interpret it. But if none
could hear the γλώσσαις λαλῶν, the Charisma was as good as un-
uttered, and we need only adduce against such a theory, the arguments which have been advanced by the author himself (p. 719).
If the sounds could be heard, then the word ἀκούειν might be
received in the signification of "understand." According to our
acceptation of the passage, which seems alone to agree with the
words, the reflection might arise, that the appearance of the
Charisma at Pentecost was perfectly of another kind, without referring to the foreign tongues then brought into operation. That
is to say, that upon the occasion mentioned, the apostles did not
appear absorbed in themselves, and conversing only with God,
they spoke to those who hasted to resort to them; these perfectly
understood the apostles, and were greatly astonished that they
heard them utter praises to God in the language of their own
nation. This may appear in some degree a contradiction; it is,
however, easily solved, for Paul here mentions the case of a person possessing only the γλώσσαις λαλεῖν as such, but the apostles
together with the same were in possession of the gift of interpretation, and certainly of prophecy. Thus they might have rule
over the spirit (xiv. 32), and be in possession of knowledge (νοῦς);
they spoke with tongues, and interpreted and prophesied at the
same time. Wieseler likewise correctly comprehends the relation,
with the exception that he too strictly separates the speaking
with tongues and the interpretation, so that according to his
opinion the crowds that flocked to the apostles at Pentecost
only really received the interpretation, and they heard not
the tongues themselves. But as the apostles were also prophets,
both must be considered co-operating with and pervading each
other. (Ver. 2. The singular form γλώσσῃ λαλεῖν occurs
again in vers. 4, 13, 14, 27; ἐν γλώσσῃ is found in ver. 20,
and in ver. 26, γλώσσαν ἔχειν. [The διὰ τῆς γλώσσης of ver. 9
is not here to reckon, for γλῶσσα signifies the tongue as a member of the body]. This use of the singular, as also Schulz and
Wieseler rightly suppose, is immaterial, they stand indifferently
for one another. But Baur (see p. 627, sqq.) attaches importance
to the two forms of expression, and asserts that the singular form

implies "to stammer indistinctly with the tongue," the plural form
"to speak with gloss." But whoever considers with some degree
of attention the remarks upon this chapter which follow, will find
that this distinction exists only in imagination. The two expressions had possibly their origin in the fact that occasionally the use
of one foreign language occurred, and sometimes that of several.
The latter form would then be styled γένη γλωσσῶν.—In ver.
3 the οἰκοδομή is the common form, and παράκλησις and παραμυθία the subordinate divisions, as Billroth, agreeing in this respect with Heidenreich, remarks. In the παράκλησις we may
distinguish the animating form of edification, in the παραμυθία
the comforting. The latter expression does not again occur in
the New Testament.—The ἑαυτὸν οἰκοδομεῖ of ver. 4 does not
imply that he edifies himself through the idea of his converse
with God, but that this elevation to a more lofty and divine element frees him more and more from dependence on the earth and
its possessions, and consequently advances his spiritual life. The
tendency of the γλώσσαις λαλῶν to progress towards the higher
Charisma of the προφητευειν must ever be borne in mind).

Vers. 5, 6. In order, however, to give no occasion for apprehension to those among the Corinthians who attached especial value
to the gift of tongues, or to the supposition that he entirely condemned this Charisma, Paul states that he rejoiced truly over the
operation of the Spirit in this form among them, but that it would
be better if they could prophesy, then those speaking with
tongues could at the same time interpret, and the church thereby
receive edification, for by γλώσσαις λαλεῖν alone it could profit
nothing. This argument is connected with the idea that under
existing circumstances the first object to claim attention was the
extension of the church, bearing the doctrine of the cross to all
lands, and collecting within its limits all who were called. This
was admitted also by those who displayed the gift of tongues,
allowing besides that all personal profit derivable from such a
source must yield to the main consideration. (Billroth correctly
observes that in ver. 5 τις does not require to be added to διερμηνεύῃ, since Paul supposes the union of both these gifts in the
same individual. He who could interpret was able to comprehend what was expressed by others in the ecstacy, and this came
very near the προφητεύων. Nevertheless, a difference then re-

mained, for the γλώσσαις λαλῶν, who had also the gift of interpretation, was excited by strong inward contrarieties. On the
first display a clear sensible explanation followed, which might
truly inform but could not arouse. The addresses of the προφητεύων are, however, to be considered powerful outpourings of a
higher character, which had the rapid effect of lightning, carrying
their hearers away in the stream of inspiration. But when Wieseler (see as above, p. 721) proceeds so far as to say "that there
never had been an interpreter who had not himself previously
spoken in the tongue which he interpreted," that consequently
the gift of the ἑρμηνεύειν was never separated from the γλώσσαις
λαλεῖν, although it did not always present itself in connexion;
such passages as vers. 26—28, in which the gift of prophecy appears perfectly independent, speak evidently to the contrary.
It stood in the same relation to the gift of tongues as the
gift of discerning to that of prophecy. My opinion certainly
is that the two gifts were often united, and that it was the
desire of the apostles that, where possible, this should always
be the case, and the same likewise with the gift of prophecy;
but in reality they often displayed themselves separately, and
from this circumstance arose the abuse; had they been always
connected, no improper use of the gift of tongues could have
occurred. In ver. 6 is to be found the presupposition, as Bleek
and Rückert correctly agree, that the speaking with tongues
was *generally* exercised in Corinth without interpretation.—
*Εἰ* is, contrary to the rule, here connected with the conjunction
[see Winer's Gr. p. 270]. It is, however, to be explained by
the pleonastic fusion of the two terms ἐκτὸς εἰ and μή.—In ver. 6
νυνί is again a consecutive particle. No stress is to be laid upon
the first person [ἔλθω]; it does not say, " even if I came," for
then ἐγώ would have been used.—The four subjects named may
be analysed, as Neander and Billroth have remarked, into two
members standing parallel. The ἀποκάλυψις is the operating
cause of the προφητεία, the γνῶσις of the διδαχή. It would appear natural to mention the forms of the γλώσσαις λαλεῖν, but
to this Charisma more useful gifts are opposed. The ἐὰν μὴ does
not refer to the whole phrase ἐὰν ἔλθω κ. τ. λ., only to the τί
ὑμᾶς ὠφελήσω. Ἐὰν or εἰ μή stand indifferently for each other.
Matt. xii. 4; xxiv. 36; Gal. i. 7, ii. 16).

Vers. 7—9. The necessity for a clear intelligible exposition is proved by Paul by a comparison taken from musical instruments; for it is requisite if the music performed is to be undertood, that the necessary intervals (διαστολή) between the tones should be observed, this alone produces melody. Eichhorn erroneously employs this passage, as we have taken occasion to observe on Acts ii., in order to prove that those who spoke with the tongues only stammered, not pronouncing articulate words. This is evidently not the fact. The single tones of an instrument may individually be regarded as true, but if the scale be not observed these single tones form no melody, they are an ἄδηλος φωνή (ver. 8); so Paul intends to say that the sayings of the γλώσσαις λαλοῦντες are unintelligible, because they want connexion. Just as inconsequently Wieseler (as above, p. 727) views the expression ἄδηλος, μὴ εὔσημος, as descriptive of tones softly uttered, while all must agree that a very loud sound may be as unintelligible as a soft one. (In ver. 7 it might be conjectured that ὅμως or ὁμοίως might be employed for ὅμως, but certainly the more difficult reading is the correct one. It is best explained by Billroth, thus, that its use sanctions the apparently inapplicable comparison of instruments not having life, as if the words were τὰ ἄψυχα, καίπερ ἄψυχα, ὅμως κ. τ. λ. Ὅμως is so employed in Gal. iii. 15. —The passage ix. 26 may be referred to, for an explanation of εἰς ἀέρα λαλεῖν).

Vers. 10—12. Paul draws a second example from the use of speech; every discourse must have a thoroughly regular succession of tones (οὐδὲν ἄφωνον), otherwise it possesses no signification (δύναμιν), and the person who speaks is as one using a foreign language (βάρβαρος). He therefore recommends the Corinthians, zealous for the spiritual gifts, to strive after such as could be understood by the church. It is highly probable that the expression γένη φωνῶν (ver. 10) refers back to the description of the Charisma in xii. 28, γένη γλωσσῶν. Neander makes it relate to the forms of the λαλεῖν, προσεύχεσθαι, ψάλλειν (see remarks on Acts ii. 4—11), and undoubtedly these are understood to be included. It is, however, possible that the name γένη γλωσσῶν refers to the form in which the Charisma appeared, really speaking in foreign tongues, as at the feast of Pentecost, and according to which few or many foreign languages might be brought into use.

(See the remarks on xiii. 1).   (In ver. 10 εἰ τύχοι is striking; for although, as shown in xv. 37, the form might stand for " as it were, for example," it would not apply here.   It would have been better to apply it in this signification to ver. 7 when speaking of instruments of music.   I therefore agree with Billroth, who receives this expression, like the Attic signification of ἴσως, as an ironical modest form of a decided assertion in this sense: " numerous as languages are, they have nevertheless their signification."—Bleek understands οὐδέν, " every rational creature," but it is better to connect its meaning to γένος φωνῶν.   The ἄφωνος is then comprehensive, without clear decided utterance.—In ver. 12 πνεύματα, for which some Codd. incorrectly read πνεύματικά, is employed to express the operation of gifts of the Spirit which are similar. The plural πνεύματα is to be considered substituted for διαιρέσεις πνεύματος, and Billroth, as also more recently Wieseler, erroneously supposes it to refer alone to the gift of tongues which we have already condemned.—I cannot agree with Bleek and Billroth in their acceptation of the ἵνα περισσεύητε: they do not supply the αὐτῶν or ἐν αὐτοῖς, but understand it, " that ye may be abundant, i. e. amply contribute to edification."   But ver. 13 clearly shows that the apostle's meaning was, that they should pray for the adding of other gifts, particularly those of interpretation and prophecy, to the one they possessed.   This seeking to advance is indicated in the ζητεῖτε, ἵνα περισσεύητε [the reading προφητεύητε facilitates the explanation, but from the connexion is rightly supposed a correction], and is grounded upon a general endeavour to possess the Charismata).

Vers. 13, 14.  Upon this foundation, then, the apostle proceeds to exhort those speaking with tongues to pray for the gift of interpretation, in order that their νοῦς may be no longer unfruitful (ἄκαρπος) and without effect.   Throughout this argument the principle must ever be remembered, though not expressly stated, that it is always a subordinate condition of the νοῦς, the faculty of knowledge recorded in men, as regeneration always tends to cultivate this power.   The acceptation of the προσευχέσθω ἵνα διερμηνεύῃ might be thus far objected to, as προσεύχεσθαι appears in another meaning in ver. 14, 15.   This has occasioned Billroth and also Winer previously to explain the passage as signifying that those speaking with tongues prayed, i. e. exercised his gift, with

the design immediately to interpret what he was saying. But
Bleek correctly calls to mind that ἵνα διερμηνεύῃ cannot be otherwise understood than as comprehending the object of the prayer;
and it would likewise be impossible to adopt the erroneous supposition of Usteri that the πνεῦμά μου in verse 14 signifies the
human mind, for the νοῦς is only considered a property of the
human mind. (See my Opusc. Acad. page 156, sqq.) Bleek has
already correctly explained πνεῦμά μου = τὸ πνεῦμα Θεοῦ ἐν
ἐμοί. In the inspired state of those speaking with tongues, it
was not the individual himself which spoke, but the higher power
through him. In conclusion, if Billroth again discovers here an
*identity* of the divine and human mind, we must again repeat
our dissent from his view. The human mind is certainly allied
to the divine, and the eye with which man discerns the beam of
divine light to the divine Spirit; but *identical* it is not. (See
remarks on Rom. viii. 16).

Ver. 15. In order to make his meaning altogether evident,
Paul declares that the gift of tongues may be employed, but the
understanding is to be included likewise. He consequently does
not desire the γλώσσαις λαλεῖν to be dispossessed, but that it
shall become more fruitful for the church and improving for individual living, by a conscientious endeavour to obtain the gift of interpretation, or, better still, that of prophecy. The dative πνεύματι and νοΐ naturally indicate the operating cause of the προσεύχεσθαι and ψάλλειν, the ecstatic inspiration and the active
power of the Spirit in knowledge. The προσεύχεσθαι and ψάλλειν appear to have been a different form in which the γλώσσαις
λαλεῖν displayed itself, according to which the Charisma was uttered
sometimes in the form of prayer, sometimes in a poetic or musical fashion. In verse 26 under the name ψαλμὸν ἔχειν, the poetic
form is treated almost like a peculiar Charisma. Certainly these
various appearances might be employed to elucidate the expression γένη γλωσσῶν (xii. 10, 28), even without taking into consideration the use of various languages. Nevertheless it does
not agree with the original language. But it might not be improbable that the first Christian hymns, such as according to Pliny
(Epist. x. 96) were sung by the Christians in their meetings,
owed their origin to those persons who were endowed with that
form of the gift of tongues called ψαλμὸν ἔχειν. (The τί οὖν

ἐστι corresponds only to the Latin *quid?* or *quid jam?* " what will we then? what is really our meaning?")

Vers. 16—19. Paul again returns to the idea in verse 2, sqq., that the gift of tongues cannot edify others. In its relation to prayer he says the hearer cannot say, Amen (which according to ancient custom was pronounced by the assembly),* for he understands not what is said. (There is no reason for Beza's deduction that the word εὐλογεῖν, for which afterwards εὐχαριστεῖν is used, contains any allusion to the Lord's Supper, for upon no occasion was the Charisma of the gift of tongues exercised in this sacrament).†
The apostle adds for the same reason, that he would rather speak a few words, διὰ τοῦ νοός, *i. e.*, in the manner of προφητεία, than many with tongues, although all these gifts were at his command more than at theirs. This assurance has something striking in it. We might imagine that in proportion as knowledge increased, the faculty for enthusiasm diminished, at least we must psychologically admit this as a rule, the uniform distribution into activity and passiveness displayed in Paul, might rarely be perceptible. We are shown in 2 Cor. xii. that a state of ecstacy was not unknown to him. (In ver. 16, the form ὁ ἀναπληρῶν τὸν τόπον τοῦ ἰδιώτου is difficult; it corresponds to the Hebrew מָקוֹם פּ״ מָלֵא אֵל, *locum alicujus implere.* But wherefore this circumlocution? Why does not Paul write at once ὁ ἰδιώτης? Acts iv. 13 has the expression in the signification of "unlearned," but it is used here, as ver. 24 plainly shows, since the idiot is to be distinguished from the unbeliever, in the signification of laity, as opposed to the officiating priests. In classical speech, ἰδιώτης also formed the opposition to ἄρχων or στρατηγός, the common soldiers were called ἰδιῶται. [See Epictet. c. 23. Xenophon de rep. Lac. x. 4. Polyb. v. 60]. If we consider well the circumstances under which the speaking with tongues took place, it will be evident for what reason Paul *could* not write ὁ ἰδιώτης, but was

---

* See my Mon. Hist. Eccl. Ant., vol. i., p. 101, vol. ii., p. 168, for the passages in the Fathers especially referring to this subject.

† This is also approved by Bleek's observation, that from this passage it may be perceived, that as yet no fixed liturgical prayers were in use. The prayer of those speaking with tongues is by no means to be regarded as essentially belonging to God's service; it came only as an addition to the established service conducted by the presbyter as πάρεργον.

obliged to employ so circuitous a form. It was perfectly possible for any one, a layman, invested with no ecclesiastical office, to have the gift of speaking, and if he exercised this in the church, he was for the moment the leader of the devotions, the liturgy. All the members of the church, even the ministers, deacons, and presbyters, stood for the time to those exercising the gift of tongues in the condition of laymen, *i. e.* the receiving portion of the community. But as they were not really in themselves the laity, Paul employs to represent their position, the expression suitable in the highest degree of ὁ ἀναπληρῶν τὸν τόπον τοῦ ἰδιώτου. Wieseler understood by ἰδιώτης those who were not furnished with the gift of tongues (see as above p. 711, note), but that is not strictly correct. Those also who possessed this gift would be an ἀναπληρῶν τὸν τόπον τοῦ ἰδιώτου, even if he did not exercise it, but another was displaying this power. In conclusion, this passage affords striking proof that the contradistinction of clerus and laity did not arise at a later period from a desire of dominion on the part of the former, but that it was an original and Christian distinction introduced by the apostles themselves into the church. The *names* alone arose at a later period, the *thing* was from the very beginning. More will be said on this subject when the pastoral epistles are brought under consideration.

Vers. 20—22. The apostle then considers the other point (see on ver. 15) the furtherance of the individual spiritual life. He recommends his readers to grow in understanding, and to observe how the gifts stand in relation to each other; they must strive to attain unto the higher gifts. The γλώσσαις λαλεῖν is a gift for children in spirit, prophesy for men. The holy Scriptures, while speaking of the gifts of tongues, immediately intimate its subordinate value; the γλώσσαις λαλεῖν may certainly become a medium to awaken unbelievers, a sign to direct them to the mightier powers present in the church, but to the church itself, the believing, the προφητεία could only bring a true blessing.—This passage is unquestionably one of the most difficult in the section, and it is only after mature consideration that I have been able to decide upon the signification here given. Neander has proffered an entirely different explanation, in which Billroth coincides. Bleek agrees with me in all important points. According to the former interpretation, the ἄπιστος which occurs in this passage

P

(ver. 22) applies not to the unbelievers who may yet believe (*in-fidelis* negative), but to the unbelieving who persevere as such (*infidelis* privative). It is employed in its first signification in ver. 24. Then, laying full stress upon the words of the quotation οὐδ᾽ οὕτως εἰϲακούσονταί μου, and accepting the εἰς σημεῖον in the signification of " as a sign of correction," the whole may be thus understood, " Be ye men in understanding! God himself has plainly intimated by his Word that the tongues shall serve for a punishment to unbelievers; the προφητεία, on the contrary, is appointed for believers." This view appears corroborated by the fact, that, 1st, a reproof may be observed to be retained in the quotation, though that is of little importance, as Paul pays no regard to the connexion of the whole passage; and 2nd, that ver. 23 appears to agree with it, because then the first impression which the Charisma of γλώσσαις λαλεῖν excites upon unbelievers, is that of offence. This, however, does not arise from the Charisma itself, but for the misuse of it; and, besides, the disadvantages of this explanation preponderate in an eminent degree. 1st, The change in the meaning of the word ἄπιστος has something constrained in it, but should it occur, it must necessarily be indicated by something else, if the passage is to be intelligible. 2nd, If the divine intention in the gift of tongues were of this nature, viz., that it should prove a means of punishment for stiff-necked unbelievers, the apostle directly labours to counteract this intention by the directions which he gives. He then must have said, Speak diligently with the tongue, in order that the divine purpose may be fulfilled; as he says at the commencement of the epistle, the doctrine of the cross shall be a σκάνδαλον, therefore the nature of it may not be hidden. 3dly, There exists not a trace that such an effect was produced by the tongues, and the idea of a punishment-Charisma is especially untenable, all the gifts of grace are subservient to blessing! Lastly, the οὐδ᾽ οὕτως εἰϲακούσονταί μου, does not agree with this construction of the words, *i. e.*, "*not once* in that manner of speech do they hear me," for it means that this manner of speaking through foreign tongues had something especially calculated to arouse attention, but that it failed when the heart was dead to holy impressions. Thus all seems to confirm our view; the quotation alone is of limited ap-

plication, as in the other exposition, and even in our notion of the
contents of this passage, prophecy conserved something of a correcting character, for, according to Paul, Israel appeared unbelieving and incapable of receiving the operation of grace.    In the
meantime we must consider, among other circumstances, that
the apostle had made so free an application of the passage Isa.
xxviii. 11, 12, that there would be no difficulty in understanding
a feature of the same in a more limited sense.    Wieseler is perfectly right in supposing (p. 736, sqq.) that the apostle does not
intend to compare the gift of tongues with what is uttered by
Isaiah, but that Paul finds this Charisma itself described in the
prophetic pages.    The independent manner in which in the quotation he construes the Hebrew text into the Greek, shows this.
But this can only be found in the free typical interpretation of
the prophetic words so often employed by Paul.    (In ver. 20 the
παιδία and τέλειοι refer to steps in the inward development.
[See thereon 1 Cor. iii. 12, 13, and 1 John ii. 13, sqq.]    It may
be inquired why φρεσί and not νοΐ is put.    The expression φρε-
νές indicates in scriptural language *understanding*, νοῦς *reason*,
*i. e.*, the capacity for discerning what is eternal.    [See my Opusc.
Acad. p. 159.]    Here it is equivalent to *intellectual* development, employing in a becoming manner the powers flowing from
the higher world, to the salvation of the whole.—In ver. 21 νόμος
stands in an extended sense for the whole Old Testament.  See John
x. 34.—Isa. xxviii. 11, 12 is certainly a rebuke against Israel and
Juda; but Paul does not employ the passage in this signification, as
we have shown already, but so that in the οὐδ᾽ οὕτως εἰςακούσονταί
μου only the inferior efficacy of the Charisma shall be indicated;
speaking with tongues cannot produce understanding, it can only
show the way to it, therefore the more perfect Charisma is to be
the object of attainment.    The quotation, besides, is not only freely
handled as to its purport, but also its form.    The LXX. read διὰ
φαυλισμὸν χειλέων, διὰ γλώσσης ἑτέρας, ὅτι λαλήσουσι τῷ λαῷ
τούτῳ—καὶ οὐκ ἠθέλησαν ἀκούειν.    The manner in which Paul
states the words, reminds us of the appearance of the Charisma,
as it presented itself at the feast of Pentecost, Acts ii. 4, and
brings before us the idea "tongues" but not " gloss."    Paul would
hardly have chosen this expression if he had been unacquainted
with the employment of several languages in this form of Cha-

risma. Wieseler fails egregiously here; he overwhelms the sense
with his hypothesis, instead of allowing the words to modify his
views.—The form ἑτερόγλωσσος is very rare, the word is employed
= βάρβαρος, one who speaks in a foreign language. It has been
erroneously supposed to be here neuter. Paul has therewith
expressed the Hebrew בְּלַעֲגֵי שָׂפָה "by (people's) stammering
lips." It may be doubted whether it should stand masculine or
neuter, but the first appears preferable, so that ἀνθρώποις is to
be supplied. In verse 22 the phrase ἡ προφητεία οὐ τοῖς ἀπίστοις is only apparently a contradiction of vers. 24, 25. It forms
the antithesis only to εἰς σημεῖον. Believers need such no longer,
the source of salvation is already pointed out to them, for which
reason it is called αἱ γλῶσσαι οὐ τοῖς πιστεύουσιν, although the
gift of tongues, viewed with reference to itself, can never be considered an object of indifference to the faithful; on the contrary, it may be said of the προφητεία, that it is not for the
ἄπιστοι, that is to say as σημεῖον, although considered in itself
it may prove advantageous even to them).

Ver. 23. It is necessary, to the correct understanding of this
passage, that the emphasis be laid on πάντες. Paul intends to
say that the speaking with tongues itself, when it takes place in
regular form, cannot offend, but only its exercise by all at the
same time, and in a tumultuous manner. But this form of the
appearance (which was certainly the one it took at the first festival of Pentecost) is not absolutely to be reproved, and the
words οὐκ ἐροῦσιν ὅτι μαίνεσθε express no such censure. As
the persons under consideration are unbelievers, μαίνεσθαι can
only mean "inspired by a God;" without προφήτης the utterance
of a μάντις cannot be understood, for which reason it may be
truly said a degree of blame is to be found in the ὅτι μαίνεσθε, but of an entirely different kind to any hitherto imputed.
The words might namely be thus paraphrased as it were: "If
unbelievers enter in, they would say, we perceive certainly that
ye are inspired by a divinity, but, there being no prophet present, we do not understand what the God says to us." Undeniably a quick excited manner of speaking is signified in the μαίνεσθαι: the expression by no means agrees with Wieseler's supposition that the individuals gifted with the tongues employed
scarcely perceptible sounds and tones, and his justification of the

opinion (see work above quoted, p. 731) is in a high degree forced. At Pentecost the manifestation could hardly be said to take place in gentle whispers; and had the gift of tongues shown itself as Wieseler describes, the term chosen and applied to it would have been γλώσσαις λέγειν, utterance being invariably implied where λαλεῖν is employed. (See on Rom. iii. 19). The addition of ἰδιῶται ἢ ἄπιστοι can only make us hesitate to accept this explanation, for this makes it appear that the laity would not so express themselves, although unbelievers had the power to do so. We might here take refuge in the admission propounded by so many expositors that ἰδιώτης stands here in a very different sense to its meaning in ver. 26, and signifies only "unlearned." But I consider this acceptation, by reason of the ἢ, perfectly unsupported both here and in ver. 24; the question is not of learning, for any reference to foreign languages or gloss is entirely relinquished. What connexion would be afforded by "unbelievers or unlearned!" But I would by no means restrict the application of the term idiots to those who themselves possessed no Charisma, but include those laymen who were likewise beginners in a Christian course, as yet unacquainted with the riches of its manifestation, and who at a later period would have been called Catechumens. What follows agrees best with this.

Vers. 24, 25. If all prophesy, no such ill consequences follow, for something is communicated which is universally intelligible, and by adapting the discourse to special circumstances the most important moral consequences might ensue. This description is taken from the life. The Gentiles might frequently, from simple curiosity or an undefined feeling of longing, resort to the Christian assemblies. The inspired language they then heard suddenly made them acquainted with their inward necessities, their sinfulness, and the necessity for redemption; and, overwhelmed as it were by the power of the Spirit, they sank down, confessing that of a truth God was not only among the Christians, but present *in them*. This was beheld at the first Pentecost, when the apostles (Acts ii.) revealed the γλώσσαις λαλεῖν, and likewise the προφητεύειν. From this relation we may plainly observe that the προφητεύειν bore the same reference to the διάκρισις πνευμάτων as interpretation to the gift of tongues; both were generally united. For the knowledge of the secrets of the heart is in itself no manifestation of the προφητεύειν, but only the discerning of spirits bound up with it. (In John xvi. 8 the ἐλέγχειν of the Spirit is especially brought to view.—Concerning the indwelling of God in man, see the observations on John xiv. 23; and for κρυπτά see on iv. 5).

Vers. 26—28. The special commands and directions arising out of the preceding observations then follow. Whoever is in possession of a gift may bring it into exercise in the assembly, but only so as to conduce to the advantage of all. Two or three alone were therefore to speak with the tongues. This must likewise be in succession, and so that an interpreter made their meaning available for the meeting. If none were present possessing this gift, then the γλώσσαις λαλῶν was to converse inwardly with God, without making known aloud the subject of his contemplations. In this verse everything is clear, and we have only to remark that the apostle acknowledged the capability of restraining the impulse of the Spirit even in those who only possessed the gift of tongues, and in whom the operation of the Spirit was least developed, so that they could of themselves keep silence. They therefore do not appear as perfectly involuntary instruments. (In ver. 26 the ψαλμόν, διδαχήν κ. τ. λ. ἔχειν does not simply mean to be in possession of one or other Charisma, but also to foresee that the Charisma will even now display itself. We must doubtless suppose that those who would speak announced it to the presbyters of the assembly, and that these secured the necessary observance of precedence in the speakers. The forms ψαλμὸν, γλῶσσαν ἔχειν, do not therefore here imply to possess the gift of poesy or of tongues, but to be aware that, in consequence of being possessed of the gift, they had to deliver a song of praise, to give utterance to the tongues. In the series mentioned, ἀποκάλυψιν ἔχειν signifies the προφητεία (see on ver. 6), consequently four gifts are enumerated, and the ψαλμὸν ἔχειν indicates a special form of the gift of tongues. Again, we must observe that no decided order appears in the mention of the gifts.—It has been already observed on ver. 15, that it is not improbable something of a musical character was connected with the poetic form of the Charisma; it may be conjectured that those speaking with tongues, delivered their psalms with singing, or perhaps as recitative; and therefore, as the Charisma of γνῶσις (see on xii. 8) was represented in the regulated course of the Christian life, by means of theology, so the Charisma of speaking with tongues was made known in Christian poetic art, and church singing.—The ἕκαστος does not exactly signify that no Christian was without a Charisma, but among those having a Charisma, some have one, some another.—In ver. 27, κατὰ δύο is to be understood "certainly two," i. e. in every assembly two, and that these should speak successively, i. e. ἀνὰ μέρος, and not at the same time. By this means the impression of the μαίνεσθαι of the entire body was avoided, and the beneficial operation remained which was subservient to the γλώσσαις λαλεῖν εἰς σημεῖον τοῖς ἀπίστοις. The εἷς διερμηνευέτω in ver. 27 is not favourable to Wieseler's hypothesis. He thus explains the words [see work already quoted, p. 720], "Let one, not several, at a time, interpret." But according to his own theory, this is a perfectly superfluous direction; by his own showing, none could interpret save the speaker having the gift of tongues. In order to parry this meaning, he therefore interprets these words at pleasure, one should interpret *after* the other, as one after the other speaks with the tongues. But the words evidently convey the precept, that they should not speak with the tongues, unless *one* at least was in the assembly who could interpret.—In ver. 28, the ἑαυτῷ λαλεῖν καὶ Θεῷ corresponds with the ἑαυτὸν οἰκοδομεῖν of ver. 4).

Vers. 29—31. It was precisely the same with the gift of προφητεία : here also they were not all to speak together, but in order, that every one might contribute whatever was in his power to the general edification. It will be naturally understood that interpretation was not necessary to the prophets; instead of this, it was called οἱ ἄλλοι διακρινέτωσαν. It has been already observed in the general remarks upon ver. 1, that the gift of διάκρισις πνευμάτων gave occasion to perceive that the prophets were not absolutely a pure medium of the divine Spirit; their old and not yet sanctified nature gave expression to much that had to be distinguished (1 John iv. 1). It was only in the apostles that the potency of the Spirit revealed itself with a power so mighty and manifold, that error retreated before them, while in themselves the one gift immediately supplied another, so that their revelations were subjected to no further διάκρισις. We may very probably infer that with those who exercised the gift of tongues, the calm and clear-sighted interpreter undertook also the διάκρισις. (In ver. 29 the article in οἱ ἄλλοι admits a reference to other not exactly active prophets, but not to all persons who were present. Ver. 37 decidedly confirms this supposition).

Vers. 32, 33. To prove immediately the practicability of these directions, the apostle concludes by laying down the principle, that according to God's will and command, the spirits of the prophets are subject to the prophets, *i. e.* the prophets should not allow themselves to be impelled as if free from the restraints of the Spirit (φέρεσθαι), but should rather conduct with regularity, and in perfect consciousness, the higher powers existing in them (ἄγεσθαι). (See thereon the remarks on Rom. viii. 14). This is founded upon the lawfulness resting in the divine Being (εἰρήνη = τάξις, ver. 40), which excludes all disorder (ἀκαταστασία), and therefore could not admit anything of like nature in the exercise of the gifts. This important principle places an effectual bar to all enthusiasm and every fanatical attempt, and especially checks the attributing any undue importance to somnambulism or other ecstatic condition which would be induced by the absence of self-consciousness. All fanatics have ever asserted that the Spirit impels them, and has commanded this or that. According to Paul's representation, the Spirit (presupposing that it is holy) shall not only yield to an examination of his claims, but the prophet who is filled with the Spirit *shall also not yield himself implicitly to the higher power, but he himself shall direct it.* But we may ask, according to this principle, is not the divine rendered subordinate to the human? This is only apparently the case, for that which in the prophet rules over the Spirit is in effect only the divine in another form of revelation. In the highest powers the Spirit always reveals itself as individual knowledge; the condition in which this is subdued or appears disturbed must be gradually overpowered and elevated into a clear perception. That the mighty powers generated by the Gospel should at the commencement intoxicate, as it were, the infant church, and excite a crowd of beatific emotions, was more than natural. It was especially thus with the susceptible Corinthians; they were overpowered by the bounty and goodness of God's house, and rejoiced as though they were already in the kingdom of God. But this marriage of love, this happy commencement of Christ's operation in mankind, could and dared not continue; the prophets must be rulers over their spirits, the great struggle after the knowledge of God must arise which was to pervade the church, and is still maintained in it; in order that the Lord may not only be in us, but we also in him.

Vers. 34, 35. The deviation of the Corinthians from the right exercise of the Charismata was further shown in permitting women who were possessed of the gifts (for such alone can be intended) to speak in public. This is reproved by the apostle, appealing likewise to the word of God (Gen. iii. 16). Women were to be submissive to their husbands in all things, and to learn, but not to teach. To what purpose, we may then ask, were they endowed by God with the gifts, if they were prohibited the exercise of them? We read in Acts xxi. 9 that the four daughters of Philip had the gift of προφητεία. To this we answer, they might apply these gifts to their own private edification (xiv. 4), or employ them in the same manner to the advantage of others, but not in public assemblies. (In ver. 34 λαλεῖν is to teach, to instruct. See John vii. 46, xii. 48; Heb. i. 1.— The ἐπιτέτραπται bears reference to ecclesiastical statutes. See xi. 16.—Lachmann has given the preference to the readings ἐπιτρέπεται and ὑποτασσέσθωσαν, which I should also recommend, did it not appear improbable that the more difficult and usual form had arisen out of the more easy).

Vers. 36, 37. The great stress which the apostle lays on this precise point leads us to suppose that the Corinthians had proved themselves especially stubborn in this particular. Probably some women had possessed the gift of tongues in an eminent degree, and their exercise of this power had been the source of much joy. So much the more Paul feels called upon to remind them, that they (the Corinthians) receiving the Word of God through the agency of teachers, must conduct themselves in all things agreeably to the general custom of the church and (what was certainly in his mind, if not uttered) his apostolic commands. Those likewise who knew themselves to be possessors of spiritual gifts were especially called upon for obedience in this particular, as his admonition regarded not his γνώμη, but a decided commandment of the Lord. (See on this the Comm. on vii. 1). He who chose to remain ignorant of such a command, thereby perilled his salvation —Billroth has justly observed, that this was said with reference to the observance of the last point, that women were not to teach publicly. Paul had certainly no communication from the Lord regarding the other declarations concerning the employment of the Charismata. For this reason the reading received by Lachmann ὅτι τοῦ κυρίου ἐστιν ἐντολή is preferable. The plural has been substituted by those transcribers who applied the principle in the text to the whole contents of the chap. xiv. (Concerning καταντάω see xi. 11.—If πνευματικὸς is here distinct from προφήτης, the former expression decidedly indicates not only the γλώσσαις λαλῶν (as Baur, p. 644, considers), but all forms of the Charismata, the signification of the words being, "If any possess the gift of prophecy, or any other gift of the Spirit." The possession of any spiritual gift supposes in the possessor a certain faculty for discerning the presence and operation of the Spirit in others.—᾿Επιγινώσκειν has here the additional signification "to acknowledge," which form of expression has something of indulgence, Paul intimating by it that the minds of the Corinthians would not wilfully strive against God).

Vers. 39, 40. With a retrospective glance at xiv. 1. xii. 31, the apostle now concludes his copious dissertation by again urging to diligent prayer (for only so can the ζηλοῦν exhibit itself together with the gifts of grace), for the gift of προφητεία: he permits alone the speaking with tongues, and commands, under all circumstances, the observance of decency (antithesis of the αἰσχρόν, that women speak in the assembly, ver. 35) and order (in opposition to the irregular speaking all at once, ver. 27, sqq.) The reading in ver. 39 accepted by Lachmann καὶ τὸ λαλεῖν μὴ κωλύετε γλώσσαις or ἐν γλώσσαις, can only be considered an error of transcription in the Codd. In no single passage is γλώσσαις separated from λαλεῖν, but ἐν γλώσσαις λαλεῖν never occurs as the name of the Charisma [which would support Bleek's hypothesis]; for in ver. 19 ἐν γλώσσῃ is to be understood ἐν χαρίσματι τῶν γλωσσῶν.—Baur (p. 640) concludes from the μὴ κωλύετε, that there were persons in Corinth who desired the suppression of the gift of tongues, in consequence of the abuses that it produced. But this supposition is not sufficiently grounded; it appears more likely that Paul added the conclusion in this form, in order to prevent future misunderstanding of his opinions, or the idea that he would altogether banish the gift of tongues).

( 235 )

## IV.

## PART FOURTH.

(xv. 1—xvi. 24).

§ 12. THE RESURRECTION OF THE BODY.*

(xv. 1—58).

This likewise very important section contains first (ver. 1—11) the information, that the doctrine of Christ's resurrection, which, as an historical fact, is perfectly ascertained, is a most essential part of the system of Christian teaching. The importance of this dogma of the resurrection for Christians especially is there averred (vers. 12—24), and it is shown that our belief of our own resurrection resting on that of Christ, any doubt of the one must affect our faith in the other, as a natural consequence. Such sceptics were to be found even in Corinth (ver. 12), and the apostle warns others against their corruptness in the most emphatic manner (vers. 33, 34). Paul then illustrates the life after the resurrection (vers. 35—58) and the glorification of the material, by showing its anology to a growing grain of corn, proving

* The doctrine of the resurrection of the body has recently been the subject of much exegetic comment, in consequence of the investigation instituted concerning the eschatology and the doctrine of immortality in particular. The principal works besides Krabbe's well-known work on the subject, which may be compared with Man's Criticism (in the joint theological work by Pelt. pt. 2), Weigel's Abhandlung ueber die urchristliche Unsterblichkeitslehre (Stud. 1836, pt. 3, 4), Lange ueber die Auferstehung des Fleisches (idem 1836, pt. 3), and Eine Kritik der Schriften von Weisse, Goeschel, Fichte, by Jul. Mueller, which were called forth by Richter's writing "ueber die letzten Dinge" (idem 1835, pt. 3). The purely speculative writings, such as those recently examined by Mueller and others, are not noticed.

that in the resurrection the perishable body became imperishable. This corporeal change would be experienced by all, even those who were living at the Lord's second coming; and death would be finally conquered, and everlasting life brought to light by this glorious transformation. Vers. 1, 2. The first paragraph of this chapter shows us that not only the *doctrine* of the resurrection of the dead (mentioned in Heb. vi. 2 as one of the principles of Christianity), but that also the *fact* of Jesus' resurrection was considered most important in the course of instruction adopted in Christian antiquity. As Christianity is essentially based upon history, and that not only upon human but sacred history, on acts of the living God, which as such are the fruition of the most elevated ideas, so it is expressly founded upon the fact of the resurrection as the great keystone of our Lord's mission, of which the ascension was the necessary consequence. (See Comm. on Matt. xxviii. 1; Acts i. 11). The apostles, therefore, first appear, not as teachers, but *witnesses;* they deliver what they have experienced, or, like Paul, received. The παραλαμβάνειν is here employed by Paul himself as in xi. 23, not as signifying a receiving from men, but from the Lord himself. The apostle recommends his readers to hold fast that which he has delivered to them, and not to allow themselves to err with respect to it. (In ver. 1, the γνωρίζω has from the connexion the signification of " to call back to remembrance." The εὐαγγέλιον refers here particularly, as ver. 3, sqq. shows, to the joyful message of the resurrection of the crucified Saviour by which his great work was sealed.—Ἑστήκατε has as usual a present meaning. The apostle indulgently considers the Corinthians as yet maintaining the faith unshaken, though threatened with danger; the εἰ κατέχετε [ver. 2] alludes to this hazard of their salvation. The construction of the whole sentence is to be explained by attraction, so that the words must regularly run thus: γνωρίζω ὑμῖν τίνι λόγῳ [in which form of the doctrine] τὸ εὐαγγέλιον εὐηγγελισάμην.—The concluding phrase ἐκτὸς εἰ μή κ. τ. λ. refers only to the σώζεσθε. [See concerning the pleonastic form ἐκτὸς εἰ μή on xiv. 5]. It will of course be supposed that the κατέχειν is not to be understood only as preserving in the memory, but holding fast in a living faith). Vers. 3, 4. This passage, in connexion with Eph. iv. 4—6,

Heb. vi. 1, sqq., 1 John iv. 2, constitutes the symbol of the apostolic church. In the places quoted, the various doctrines relative to the person of the Redeemer are assumed to be understood, but here they are stated, and other doctrines are not especially mentioned. The πρῶτα, among which he names the following subjects, are the θεμέλια or στοιχεῖα quoted in Heb. vi. 1, sqq. The expression πρῶτα does not consequently signify the *origin*, but the *important* points of the Christian doctrine. Death, burial, and resurrection, are the objects which, in accordance with his intention, are held up to view by Paul; burial is alone to be considered as the decided perfecting of death; this is not, therefore, expressly said to be confirmed by the Scriptures, although Isa. iii. 9 might be alleged in confirmation. Death and resurrection are, on the contrary, necessarily correlative. Resurrection presupposes death, death without resurrection following could not warrant salvation, or any death be εἰς ἄφεσιν τῶν ἁμαρτιῶν. (By the addition κατὰ τὰς γραφάς, Paul intends to represent the preaching of Christ's death and resurrection as the fulfilment of all the prophecies of the Old Testament, so that the latter were renounced if the resurrection were denied. With reference to the death, he evidently had in mind such passages as Ps. xxii., Isa. liii., and it is possible that, with reference to the resurrection, typical prophecy, such as the history of Jonah [see on Matt. xii. 40, vi. 4], to which also Ps. xvi. 10, and Hosea vi. 1, 2, might be added, presented themselves).

Vers. 5—8. Paul now mentions various relative occurrences, in order to strengthen the reality of the fact. These have been individually considered and commented upon in the account of the resurrection given in Matt. xxviii. 1, sqq., as well as the statement which so decidedly speaks against any mythic view of the resurrection, that more than five hundred brethren were present, of whom many were still living. Evangelical history makes us no further acquainted with the circumstances under which James saw the Lord. Without doubt it is the brother of our Lord who is mentioned, subsequently Bishop of Jerusalem, and who, according to John vii. 5, could not believe in Jesus. This reappearance might have convinced him of Christ's divinity, for we find him ever after (see on Acts i. 14) in the company of the apostles. Concerning the reason that Paul includes the appearance vouch-

safed to himself with the before mentioned, see in Comm. volume
ii. on Acts i. 9—11.—In ver. 8, ἔκτρωμα = נֵפֶל, is unripe fruit,
untimely birth of ἐκτιτρώσκειν,* and the context shows upon
what ground the apostle so styles himself).

Vers. 9, 10. The remembrance that the church is to be extended
by his labours accompanies the apostle throughout his life.  He
expresses himself here as in Ephes. iii. 8 ; 1 Tim. i. 15.  The
greatness of the divine mercy, however, kept pace with the greatness of his sins; the enemy of Jesus was called to be his apostle,
and he, obeying the summons with faith, laboured more abundantly
than they all, or rather grace working through him.  These remarks were necessary in this place to confute the antagonists of
his authority.  It has been already observed (Exposition of Epist.
Rom. p. 7) that the extended activity of Paul was in a great measure due to the fact that the Jews were not included in his mission.  The Twelve being especially appointed for them, their field
of labour was more circumscribed.  That the words οὐκ ἐγὼ δὲ,
ἀλλ᾽ ἡ χάρις τοῦ Θεοῦ, do not abrogate liberty needs no proof.
Augustine rather is perfectly right, when he remarks on this passage, *Nec gratia Dei sola, nec ipse solus, sed gratia cum illo!*

Ver. 11. Paul now proceeds to state expressly the perfect harmony subsisting between himself and the other apostles, in order
to prevent any occasion for supposing that in this respect there
existed a difference of doctrine between them; this makes the ir-
regularities of false teachers the more apparent, and we may besides conclude with certainty from this slight allusion, that the
opposition offered to Paul and his authority by parties in Corinth
had not assumed so decided a form when the first epistle was
written as when the second was sent, in which the apostle (chap.
xi. 12) expressed himself far more strongly.

Ver. 12. The errors of these persons are thus expressed: λέγουσί
τινες ἐν ὑμῖν, ὅτι ἀνάστασις νεκρῶν οὐκ ἔστιν. The τινὲς ἐν
ὑμῖν does not justify the acceptation of foreigners, who had only
for some time resided in Corinth; it signifies members of the
church.  But the words ὅτι ἀνάστασις νεκρῶν οὐκ ἔστιν cannot

---

* Fritzsche, in his Diss. in Epist. ii. ad Corinth. p. 60, note, has well proved
that Schulthess is mistaken in supposing that the ἔκτρωμα should be translated
" posthumous, born in old age."

possibly mean that Jesus is not risen from the dead, for ἐκ νεκρῶν would then be employed, but that the general resurrection looked for, will not take place.    In the Introduction to the Epistle to the Corinthians (§ 1) it has been already observed that we may not regard those Epicureans, nor those formerly Sadducees, as promulgators of this view, for neither of these sects exercised a direct influence on the church.    Billroth likewise remarks very appositely that verse 32 opposes this idea, for it states that the very defenders of the view themselves abhorred such a principle φάγωμεν καὶ πίωμεν κ. τ. λ.    It would, therefore, certainly be more correct to suppose it was the *Christianer* who tolerated this opinion.    (See Introduction to this Epistle, § 1).    These, imbued with a Gnostic, spiritual bias, might easily take offence at the resurrection of the body, in which a gross materialism appeared to them to exist.    It is possible that, like Hymenæus and Philetus, they understood the ἀνάστασις spiritually.    Of them it is said, 2 Tim. ii. 18, λέγοντες τὴν ἀνάστασιν ἤδη γεγονέναι, which without doubt signifies that they regarded the spiritual quickening of the world, effected through Christ, as the promised resurrection.    Only we might hesitate, and ask how, with such principles, these heretics understood Christ's resurrection?    The whole discussion shows that they did not deny this, for Paul's argument is always this: if there is no resurrection of the dead, then cannot Christ have arisen.    This conclusion is only intelligible when "which ye acknowledge and would also not have denied" is supplied.    We must therefore unhesitatingly admit that the false teachers had not yet developed their views as a perfect system; they rather tended towards a doketic conception of the whole life of Jesus, as displayed in their principles at a later period.    But if they had early and decidedly uttered such opinions, Paul would immediately have resolutely opposed them and required their excommunication. Billroth has expressed himself in a very remarkable manner upon this passage.    He asserts that the same apprehensions prevailed in Corinth which had arisen in Thessalonica (1 Thess. iv. 15, sqq.)    These believers feared that the faithful who died before the coming of Christ would have no portion in the kingdom of God, and the learned man quoted, thinks that individuals in Corinth entertained the same opinion.    But between the position of the Thessalonians and these Christians there existed a very important difference; for the former, who were scarcely converted, and had only enjoyed for the space of a few weeks the apostolic instruction, were in uncertainty concerning the course of events in the establishing of God's kingdom. They did not hesitate at the dogma of the resurrection, but doubted if their dead were already risen to the kingdom of God; in a word, the difference between the first and second resurrection was unknown to them. But the Corinthian Christians, as well as the two individuals named, Hymenæus and Philetus, *doubted the doctrine of the resurrection itself*. They were well acquainted with it, but held it to be a Jewish-materialist opinion, and believed in a pure continuing of the spirit without material covering, the employment of which in relation to the spirit appeared to them possibly as pollution. If Billroth's supposition were correct, Paul would have expressed his idea very unsuitably, for the main point of the whole dissertation ought to have been the remark only incidentally mentioned by Paul, that the dead arise, but the living shall be changed (vers. 51, 52), whilst the argument in favour of the resurrection entirely appropriates the first place. —If, in conclusion, Mueller (Stud. 1835, part iii., p. 748, note) and Weizel (idem. 1836, part iv., p. 909) imagine that in the passages quoted from our chapter, they may infer that no difference is made in the New Testament between ἀνάστασις νεκρῶν and ἐκ νεκρῶν, they are clearly mistaken, for when ἀνάστασις νεκρῶν occurs (vers. 13, 21, 42) it relates generally to awakening from death. The expression is consequently entirely according to my definition; but where the special reference is to Christ (ver. 12) ἐκ νεκρῶν is correctly applied.

Vers. 13, 14. Paul then draws the most important deductions from the conclusion that, if there be no resurrection, Christ cannot be risen. These affect first the apostles, for then their preaching could be nothing and their faith even vain. It is evident that this argument only applies if the ἀνάστασις is understood as transfiguration of the corporeal, and therefore an overcoming of death, as already laid down on Matt. xxviii. 1. Had the apostle only thought of a reanimation of the body or substantial change in it, Jesus might be reanimated without proving anything for a general resurrection, even as Lazarus was reanimated in an unusual manner, but only subsequently to die again. If on the contrary the ἀνάστασις is understood as a glorifying of the material, the restoration of a σῶμα πνευματικόν, and it should be asserted to be absolutely impossible; so naturally the resurrection of Jesus himself is denied, or can only be maintained by an inconsequent application of the principle. Billroth is, therefore, perfectly right when he draws attention to the necessity of urging the *conformity* of Christ's *substance* with man's; otherwise it might be said, Christ can have an advantage beyond that of all other men; he may have arisen as a distinguishing sign, it does not follow that others also must rise again. But his resurrection concerning even the true corporeal body, it is impossible that this should be glorified and yet unchanged. (I prefer the reading πίστις ἡμῶν to the more usual ὑμῶν. The latter might easily have been adopted here from verse 17. The ἡμῶν throws especial light on the context, showing us that, after amply dilating on the evil consequences to the apostles arising from such a doctrine, Paul proceeds to state its influence on the whole church. See on verse 17, 18).

Ver. 15. A condition is now supposed highly derogatory to the apostles, the mention of which is again introduced with δὲ καί. The apostles would be false witnesses, having testified of a fact, not willed by God, that it was his deed, if the assertion of the antagonists were well grounded. The idea is carried out in three positions. First, it states that the preaching of the apostles, drawing its power chiefly from the announcement of the resurrection, would be without effect, and their labour consequently vain. Next, their personal belief would be void, if Christ were not arisen. Lastly, they would be false witnesses, sinners, if they testified to a fact which could not take place. We may observe how the reading πίστις ὑμῶν (verse 14) interrupts the connexion. (The expression ψευδομάρτυρες τοῦ Θεοῦ is best explained with Grotius by " witnesses who misemploy the name of God as testimony;" so that the κατὰ τοῦ Θεοῦ which follows is exegetical. Billroth, on the contrary, considers the genitive as gen. subj. " witnesses of God, who, however, are false witnesses;" but this interpretation appears to me to possess a degree of severity.—The εἴπερ ἄρα, " if it were otherwise, as ye assert," argues *e concessis*. When it is affirmed [see Winer's Gr. p. 416, Billroth also agreeing] that ἄρα is employed in preference in

Q

stating the demonstration arising from heterogeneous assertions, I can by no means coincide.  In this place ἄρα is certainly not a conclusive particle, but an expression of astonishment, which is the original signification of the word [see Hartung's Partikel-lehre, volume i. p. 422], so that the passage is to be understood, " if it were otherwise, as ye wrongly suppose," &c.)

Vers. 16—18.  Paul then passes to what is of general application, and proves to his readers, that if there is no resurrection their own faith is as nothing, for neither they nor those believers already dead could have forgiveness of sins.  (Ἀπο-λέσθαι = ἐν ἀπωλείᾳ εἶναι stands parallel with the ἐν ἁπαρτίαις εἶναι).  As the forgiveness of sins appears closely linked to the resurrection, and not to the death of Christ, it clearly establishes the fact that both are necessary correlatives; the resurrection corresponds with death, vanquishing all by the resurrection, and the death resembles the resurrection, inasmuch as by it death is annulled.  (See remarks on Rom. v. 25).

Vers. 19, 20.  If, therefore, there were no resurrection, and consequently no kingdom of God, no restoration of Paradise, the Christians sacrificing everything in this life, in order to gain all in the next, were certainly most worthy of compassion.  But Christ being security for our resurrection, the first-fruits only of those who slept, the resurrection commenced with him.  Billroth justly remarks that ἀπαρχὴ τῶν κεκοιμημένων is not to be supposed simple apposition to Christ, but as the prædicate of the whole sentence: Christ arises as first-fruits, i. e. in order to be the first-fruits.  This idea is striking, for it seems as if the apostle might be answered: if the body is not raised, the spirit of the men may yet continue to exist; and to this it is indifferent whether the life of the man has been one of stern self-denial, or self-indulgence.  But the apostle by no means recognises the possibility of continuing to exist as a pure spirit without bodily organs; the *doctrine* of the immortality of the soul is as unknown to the entire Bible, as the name; and certainly truly, because a *personal perception* in created beings is necessarily counteracted by the limits of corporeality.*  The modern doctrine of immortality is not materially different from the supposition,

---

* See Usteri's remarks in the Paul. Lehrbegr. p. 365, and the passage there quoted from Athenagoras de Resurrect. c. 25.

that the soul flows back, like a drop in the great sea of universal
life. The circumstance that, even according to the Bible view,
the soul must be considered self-subsisting in the interval between
death and resurrection, appears to contradict our opinion. But
first, the power of perception in this state, at least with many,
can only be regarded as a glimmering, for which reason the dead
are called κεκοιμημένοι, without admitting an absolute want of
perception in them as the psychopannychites do; secondly, it
must be supposed that a certain relation is always maintained
between the element of the body and the separated soul, intimate
in proportion to the sanctification of the organ which had invested
the soul on earth. (See further on this subject in my Opusc. Theol.
Diss. vii. p. 165, sqq.) Lastly, as Christ here is styled ἀπαρχὴ
τῶν κεκοιμημένων, so in Rev. i. 5, Col. i. 16, ὁ πρωτότοκος τῶν
νεκρῶν. Enoch and Elias likewise tasted not of death. (Gen.
v. 24; 2 Kings ii. 11). In the ἀπαρχή is not only contained
the idea of the first, the earliest, but also that of the most costly,
and as such dedicated to God.

Vers. 21, 22. In the same manner as in Rom. v. 12, sqq., (to
the explanation of which I beg to refer), only that there the reference is pre-eminently to the spiritual life, Adam and Christ
are represented by the apostle as the hinge affecting the movement of man's life. As Adam sinned not in himself alone, but
all in him, so in Christ's resurrection there is a resurrection of all.
To every one unprejudiced, it must be clear that the expression δι'
ἀνθρώπου, ἐν τῷ Ἀδάμ, indicates Adam not only as the *beginner* of
sin and its consequences, death, but as the *origin*,* just as Christ
is the origin of life and its most elevated display the ἀνάστασις.
The resurrection of the evil and the good is equally implied in the
πάντες (see on John v. 29 ; Acts xxiv. 15). Billroth thinks it
can only apply to the believers, as the others cannot be considered
ἐν Χριστῷ, but Christ represents mankind, his power awakens
both good and evil ; for as human the former may be considered
in him, although they are immediately in judgment separated.

---

* The present occurring in verse 22 is worthy of remark, ἀποθνήσκουσι. Commencing with Adam, the process of decay was present in, and as it were advancing
in the human race, but with Christ began the principle of reanimation. But as,
however, the reference is here pre-eminently to the resurrection of the body, the
future ζωοποιηθήσονται is employed.

Mueller also follows Billroth (Stud. 1835, pt. iii. p. 749) in receiving the ζωοποιηθήσονται as equivalent to the ἀνάστασις εἰς
ζωὴν. But verse 23, sqq., which refers to the totality of the
species, seems to demand the application of the most extended
sense to the making alive. Those who defend the restoration
might apparently quote the πάντες in favour of their views, but
how far the paragraph justifies the doctrine, will be brought under
consideration in the Comm. on verses 24—28.

Ver. 23. As according to the divine regulation everything de-
velops itself by degrees, so the new world of the arisen will be
gradually perfected; Christ is the seed-corn of the same, and likewise the first early ripe fruit; to himself succeed his own at his
second coming, afterwards at the end of the whole course of the
world, and the commencement of eternity, all the dead in the
graves shall arise. This passage is one of those from which we
may undeniably conclude that the New Testament acknowledged
and accepted the Jewish doctrine of the twofold resurrection, viz.,
that of the righteous, and the general one. (See Bertholdt Christ.
Jud. p. 176, sqq., 203, sqq.; Eisenmenger entd. Judenth. vol. ii. p.
901, sqq.) This distinction has already been entered upon on Luke
xiv. 14; John v. 25, sqq.; Acts xxiv. 15; the Apocalypse alone
fully developed the doctrine (xx. 5, sqq., xxi. 1, sqq.) Without
any foundation, Billroth, following Usteri, declares that Paul's
doctrine deviates from that laid down in the Apocalypse; the
Revelation, treating the subject *ex professo*, is only more copious.
The circumstance that after the establishment of God's kingdom
Satan will be again unbound (Rev. xx. 7, sqq.), is truly not entered upon by Paul, but nothing expressed by the apostle contradicts the declaration. For the giving up of all dominion to the
Father, which is the subject of what follows, is to take place after
the coming of the kingdom of God, and consequently after Satan
is fully vanquished. Christ's dominion begins truly with his own
resurrection, and sitting at the right hand of God, but it appears
perfected with the Parousia, which is thenceforward the same with
the establishment of God's kingdom on earth (Acts i. 7). If after
the εἶτα τὸ τέλος the express mention of the general resurrection
of the good and bad does not occur, it is sufficiently accounted
for by the fact, that the apostle throughout the whole representation had ever the believers first in thought, for which reason we

shall find from ver. 40, sqq., only a description of the bodies of the blessed, and not of those of the unhappy also, is given. But though not expressly uttered, it is necessarily included in the idea. The ἕκαστος ἐν τῷ ἰδίῳ τάγματι shows that Paul desired to describe the gradual order of the resurrection, and as the εἶτα τὸ τέλος plainly joins the ἔπειτα, the expression must inclusively signify the general resurrection. This opinion is rejected by Weizel (see work already quoted, p. 915). But it is most certain that the resurrection of the godly men of the Old Testament with Christ is not here mentioned, and therefore the views of those who apply Matt. xxvii. 52, 53, only to apparitions of the dead find powerful support in our passage. This opinion has been particularly advanced by Steudel.

Vers. 24—28. The apostle considers himself called upon to define more closely the nature of this τέλος, and to place it in juxtaposition with Christ's βασιλεία. The whole passage is the more remarkable as it stands alone in the holy Scriptures, for even the Apocalypse contains no such information as that conveyed by Paul. Mention alone is made of the new heaven and the new earth (Rev. xxi. 1, the establishment of the κτίσις has already taken place in the Parousia; see on Rom. viii. 19), without any explanation of the relation of the Redeemer to this new condition of things. But precisely because this information stands so isolated, the difficulties contained in it are nearly incapable of solution. If we take into consideration, first, the description of the βασιλεία of Christ, the prophecies of the Old Testament, Ps. cx. 1, viii. 7, lead the apostle to infer* that Christ's dominion shall be *universal*. *All* enemies shall be placed under his feet, but the last enemy† subdued is death. This is effected by means of the general resurrection, consequently Christ's kingdom extends as far as this termination. Though the Father has subjected all things to the Son, it is nevertheless manifest that he is to be excepted from the things placed under him; he rather exalts the Redeemer, in so far as he took man's nature on himself, Ps. cx. 1,

---

* Concerning the mention of the Messiahship in Ps. cx. and Ps. viii., see further on Heb. i. 2. The 8th Psalm refers first especially to man, but inasmuch as the idea of manhood was truly realised in the Messiah, certainly to him. (See Umbreit's Erklärung des achten Psalms in the Stud. 1838, pt. 3).

† The expression ἔσχατος ἐχθρός contains not only a reference to the period of the victory, but also to the *greatness* of its *resistance*. The overcoming death demands the highest revelation of the ζωή.

*i. e.* the Father reigns through the Son. It is evident that in this description Paul makes no difference between the hidden and revealed kingdom of Christ. (See Comm. on Matt. iii. 2). Although the evil has a predominating power over the good in the αἰὼν οὗτος, nevertheless the kingdom of Christ is intimately and truly present in the latter, and further daily displays itself. In his Parousia the good will indeed in the αἰὼν μέλλων gain dominion over the wicked, but the evil is not absolutely removed until the general resurrection totally destroys death. This explanation appears favourable to a general restoration, for the enemy is only truly vanquished when he is transformed to a friend, the *plus* of power alone cannot be a reason for Christ's victory, for that was *his* from the beginning. But death is first really done away with when the ζωή has drawn all things in its nature; as long as the other death reigns over a portion of creation (Rev. xxi. 8) it appears yet to maintain its sway. This impression is considerably strengthened by the further description of the nature of the τέλος in vers. 24 and 28. It states in the first verse that the Son yields the dominion to the Father when he has destroyed all power (the second ὅταν is to be considered antecedent to the first, the καταργεῖν δύναμιν is still an act of his authority); or in other words, that he will destroy his own as well as all other dominion, and give them over to the Father. (Concerning Θεὸς καὶ πατήρ see on 2 Cor. i. 3). It is evidently an assertion without ground to maintain that the parallel expressions ἀρχή, ἐξουσία, δύναμις indicate only the various classes of bad angels, or earthly powers and governors; the πᾶσα which is added and even repeated may signify good and bad, or briefly all dominion without exception, as the power of the Son is included in the removal. God remains sole Lord, for, according to ver. 28, the Son himself is *subject* to him, in order that he may be τὰ πάντα ἐν πᾶσιν. How can we comprehend this idea? In the destroying all dominion is evidently included the removal of all distinction, therefore the *restoration of equality*. That which human imprudence mischievously desires to realize in this sinful world, freedom and equality among men, the Spirit of the Lord effects in a lawful manner. The possibility and necessity for dominion depends only upon the fact that self-control, and the consciousness of

the highest aims, are wanting not only in the individual, but
in the whole race of man. Were self-government proportionate
in all beings, we might say that all dominion is destroyed;
the ruling principle, the Spirit of God, is equal in all. The idea
would therefore be similar to the prophecy in the Old Testament,
which promises that the knowledge of the Lord shall cover the
earth as the waters cover the sea, that one shall no more inquire
of the other, because every one knows and observes his own
standard in all things. (Isa. xi. 9 ; Habak. iii. 14). We must
accordingly regard the individuality as preserved in the removal
of the dominion, for we are not speaking of the swallowing up of
the individual in the sea of the universe. For even of the Son
himself is said παραδοῦναι τὴν βασιλείαν, the ὑποταγῆναι τῷ
πατρί does not refer to the merging of the Son's personality in
the divine substance (as the *Logos* was from the beginning separ-
rate from the Father, [John i. 1], so he also remains in eternity
separate from him), but these expressions rather indicate the
*dignity* of *Christ* as *Messiah*, into which he entered by becoming
man. It is only of Christ as the Messiah, as the way and medi-
ator, that it can be said that God has put all things under him,
*i. e.* that God has surrendered the kingdom to him, and when
through his instrumentality all is atoned for, that terminates his
rule, all are come to God, God is in all, the Redeemer is then only
the first-born among many brethren (Rom. viii. 29); or on the
other side, those sanctified through him, are become like unto
him (1 John iii. 2). But the whole argumentation only applies
when *all* is included in the meaning. For if a portion of God's creatures remained excluded from the restoration after God's image, of
necessity this portion would need government; to which may be
added, that the ἵνα ᾖ ὁ Θεὸς τὰ πάντα ἐν πᾶσιν cannot be textually interpreted otherwise than so, that in *all* created things God
appoints all, accordingly the evil God resisting human will, finds
no more room for exercise. For if we assign its full signification
to τὰ πάντα, but limit the ἐν πᾶσι to those sanctified through
Christ, it appears perfectly discretionary to assign the most comprehensive sense to passages such as Rom. xi. 36, ἐξ αὐτοῦ καὶ
δι᾿ αὐτοῦ καὶ εἰς αὐτὸν τὰ πάντα. It cannot, therefore, be denied,
that if the restoration is sanctioned in any passage, it is in

this.* However, the defenders of this doctrine should not overlook the fact, that neither here nor in any other passage of the
sacred Scriptures is the final leading back of all evil men, yea,
even demons and Satan himself, laid down as an open and decided form of doctrine; this circumstance is calculated to awaken
serious reflection as to the advisability of introducing such an
opinion or making it the subject of public instruction.

Ver. 29. After this digression the apostle returns to the
principal position, and argues first on the subject of the resurrection from the βαπτίζεσθαι ὑπὲρ τῶν νεκρῶν. This difficult expression is well known to have deeply engaged the attention of
exegetical writers, from which numerous explanations have arisen.
But before we proceed to examine the most important of these,
we shall attempt ourselves to elucidate the passage. It is evident that the connexion here is not so loose as Billroth, among
others, supposes. To the βαπτίζεσθαι, the κινδυνεύειν of ver. 30
connects itself by means of the τί καί, which is not to be neglected. If we are not entitled exactly to attach the meaning of
"the baptism of suffering" to the βαπτίζεσθαι, it is nevertheless
undeniable that with the idea of baptism is likewise intimated as
accessory all the sufferings which might affect the baptized. The

---

* The most plausible argument against our explanation of the passage relative to
the restoration is this. The apostle treats in the whole chapter of believers only
and their resurrection, as we have already observed on ver. 23 ; therefore the whole
connexion requires, that to the class restricted to "all believers, all who are in
Christ," the πάντες ζωοποιηθήσονται (ver. 22), and the ἐν πᾶσι (ver. 28), should
be also added. That the evil arise, and what their possible fate may be, is not now
entered upon by the apostle, his doctrine in this respect must be ascertained from
other examinations of the subject. (See on Rom. xi. 32). Mueller likewise in the
Stud. 1835, pt. iii., p. 749, has given an explanation of Rom. viii. 11, and also Mau
(Theolog. Hitarb. pt. ii., p. 104). Candour, however, compels us to confess that
the first impression arising from the apostolic representation is not favourable to
these explanations, even omitting the fact that the absolute removal of dominion
and death appears to exclude the possibility of continuing death's dominion over
any portion of creation. The verses 23, sqq. are of a nature to lead us to infer
that the apostle comprehended all mankind in the view taken, because he speaks
of the end, consequently of the general resurrection of all. Weizel (Stud. 1836,
pt. iv., p. 909) is of my opinion. This opinion appears yet more to commend itself
to our consideration *when we reflect, that Paul never openly speaks of the resurrection
of the wicked.* However, there certainly appear in the Holy Scriptures, and doubtless from wise motives, apparently contradictory doctrines on this important point ;
and for this reason we should do well to leave them in the hieroglyphical uncertainty in which they have been given to us. (Concerning Paul's description of the
last judgment, see further the observations on Rom. ii. 6—8).

τί μοι τὸ ὄφελος of ver. 32 is, however, to be considered as an interpretation of the τί ποιήσουσιν (ver. 29), and ποιεῖν = עָשִׂיר is accordingly to be received in the sense of " to gain somewhat, to acquire something, to attain." The construction would then shape itself thus : for what then would they gain who (at a later period) received baptism ? (The answer implied is : they would not only gain nothing, but would be, as stated in ver. 19, the most miserable among mankind). For what reason should we ourselves, who have long taken upon us the profession of Christians, tempt the dangers which hourly await us in that character ? To what purpose the daily strivings, if there were no resurrection, and no eternal reward in Christ's kingdom ? But it must be evident that the explanation of ver. 29 is closely linked with the verses preceding the 24th, and that the declaration concerning the τέλος (vers. 24—28) appears only a digression. In ver. 23 the οἱ τοῦ Χριστοῦ are represented as those participating next in order to Christ in that resurrection of which he was the first-fruits ; and this idea, taken in connexion with the ἐπεὶ τί ποιήσουσιν of ver. 29, authorises the construction which follows : " For were it not so, if believers were not to arise at Christ's coming, what would those gain who had received baptism ? " Billroth's conception of ποιεῖν appears to me entirely erroneous. He translates: what will they do who permit themselves to be baptized? Answer: something very foolish. But for what purpose employ the future thus ? He says it may be explained, *quid eos facere* APPAREBIT, or *quid ii facere* INVENIENTUR ? But allowing that it is capable of being so understood, although a difficulty presents itself, such admission entirely destroys the connexion with what precedes, and which we think is sufficiently evident. There still remains that difficult form βαπτίζεσθαι ὑπὲρ τῶν νεκρῶν to be explained, a passage hitherto received as if only βαπτίζεσθαι stood, of which the signification could not be mistaken. It is highly important that the article should stand here (τῶν νεκρῶν) which is in the *text. rec.* immediately repeated in what follows, but in this passage αὐτῶν is decidedly to be preferred. The use of the article does not imply dead persons without distinction, but the allusion is to certain well-known dead. The connexion with ver. 23 shows the reference to be to those departed in the Lord. If we maintain this reference it thence ap-

pears that ὑπέρ cannot here mean "instead," for the dead are
certainly already baptized, but that it signifies "for, to the
advantage of." But how far can the apostle declare that believers about to be added to the church were baptized for the
advantage of the dead? Inasmuch as a certain number, a πλήρωμα of believers is required (see on Rom. xi. 12, 25) which must
be complete before the Parousia, and with it the resurrection,
can take place. Every one, therefore, who receives baptism be-
nefits thereby the body of believers, those already dead in the
Lord. This conception appears to me to explain the passage;
all other expositions* bear traces of weakness on important points.
Billroth has again quoted the explanation of the *baptismus vica-
rius.* Tertullian (adv. Marc. v. 10) mentions this as only a heretical custom, which is also confirmed by Epiphanius (Haer.
xxviii. c. 6); but it is incredible that so early as the apostolic
times a superstition of this nature, in which the living became as
it were proxy for the dead in baptism, should have existed, or
become so general, that the allusion to it should have been universally understood. But, allowing this, what has given rise to
the supposition that Paul sanctions so rank a superstition? An
authority for the βαπτίζεσθαι ὑπὲρ τῶν νεκρῶν is undoubtedly
found in the passage, for it is evident that the foundation of the
whole question is the opinion that, if the dead arise, they gain
something by means of the βαπτίζεσθαι ὑπὲρ τῶν νεκρῶν. To
this may be added that, in such a view, the article must be
omitted before νεκρῶν. Billroth endeavours to explain it by supposing that certain dead persons were intended, it might be rela-
tives or friends, in whose place the βαπτιζόμενοι suffered themselves to be baptized. But if this explanation fails, neither
baptizing on the graves of martyrs (of which custom not a trace
existed in the apostolic ages†), nor the being baptized to the
confession of the resurrection,‡ which cannot be literally expressed

---

* Especially in the writings of Calov, Wolf, and Heumann on this subject; the
greater part of these, however, contradict themselves so fully as to require no
other refutation.

† The custom which undoubtedly existed in later times (Euseb. H. E. iv. 15,
August. de Civ. Dei xx. 9) of baptizing upon the graves of the martyrs, may possibly have arisen from a misunderstanding of the present passage.

‡ This explanation is the prevalent one among the Catholic Fathers. They
argue from the practice of their times, according to which the persons to be bap-

by ὑπὲρ τῶν νεκρῶν, or being baptized in the name of those already dead, can lay claim to be recognised. The latter explanation would, indeed, according to the meaning, be most appropriate, if only the form βαπτίζεσθαι ὑπὲρ instead of εἰς, or ἐν ὀνόματι were grammatically supported, and the plural were not so at variance with the article, as by the dead who are baptized, only Christ can be understood. The explanation propounded by Superintendent Meyer (in the Hanoeverschen Nachrichten von Brandis un Rupstein Jahrg. 1034, pt. iv., pp. 179, sqq.), according to the views of Abresch and others (see Poli Synopsis ad h. l.), appears to me very difficult of reception. According to this, σωμάτων or μελῶν is to be supplied to νεκρῶν, and the meaning to be: what shall avail this grave of water (viewing baptism according to Rom. vi. as the image of death and resurrection) for your dead members, if there be no reanimation to expect? But in opposition to this, the fact seems to deserve attention, that in this view the νεκροί would become the βαπτιζόμενοι themselves, in which case the idea would certainly be more intelligibly expressed. Calvin considers the reference is to those who, being near to death, were desirous of receiving baptism before their end; *non tantum baptizantur,* he says, *qui adhuc victuros se putant, sed qui mortem habent ante oculos.* But it is not very clear how this thought is to be found in ὑπὲρ τῶν νεκρῶν.—In conclusion, I will not deny that a certain feeling of doubt remains in my own mind with reference to the passage I have adduced relative to the πλήρωμα of the church. The idea is one so remotely bearing on the subject, that Paul could not justly assume it would be correctly understood by all his readers. Now the whole passage conveys the impression that Paul was treating of what he felt was thoroughly comprehended. I therefore, with a view to further the explanation, propose to admit the following modification, viz., to receive ὑπέρ = ἀντί in the signification of "instead, in place," which presents no difficulty. (See remarks in Comm. on Matt. xx. 28). The tenor of Paul's writing as far as ver. 19 was to show how, amid the self-denyings and persecutions which awaited the Christian in this world, he would

tized confessed belief in the resurrection of the dead, before baptism, and apply it to the circumstances of apostolic times. But in the most ancient periods belief in Christ alone was indispensable to baptism, as passages from Justin Martyr prove. (See my Monum. Hist. Eccl. vol. ii., p. 167).

be the most miserable of men, if there were no resurrection. This view of the misery of the Christian in this world continues to form the groundwork of the further argument. He endeavours to prove that those persons *who were baptized in the place of those members removed by death from the church* (ὑπὲρ τῶν νεκρῶν), would gain nothing thereby, if there were no resurrection for the dead. And likewise the patient endurance of persecution by those already Christians, having become so by baptism, would profit them in no degree, if their reward was not to be found in the resurrection. This view, it appears to me, commends itself by its simplicity, and it is rather striking that it had not been touched upon at an earlier period; but we have only to suppose that Paul considered, that as the ranks of the body of believers were thinned by death, the deficiencies were supplied, and their places filled by those newly baptized. What will these gain thereby, Paul intends to say, or what will avail their being baptized in the room of the dead, *i. e.* occupying the place of those departed? if there should be no resurrection, there can exist for neither the hope of reward, as an inducement to enter into the conflicts which await the Christian. In this sense the καὶ is not without signification in the sentence τί καὶ βαπτίζονται, for what reason do ye yet permit yourselves to be baptized? is it not sufficient that the dead have hoped in vain, why draw others into error? The τί καὶ ἡμεῖς κινδυνεύομεν which follows in ver. 30 also connects itself thoroughly with this idea; for, passing from those who, after uselessly enduring sorrows and persecutions, have died (supposing the hope of the resurrection to be proved a fallacious one), Paul proceeds to mention the living members of the church, who are foolishly sacrificing the certain for what is without certainty. (Regarding the connexion of the phrases, Griesbach has connected the εἰ ὅλως νεκροὶ οὐκ ἐγείρονται with what precedes; but with Lachmann I prefer connecting it with what follows, as otherwise the phrase τί καὶ, &c., seems inappropriate).

Vers. 30, 31. The ἡμεῖς indicates in the first place the apostle himself, but in such a manner that all those belonging to the church are represented as more or less in similar circumstances; the ἀποθνήσκω refers entirely to his individuality. (In ver. 31 ἀποθνήσκω implies "to find oneself in danger of death." See

2 Cor. iv. 10, 11.—Νή, though only occurring in the New Testament in this place, is very generally employed in the form of taking an oath.—The reading ἡμετέραν is evidently a change from the more difficult ὑμετέραν, i. e. "by my glory, that I have in you.")

Vers. 32—34. That the apostle was exposed to numerous dangers in Ephesus, is shown by Rom. xvi. 4, where it is said that Priscilla and Aquila had offered themselves in his place. (See also Acts xx. 19). Nevertheless θηριομαχεῖν must certainly only be employed metaphorically, for Paul's privilege as a Roman citizen secured him from the arena. It is also improbable that before Nero's persecution of the Christians, any were so exposed on account of their faith. But the reference in the κατὰ ἄνθρωπον is obviously to human and earthly affairs; if these were any spring of action, to what purpose the daily strife? it would be more prudent to enjoy the pleasures of life! We may observe that the apostle sets completely aside the possibility of a pure spiritual existence; if there is no resurrection of the dead, the destruction of the individual is unavoidable. Billroth correctly remarks on this passage, as we before noticed, that this by no means implies a charge of epicurean principles against his antagonists; on the contrary it supposes that they likewise entertained a horror of such doctrines. The words are quoted strictly from Isa. xxii. 13, according to the LXX. The two verses 33, 34, might easily be understood to contain Paul's counsel that the better-disposed should entirely separate from the evil-minded; but this is not justified by the whole contents of the epistle; and even in the second epistle, so much more reproving in its tone, nothing of the sort is to be found. I am, therefore, of Billroth's opinion that the τινές, with whom they were advised to avoid association, are not the persons mentioned in verse 12, but possibly foreign emissaries who laboured to introduce error into the church in Corinth. We may, however, safely infer thus far, that Paul desired by these strong expressions to signify what the result might be, if the erring members of the Corinthian church failed to return to the undefiled truth. (In verse 33, concerning μὴ πλανᾶσθε see vi. 9.—The quotation is, according to Jerome, from Menander's Thais. On account of the iambic trimiters we must read χρησθ', which Lachmann has again inserted in the

text.—Only in ver. 34 does ἐκνήφω occur, the *simpler* form being
more frequently used in the New Testament. The *compositum*
alludes to the intoxicating nature of the evil influences already
at work. Δικαίως here only defines the nature of this shame " in
a just and becoming manner."—The form ἀγνωσίαν Θεοῦ ἔχειν
is not precisely the same as Θεὸν οὐ γνῶναι, the latter is pure
negative, while in the former the ἀγνωσία itself becomes positive,
*i. e.* positive errors concerning God and divine things are concealed in it).

Vers. 35—38. It is plainly to be inferred from the fact of the
apostle now passing to the supposed inquiry into the nature of
the resurrection, and of the new body, that difference of opinion
on the subject prevailed in Corinth. Although the ἄφρων is not
to be viewed as a decided characteristic of an individual or class
of persons, but may rather be regarded as a rhetorical form ; the
strict examination of the subject nevertheless sanctions the supposition that some (at least in Corinth) had given currency to opinions that the same body was to arise which had been given to us
on earth. To the materialist Jewish Christian it was certainly
easy, especially when combating the inferences of Gnostically inclined Christians, to identify the body of the resurrection with
that of corruption, which was an error in no degree less than
that Gnostic tendency declaimed against by Paul from the
very first. The apostle seeks his proof in the image of the
grain of wheat (κόκκος); this, which is sown, *i. e.* entrusted to
the earth in order to be changed, is not identical with that
which springs forth (the σῶμα γενησόμενον), but is only the
parent of that σῶμα, whose nature is permitted by God to be
after the nature of the grain of wheat. But this comparison does not appear to be entirely applicable, inasmuch as the
plant again produces as fruit the same wheat from which itself
was raised. Paul, however, has no intention of carrying his metaphor so far: he compares with the dead grain the fresh living *plant* which springs into being from its decay, not the fruit.
His idea might also have included the blossom, in which the impulse of the plant to exalt itself is most plainly manifested. The
formation of the fruit may be regarded as *retrogression* from the
highest point of perfection, because it involves in itself a return
to the first principle, and shows the conclusion of the entire course

to be at hand. (See concerning the tendency of nature to perfect itself, which nevertheless sinks powerless back to its origin, the remarks on Rom. viii. 19, sqq.) If Billroth understands in this passage an allusion to the indwelling imperishableness of human nature, it does not appear to me capable of this construction.* This imperishableness must be the spirit essentially such, while the apostle is treating of the capacity residing in the human organism for producing a higher corporeality, by no means to be considered without the Spirit, but which may nevertheless not be identified with it. (In ver. 36 the reading ἄφρων employed by Lachmann is doubtless preferable. The ἄφρον could only apply to the question, which is by no means unreasonable, but only presupposes the erroneous operation of the identity of the present with the new body.—Ver. 37. The ὃ σπείρεις—οὐ σπείρεις has been already correctly explained by Heidenreich thus: *quoad seminas, quodcunque id sit, non seminas certe plantam nascituram.*—Concerning εἰ τύχοι see remarks on xiv. 10).

Vers. 39—41. Paul does not pursue the comparison to the end, making it complete, but leaving the idea touched upon in ver. 38 that there are various kinds of seed, he passes to the variety of formations existing in the universe. He first adverts to the difference of substance of the σάρξ in the various classes of creatures (man being included here according to his animal nature). He then discriminates between heavenly and terrestrial organisms, and again among the heavenly bodies asserts that differences exist in degree of glory. Calvin has very judiciously remarked that the tendency of the apostle's argument was not to assert that, according to the degree of sanctification attained by individual believers, the properties of their glorified bodies and the degree of glorification they attained would be proportionate; he intended only to express the difference between the body of the resurrection and this corruptible body. It may not, however,

---

* Billroth's views concerning this passage might not be considered inappropriate if he had substituted "glorification" for "resurrection" in that which follows. "Paul does not admit the resurrection to begin with the natural death as modern views do (or rather these may be said to deny the resurrection altogether, allowing only a pure spiritual immortality), but with the admission of the man into the kingdom of Christ." As soon as the spirit is subjected to the influence of Christ's living the same works to the glorification of the body (see on John vi), but the resurrection i. e. the perfected glorification, is still deferred until the end.

be altogether denied that the former idea.is associated with the apostolic observations. Were it not so, it had been sufficient to draw attention to the specific differences between things heavenly and those of earthly design. The division of these objects into several denominations clearly shows the existence of an idea accessory and subservient to the more prominent one. (Lange is also rightly of this opinion, p. 703). In conclusion, it may be stated that σῶμα (ver. 40) is not to be precisely understood of the body, as if σῶμα ἐπίγειον corresponded to the σῶμα ψυχικόν (ver. 40), and σῶμα ἐπουράνιον to the σῶμα πνευματικον, but σῶμα has rather here the more general signification "unity composed of members, organism." Ver. 41 shows that Paul especially reckoned the stars among the heavenly organism; nevertheless nothing concerning the apostle's astronomical views can be concluded from this circumstance; in ver. 38 he has also styled the vegetable formations σώματα.

Vers. 42—44. The application of the parable now follows, with very evident reference to the image employed, the grain (ver. 36, sqq.); since the σπείρεται applies to the decay, ἐγείρεται to the awakening, or springing up of plants. As there are many sorts of organisms, so likewise has man a σῶμα ψυχικόν as well as a σῶμα πνευματικόν. Man standing in an especial manner upon the limits of two worlds, being equally allied to earth and heaven, possesses likewise a twofold corporeality. The earthly body has the predicate of all things earthly, the divine the attributes of the heavenly. But it is doubtless an introduction of modern philosophic views,* to ascribe, as Billroth does in this place, the following idea to the apostle, viz., "that the spiritual body is the power of the Spirit, which is aware that its true immortality is to

---

* Goeschel appears to understand the doctrine of the glorified body differently; see his writings on the proofs of the soul's immortality (Berlin, 1835), p. 253. It sometimes seems as if the respected writer did not regard the higher corporeality as glorification of the matter, but *only* as a *limitation* of the *personal attributes*. But how a limit can be imagined without a limiting power is not very clear, consequently it must be considered as a self-limitation. But in what sense can this be styled a body? Mueller decidedly intended the same when he distinguishes the resurrection of the body from that of the flesh, maintaining the former, but denying the latter. At all events, the expression "resurrection, glorification of the flesh," is wanting. But it is certainly accidental that John, in chap. vi., speaks of the eating Christ's flesh, that has life in it. Flesh is the necessary substance of the body, the glorified body has glorified spiritualized flesh for its substance. (See also Lange, Stud. 1836, P. 3, p. 695, sq.)

be found in its unity with God and Christ, that although continually renewed in mortality, it maintains itself therein as immortal." The πνεῦμα cannot be identical with σῶμα πνευματικόν. The entire doctrine of a spiritualized, glorified, material body is considered by Billroth unreal, as it must be necessarily acknowledged exegetically such, which is implied by the apostle in the expression σῶμα πνευματικόν: yet this learned man himself admits it, in regarding the apostle in the point under consideration, as not yet freed from the differences of spirit and matter. To this representation we ascribe, according to the testimony of revelation, not only a transient subjective truth, but a permanent objective one. As without body, no soul, so without corporeality no eternal happiness ; corporeality and the concomitant personal qualities are the object of God's work. The unity of the person of God in the process of creation is an eternity of personal powers which have in the glorified body the limit, and wherein alone they have a perception of the glorified nature of their basis. As the spirit first *earthwards* clothes itself with the body, so afterwards *heavenward* is the body glorified in the spirit. Regeneration does not destroy the old man, but as the Spirit causes the new to proceed from him as the parent, so the power of the Spirit creates from the covering of the earthly body a spiritual one. The natural body is the clothing which the unenlightened ψυχή effects for himself, thence σῶμα ψυχικόν, the spiritual body, is the garment in which the soul, having become celestial and glorified through the Spirit of Christ, arrays itself. The earthly and celestial body are not identical, but not absolutely different: the elements of the former are employed in the formation of the latter, the operation of Christ in believers gradually transforms the one into the other. All waverings, therefore, in the spiritual life are hinderances and checks for the higher corporeality ; an idea calculated to produce a becoming seriousness and truth in all things which concern the body, as indifference in these matters may give occasion for disregard of sinful offences against it. (In verse 44, the reading εἰ ἔστι σωμα ψυχικὸν, ἔστι καὶ σῶμα πνευματικόν is certainly not inapplicable [it conveys the idea that if the ψυχή possessed the power to form for itself a corresponding organ, this must be the case, and in an enhanced degree, with the πνεῦμα]. Nevertheless, the form generally in use appears to me preferable, for this sen-

R

tence, ver. 44, is nothing more than an exposition of ver. 42, οὕτω καὶ ἡ ἀνάστασις τῶν νεκρῶν. Erasmus, Mill, and Semler recommend the entire omission of the passage, but this appears by no means advisable; it leads the way to what follows, and cannot therefore be omitted).

Vers. 45—47. Paul still continues his subject, and traces back the differences mentioned to a higher point, in which the source of the two-fold corporeality is to be found. *Adam* and *Christ* (see on ver. 22) are again indicated as the origin from whence the corruptible and incorruptible body of man proceeds; its influence governs the race, and appoints the most inward nature of the individual. They are not men as the others are, but the point originating the entire course of development, therefore Christ is also styled ὁ ἔσχατος Ἀδάμ, as in Rom. v. 14 τύπος τοῦ μέλλοντος is applied to Adam; but if Paul here refers to the passage Gen. ii. 7, which the LXX. translate καὶ ἐγένετο ὁ ἄνθρωπος εἰς ψυχὴν ζῶσαν, the foundation lies only in the expression σῶμα ψυχικόν (ver. 44). No analogy for the second half ὁ ἔσχατος Ἀδὰμ εἰς πνεῦμα ζωοποιοῦν is to be found in the Old Testament. We may therefore suppose, as the words of the entire passage cannot be received as a quotation, that the apostle himself added them as a period to his strain of argument; for although οὕτω καὶ refers to the preceding sentence, yet it is impossible to conclude that in the contrast laid down between Christ and Adam, Paul drew the incomprehensible character of Christ from that which was understood of Adam. The circumstance of the passage quoted having no mention of the body, shows above all how little the allusion to Gen. ii. 7 is to be viewed as a corroborative and real citation. It is very probable that Paul presupposed the knowledge of the body being formed from the dust of the earth, as stated in Gen. ii. 7; this is sanctioned by the χοϊκός following in verse 47; ψυχικὸν σῶμα therefore is applied to a body formed of base materiel, animated by a ψυχή. The free use of the quotation shows the different sense in which it stands in the former text, and in the apostle's argument. That is to say, in the history of the creation the expression ψυχὴ ζῶσα = נֶפֶשׁ חַיָּה by no means implies something inferior, an antithesis to the πνεῦμα, but it signifies there, that the image formed out of dust became, by the hand of God, an animated organism.  When employed by the Apostle Paul, on the contrary, ψυχὴ and ψυχικός possess a lower signification (see the observations on ii. 14), standing parallel to the χοϊκός (ver. 47), and indicating not the sinless creature proceeding from the hand of his Creator, but the fallen being, betrayed into the power of the φθορά.  The employment of the biblical parallel is accordingly only to be considered a slight expression of an entirely independent train of thought arising from a passage of Scripture.  It has been asserted that by the quotation from the Old Testament Paul appears to have had Adam in his original condition in view, and not the fallen Adam.  This view has especially been adopted by Mau (Theol. Mitarb. pt. ii., p. 94, sqq., p. 100), and an opinion founded thereon, that death is not to be considered a consequence of sin, but a natural property of the body; only the manner of the death, and the descent into Hades, is the consequence of sin.  But though the author labours to establish this view, employing principally this passage for the purpose, I have not been able to convince myself that his opinion is well-grounded.  It is undoubted that Adam's body likewise needed glorification; but had he not sinned, he would without θάνατος have proceeded on the way to be clothed upon. (2 Cor. v. 1, sqq.)  Death is ever the powerful struggle of soul and body with corruption and its horrors, not ordained such of God, but following as the simple consequence of sin.  Paul here makes no allusion to the fall, but employs the Old Testament description of Adam, without distinguishing between the time before and after the fall; nevertheless what precedes (especially the φθορά, ver. 42), as well as that which follows (vers. 48, 49), compels us to believe that Paul had the fallen Adam in his mind.  We might with perfect right observe silence respecting the fall, because there existed the same necessity in Adam's body for glorification before that event, as afterwards, in order to become a σῶμα πνευματικόν. Upon this subject more will be found in Krabbe's striking controversy with Neander (von der Suende, p. 191, sqq.), the latter entertaining similar views to Mau (Pflanz. vol. ii., p. 519, sqq.)— From the predicate of Christ πνεῦμα ζωοποιοῦν, for which in ver. 47 ὁ κύριος ἔξ οὐρανοῦ stands as an explanation, it may be concluded that the apostle does not consider the natural πνεῦμα in a condition to form the σῶμα πνευματικόν, but only the divine spirit of God,

who took upon himself man's nature as Christ. For this cause
he is called the resurrection (John xi. 25), and he only who be-
lieveth in this hath life, and shall arise at the last day. (John
vi. 54). The idea expressed in verse 46 is, that the laws of development require that the lower precede the higher, and con-
trary-wise that the higher follow the inferior, even as the human
birth must necessarily precede the new birth or regeneration. (It
seems to me that Billroth discovers too many difficulties in verse
47; the ἔξ οὐρανοῦ corresponds entirely to the ἐκ γῆς [an allusion to
Gen. ii. 6] with reference to the origin; the χοϊκός appeared to present to the apostle no suitable adjective form, he therefore employs
ὁ κύριος, by which the χοϊκός acquires an idea of ministering to.
The omission of ὁ κύριος certainly arose from the fact of the transcriber seeing some difficulty in the use of it).

Vers. 48—50. In order to establish the connexion of every man
with the two states mentioned, the writer remarks that the nature
of the one passes into that of the other; in the first Adam by
the natural birth, in the second through the spiritual. Referring
to the history of the creation (Genesis i. 27), the expression
εἰκών is chosen to signify the relation of created beings to each
other. The natural birth imprints the image of the fallen
Adam in the soul (Gen. v. 3), the new birth (which is first truly
accomplished with the glorification of the body), the image of
Christ, by whose sacred influence the body is glorified. (See
on Rom. viii. 11; 2 Cor. iii. 18). The reading φορέσωμεν includes
in the idea that of admonition, which does not agree with scriptural
doctrine; regeneration can never be attained by striving or even
faith itself; it is an act of positive grace, to the obtaining of which
admonition would be in vain employed. The apostle then, with
reference to the subject treated on in vers. 35, 36, concludes with
the assertion that this mortal corruptible body can have no part
in the kingdom of God, but only the incorruptible body of the
resurrection. In the τοῦτο δέ φημι a concession to the spiritua-
list and an opposition to the materialist opinions is to be seen.
(Concerning the formula σὰρξ καὶ αἷμα see Comm. on Matt. xvi. 17,
xxvi. 26. It indicates earthly corporeality in its mortality and
sinfulness. It may not be argued from it that the immortal body
can have no σάρξ: a σῶμα can never be considered without
σάρξ [in the sense of spiritual restraint], as we have already

seen.    But the σάρξ itself is likewise a σὰρξ πνευματική* as Christ's body in the holy communion.—By the expression βασιλεία Θεοῦ we are here to understand the kingdom of God upon earth, the re-establishment of Paradise, which the Scriptures inform us will undoubtedly attend the coming of our Lord.    See the observations in the Comm. on Matt. iii. 2).

Vers. 51, 52.  Paul now enters upon the consideration of another point, which Billroth has erroneously viewed as the main subject of the argument.    He explains the relation which the living will bear to those already dead in the faith at the looked for coming of Christ.  It appears that many of the Corinthian Christians entertained the idea that those still living at that event would with earthly bodies have part in the kingdom of God.  This Paul declares to be an error, and teaches that these receive a new body as well as those who are raised; that is to say, they are all changed upon Christ's appearance, and that suddenly. An authentic interpretation of the few words here given is formed by the passages 2 Cor. v. 1 ; 1 Thess. iv.    Paul terms this a μυστήριον, while he even expresses the fact; but that which may be regarded as the mysterious in it is the *how*, not the *fact*.   The power of the Spirit, which at that dread moment will pour itself upon the church like a life-bestowing dew (Isa. xxvi. 19), will effect the bodily transformation in a mysterious manner.    The act of changing is called in 2 Cor. v. 2, τὸ οἰκητήριον τὸ ἔξ οὐρανοῦ ἐπενδύσασθαι, the farther consideration of which will then occur.   The apostle here chiefly dwells upon the suddenness with which the bodily transformation will take place, and as Billroth justly observes, for the purpose of removing any apprehension from the minds of the Corinthians that some might arrive too late to participate in God's kingdom upon earth.   This dread might display itself in a twofold form.    It might be feared that the living would find entrance before the dead, see 1 Thess. iv. 15, or, on the other hand, that the latter should obtain precedence. It is certain, however, that the idea of the change occurring suddenly does not vitiate the supposition of a gradual preparation of

* How far removed Calvin was from denying the glorification of the body is proved by his remarks on this passage : *Cœterum carnem et sanguinem intellige, qua nunc conditione sunt, caro enim particeps erit gloriæ Dei, sed innovata et vivificata a Christi spiritu.*

the glorified body during the earthly course by the operation of Christ. The suddenness only bears reference to the momentaneous bursting forth of the already perfected new body,* as the beautiful butterfly which is gradually perfected in the less attractive larva frees itself suddenly from the obstruction of its dark envelope and springs into light of the sun.—Paul likewise appoints the time by the expression ἐν τῇ ἐσχάτῃ σάλπιγγι. As seven trumpets are mentioned in Rev. viii., the expression ἐσχάτη cannot well imply, as Billroth thinks, " trumpet, sounding in the last day," but it may rather be understood of last-sounding trumpet. But the expression is naturally only a figurative one, to describe the awakening spiritual operation which shall arouse mankind in awe and trembling. (See on Matt. xxiv. 31). Similar consternations, excited by higher causes, pass from time to time through mankind; but those which occur at the period immediately preceding the last day will be of the most powerful nature, and arouse the most secret things of the inward life. See further on 1 Thess. iv. 16, and Rev. viii. In the Old Testament the prophetic and typical passages in Exod. xix. 16, Isa. xxvii. 13, Zach. ix. 14, may be consulted. (With respect to the text in verse 51, many various readings occur, partly occasioned by the position of the οὐ. This negation would appear more suitably placed before πάντες than before κοιμηθησόμεθα, for in the latter case the words would really imply " none will die." Billroth has correctly remarked upon this that the emphasis belongs to ἀλλαγησόμεθα, and the οὐ κοιμηθησόμεθα is only an accessory idea; all it is true will not die, but all will certainly be changed. The most part of the deviations arise from the circumstance, that offence was taken at the idea that *not* all should die, death being appointed to all men. [Heb. ix. 27]. In later times, as the expectation of the near approach of Christ's coming diminished, the idea must have certainly acquired importance. Lachmann had decided that the negation should be omitted, but the connexion urgently requires it, because, as remarked, Paul defines the posi-

---

* The idea of the sudden transformation indicates that no development is to be expected after death, but that every individual is called to publish the character of the course he has hitherto followed on earth. Children will not arise as men, nor aged men retreat to the period of youth, but every glorified body will represent clearly his degree of age, with the exception of all that is perishable, so that all taken together may declare the entire human race in its degrees and varieties with the most perfect clearness.

tion of those alive at Christ's appearing; these die not, but will be changed.—The sentence σαλπίσει γάρ as far as ἀλλαγησόμεθα, that is suitably enclosed within brackets, throws yet more light on the immediately preceding idea of the instantaneous transformation which takes place, and likewise upon the manner of the resurrection.—Concerning the form σαλπίσει, see Winer's Gr. p. 80, it would be best to consider it impersonal: it will sound. Without doubt Paul included himself also in the ἡμεῖς, because he hoped to live until the coming of Christ.　See on 2 Cor. v. 2, sqq., 1 Thess. iv. 17).

Vers. 53—54. Employing the image of a garment, the apostle further describes the forming of the new body, finding in the same the fulfilment of Isaiah's prophecy (xxv. 8), that death shall be destroyed.　It is very striking that the φθαρτόν and θνητόν are not described in this passage as destroyed, but only as clothed upon.　(See on 2 Cor. v. 2, sqq.)　Doubtless Paul intends by this to signify that the elements of the mortal body are as it were absorbed, swallowed up by the omnipotence of the glorifying Spirit.　We cannot deny that the words κατεπόθη ὁ θάνατος appear as in verse 26 to favour the restoring.　It evidently not only implies that death has for ever lost its power over some (the faithful), though retaining over others its might as the second death,* but that it ceases everywhere, which can only happen when the ζωή accepts all in himself, and God is all in all.　(Λόγος is used here = προοφητεία, according to the context.—Νῖκος is a more recent form for νίκη.　The Hebrew לָנֶצַח is frequently so given by the LXX., even when that which is to be represented as enduring or lasting is not precisely of a joyful nature. [See Lam. v. 20 ; Amos viii. 7].　Paul follows the Hebrew text in the translation from Isa. xxv. 8 ; the LXX. read κατέπιεν ὁ θάνατος ἰσχύσας, from which it is probable that they followed another reading).

Vers. 55—57. The apostle then employs a passage from Hosea xiii. 14, in which the prophet rejoices triumphantly in the victory gained over death and his kingdom, and the consequent loss

---

* The expression θάνατος δεύτερος only occurs in the Apocalypse (ii. 11, xx. 14). In the latter passage the second death is represented as like a sea of fire, but the first death appears in the Revelation to be destroyed together with Hades, being cast into the sea of fire.　The tenor of this entire representation can, however, only be satisfactorily explained by taking it in conjunction with the series of Apocalyptic images in that book.

of his prey by the resurrection. The explanation in the Comm. upon Rom. vii. 11, sqq., is likewise adapted for an interpretation of the passage in which sin is represented as the sting of death, and the power, *i. e.* the strength creating sin, the law; the reader is therefore referred to the Comm. In the prophetic connexion κέντρον signifies nothing but the bitter feeling, the sorrow of death ; Paul, however, employs it as parallel with δύναμις in the signification of calling forth the display of power. The slumbering power of death awakens sin, and again that of sin, the law. But Christ in his mercy destroys first the law (in the sense laid down in the Comm. on Rom. vii. 24, sq. viii. 1), and then sin and death itself. (In ver. 55, Lachmann reads θάνατε for ᾅδη, and the critical authorities are in fact strongly in its favour. B.D.E.F.G. have it likewise. However, as the Hebrew text reads ᾅδη as well as the LXX., I myself prefer retaining the usual reading. It is possible that the reading θάνατε arose from an exposition to be applied to the word ᾅδη).

Ver. 58. In conclusion, the apostle exhorts his readers, having this certain hope of the resurrection, to continue steadfast in the faith, and earnest in the work of preaching the gospel, knowing that their labour would be well rewarded. This is the correct construction of the οὐκ ἔστι κενός: the words do not signify that preaching shall be successful, for many shall be converted, but that the labour shall receive its reward in the resurrection. The apostles were by no means insensible to the hope of future happiness as a spur to their zeal. (ʽΕδραῖος is also found in 1 Cor. vii. 37. See also Coloss. i. 23.—Ἀμετακίνητος = βέβαιος is only found in the New Testament in this single passage).

## § 13. THE COLLECTION.

### (xvi. 1—24).

Vers. 1—4. The subject of the collections in money made by Paul for the use of the Christians in Jerusalem and Palestine has been mentioned already in Acts xi. 29, xxiv. 17 ; Rom. xv. 26, 27. But in this chapter, and likewise in the second Epistle (chap. viii. ix.), the apostle enlarges so considerably upon the fact, that his conduct in this particular requires further consideration. It appears very striking that Paul, during the entire period of his ministerial labours, was continually mindful of this collection, and that too for the advantage of the Christians in Jerusalem. In the Comm. on Acts iv. 32, sqq., it has been remarked that the possessing all goods in common in the church at Jerusalem, was probably the cause of its becoming impoverished, and rendered these collections necessary. We, however, saw in the same passage that a community of goods, in the sense of providing a living for all the members of the church out of funds common to all, was not very probably established; it would therefore be only some individuals, acting from an excess of zeal upon the first impulse of brotherly love, who would be so destitute. But this view would not be sufficient to explain Paul's collections. It is possible that the apostle desired to express his piety towards the mother church, and the acknowledgment of his dependence. As all Jews* down to modern times paid half a shekel to the temple at Jerusalem, and after its destruction continued the contribution in order to meet the necessities of the Jews living there, Paul probably considered himself also bound to express his gratitude to the mother church by a similar collection in her behalf. This explains how again, in Gal. ii. 10, the determination to support the poor could be made the subject of a formal regulation among the apostles. These collections may be considered the acknowledgment of the connexion with the mother church. And besides, as the apostle's rules brought him into a species of conflict with the Jewish Christians, the apostle might the more zealously urge these contributions in order to signify by deeds his personal inclination towards the mother church. Paul therefore recommends the Corinthians, in order to collect without inconvenience to themselves, to lay by something each Sunday; he would then appoint a deputy to receive the money, which should either be transmitted to Jerusalem by the same means, or if necessary, he would accompany it thither himself. (In ver. 1, λογία = συλλογή according to Suidas' collection. The mention of a collection in Galatia, leads to the supposition of another epistle, besides the one we possess; nothing is there said of collection, yet

* See Haymann on the marriage ceremonies of the Jews, in the Zeitschrift für Phil. und Kath. Theol. Koeln. 1835, pt. 1, p. 42, sqq.

Paul might have introduced this personally to their notice, when he was last among them.—In ver. 2 consult the Comm. on Matt. xxviii. 1, on μία τῶν σαββάτων. Certainly it may not be inferred from this passage that collections took place among the congregations on the Sabbath, for it was Paul's intention that each should make a suitable contribution at home; but it decidedly proves that it was already the practice to distinguish the day of our Lord's resurrection, to sanctify the day by the exercise of benevolence.—Εὐοδοῦσθαι means properly to have a prosperous journey, to be fortunate, in happy condition. To the ὅ, τι ἄν, ἕκαστος is to be added, " as far as the circumstances of each sanction it." In a similar connexion, καθὼς ηὐπορεῖτό τις is said in Acts ix. 29, and καθὸ ἐὰν ἔχῃ τις in 2 Cor. viii. 12.—In ver. 3, the epistles are γράμματα συστατικά [2 Cor. iii. 1], the use of which is ancient, since the nature of circumstances rendered it necessary, although their peculiar form was assumed at a subsequent period.—In ver. 4 the ἐὰν ᾖ ἄξιον refers to the amount of the collection, with which the deputation who were to deliver it over were to charge themselves, and have reference. See thereon on 2 Cor. viii. 18, sqq.)

Vers. 5—9. The mention of his arrival in Corinth, affords an opportunity to the apostle to explain himself concerning the arrangements for his journey. We learn from 2 Cor. i. 15, that he desired to go direct to Corinth (possibly through Asia and by sea), and from thence to Macedonia ; but the desire to leave time for his epistle to produce its effect may have caused him to proceed directly into Macedonia. In the meantime, he announces his intention to his readers of becoming their guest for a considerable period, probably even for the winter. Until Pentecost, he thinks that circumstances would justify his remaining at Ephesus, which leads us to conclude the epistle was written in the spring. Concerning this, the Introduction may be consulted, § 2. (In ver. 6 τυχόν, forte, see εἰ τύχοι 1 Cor. xiv. 10.—In ver. 9, θύρα is figuratively employed for sphere of action. See 2 Cor. ii. 12; Col. iv. 3. The epithet ἐνεργής arises from the image used. —The antagonists require the presence of Paul, in order to be kept in check.

Vers. 10—12. Here follow some notices concerning Timothy and Apollos. The former is commended to a good reception, and of the latter it is observed, that he could not come at that time, but would shortly visit Corinth.   (In ver. 10 the μή τις αὐτὸν ἐξουθενήσῃ, according to 1 Tim. iv. 12, is plainly connected with Timothy's youth.—Ver. 11. According to Acts xix. 22, Erastus was clearly among the brethren named, perhaps also others.—In ver. 12, the brethren mentioned are probably the Corinthian deputies named in ver. 17).

Vers. 13, 14. It may be supposed that Paul here thought to conclude, but the exhortation which follows occurred to his mind, and led to the special observations which follow.   (Upon στήκω see Rom. xiv. 4.—Ἀνδρίζεσθαι, " to act as a man," is only found in the New Testament in this passage, though frequently in the LXX., and also in 1 Macc. ii. 64.—Κραταιοῦσθαι is used in the signification of " to become strong," Luke i. 80, ii. 40).

Vers. 15, 16. The apostle feels himself called upon to recommend to his readers Stephanus, who had conveyed the epistle from the Corinthians to Ephesus, and also had delivered Paul's epistle at Corinth.   Probably, as a man observing an impartial course, he had drawn upon himself some bitterness from parties in Corinth.   (In Rom. xvi. 5, Epenetus is called the first fruits of Achaia, though Ἀσίας is certainly the correct reading ; he must then have belonged to Stephanas' οἰκία.—The ἔταξαν ἑαυτοὺς εἰς διακονίαν cannot refer to the administration of the office of deacon [for which reason ὑποτάσσεσθαι does not convey the impression of ecclesiastical subordination among the heads], to which no one was self-appointed, but signifies such services out of the common order as delivering the epistle might be considered. These were of a nature to require acknowledgment, as the exercise of them involved both trouble and neglect of business).

Vers. 17, 18. Together with Stephanas, both Fortunatus and Achaicus are here mentioned, the two latter appearing to belong to the former as principal.   Paul describes their presence as supplying the deficiency occasioned by being absent from the Corinthians, and claims from the latter gratitude towards them on this head.   The ἀνέπαυσαν πνεῦμα ὑμῶν is either to be understood, they refreshed me so, as ye yourselves formerly ; or, by their diligence towards me they have benefitted you.—In the ἐπιγινώσκειν is implied the conduct arising from understanding, and

truly in a good sense corresponding to the τιμᾶν or ἀγαπᾶν. Ἐπιγινώσκειν is employed in a similar manner in 1 Thess. v. 12).

Vers. 19, 20. Greetings now follow, including those of Aquila
and Priscilla, who had quitted Corinth for Ephesus. (Acts xviii.
18, sqq.) These zealous believers had also here a place of meeting in their house. (Rom. xvi. 3). The exhortation to greet one
another with a holy kiss, refers to the public assembly, in which the
epistle was read aloud. (See the Comm. on Rom. xvi. 16). Φίλη-
μα τῆς ἀγάπης occurs in the passage 1 Pet. v. 14.

Vers. 21, 22. As far as this place, Paul had dictated the subject (probably to Sosthenes, i. 1), but the apostle now appends a
salutation written with his own hand, as spurious letters were
already circulated as from him (2 Thess. ii. 2). He selects for
this purpose an idea which is not carried further, and for which it
is not necessary to seek the connexion. I cannot yield to the
probability of Billroth's supposition that μαρὰν ἀθά is only added
by Paul in order also to show his Syrian handwriting, and that
the words were afterwards transcribed by Greek transcribers with
Greek characters. The thought "the Lord comes!" κύριος ἔρ-
χεται! is rather calculated to heighten the tenor of the preceding
warning : Be ye quickly converted, for the time of decision is near
at hand ! The Syriac form might be employed by the apostle
as more fluent. In the ἤτω ἀνάθεμα is expressed not only the
exclusion from the church, but also the delivering over to the active power of the enemy without. (See on ἀνάθεμα Comm. 1
Cor. xii. 3).

Vers. 23, 24. The usual form then concludes the writing, but
as the epistle contains many severe words, Paul hastens to assure
all without exception of his love, in order to prevent any personal
application of his strictures.

# EXPOSITION

# SECOND EPISTLE TO THE CORINTHIANS.

# EXPOSITION

OF THE

# SECOND EPISTLE TO THE CORINTHIANS.

I.

## PART FIRST.

(i. 1—iii. 18).

§ 1. THE CONSOLATION.

(i. 1—14).

After the greeting (vers. 1, 2), the apostle proceeds to thank God for the comfort with which he had refreshed him in all his sorrows and conflicts. The commencement of the epistle is especially directed to the better-intentioned among the Corinthians, Paul declaring that on his part he glories in nothing so much as preaching the word of God in its holy simplicity, without adding aught (3—14).

Vers. 1, 2. The greeting resembles that of the first epistle in all important points, only instead of Sosthenes, Timothy is mentioned as the writer, who consequently must have already returned from his mission to Corinth (1 Cor. iv. 17, xvi. 10) when Paul commenced his second epistle. According to ver. 1, the second epistle being directed as a circular letter to all believers in Achaia, it addresses the Athenians likewise (for according to the Roman division Hellas and the Peloponnesus were included in Achaia), though Corinth alone, as the principal city, is specially mentioned.

Vers. 3, 4. The epistle itself commences with a thanksgiving to God for the consolation bestowed upon him (the apostle) in his necessity, which inspires the desire to communicate the same comfort to others who may be in similar affliction. Paul, however, does not represent this true comfort of a nature to be appropriated at discretion, but rather as the operation of the Spirit, which is the source of mercy and perfect consolation; he exhorts his readers to trust steadfastly in all difficulties to this living God. (In ver. 3 εὐλογητός = בָּרוּךְ, when employed to signify the relation of the low to that which is high, is in the sense of "to praise, to extol;" when the circumstances are reversed, on the contrary, "to bestow a blessing."—The expression Θεὸς Ἰησοῦ Χριστοῦ, which has already occurred in Rom. xv. 5; 1 Cor. xv. 24, calls to mind the expression, God of Abraham. [See on this the observations in Comm. vol. i., Matt. xxii. 31, 32]. God is thereby indicated in the peculiar form of revelation, and understood under those special circumstances which are revealed in Christ. —The subsequent πατὴρ τῶν οἰκτιρμῶν καὶ Θεὸς παρακλήσεως corresponds to the Θεὸς καὶ πατήρ, Θεὸς expressing the idea of the origin, the source, just as in Ephes. i. 17, God is called ὁ πατὴρ τῆς δόξης. Consolation is by no means to be regarded here as the simple phrase of sympathy, but as an actual power of the Spirit, issuing from God, and capable of henceforward leading him who receives it to himself. In Matt. x. 13, the same idea is applied to peace; all such subjective circumstances have their foundation in the Spirit which God bestows upon his own).

Ver. 5. According to the principle, such as he is, so likewise are we also in this world (1 John iv. 17); the apostle places in parallel the sufferings and consolation of believers, with the sufferings and consolation, and even the gloriousness of Christ. The παθήματα τοῦ Χριστοῦ are, as Billroth correctly asserts in corroboration of Winer, the sorrows endured by Christ; these repeat themselves in the believer, and likewise the comfort and the glorification experienced by the Redeemer. Had the parallel been completely carried out, it must have been said ἡ παράκλησις τοῦ Χριστοῦ εἰς ἡμᾶς. At the least it is signified in the διὰ τοῦ Χριστοῦ that the Lord received the consolation he imparts to others; for to him may be applied, in the highest sense, that God comforted him, εἰς τὸ δύνασθαι τοὺς ἀνθρώπους παρακαλεῖν ἐν πάσῃ θλίψει, Heb. ii. 17, 18). To attribute to the expression παθήματα τοῦ Χριστοῦ the signification of "sufferings for Christ and his cause," will hardly occur to the mind of any one; nevertheless it would not be unreasonable to inquire (according to such passages as Col. i. 24), whether Χριστός may not here, as in 1 Cor. xii. 12, signify all believers collectively, the church, making the sense of the words "sufferings, which the church has to endure." The idea is by no means unsuitable, although I prefer the former explanation, as otherwise Χριστός must be taken in two significations in the same sentence.

Vers. 6, 7. The inward spiritual fellowship, the κοινωνία, which the apostle perceives to exist between himself and the Corinthians, does not permit him to refer his sufferings and his consolation to himself as an isolated individual, but inclusively to all believers. As, however, Paul desires to allow that which is consolatory to predominate, he does not say, When we suffer, suffer ye also, but, it takes place for your comfort and your salvation, i. e., as Billroth correctly explains, "Inasmuch as I suffer in the service of the Gospel, through which ye receive consolation and salvation." The participation of the Corinthians in the sufferings is not denied by Paul, but he only desires to make it a secondary feature, and therefore mentions it in the same sentence as, and under the support of consolation, which therefore neutralizes it. Billroth correctly observes that the words τῆς ἐνεργουμένης ἐν ὑπομονῇ τῶν αὐτῶν παθημάτων, ὧν καὶ ἡμεῖς πάσχομεν do not imply *similar* sufferings which the Corinthians were called upon to bear at the same time with the apostle, but *those* sufferings felt by Paul, and which all believers, according to their bond of love with him, would feel as their own. The concluding words καὶ ἡ ἐλπίς—παρακλήσεως, express as it were the principle upon which the former deduction rests; for which reason the phrase καὶ ἡ ἐλπὶς ἡμῶν βεβαία ὑπὲρ ὑμῶν is not to be in a parenthesis as Fritzsche has thought, but the εἰδότες which follows is rather to be connected with ἐλπὶς ἡμῶν in the manner of an anacoluthon. (In verse 6 several readings occur. The *text. rec.* has the sentence τῆς ἐνεργουμένης—πάσχομεν immediately annexed to σωτηρίας, then follows the εἴτε παρακαλούμεθα, while to the ὑπὲρ τῆς ὑμῶν παρακλήσεως is again added καὶ σωτηρίας, as in the first half. Several Codd., especially B.D.E.F.G.I., have moreover the phrase καὶ ἡ ἐλπίς—ὑμῶν before the εἴτε παρακαλούμεθα. This reading, backed certainly by weighty authorities, is assented to by Lachmann; he only objects to the second καὶ

s

σωτηρίας as doubtful. We may, however, suppose that a transposition by the transcriber may have early taken place, owing to the repetition of the ὑπὲρ τῆς παρακλήσεως. We would with Griesbach adopt this view, if Billroth's observation were correct, that the subject does not sanction the annexation of the τῆς ἐνεργουμένης κ. τ. λ. to the first phrase εἴτε θλιβόμεθα. He thus expresses himself: "How can it be said, if we bear sufferings, it is sufficient for your comfort and salvation that ye likewise endured them?" But we cannot see wherefore this should not be said. Is it not a general feeling that a comfort exists to those who love in sharing the suffering likewise, and are not the sorrows laid upon us by God profitable to the believer? Certainly this idea exists in the words, and may be equally deduced from the first and second part of the sentence. The contents undergo no change from altering the position of the words; both ideas of consolation and suffering are indifferently found in the apposition and in the antithesis of the εἴτε θλιβόμεθα and the εἴτε παρακαλούμεθα. With regard to Griesbach's opinion, it can only be alleged against it that it does not appear desirable to separate the εἴτε παρακαλούμεθα from the εἴτε θλιβόμεθα by the long intermediate sentence. But this may precisely have proceeded from the change in transcription alluded to, and it does not in the least outweigh the advantages of Lachmann's reading, for which the authority of the Codd. can be alleged).

Ver. 8. A closer description of the magnitude of the sufferings spoken of by the apostle in the preceding verses now follows. It is most probable from the phrase ἐν τῇ Ἀσίᾳ that Paul alludes to the persecution by Demetrius (Acts xix.), for to imagine with Heumann and Rückert that diseases which afflicted the apostle are signified, is by no means justified by the expression παθήματα τοῦ Χριστοῦ: Christ never suffered from sickness. It may not be concluded from the οὐ θέλομεν ὑμᾶς ἀγνοεῖν that the Corinthians were until this period unacquainted with the apostle's sufferings; it is not the sufferings themselves, but the greatness of them, which is exposed to view. (For ὑπὲρ τῆς θλίψεως Lachmann reads περί, which is supported by Billroth. Certainly, however, he goes too far, when he believes that ὑπέρ can on no account be employed in this passage.—The prepositions ὑπέρ and περί, it cannot be denied, occasionally stand for each other in the New Testament, for which reason the same frequently occurs in the Codd. [See Winer's Gram. 4th edit. p. 389].—The ὑπὲρ δύναμιν is in no degree synonymous with καθ' ὑπερβολήν, it rather shows forth the subjective position of the sufferings, the greatness of which is rendered objective by the καθ' ὑπερβολήν. The ὑπὲρ δύναμιν still further heightens the ὥστε καί.—'Εξαπορεῖσθαι only again occurs in the New Testament in iv. 8 of the present epistle ; these passages prove that it is the heightening of the ἀπορεῖσθαι).

Vers. 9—11. The extent of the sufferings, which according to the apostle's conviction could hope for no diminution, is conceived by him in an ethical point of view. It had the effect of freeing him from all self-confidence, and leading him to trust entirely to God, who could not only deliver him from impending death, but likewise restore those to life already become his prey. (The form τὸ ἀπόκριμα τοῦ θανάτου ἐν ἑαυτῷ ἔχειν can only be understood of the sentence pronounced. Hesychius explains ἀπόκριμα by κατάκριμα, ψῆφος. Paul considers the Almighty as Lord of life and death, uniting in himself the power of judgment and of pronouncing the sentence. Billroth's supposition appears less apposite, for he regards it as if the apostle had inquired of himself whether he could be preserved, to which he replies in the negative). The divine assistance upon which Paul relied for present and future aid appears, however, in some degree connected with human means (ver. 11) by the thanks returned for the support granted to the intercession of believers. However, according to the meaning of the apostle, the συνυπουργεῖν may not be so strained as if God and the faithful were two parallel powers, for it is rather God who by his Spirit inspires the intercession and lends power to it. This help which comes to the suffering brother by means of intercession must again, however, bear evidence of the blessing of the κοινωνία. The help is then a source of joy to all, and awakens thanksgiving in the hearts of those for whom intercession is made. (See iv. 15, which is entirely similar). Regarding the connexion of the text, we may be doubtful whether ἐκ πολλῶν προσώπων is to be connected with εὐχαριστηθῇ ὑπὲρ ἡμῶν, and if τὸ εἰς ἡμᾶς χάρισμα διὰ πολλῶν indicates the subject of the thanks, as Billroth supposes, or if, according to Fritzsche, διὰ πολλῶν εὐχαριστηθῇ ὑπὲρ ἡμῶν should be connected, and ἐκ πολλῶν προσώπων τὸ εἰς ἡμᾶς χάρισμα considered the subject of the thanks. We must especially regard the difference between the propositions ἐκ and διὰ in forming our decision. It is evident that διὰ refers to the actual assistance vouchsafed to the intercession, for which reason it would be better to connect διὰ πολλῶν with χάρισμα. According to the other arrangement, the article must be placed before ἐκ πολλῶν προσώπων, because then all as far as χάρισμα would form one subject; γενόμενον may be supplied to διὰ πολλῶν. The ἐκ, on the contrary, signifies the breaking forth of the inward feelings into thanksgiving, and from thence ἐκ πολλῶν προσώπων could be more correctly annexed to εὐχαριστηθῇ. But when Billroth attempts to construe προσώπων by oribus, so that it stands = to στομάτων, so is it without analogy ; it certainly only implies person. The διὰ πολλῶν, again, may only be understood to refer to persons, not words signifying prolixe, as Storr considers, because that would be a contradiction of Christ's command. (Matt. vi. 7).

Ver. 12. The mention of his sufferings now ceases, and Paul passes to himself and his position with regard to the Corinthians. The γάρ forms the change in the subject, so that the apostle grounds his claim to the sympathy of the Corinthians upon his sincerity, as if, And I am not unworthy of your intercession, had been supplied. The ἁπλότης is placed in contrast to the whole combination, and the εἰλικρινεία to those who were in trouble, both being characteristics of the σοφία σαρκική.—The addition of Θεοῦ refers to both subjects, simplicity as well as sincerity, and expresses the source of the same as existing in the operation of God's grace, ἐν χάριτι Θεοῦ, as it is styled in what follows. (See ii. 17, where ἐκ Θεοῦ stands parallel to the ἐξ εἰλικρινείας). This expression conveys the idea of simplicity and sincerity as its effect, just as the opposite qualities accompanying the σοφία σαρκική. (Concerning human wisdom, i. e. the wisdom proceeding from unsanctified human nature left to its own impulses, see the remarks on 1 Cor. i. 17, ii. 1.—Griesbach has, in a very unnecessary manner, enclosed in brackets the sentence οὐκ ἐν σοφιᾳ σαρκικῇ ἀλλ᾽ ἐν χάριτι Θεοῦ: it needs no separation from the context, as it belongs to and forms part of it).

Vers. 13, 14. Paul asserts his simplicity and sincerity throughout the scriptural connexion in which he stands to the Corinthians.　He thinks and writes nothing but that which they read in his writings, or acknowledge as his opinion.　The apostle hopes they will always continue thus to know him (for divine truths are as immutable as the element of their source), having already in a degree learned to acknowledge him.　This ἀπὸ μέρους cannot, without straining the sense, be explained to apply to anything but the existing divisions in Corinth.　Billroth's opinion is entirely untenable, when he states that the expression justifies the conclusion that Paul had now first the opportunity of manifesting his love towards them.　However, the apostle does not desire to pursue the subject of the dissensions further, but presses upon their attention their mutual relation to each other, as shall be made manifest in the day of the Lord, when all secrets shall be revealed; one is the glory of the other, *i. e.* one has joy in the salvation of the other without mixture of envy.　(In ver. 13 the ἀλλ' ἤ—ἤ presents a difficulty.　Fritzsche thinks [Diss. i. p. 11, sqq.] the ἀλλ' ἤ should be separated, so that the words might be understood : *neque enim alia ad vos perscribimus, quam aut ea—aut ea.*　But wherein should the antithesis of the ἀναγινώσκειν and ἐπιγινώσκειν consist?　It is evident that the ἐπιγινώσκειν does not declare anything materially different from ἀναγινώσκειν, but simply in a degree confirms the special idea " to draw from the writing," so that the meaning may be, or what ye already know, *i. e.* through my epistle ; ἀλλ' ἤ can therefore only be received as belonging to the connexion, as in 1 Cor. iii. 5.　[See Emmerling on this passage.]—In ver. 14, I cannot persuade myself of the correctness of the connexion between the ἐπέγνωτε with the ὅτι καύχημα κ. τ. λ. following, which is maintained by Billroth.　First, the ἡμᾶς by no means agrees with it, and then the ἐν τῇ ἡμέρᾳ κυρίου is especially inapplicable ; for how can it be said that the Corinthians were already acquainted with that which should be made manifest in the day of the Lord?　It would be far more reasonable to consider ὅτι καύχημα κ. τ. λ. as a separate sentence, whereby the conviction of Paul is proved that the Corinthians in part rightly acknowledged that apostle.　This conviction justifies him in feeling secure [through the illumination of the Spirit] that the church of Corinth was truly a divine creation through his agency, and would remain his for eternity).

## § 2. THE PLAN OF PAUL'S JOURNEY.

### (i. 15—ii. 17).

The fact of the apostle's expressing himself so amply upon the
subject of his projected journey may be accounted for by his antagonists having employed to his prejudice the changes he had
been called upon to make with regard to it. They had taken
advantage of this opportunity to charge him with fickleness, and
in order to refute this accusation he proceeds to explain the
grounds upon which he had made these alterations.

Vers. 15, 16. What Paul here states as his original intention
with reference to the journey to Corinth must have been written
in the epistle which is lost, for he expresses himself differently in
1 Cor. xvi. 5. The sentence ἵνα δευτέραν χάριν ἔχητε might
appear to imply that Paul was now for the first time in Corinth ;
but it has been already remarked (Introd. § 2) that there exists
foundation for the supposition that the apostle was frequently
there. Accordingly this expression must be considered to refer
only to the visit to Macedonia, the journey thither, and return
from thence. (In ver. 15 πεποίθησις, which only appears in the
New Testament in the writings of Paul, occurs frequently in this
epistle. It is closely allied to πληροφορία, firm assurance, certain conviction.—The reading χαράν is certainly to be rejected.
Some, however, e. g. Emmerling, receive χάριν in the signification
of χαράν, because it appears striking that the apostle should indicate his visit to be a favour. But in Rom. i. 11 the apostle
declares himself in the same manner. It would have been false
modesty to dissemble his own consciousness of the power which
the Lord had invested him with.—Ver. 16. In the journey to
Judea, Jerusalem was the apostle's principal object of interest.
See Acts xix. 21, xxi. 10, 13).

Ver. 17. This passage, which stands in strict connexion with
vers. 18—20, presents difficulties not unimportant. It is susceptible of two explanations, both of which, however, appear constrained. If it be construed thus, " Have I taken this determination as it were lightly, after the manner of man, in order that
with me the yea, yea, may also be nay, nay?" it really does ap-

pear that the yea became nay with the apostle, as he changed his
conclusion, even if small weight is laid upon the repetition of the
ναί and οὐ as in other places, e. g. Matt. v. 37, where the simple
expression is fully adequate. But if the words are understood
thus : " Did I act in some degree with lightness, or do I take my
resolutions in a carnal manner, in order that under all circumstances yea may remain yea, and nay continue nay ?" it agrees so
far, as the apostle changed his intention and the yea became nay.
But greater difficulties arise, which I am surprised should escape
Billroth, who has declared himself decidedly in favour of this explanation ; for then the two questions certainly do not stand
parallel, which agreeably to the apostle's purpose they should.
In the question, Have I acted in some degree with lightness ? is
signified the imputation of his opposers that he had conducted
himself with fickleness. According to this view there could be
no reference in the second question to the accusation made by
Paul's enemies, for none had charged him with stubbornness.
Should, however, this idea be involved in the words, it must
be expressed as follows : Have I, in concluding thus, acted
as it were lightly ? Should I not rather then have determined
according to the flesh, if my purpose had only been to achieve
my own intention under all circumstances, that thereby nay
might alway continue nay, and yea, yea ? To this, however,
may be added, that the context does not perfectly agree with this
construction. It is evidently wholly gratuitous to understand
the λόγος ἡμῶν which follows *solely* of the publishing of the
Gospel ; it must signify the apostle's discourse. But if this be
the case, how can the ναὶ καὶ οὔ of ver. 18 agree with the above-
mentioned conception of ver. 17 ? The difficulty can only be
solved by a third supposition, the key of which is presented in
vers. 19, 20 ; that is to say, the apostle employs in this passage ναί
and οὔ in a very peculiar manner. The expressions are not marks
of affirmation and dissent, but of truth and falsehood, whilst according to the use made of them it is possible for the affirmation
to be an error, and the answer in the negative a truth. For this
reason he denies the co-existence of the ναί and οὔ in himself, as
in Christ all is simply yea, so likewise by his Spirit all is yea in
him. The words may accordingly be thus construed : " Or have
I conceived my determination in a carnal fashion, so that with

me yea is yea, and nay is likewise nay? *i. e.* that truth and false-hood are blended together, that I am wavering, without firmness?" The only thing which can be observed against this is that ἵνα must be taken in a weakened signification, which, however, is de-cidedly admitted in several passages in the New Testament. The advantage of this reception to the connexion with the context, and the sense of the subsequent verse, is, however, so apparent, that this circumstance cannot be considered. (For βουλευόμενος good MS. read βουλόμενος, which is adopted by Lachmann in the text; but it is probable that the βουλόμενος has here been changed on account of the repetition of βουλεύομαι which follows. The internal evidence which Lachmann adduces in defence of βουλό-μενος appears to me without weight. He considers the parti-ciple of the present creates a difficulty, because no contempora-neous exercise of the resolution and of the ἐλαφρία can take place. But for what reason? The bitter antagonists of Paul certainly with the ἐλαφρία proposed to accuse him of an insin-cerity.—Billroth on the other hand is correct in his view of the article placed before ἐλαφρίᾳ, considering it as indicating the lightness of which his opponents accused him.

Vers. 18—20. The unsubstantiality of this view regarding ver. 17, defended by Billroth, is especially established by the joining of ver. 18 and the following verses. The apostle may imagine an objection on the part of the Corinthians: if he in one matter can have so changed his plan, he may likewise certainly change his doctrine. To which Paul replies, he changes not his doctrine, that is unchangeable. But what justifies this addition? The expression λόγος ἡμῶν may, as already observed, just as well indicate the speech; the sentence ὁ ἐν ὑμῖν δι᾽ ἡμῶν κηρυ-χθείς is only a current observation that the Christ in whom all is yea, is the same which he has preached to them; the sentence might be entirely omitted without the principal subject suffering thereby. Nothing further relative to the preaching of the Gos-pel occurs in the passage. Although Grotius makes the ναὶ ἐν αὐτῷ γέγονεν of ver. 19 relate to preaching, and to the confirming of the same by miracles, it is evidently an error to do so; for Christ himself is the subject to γέγονε. Ac-cording to our exposition of the meaning of ver. 17, the con-nexion with the context forms itself in the following simple

manner.    A negative reply must be presupposed to the question in ver. 17, and then continue thus : " God is faithful, in
that (by his help) our preaching to you (as well in publishing the
Gospel, as every other respect), was not yea and nay.  For the
true Christ was not yea and nay, but in him is only yea, and God
hath founded us upon Christ, and infused his Spirit into our hearts
(vers. 21, 22) ; we thence possess the same spiritual character as
Christ, in us is only yea, not yea and nay." If we, according to
this, view the δέ of ver. 17 as not adversative, but the particle which
contains the connexion of the discourse. it need occasion no hesitation, as it is well known to occur frequently thus in the language
of the New Testament.    (See Winer's Gram. p. 414, sqq.)    Exception may, however, be taken to the proffered signification of ναὶ
and οὔ: we will therefore examine more closely vers. 20 and 21,
for if we except it in the sense laid down, we are also compelled
to apply the same to ver. 17, as the connexion of the whole deduction is adverse to a different signification of the words in that
passage.    The usual explanation of the words Χριστὸς οὐκ ἐγένετο
ναὶ καὶ οὔ, ἀλλὰ ναὶ ἐν αὐτῷ γέγονεν, is this, "Christ is ever asserted by us, our preaching of him remains always the same."
But the words speak certainly not of the preaching of Christ,
but of Christ himself, as is plainly proved by the sentence, " all
God's promises are in him yea," which according to the usual
explanation would be here thoroughly inapplicable.    Our conception of the passage, however, agrees entirely with this.    Christ as
the manifestation of God (τοῦ Θεοῦ υἱός is therefore employed) is
the absolute Truth, merely the *position*, in him is the actual fulfilment of all God's promises, the *negation* does not exist in him.
This absolute, divine, and positive principle of Truth is imparted
by God to his own people, through Christ in the Holy Spirit, so
that in them likewise the position only exists, and not as in the
natural man, the negation also.    Paul thence argues that it would
be impossible for him to be wavering, in the manner of the world
(κατὰ σάρκα).    In ver. 19 the sentence ὁ ἐν ὑμῖν δι᾽ ἡμῶν κηρυ-
χθείς has probably a current reference to the false preaching of
the teachers of error ; their Christ was no absolute position, because he was not in all respects the true one.—Concerning Sylvanus, see Acts xviii. 5, where he is called Silas, and 1 Pet. v.
12.—In ver. 20 αὐτῶν is to be supplied to the ἐν αὐτῷ τὸ ναί.

The sentence ὅσαι—ἀμήν is not to form a parenthesis, as Griesbach supposes; it connects itself strictly with the train of thought.
—As regards the reading of the last words of ver. 20, the general
one admits of clear explanation, nevertheless it appears with
Lachmann preferable to admit the καὶ ἐν αὐτῷ τὸ ἀμήν for the
following reasons. First, weighty authorities are in its favour,
especially A.B.C.F.G. and six other Codd.; and secondly, a far
more free connexion is thereby gained for the concluding words,
τῷ Θεῷ πρὸς δόξαν δι᾽ ἡμῶν).

Vers. 21, 22. Both verses, according to the preceding passage,
have for their object the communicating to the apostle whatever is
in the possession of Christ. We are not therefore to view the βε-
βαιοῦν εἰς Χριστόν as an outward union, a simple reception into
the public community of the church, but as inferring an essential
union—an engrafting, as it were, in the Lord—so that his life is
the life of Paul and of all believers. As χρίσας is distinguished
from σφραγισάμενος and δοὺς ἀῤῥαβῶνα, the former would be
best understood to designate the call to the spiritual offices of
priest and prophet, as experienced in the fullest sense by the
apostle. The σφραγίζειν (Rom. iv. 11; 1 Cor. xi. 2), and ἀῤῥαβῶνα
δοῦναι signify the operation of the Spirit which follows the calling, whereby the creature is confirmed in the same, and receives
the Spirit as a pledge of happiness in everlasting life. (In ver.
21 the participles βεβαιῶν and χρίσας are best connected adjec-
tively with Θεός, supplying ἐστί before the ὁ καὶ σφραγισάμενος
ἡμᾶς.—An allusion to the name Χριστιανοί possibly lies in the
χρίσας, the anointed by the Spirit, the kingly priesthood.—Ver. 22
expresses in the δοὺς ἐν ταῖς καρδίαις ἡμῶν the idea of excitement,
connecting with it, at the same time, that of subsequent repose).

Vers. 23, 24. That which the apostle has hitherto mentioned
generally is now specially enforced. The change in the plan of
his journey was founded upon no fickleness, but was called forth
by his love; he desired to be considerate towards the Corinthians,
to leave them time to collect themselves, and return from their
errors. The forbearance is further explained by him, as that a
repeated appearance in Corinth would seem urgent and vexatious,
and he desired not to have dominion over their faith, but only to
participate in their joy; he therefore leaves them the opportunity
of finding the right way, for being themselves certainly in the

faith, they could not be dealt with as unbelievers. (In ver. 23 ἐπὶ τὴν ἐμὴν ψυχήν may not be understood as if it were, I call God and my soul as witness, meaning that both God and soul should witness ; but, I call God as a witness against my soul, *i. e.* my soul shall suffer if I am saying that which is untrue.—The concluding sentence of ver. 24, τῇ γὰρ πίστει ἑστήκατε, is received by Grotius as an explanation of χαρά, " Ye may hope for joy, for by faith ye stand;" but as the mention of joy is only incidental, it appears more suitable to connect it as stated above with the more important οὐχ ὅτι κυριεύομεν (κ. τ. λ).

Chap. ii. 1, 2. On his own account also, Paul continues, he had avoided coming again to Corinth, not wishing to appear as a reprover, and thus to prepare sorrow for himself and others. When the necessity for reproof was urgent, the consciousness that a spiritual blessing might be thereby awakened was his sole consolation. The idea contained in the λύπη is especially to be observed in this and the following verse. Hitherto this has been erroneously considered entirely active, or entirely passive, as arousing sorrow, or experiencing it, but both these conditions are found in it. The affectionate nature of the apostle suffered very sensibly when he was compelled to inflict sorrow. The contrasts, therefore, of joy and sorrow prevail in the λύπη. The λύπη over sin is the purest source of joy, as the joy which is entirely sinful, and without the λύπη is the certain foundation of sorrow. This leads the apostle to say he did not desire to introduce ἐν λύπῃ again in Corinth. To understand this, on account of the ἵνα μὴ λύπην ἔχω of ver. 3 as simply passive, is clearly an error on the part of Billroth, for εἰ γὰρ ἐγὼ λυπῶ ὑμᾶς immediately follows, which refers to the ἐν λύπῃ ἐλθεῖν of ver. 1. But to prepare sorrow for another, is a pain to himself, thence ἔκρινα ἐμαυτῷ (*dat. comm.*), " I have conceived it advantageous to myself." The connexion between vers. 1 and 2 has something obscure in it, especially on account of the καὶ τίς ἐστιν ὁ εὐφραίνων με, εἰ μὴ ὁ λυπούμενος ἐξ ἐμοῦ; the singular ὁ λυπούμενος does not refer to any definite person,—the excommunicated person, for example, who is presently mentioned,—but is occasioned by the preceding ὁ εὐφραίνων. Certainly the plural might have been employed on both occasions, but the singular makes the text more concise and sententious. " He only can cause me joy, who permits me (*i. e.*

as the servant of God) to occasion him sorrow. But how is this connected with ver. 1 by means of εἰ γὰρ ἐγὼ λυπῶ ὑμᾶς? Doubtless thus, Paul will for this reason not journey *again* ἐν λύπῃ towards Corinth ; because he cannot foresee that circumstances there will prove the source of rejoicing to him, or that the condition of those who were from his former reproof λυπούμενοι, would be productive of more satisfaction to him. The passage thus contains an indirect recommendation to apply his reproofs better to heart, for the λυπούμενος is really one who displays genuine penitence, and real sorrow for his sin, and in whom therefore one may really rejoice. Grotius finds the following meaning in the words, " If I occasioned you sorrow, then should I have no one in Corinth who would cause me to rejoice." But the εἰ μὴ is decidedly against this, as by it the λυπούμενος is explained to be the εὐφραίνων. Rückert supposes an Aposiopesis, making a new question to commence with the καὶ τίς ἐστιν in the sense of, " And yet who maketh me to rejoice, but those whom I have caused to sorrow ? " But it is evident that the sentence forms a whole. According to our explanation, the only objection which presents itself is the present tense λυπῶ: certainly the ἐλύπησα is expected as antithesis to the πάλιν of ver. 1. But the present form may proceed from the fact of the effects of the sorrow being regarded as permanent. (In ver. 1 the πάλιν alludes to another stay of Paul in Corinth, in addition to the considerable one, during which he laid the foundation of the church there. See the Introd. § 2.—In ver. 2 καὶ τίς, in the signification of *ecquis quis tandem*, occurs also in Mark x. 26 ; Luke x. 29 ; John ix. 36).

Vers. 3, 4. Paul desires by the present written exhortation to effect an object not hitherto attained ; and in this view expresses the earnest hope that the Corinthians would receive that which was joyfulness to him, as a source of rejoicing to themselves. In order powerfully to stimulate their love, he describes the frame of mind in which he found himself at the time of writing to them. The Fathers (and among the moderns, Emmerling) have correctly referred the ἔγραψα αὐτὸ τοῦτο to the epistle before us ; but Billroth maintains its application to the earlier epistle, which renders the whole passage perfectly unintelligible. If it appears inconceivable that he can suppose the following to be the correct inference from the words, viz., " that Paul's object in this epistle is not the amendment of the Corinthians, but to address those already improved in grace." The words which precede certainly evince a desire on the part of the apostle that the present epistle may conduce to the improvement of the Corinthians, and this desire is yet more evident in the second part of the writing. Rückert likewise applies the sentence to the second epistle, although he finds the τοῦτο αὐτὸ an obstacle, and will therefore receive this expression in the signification of "even for that cause," but this is thoroughly incompatible with the Greek construction. (In ver. 4 consult Luke xxi. 25 concerning συνοχή. The affliction here described does not proceed from any outward necessity, but simply from the grief experienced by the apostle at being compelled to adopt such a style of writing. The οὐχ ἵνα λυπη-θῆτε appears a contradiction of ver. 2, where it says that only the λυπούμενος were to him a source of rejoicing. But here Paul employs the sorrow in an outward sense, and in ver. 2 it is not the end but the means to an end).

Ver. 5. After the apostle has thus cast a glance at the future, and taken due precaution to avoid many subjects of uneasiness upon his next arrival at Corinth, he turns to the past. If any have awakened grief, he has not caused it to him (Paul) but to all, and from this place to ver. 11 it is further impressed upon them that the love he has shown towards them they are now called upon to exercise towards this sinner. It is only in this manner that we can obtain a free and clear connexion with the foregoing passage. Ver. 4 plainly appears to be an additional sentence describing the circumstances under which the apostle wrote; the εἰ δέ τις λελύπηκεν is therefore immediately connected with the ἵνα μὴ ἐλθὼν λύπην ἔχω (ver. 3). "The intention of this epistle is so to dispose your minds that I may have joy in you; but should any one have caused you grief, let me not be regarded, but have a view to yourselves." A stop is not therefore to be introduced between vers. 4 and 5, as Griesbach supposes, but one verse closely follows the other, in the manner correctly printed by Lachmann. Billroth's declaration of the connexion is erroneously conceived, but this is necessarily a consequence of his incorrect understanding of the ἔγραψα ὑμῖν (ver. 3). He considers that ver. 5 stands connected with ver. 4 in the manner following. Paul states in ver. 4 that he had written in much affliction; but in order that he may not appear to be directing fresh reproofs to the sinner formerly addressed, he adds he had not troubled him. But how could the apostle justly assert this? The description in 1 Cor. v. 1, sqq., decidedly proves that this occurrence had greatly affected Paul. The words οὐκ ἐμὲ λελύπηκεν can only be conceived true by supposing that the apostle thereby intended indirectly to condemn the wrong position of some of the Corinthians to the above-mentioned sinner. Several among them might possibly (the impenitent, for example, or those who avoided all occasion of trouble to themselves) have compassionated the apostle for the affliction caused him by the same unfortunate person; therefore, in order to direct their thoughts to themselves, he says he was not then treating of its reference to himself but to them. It will of course be supposed that the apostle neither wished to deny or conceal the personal suffering produced by the circumstance; he only desired to make them perceive that it was unnecessary to occupy themselves with him, and had only to look to their own sorrow. But as this sorrow was by no means either deep-seated or general (as it would have been had their spirit of unity been truly awakened, (Paul adds with delicate irony, ἀπὸ μέρους, ἵνα μὴ ἐπιβαρῶ. For according to him the highest praise he could have awarded would be to say, that he had troubled all without exception, and yet no complaint proceeded from the Corinthians; but as he could not assert this, he ingeniously turns the phrase thus: he has not troubled me, but partly you, in order not to burthen all with this grief. According to this acceptation of the words, we prefer with Mosheim the interpretation ἀλλ᾽ ἀπὸ μέρους, ἵνα μὴ ἐπιβαρῶ πάντας, ὑμᾶς. But if πάντας ὑμᾶς must be connected, then not αὐτόν but only ὑμᾶς requires to be supplied to ἐπιβαρῶ. According to the usual explanation the passage is expressed quite differently. They translate: he has not only grieved me, but also you. To agree with this, the ἵνα μὴ ἐπιβαρῶ, must be understood to include a commendation; in order to avoid reproving all with their indifference. But there exist no just grounds for the interpolation of a μόνον, Paul absolutely negatives of himself that which he asserts of the Corinthians. (Fritzsche [Diss. i. p. 16, sqq.] receives ἀπὸ μέρους in the sense of non admodum, which comes tolerably near the meaning given, as the apostle likewise intends to reprove the

feeble grief of the Corinthians;* nevertheless the reference to πάντας ὑμᾶς is too strict to allow us to depart from the first meaning,
especially as in verse 6 the ὑπὸ τῶν πλειόνων is only another expression for ἀπὸ μέρους).

Vers. 6, 7. The apostle then proceeds without further irony;
nevertheless, if the necessary severity against the immoral offender be not exercised by all, but only by the greater number
(the majority truly standing as the whole community), it is amply
sufficient; and it becomes the sincerely penitent to practise that
indulgence towards the individual, of which he knows himself
to stand in great need. Rückert's supposition that the punishment of excommunication mentioned by the apostle had by no
means been employed by the Corinthians, but could only be
considered as a severe reproof (ἐπιτιμία should stand = ἐπιτί-
μησις) must be rejected as thoroughly untenable. In ver. 6 ἱκα-
νόν must be received substantively "it is a sufficiency." See
Winer's Gr. p. 331. Kühner's Gr. Pt. ii. p. 457.—In ver. 7 the
infinitive must be inferred from the presumptory form of ver. 6,
if it be not altogether necessary to supply ἔστω. In the καταποθῇ the idea is possibly expressed that, urged by despair, the
λύπη might hurry into the world and there fall a prey to its
prince [ver. 11]).

Vers. 8, 9. The apostle then adds an express command to receive again the excommunicated person, supposing they would
show the same obedience to this precept, as they had already done
the one (contained in the first epistle, chap. v.) requiring his exclusion. The form of this command Paul tempers by explaining
himself historically as to the tendency of the epistle. It need not
be stated that the meaning is not, that this was the sole intention of writing, for it contains much besides on various subjects.
The command for the excommunication also may not be regarded
as simply a trial of obedience, the main object was the salvation
of the church and of the individual. The assertion of these points
has for its object the exhibiting the reproof as forbearing. In
conclusion, this passage places fully before us the plenitude of the
apostolic power; the apostle retains and forgives sins, as taught

---

* Fritzsche certainly only regards ἵνα μὴ ἐπιβαρῶ as an explanation of ἀπὸ
μέρους: but in what manner this idea may accord with the meaning of ἀπὸ
μέρους as laid down, or correspond with the whole connexion of the passage, is
not perceptible.

by the spirit. (In ver. 8, κυρῶσαι ἀγάπην has not only the usual signification " to show love," but " to confirm love," that is to say, by reception into the communion of the church. The expression does not occur again in the New Testament. Emmerling compares הֵקִים, which the LXX. in Gen. xxiii. 20 render κυροῦν).

Vers. 10, 11. If a section is to be formed, it is certainly in this place, not, however, to include verse 12 or verse 14, as Griesbach thinks, for the connexion of idea is very apparent in both passages. But Paul here passes at once from the special circumstance of the reinstatement of the incestuous person to the idea of general forgiveness. The words ᾧ δέ τι χαρίζεσθε, and εἴ τι κεχάρισμαι, do not allude to any decided *Factum;* the extremely vague τί forbids this, and indeed the manner in which mention is made of the χαρίζεσθαι will not sanction their application to sin. These words must be considered to bear decided reference to the prevailing dissensions in Corinth. In these disputes all parties were in error, and must equally abandon their false notions; and Paul, therefore, commences by proclaiming his own unanimity of feeling towards the Corinthians, and that from a sentiment of love. Where the spirit of dispute is not vanquished by love, Satan is gratified, and seeks to ruin souls. From what has already been laid down, it will be evident that the ἵνα μὴ πλεονεκτηθῶμεν ὑπὸ τοῦ σατανᾶ does not contain a reference to the above-mentioned sinner alone, although it undoubtedly includes him; it expresses generally the danger of yielding an entrance to feelings of hatred. (In ver. 9, the δέ may certainly be explained thus, " As I expect perfect obedience from you in this matter, so am I likewise ready on my part to agree with you in conferring forgiveness on any."—Ver. 10. The εἴ τι κεχάρισμαι is an expression of humility: " If I perchance have anything to forgive." The reception of the κεχάρισμαι in a passive signification, as defended by Rückert, thus, " For to me also much has been forgiven, especially my offence in persecuting the church," is textually allowable; it nevertheless has the εἴ τι κεχάρισμαι against it, which will admit of the medial interpretation only, for that he was forgiven could certainly not be a subject of doubt.— The ἐν προσώπῳ Χριστοῦ represents the indulgence and readiness expressed by Paul, as sanctified and pure; they are such as may

be displayed in the sight of the Lord, and can, therefore, have no
admixture of a carnal nature.—Verse 11 shows how decidedly and
really dangerous Paul considered the betrayer and enemy of man
in his sphere of activity.   See Ephes. vi. 12).

Vers. 12, 13.  The joining these verses with the mention already
made of the journey, is so little adapted to the sense, that we
cannot understand the reason it is done.   Passing by the fact,
that we must return to i. 16, nothing further concerning the
journey is learned from these verses; plans only, and not actual
journeys, were discussed in i. 16, and in i. 23, and ii. 1, simply
Paul's design not to visit Corinth.   It would be far more to the
purpose, to see in these verses a declaration of Paul's great love
towards the Corinthians, forming thereby a commentary on the δι᾽
ὑμᾶς.   At all events the δέ of verse 12 must then be again received in the signification of "furthermore."   (See Comm. on i.
18).   The sentence θύρας μοι ἀνεῳγμένης ἐν κυρίῳ thus obtain
significance; for these good expectations might have detained
him in the place in which he then was, but his love to the Corinthians was so great, that he hastened on towards Macedonia, in
order to receive intelligence from them through Titus, as early as
possible.   It appears, however, very striking that the apostle, in
order to obtain early information from Corinth, should neglect a
favourable opportunity of publishing the Gospel.   It would seem
as if he had yielded too readily to human impulse, and abandoned
that which was of high importance for an object of less moment.
But the expression τῷ πνεύματί μου proves that this was not the
case; it was not purely human impulse that caused him to leave
Troas so hastily, but the consciousness that very important matters affecting God's kingdom in Corinth were coming under notice
at this time, and that he should be thereby justified in leaving
his present promising position for a time, in order to receive an
accurate report of them.   (In verse 13 the ἀποταξάμενος αὐτοῖς
refers to those inhabitants of Troas who were inclined to receive
the Gospel).

Vers. 14—16.  Nevertheless, continues the apostle, even in this
restless struggle, on account of the Corinthian Church, God always
gave us the victory.   Truly this victory displayed itself in the
person of the Lord himself (Luke ii. 34), and likewise in his
faithful servants, not only in the attractive, but also by means of

T

the repelling power. Although the apostle does not expressly
apply this to the circumstances of the Corinthians, it is yet evident that he intended to signify that this likewise might be said
of them, especially as he also alludes to the divisions in Corinth,
in ver. 17. His preaching was to the humble-minded and pure
a blessing, but a curse to his antagonists. By means of a twofold image, this idea is farther expressed, by *triumph* and *sacrifice.* God prepared for him, decreed him, as it were, like a con-
quering emperor, the triumph, but in Christ; *i. e.* inasmuch as
the apostle himself was in Christ, and likewise in and for the
things which are of Christ. In the second image the creature
appears passive, he gives himself to God as a well-pleasing sacrifice, but the savour of this sacrifice is permitted by God to be
manifest everywhere, to good and bad indifferently. The question
here presents itself, how far the apostle is speaking of the ὀσμὴ
τῆς γνώσεως Χριστοῦ, of the εὐωδία Χριστοῦ? Doubtless inasmuch as it is not Paul's own life which renders the sacrifice well-
pleasing to God, but Christ's life in him, and the γνῶσις is especially here held forth to view, because the idea of the sacrifice is in
the first place employed with reference to Paul's labours in preaching the Gospel, while he also applies it to his internal and external
conflicts at another period of time. The sweet savour's relation
to the sacrifice is exposed, according to the biblical expression,
רֵיחַ־נִיחֹחַ לַיהֹוָה. (See Lev. i. 9—17; Num. xv. 7). The sweet
savour is as it were the manifestation, the utterance of the dumb
sacrifice. The savour of life shed abroad by the apostle appeared
as a mighty power, attracting to itself as to a magnet all things
possessing affinity, but repelling antagonistic qualities. The σωτηρία and ἀπώλεια are the terminations of one as of the other,
of life and of death. Paul by no means intends to designate two
unalterable classes of mankind by the expression ἐν τοῖς σωζομένοις καὶ ἐν τοῖς ἀπολλυμένοις, but only to describe the result
produced by the one operation of the Gospel or the other. The
effect itself is by no means dependent on God's constraining
power, but on the devoting himself to the Gospel, a state within
the power of every individual.

Ver. 17. The words καὶ πρὸς ταῦτα τίς ἱκανός, must be especially considered with regard to the context. The idea "who is
thereunto worthy" (to exercise such operation), might as in iii. 5

be applied to man *without* God; and indeed in what follows we
are made aware that it is only speaking *from* God through Christ
that qualifies, and not the power of the individual, be it ever so
great. But this is not the chief idea in the present passage, the
intention of the apostle is rather to abate the arrogance of his
Corinthian antagonists. These also laid claim to apostolic prerogative (see chap. xi. 12), for which reason the apostle asserts
that only the sincere mind, the condition of εἰλικρινεία, constituted the capacity for such a position. The καπηλεύειν =
δολοῦν of iv. 4, indicates the antithesis, or confounding things
divine with those merely human, as reproved in 1 Cor. i. 2. But
if the state of sincerity implies the negative human side, the concluding words of the chapter and the verse must describe the
positive divine side. Unless the passage be in a degree pleonastic,
a reference must exist here, as in Rom. xi. 36, and other places,
to the circumstances of the Trinity. It is easy to explain ἐκ of
the Father, and ἐν of Christ; the former indicates the origin of
the exalted life which filled the apostle, the latter the life as the
enduring element of the same ; but it is unusual to regard κατενώπιον or κατέναντι (preferred by Lachmann) as of the Spirit.
According to this representation the Holy Spirit is considered as
the divine element which hovers, as it were, over the Church, before whose eyes and under whose sacred egis the latter extends
itself. In conclusion, it will be readily understood that the τοῦ
must be erased after κατενώπιον: Lachmann has already correctly
omitted it. (The expression οἱ πολλοὶ with the article refers to
well-known personal qualities. In iii. 1 τινὲς stands for πολλοὶ
as a proof that it is not to be pressed.—The doubled ὡς ἐκ is not
to be explained by the *Caph veritatis,* but it describes the nature of
the preaching as adapted to the views and judgment of the hearers :
we speak so, that they must confess that we speak from God, and
as enlightened by God. It also does not mean that they are
really not enlightened, but their enlightenment is viewed and
represented by the standard of others.—The repetition of ἀλλὰ
only marks more strongly the antithesis).

## § 3. THE APOSTOLIC OFFICE.

### (iii. 1—18).

After the apostle has stated that from his position towards the Corinthians, he required neither from himself nor others any commendation to them, they themselves being his living epistles, he proceeds to declare that this firm conviction did not rest on a consciousness of his own power, but of the gloriousness of his office, which he brilliantly illustrates by a parallel with the ministration of the Old Covenant.

Ver. 1. Although, as we have already observed on i. 1, the first part of our epistle is specially addressed to the well-intentioned, a reference nevertheless frequently occurs to his adversaries and their manifestations. It is precisely so in this place; he knew that his antagonists had charged him with self-commendation, and, therefore, he now inquires if he desired again with self-sufficiency to commend himself. Besides this, the apostle, by a side remark, exposes the weakness of his haughty opponents. These had, from a sense of their deficiency in divine authority, sought to assist themselves by letters of recommendation to the Corinthians, and from the latter to other churches. But Paul was superior to such proceedings, and in bold speech he compares his divine labours in his sphere of action with these artifices. (I prefer the reading εἰ μή, accepted by Griesbach and Lachmann; in the first place, the critical authorities in its favour are not slight, and then, although it appears rather more difficult, it applies better to the sense. In the second question the intention is obscure, for in the main point it is only a repetition of the subject of the first. Doubtless with the εἰ μή the connexion shapes itself thus: Do we then again begin to commend ourselves? In nowise; else should we as others employ commendatory letters to or from you, and for such we have no occasion, &c.—Paul's Corinthian antagonists might have brought with them letters of recommendation from Peter, James, and perhaps even John, and pleaded the authority of these apostles. But certainly these apostles could not agree with their views, but were rather deceived by them concerning the nature of their proceedings. [See

Comm. on xi. 13, sqq.] The position of the church with regard
to the various sorts of sectarian connexions existing within her,
might have early inculcated the necessity for γράμματα συστατικά, but it is unnecessary to state that in this passage such formal letters of credence are not intended).

Vers. 2, 3. The apostle explains the dependence of the Corinthians upon himself in a bold metaphor; he required no commendatory letter to them, they being his living epistle to the
world, an impressive document of his apostolic calling, addressed
to the whole world. He who could establish a church of God in
a city like Corinth must bear within himself the Spirit of the
living God, from whose body streams of living water flow. The
image is simple and intelligible, for if in verse 2 the Corinthians
are styled an epistle of Paul, and in verse 3 an epistle of Christ,
which he presents to the world, the latter verse is only a closer
definition of the former; and the apostle desires to make it apparent, that his labours have been perfected not in his own, but in
Christ's power. In the description of the spiritual nature of this
epistle, the apostle draws a parallel between it and the Old Testament, which is hereafter more fully carried out. The latter was
likewise an epistle of God to the world, but engraven by the
finger of God on tables of stone, while the former epistle is written on the tables of the heart. Because this was evidently so
among the Corinthians, this epistle was published, and, as it were,
read by all the world. The only difficulty in the passage is
caused by the sentence in ver. 2, ἐγγεγραμμένη ἐν ταῖς καρδίαις
ἡμῶν. If we lay aside the reference to i. 19 in the plural, and
say that Paul spoke inclusively of his fellow-labourers, Timothy
and Sylvanus,* the ἡμῶν nevertheless remains striking. We expect ὑμῶν, as the Corinthians collectively formed a living letter,
the individuals composed, as it were, the words of the same. A
few Codd., it is true, read ὑμῶν, but this change has evidently
been made on account of the difficulty, and may not be received
as correct. It is Emmerling's opinion that *literæ nobis in-
scriptæ* only means so far as "dwelling in us, as it were, so that

---

* That καρδίαι can be employed plurally, like σπλάγχνα, as Billroth thinks,
I much doubt. The ἡμεῖς employed alone by Paul cannot, under any circumstances, be accompanied by καρδίαι; we must, therefore, suppose that Paul spoke in
several names.

we bear it about with us everywhere." But this does not remove the chief difficulty, the real existence of the Corinthian church is the letter read by the world, not the subjective remembrance of their existence in the apostle. Fritzsche (Diss. 1, p. 19, sqq.) thinks that the apostle first principally refers to the Corinthians themselves, and afterwards to the epistle, to which he compares them : that the ἐγγεγραμμένη κ. τ. λ. comes under the former head, making the sense : *conscius mihi sum, vos mihi commendationi esse.* It seems to me that it may be necessary to adopt a modification of the reference, only it may be requisite to point out the means by which this would be obtained ; probably through the parallel of the apostolic office with the office of the Old Testament, which was floating in the apostle's mind. The high priest was the visible representative of the latter, who, among other rich symbolic ornaments, bore on his breast the insignia of his office, composed of twelve precious stones, upon which were engraven the names of the children of Israel. He wore this on his breast when he entered the holy temple, as a remembrance before the Lord continually (Exod. xxviii. 15, sqq.) The stone tables here mentioned are, according to this, not the tables of the law, but these precious stones engraven with the names of the children of Israel. This emblematic regulation is received by Paul in a spiritual sense, and applied to the relation of himself and other teachers of the Gospel, towards their spiritual children ; they bear their names engraven in their hearts, and bring them continually before God in prayer. There can be no doubt that the idea was passing through the apostle's mind that the bond between those become regenerate, and the teacher whose preaching produced the new birth, was in no case simply an outward one, but that an essential inward connexion took place between them. The regenerate are linked to the heart of their spiritual father by means of a spiritual bond ; precisely as Christ is in us, and we in Christ, so should believers also exist in one another. Under this view the Corinthians were actually in two respects an epistle ; first, by being engraven on the heart of the apostle, and secondly, inasmuch as they from this source of their life had gained an outward existence likewise.\* In

---

\* The idea that the power of faith and divine love, the inward emotions of the heart, as expressed in preaching, and the sigh and prayer of the contrite sinner,

conclusion, σαρκινὸς has in this passage, as the antithesis to λιθινὸς, only the signification of "living," without reference to the idea of weakness or sinfulness which is otherwise found in the σάρξ. Vers. 4—6. After Paul has declared the steadfastness of his faith, resting upon God, he again impressively states that his connexion with the Corinthians is indestructible, and that he does not ascribe to himself the fitness for the exercise of such powers, but imputes all to God, who has endowed the exalted office which he fills with extraordinary power. In ver. 5 the apostle strongly exposes the unfitness of the natural man (for what he here says of himself is applicable to mankind generally) to work the works of God. The λογίσασθαι stands in opposition to the ἐργάζεσθαι: if the man cannot even think that which is good, how much less shall he have the power to do it? (It is not necessary to supply ἀγαθὸν to the τι: the apostle considers the evil as the μὴ ὄν). The καί at the commencement of ver. 6 refers to this doing, " God gave us not only good thoughts, but made us also capable, as ministers of the new covenant, of putting them in practice. The ἀφ᾽ ἑαυτῶν and ἐξ ἑαυτῶν are in no degree pleonastic, but the ἐξ rather more closely determines the ἀπό. That is to say, in a certain sense the foundation of the Corinthian church proceeded *from* Paul, but the groundwork of the necessary power for his work was not his own. This proceeded not from him, but was shed abroad from God through the apostle. —The apostle now explicitly contrasts the new covenant with the old, but as in the πνεῦμα the new, so in the γράμμα the old is signified, and the following parallel between the two shows that Paul had the followers of Peter especially in view. (Concerning the antithesis between γράμμα and πνεῦμα see the observations on Rom. vii. 6). The letter corresponds to the body,

displays itself also in the outward and visible existence, is beautifully and significantly exhibited by Albert Knapp on the 87th Psalm. (Christoterpe 1835, pp. 348, 349.

> God effects all—what the spirit aspires to
> Is by him consummated,
> And all sighs that are like seed
> Scattered 'mongst regions of dark heathenfolk,
> Will one day wave in ears of gold.
> The heartfelt supplication—in eternity
> Receives its answer through the Lord.

which the Spirit forms to himself, and which he fills. The Spirit never appears here below without form; the Spirit of the New Testament, therefore, has also created for itself a form in the visible church and its institutions. But the Spirit rules with so predominant a sway in Christianity that it may be called *the Spirit*, upon the same grounds as the Old Testament is styled *the letter*, on account of the prevailing dominion of form. In a short significant expression Paul defines the difference of the two economies: τὸ γράμμα ἀποκτείνει, τὸ πνεῦμα ζωοποιεῖ. As, according to the connexion the ζωοποιεῖν refers to the imparting a higher life by means of the Gospel, to the power of creating men again in the new birth, it might be supposed that the ἀποκτείνειν was only to be received negatively: "the Old Testament can communicate no life." This view might appear the more correct, as the context would reject the notion of attaching censure to the Old Testament, but is calculated to represent it as the stepping-stone to revelation. But the expressions διακονία τοῦ θανάτου (verse 7), and τῆς κατακρίσεως (verse 9), prove that the apostle maintains the positive idea of the ἀποκτείνειν. It is clear from Rom. vii. 9, sqq., that Paul attributed to the law a power to kill, to condemn, and to impose a curse, for it required absolute holiness and the fulfilment of all commandments.* But by the power of grace this condemnation and this death became the source of life and forgiveness to the penitent. *Without* the New Testament, as a necessary extension of the Old, this characteristic of the economy of the Old Testament would truly be an imperfection; but *with* it, it becomes necessary for the instruction of man. (See on Galat. iii. 24). It was when the Old Testament was still maintained to be of this preparatory character, after the economy of the Spirit had manifested itself (as was done by the false teachers in Corinth, at least by Peter's party, with reference to whom these parallels appear to have been delineated), it was then that positive error and the abuse of the law commenced, which was opposed so strongly by Paul in the epistle to the Galatians. But to receive the Gospel without the law which should prepare for its acceptance is again the error of

---

* Fritzsche accepts this idea in too restricted and outward a sense when he says with respect to it: *Mosis munus fuit* διακονία θανάτου, *quoniam ille legem tulit, quæ plurima supplicia sanciret.* (Diss. i. p. 27).

Antinomianism. The apostle is not here speaking of the law as
it was of importance in the economy of the New Testament,
but of the law as applicable to outward institutions, in which
view it is perishable. (See on ver. 11). In order to signify this
the apostle makes use of the expression διακονία. For although
the law is not destroyed under the new covenant, there nevertheless no longer exists any διακονία τοῦ νόμου or θανάτου, the
διακονία τοῦ πνεύματος includes the law within itself. (Concerning the connexion of the concluding words by means of γὰρ
with that which precedes, Fritzsche and Rückert have correctly observed that this conjunction does not refer itself to the
principal phrase ἱκάνωσεν κ. τ. λ., but only to the preceding antithesis of γράμμα and πνεῦμα, for the purpose of making it
clearer, so that the meaning is, ἥτις διαθήκη γράμματος ἀποκτείνει, πνεύματος ζωοποιεῖ).

Vers. 7—9. The apostle further carries out his spirited parallel, proceeding from the minor to the superior particulars composing it. If the ministration of death and condemnation
were already so glorious, how much greater must be the glory
of the Spirit and of righteousness! The antithesis of the condemnation defines more strictly the idea of the δικαιοσύνη. As
the former was the announcement of rejection, the latter conveyed the tidings of righteousness, which, as a divine proclamation, may be concluded of active efficacy, producing righteousness.
Strictly speaking, life should have been employed in opposition to
death; but the Spirit is considered as the life-creating principle,
according to the words which occur previously, πνεῦμα ζωοποιεῖ.
The idea of the θάνατος is also to be defined in the same way
from the γράμμα ἀποκτείνει which precedes. The ἐντετυπωμένη
ἐν λίθοις only incidentally refers to the διακονία: its more avowed
reference is to the Decalogue inscribed upon the table of the law.
The ἐν λίθοις is consequently not the same as the ἐν πλαξὶ λι-
θίναις of ver. 3. But inasmuch as this forms the quintessence of
the whole law, upon which the office itself rests, and in the application of which its existence consists, the apostle likewise applies
that which concerns the Decalogue to the office itself. The
greatest peculiarity, however, in this passage is the typical application of an historical subject. According to Exod. xxiv. 12,
sqq., xxxiv. 1, sqq., Deut. x. 1, the countenance of Moses, when

he descended from Sinai was so bright, through the reflected glory emanating from the presence of the Lord with whom he had spoken, that the Israelites could not endure to behold his countenance. Regarding Moses as the representative of the law, the apostle considers this brightness of his face as the definition of the glory resting on the economy of the old covenant. As in the latter all was outward, so likewise was the brightness external, transitory, continually passing away: in the new covenant, on the contrary, all was of internal signification, the gloriousness was of a concealed character, but infinitely greater and more enduring. Such passages as 1 Cor. x., Gal. iv., prove that this application of an occurrence related in the Old Testament is in no respect to be regarded as an ingenious play upon words, but is based upon the fact that in the apostle's fundamental views of the Old Testament, and its history, it was ever considered as a type or precursor of the New Testament. In the 12th and following verses the comparison takes another direction; but had the apostle desired to continue the comprehensive parallel already entered upon, there still remained abundant materials for it. He might have illustrated the difference between the two economies from the circumstance, that the Israelites were not even in a condition to behold the transient glory of Moses' countenance, while the believer in the New Testament may himself become the recipient of an infinitely more glorious and mighty spirit. (In verse 7, Fritzsche has correctly observed, in opposition to Emmerling, that the τὴν καταργουμένην refers to τὴν δόξαν, understanding thereby the gradually vanishing light imparted to Moses' countenance, after his interview with Jehovah; whilst Emmerling, on account of verse 11, refers it to τὰ γράμματα, with which it is incidentally connected, thus making the reference to the economy of the Old Testament to declare that it is of a transitory nature. Decidedly this type may contain such an allusion, but in ver. 7 the reference is to the type itself, and not its signification).

Vers. 10, 11. In order yet further to enhance the idea, the apostle declares that in presence of the greater gloriousness, that which was less has ceased to exist; for if the perishable institution had already passed through its period of glory, that which was imperishable must continually endure in (increasing) gloriousness. (See on ver. 18). In ver. 10 the only doubt is excited by the ἐν τούτῳ τῷ μέρει and its meaning. I prefer, with Beza and Billroth, the connexion with δεδόξασται, so that then ἕνεκεν τῆς ὑπερβαλλούσης δόξης is added epexegetically. Compared with heathenism, the Old Testament certainly possesses glory; but according to the view here held before us, its gloriousness is no longer glorious, being overpowered by the preponderating light of the New Testament; the moon reigns pre-eminent in the presence of the stars, yet her light is as nothing compared with that of the sun. Fritzsche understands it differently ; he translates it, *quod collustratum fuit hac parte, i. e.* so that it was bright and glorious, through Moses' shining countenance. But in this view, which is nevertheless reasonable in itself, the chief position of this verse, viz. that the gloriousness of the Old Testament retreats so entirely before the glory of the New Testament, that it ceases to exist, is not made sufficiently prominent. Concerning the τὸ καταργούμενον and τὸ μένον of ver. 11, it is certainly correct, that from ver. 7 the subject under consideration is the ministration of the letter and of the Spirit, not of the law and the Gospel, nevertheless the former shares the character of the latter, and *vice versa.* Not only the ministration of the law, but the law itself, regarded as an institution, was considered on the decline when Paul wrote ; therefore καταργούμενον, the present is used. Billroth has correctly observed that διὰ δόξης and ἐν δόξῃ are not to be considered entirely parallel ; the former indicates that which is transitory, the latter, the enduring. Ver. 11, with its γὰρ, must be understood as a repetition of the proof for the ὑπερβάλλουσα δόξα: if it is conceived to refer to the preceding verse, πολλῷ μᾶλλον does not agree with it.

Vers. 12, 13. The apostle, returning again to the subject of ver. 4, expresses his determination to labour afresh in the strength of God's power, and the exalted nature of the office conferred upon him by God, and this likewise in antithetical parallel with Moses ; the latter veiled his countenance, but the ministers of the New Testament labour with uncovered face (ver. 18). Fritzsche is certainly right when he views in the ἐτίθει κάλυμμα a reference to the mystery which the priesthood possessed in the Lord, and in the Holy of Holies, with which we may contrast the open proceedings of the ministers of the new covenant

The correct meaning of the εἰς τὸ τέλος τοῦ καταργουμένου is perfectly reconcilable with this. These words can be no otherwise understood than of the passing away of the brightness from Moses' countenance; this brightness is called τὸ καταργούμενον, and the fact of its vanishing τὸ τέλος. The meaning of the words is then this: "Moses covered his countenance with a veil, in order that the children of Israel might not behold the end of that which is abolished;" i. e., abandoning the employment of typical language, that they might not perceive that they belonged to an economy about to cease. This reception is not contradicted by our accepting τὸ καταργούμενον in another sense in ver. 11, viz., as there referring to the institution of the law, and not to the gloriousness, for in the apostolic description they are both represented as abrogated together. Only when the type stands clear, as in ver. 13, the expression must be admitted in its actual sense; but when, as in ver. 11, the explanation of the type is brought forward, the inward sense must exercise sway. Yet because Christ is called the end of the law (Rom. x. 4), it has been thought that Christ was here intended, which is, however, perfectly unjustifiable, for how could Paul say that Moses covered his countenance in order that the Israelites should not behold Christ? From this the question naturally arises, do the words in Exod. xxxiv. 33 contain such a reference? According to the relation in that passage the object in covering the face would appear to be of an entirely different kind, viz., to render it possible for them to look upon Moses, and not to conceal from the Israelites the vanishing of the glory. History may not, however, be transformed in order to aid the typical explanation of its signification; it must be taken precisely as it stands. We have ever maintained this as a fundamental principle, nevertheless a certain degree of freedom to be granted in the use of history is also sanctioned in the type. That which is not expressly related, or intended to be apparent as the object of a definite proceeding, may be modified to a certain extent when adopted in the sense of a type. These observations are applicable to the present passage. The apostle was able to allude to the veiling of Moses' countenance in the manner he has done, because the Old Testament does not expressly state that the reason for the wearing of the veil was, that the Israelites were unable to bear the brightness of his face; this intention in such a proceeding is only inferred from the context. Besides this, another inference may be drawn from the action described, and this bears relation to the weakness of the Israelites; they were not able to bear the view of the truth. On this foundation the apostle proceeds with the typical application of the passage.

Vers. 14, 15. The type is now in some degree modified. Hitherto Moses has been the early type of the economy of the Old Testament, but now the book itself, whose sense cannot be understood by the children of Israel, is constituted the type. (In ver. 15 Μοϊσῆς, i. e. the books of Moses, stands by synecdoche for the entire Old Testament); and while in ver. 14 the veil appears to be on the Old Testament itself, it is called in ver. 15 κάλυμμα ἐπὶ τὴν καρδίαν αὐτῶν κεῖται. However, these are freedoms in the employment of the type, which do not suit the nature of the comparison ; this might appear to have arisen from the subject of ver. 13 being only the veiling in order that the Israelites should not observe the disappearance of the brightness, while want of power to understand the Scriptures is immediately afterwards introduced. But, as already signified, these are only apparently incongruous. The Israelites were, from their weakness, incapable of witnessing the disappearance of the brightness, not being able to discriminate between essence and form; their incapacity in this particular forbade their comprehending how the nature of the Old Testament could continue to exist in the Gospel, even if the appearance of the former as an especial institution were removed by the fulfilment of the latter in Christ. Inasmuch as this weakness and blindness was of a guilty nature, the apostle pronounces thereon the reproving ἐπωρώθη τὰ νοήματα αὐτῶν. (See on Rom. xi. 25). But how does the apostle introduce the condition of the Israelites, for his description of them does not appear to be relevant to the strain of his argument? It must here be inquired how the ἀλλά before the ἐπωρώθη is to be understood. It cannot form, as it would seem, the antithesis to the καὶ οὐ of ver. 13, if that is expressed by Paul in ver. 18; thus ver. 14—17 forms a digression distinguished by Griesbach by being placed within a parenthesis. Billroth translates it, " but therefore also were their minds blinded!" But the " therefore" does not stand in the text, and may not be added, for the condition of the Israelites described in verse 14, 15 is the same as that represented in verse 13; it is only by means of the *ἄχρι, ἕως τῆς σήμερον*, stated to be one which still continues. We must therefore receive ver. 14 as the antithesis to *καὶ οὐ*, and in the following manner: "We conduct ourselves freely and openly, hiding neither ourselves nor our works, but this candour has no effect upon the Jews, their senses are blinded." In verse 18 the antithesis is resumed, but in such a manner that the connexion with verse 17 is perfect; the brackets including verses 14, 15, 16, 17 are therefore to be erased. The assertion of the blindness of the Israelites is so strong in this passage, because the principle objection of the entire Judaizing party to Paul was that he seemed to take from them the glory of the Old Testament.* It is probable that he bore them especially in mind in the words which occur in ii. 17, iii. 1, and after the parallel of the two economies the reference to Jews and Jewish Christians naturally arises. These passages indirectly contain the exhortation to free themselves perfectly from the veiled Moses, and to behold the countenance of the unveiled Christ, whose glory is reflected from his faithful followers. (Ver. 14 is the only passage of the New Testament in which the *παλαιὰ διαθήκη* precisely indicates the writings of the Old Testament.—The general reading *μὴ ἀνακαλυπτόμενον ὅ, τι* is decidedly to be preferred to the one received by Griesbach and Lachmann, who read *ὅτι*. The meaning of the words is, " The veil is not uncovered, *i. e.*, cannot be uncovered [by human means, 2 Peter i. 20], because it can only be removed in Christ." —The *ἡνίκα* of verse 15 does not again occur in the New Testament, the interrogative form *πηνίκα* is never found).

Vers. 16, 17. If the removal of the veil is here made dependent upon the turning of the heart to the Lord, while in verse 14 it is said *ἐν Χριστῷ καταργεῖται*, it involves no contradiction, for Christ first manifests himself to mankind as the living Saviour in the conversion. It is only when internal light is bestowed that man can discern Christ also in the Scripture. But how does verse 17 connect itself? If we receive *τὸ πνεῦμα* as the indication of the substance of the Son, as in John iv. 24, or if we admit with

---

* Lakemacher (Obs. Sacr. iii. 2) thinks he here discovers an allusion to the Jewish custom of veiling the head when the Holy Scriptures were read. (See Jahn's Altherth. vol. iii. p. 439). But this is decidedly excluded by the reference to the fact of Moses veiling himself.

Usteri (Lehrbegr. p. 335) the Son and the Spirit are identical, still the connexion is not clear. To the circumstances of the Trinity there is absolutely no reference; but, as Calvin and Beza have correctly remarked, the apostle casts a retrospective glance to ver. 6, in which he has contrasted the letter with the Spirit. He concludes his argument by saying, "The Lord is even that Spirit of which we have already spoken. The δὲ especially is not to be taken, as Fritzsche and others have done, in the same sense as γὰρ, for it continues the passage and the argument. But a degree of objection might be urged against this view, inasmuch as we might suppose that Christ was not the Spirit, *i. e.*, the spiritual institution, the economy of the Spirit itself, but that he had only founded it. But according to the apostolic declaration Christ himself is all, he fills the church with himself, it is therefore Christ himself. (1 Cor. xii. 12). The apostle can therefore immediately continue: οὗ δὲ τὸ πνεῦμα κυρίου, for the New Testament is only called πνεῦμα because it is the sphere in which the Spirit of the Lord works. In the Old Testament a divine Spirit was certainly also efficacious, but it was after Jesus' glorification that the Holy Ghost, in a specific sense so called, first manifested itself. (John vii. 39). The apostle mentions the ἐλευθερία as the effect of the Spirit of Christ, because these form the antithesis to the *weakness* of Israel, which hindered them from beholding unveiled the glory of God as displayed in the brightness of Moses. Such weakness is *bondage*, a fettering the spiritual life with the flesh, and this is removed by the Gospel.

Ver. 18. Paul, in conclusion, presents to himself and all believers a description of this liberty effected by the Spirit of the Lord. This freedom effected by the Lord (ἀπὸ κυρίου) manifests itself by imparting its gloriousness to the believers, who behold as with open face, and in whom he is reflected as in a glass. In Christianity all became like Moses; with each regenerate creature the Lord speaks, as a man with his friend, and this glorious state increases in itself until the believer is changed into the image *of Christ.*—This explanation of the passage agrees in the strictest particular with the connexion, the κατοπτρίζεσθαι alone forms a difficulty. This expression elsewhere occurs only in the signification of "to reflect oneself, to behold oneself in a mirror," or to see something in a glass; and if this acceptation is retained, the idea loses much in perspicuity. The μεταμορφούμεθα plainly proves that the apostle considers the Christians as those in whom the glory of the Lord is displayed; for, from the continual operation of the same, they are described as gradually becoming transformed into the image of Christ. It is, therefore, impossible that Paul should previously say that they behold the glory as not from themselves, but truly only in a glass. Κατοπτρίζεσθαι is rather here employed* in the sense of to reflect as from a mirror, *i. e.*, to beam forth, to reflect back the glory," so that the parallel with Moses again presents itself; only whilst the latter veiled his countenance, and the brightness thereof speedily vanished (ver. 13), Christians walk with uncovered faces, for their glory steadily increases, they are conducted from one degree of glory to another (ἀπὸ δόξης εἰς δόξαν), and changed into the image of Christ. The μεταμορφοῦσθαι doubtless implies not only the inward glorification, but also the glorification of the body, concerning which Paul immediately proceeds to explain himself further (from iv. 7). See also Phil. iii. 20. (The accusative τὴν αὐτὴν εἰκόνα is best explained with Fritzsche from the notion of emotion, comprehended in the μεταμορφοῦσθαι, which is frequently connected simply with the accusative, and without any preposition. See Kuehner's Gr. vol ii., p. 204.—The αὐτήν refers to the preceding δόξαν κυρίου: the glory of the Lord, which beams forth from the faithful, becomes the image of Christ in them.—Πνεύματος is, according to ver. 17, to be understood in apposition to κυρίου, " The Lord's, whose Spirit it is," but not as if the Spirit were added to the Lord, the Lord's Spirit, *i.e.*, Christ. A third supposition, supported by Billroth, and, according to which, πνεύματος is considered dependent on κυρίου, is for this reason inadmissible; the expression, " Lord of the Spirit " never occurs. But if we connect πνεύματος with κυρίου, in the manner proposed, we may not, with Rückert, suppose κύριος πνεῦμα an idea, as do the church Fathers. Θεὸς λόγος, to bind; but πνεῦμα is here, according to ver. 17, the antithesis of γράμμα).

---

* Winer (Gr. p. 232) receives the expression in the sense of *sibi intueri;* " to behold oneself in the glory of the Lord, as in a looking-glass," *i.e.*, for one's satisfaction and strengthening. But this is certainly inapplicable; the beholding must be considered of an inward character, as in the mirror of the soul; in which case, according to its nature, it represents a reflecting back of the Lord's image.

II.

# SECOND PART.

(iv. 1—ix. 15).

§ 4. THE CONFLICT.

(iv. 1—18).

---

IN the first verses the apostle condenses into few words the subjects touched upon in the preceding chapters, and introduces himself as the minister appointed by God, whose labours should not fail, and to whose preaching the blind alone could remain indifferent (1—6). He contrasts the gloriousness of the intention of his calling, with the weakness of external things, in a comprehensive parallel, from which he proves that the trials and struggles of his earthly life in no degree remove his efficacy, but that they are subsidiary to the great end of perfecting himself and the church (7—18).

Vers. 1, 2. The conviction that his office proceeds from God's grace alone, and not from his own worthiness, enables Paul to assure them that no difficulties have had power to weary him, (this indirectly attacks the state of affairs in Corinth), and that he has never employed unworthy means or deceit in order to support his authority, but that in the power of truth it commended itself to men in the sight of God. This idea takes a retrospective glance at iii. 1, ii. 17, in which the mixture of divine truth with human wisdom by the opponents of Paul was reproved. The πανουργία (see 1 Cor. iii. 19) is to be understood of this same impurity of sentiment which disfigures divine truth itself. It refers as little to moral offences (as Kypke, Krebs, &c., erroneously suppose, seeing in it an allusion to the vice prevalent in Corinth), as the κρυπτὰ τῆς αἰσχύνης: both expressions signify the crafty mode of proceeding which characterised the antagonists of Paul, and which could not bear the light. (In ver. 1 consult, concerning καθώς, Winer's Gr. p. 418.—In ver. 2 ἀπέπομαι, implying to deny one-self something, i. e., to avoid something or to renounce it, only occurs in the New Testament in this passage.—The expression κρυπτὰ τῆς αἰσχύνης indicates secrets which bear in themselves marks of shame : secrets may, however, be supposed to exist which do not necessarily bear this character. The expression πρὸς πᾶσαν συνείδησιν ἀνθρώπων marks the opposition of the divine nature to the human in its most extended sense. The purity and openness of the former must be alike evident to friends and enemies).

Vers. 3, 4. To a winning of all to the Gospel, although pro-fessed by the apostle, he does not attach an unconditional hope, and for this reason the hearts of so many persons were brought under the influence of Satan, and thereby became ἀπολλύμενοι, that to these light itself must appear darkness, because they maintained their darkness to be light. The expressions φωτισ-μὸς εὐαγγελίου and δόξα Χριστοῦ contain also an allusion to the image employed in chap. iii. relative to the veiling of Moses. Instead of withdrawing the veil from their hearts (iii. 15) and permitting Christ's light to shine through them, they draw it yet closer, thereby obscuring for ever the source of their bliss. But when to Christ εἰκὼν τοῦ Θεοῦ is added, not only the Gospel in all its glory shall be brought to light, but the opposition to Satan to the Θεὸς τοῦ αἰῶνος τούτου must become heightened. The devil is a defaced image of God ; Christ, the God of the αἰὼν μέλλων, the pure unclouded image of the Father. As, however, throughout the universe all the manifestations of the principle of good preserve a unity and connexion with each other, so like-wise do the evil, and Satan is the centre from which all sinful development emanates, the origin of each wicked human deed. His predominance, however, presupposes a turning away from God on the side of the man, and an inclination towards evil. It is not necessary to view the ἄπιστοι as an absolute prolepsis, with Fritzsche and also Billroth, as if Paul considered the ἀπιστία the consequence of the blindness, and immediately connected this latter result with the power which called it forth ; but Paul rather

conceives mankind through the divine omniscience, as chosen or
not chosen. (The ἐν οἷς—ἀπίστων of ver. 4 is a kind of Hebrew
construction. It is entirely erroneous to understand the ἐν οἷς as
indicating the ἄπιστοι to be individuals among the ἀπολλυμένοις:
both are identical. The ἐν οἷς indicates the operation of the
devil to be of an inward spiritual nature.—The name Θεὸς,
τ. ἀ. τ. only occurs here in the New Testament.* The devil
is more frequently styled ἄρχων, τ. ἀ. τ.; John xii. 31, xiv.
30, xvi. 11. The Rabbins also have the name "God of
this world." [See Schöttgen Hor. Hebr. i. 688].—The εἰς τὸ
μή is selected according to the satanic intention. The readings
here are very various. Instead of the *simplex* form, some Codd.
read καταυγάσαι, others διαυγάσαι: the *text. rec.* interpolates an
αὐτοῖς, which certainly ought to be supplied, but does not belong
to the text. Receiving the MS. as authority, the reading of αὐγά-
σαι τόν, already accepted by Griesbach and supported by Lachmann, is to be maintained. The conclusion of the verse τοῦ
ἀοράτου is likewise certainly a gloss out of Col. i. 15, concerning
which the Comm. on the expression εἰκὼν τ. Θ. may be consulted.
—Φωτισμός, which again immediately occurs in ver. 6, has been
chosen by Paul, and not φῶς, because the latter signifies the ray
of light, and the former the action of the same, for which αὐγή is
also employed).

Vers. 5, 6. If the observation that he preached not himself
occurred in any other connexion, we might suppose that Paul
thereby intended to caution his followers against too strict a de-
pendance on his person. But the context, as well as the expression Ἰησοῦν κύριον, in antithesis with the ἑαυτοὺς δούλους, shows
that the apostle rather designed a polemic against the followers
of Peter and the *Christianer;* that he considers himself only as a
weak, subordinate creature, whilst in Christ the Lord of all appeared manifest. He alone, therefore, could be the object of the
preaching to the world. It appears to me unnecessary to include
ver. 5 in a parenthesis, as Lachmann has done, making ver. 6
succeed immediately to ver. 4; the ὅτι of ver. 6 rather refers to

---

* The expression assumes a somewhat ironical tone ; instead of the true God
the world has chosen for its God that which is the most perfect contrast to all
that is divine. Schöttgen (on this passage) has quoted the words : *Deus primus
est Deus vivus, sed Deus secundus is Sammael,* out of Jalkut Rubeni.

the preceding idea in this manner: " We preach not ourselves,
but Christ, for if we appear to be the speakers, it is nevertheless
Christ who works by us, and who inwardly enlightens us, in order
that we again should enlighten others." This idea is expressed
by Paul by means of a parallel of the creation and regeneration;
as God (according to Gen. i. 1) called light to shine forth out of
the darkness of the physical world, so he likewise permits spiritual
light to beam forth out of natural darkness, in those who are born
again; thus they appear as lights of the world (Eph. v. 8). Emmerling erroneously understands ἐκ σκότους "after the darkness
he created the light;" ἐκ has rather its real signification, " out or
forth from the darkness." (See Winer's Gr. p. 351). In the
second hemistich of the verse, the penetrating of the light into
the πρὸς φωτισμόν is expressed, the words bearing this translation, " The God who said, light shall shine forth out of the darkness, shines also in our hearts (on the first conversion), thereby
making the inward darkness light, and enabling us to shed light,
i. e., to the enlightenment of others." The idea of the peace re-
sulting from the light dwelling in the heart, and the motion of
the penetrating light, is connected in the expression ἔλαμψεν ἐν
καρδίαις. The γνῶσις τῆς δόξης τοῦ Θεοῦ is not to be considered
as the apostle's own knowledge, but that which he calls forth in
others, by means of the light emanating from him. The connexion of the ἐν προσώπῳ I. Χρ. alone can make us doubtful.
Fritzsche and Billroth would connect it with the πρὸς φωτισμόν:
but it is not correct to do so, for this reason, not ἐν but ἀπό must
then stand, because the outpouring operation of the light is described in the πρὸς φωτισμόν. I therefore give the preference to
the connexion with the δόξα τ. Θ. In this view the repetition of
the article τῆς before ἐν προσώπῳ is justifiable, but not absolutely
indispensable. In verse 6 I prefer with Lachmann the future
λάμψει, instead of the usual reading λάμψαι, so that God may
be deemed speaking. The Codd. A.B.D. support this reading,
according to which the construction of the sentence appears much
clearer.—The ὃς before ἔλαμψεν presents a difficulty. In some
MSS. it is certainly omitted, and in others οὗτος stands for it,
but that may only have been substituted in order to render it
easier; the difficult reading is unquestionably the original one;
either ἐστὶ must be supplied to the premises, as Fritzsche and

others suppose, or the ὅς must be taken for οὗτος καὶ with Rückert. The latter appears to deserve the preference). Vers. 7—10. Paul appends to the preceding representation a description of the outward weakness in which the glory of the internal life was displayed in his person. The intention of this contrast is to show that all is to be ascribed to God, and not to men, as he has already stated in iii. 5. For throughout the apostle's sorrows and necessities, and the same may be said of all believers, the protecting power of God displayed itself; they were intended only to humiliate him, to divest him of all trust in his own strength, but were neither allowed to corrupt or destroy the object of them. The life of the Redeemer himself is here a type for those who believe in him; they bear about his dying with them, in order that his life may be manifest in them. It may be inquired how the σκεύη ὀστράκινα of this beautiful passage is to be understood. We might imagine that the expression referred to the whole man, making the sense, " we possess the everlasting, the divine, in the weak and sinful form of that which is human." But the following passages prove (iv. 10, 11, 16, v. 1) that the first and prominent idea of the apostle bore reference to the body, by means of which all the sorrows of this life are conveyed to the inward man, because it is the bond connecting him to the κτίσις.* The form of speech also agrees best with this view, for σκεῦος = כְּלִי is called the body, as the vessel containing the soul (1 Thess. iv. 4; 1 Sam. xxi. 6), but the expression is never employed for the whole man. The ὀστράκινον refers to the עָפָר of Gen. ii. 7, for which in v. 1 ἐπίγειος stands. By adopting this supposition it becomes perfectly intelligible how Paul, in ver. 10 should pass over to the σῶμα, and contrast the glorified body which the living power of Christ will evoke in believers (see Comm. on John vi. 40) with the frail and sinful one belonging to this temporal life. (In ver. 7 ὑπερβολὴ τῆς δυνάμεως may be correctly understood as Hendiadyoin.—The ἐξαπορεῖσθαι of ver. 8 has already appeared in i. 8.— Ἐγκαταλείπεσθαι properly means to be overcome in the course or race, so as to be left behind:† it agrees well with διώκεσθαι.—

* Artimedorus (Oneirocr. vi. 25) employs the same expression : ὁ θάνατος μὲν γὰρ εἰκότως ἐσήμαινε τῇ γυναικί, τὸ εἶναι ἐν ὀστρακίνῳ σκεύει.

† See Herodotus viii. 59 : οἱ δέ γε ἐγκαταλειπόμενοι οὐ στεφανοῦνται.

The καταβάλλεσθαι, "to be cast down," is borrowed from the
terms of wrestling, consequently the image of a conflict passed
again before the apostle's imagination.—In ver. 10, the νέκρωσις
indicates the gradual death. Paul views the whole term of Christ's
abode on earth as a continual dying, the accomplishment of which
was the death on the cross. But the genitive 'Ιησοῦ may certainly not be received as = διὰ 'Ιησοῦν, for Jesus is here regarded
as a type, but the real type itself, consequently Christ essentially
bears within himself the dying and rising again in man's nature.
Upon the opinion that Christ represents the former also see my
Comm. on Rom. viii. 3).

Ver. 11. This verse throws some further light upon the striking idea of the πάντοτε περιφέρειν νέκρωσιν. That εἰς θάνατον
παραδιδόμεθα διὰ 'Ιησοῦν stands here, affords no just grounds for
explaining the genitive of verse 10 by διά, for the typical parallel
now ceases. Emmerling, moreover, is of opinion that here, as in
verse 10, the ἵνα is to be understood ἐκβατικῶς, but erroneously.
Paul understands his dangers and circumstances of suffering which threatened his life *teleologically*, and signifies
that it was God's intention in permitting them to render them
conducive to the perfecting of man. This presupposes that
Paul regarded the glorification of the body as taking its rise on
earth, and accomplishing itself gradually, and does not in the
least contradict the opinion, that the nature of this new body,
fashioned in secret, will first manifest itself at the coming of
Christ and in the act of the resurrection. (The ἐν τῇ θνητῇ
σαρκί of verse 11 proves that the expression σὰρξ πνευματική was
not contrary to the apostle [see on 1 Cor. xv. 44], for the manifestation of Christ's life in the mortal body is nothing else than
the glorifying of the body).

Ver. 12. The apostle now passes from himself and the effect
of his sufferings to his readers. He, the living creature, is also
the gradually dying servant of the Lord. They being dead will
be made living by his means, just as Christ died and by his death
brought life to the whole world. Paul, however, by no means desires to attribute to himself an effect *equivalent* with Christ; it
is rather Christ who works in him. We must also observe that
too much stress is not to be laid upon the chief point of this passage; for, strictly speaking, we must admit that believers, made

living by the apostle's preaching, must also participate in Christ's death in order to live again with him.  In a total and scarcely conceivable misunderstanding of these words Rückert refers them to mortal life and death, and thinks that certain maladies are alluded to from which the apostle and Corinthians had suffered, but which had now yielded to an improved state of health.

Vers. 13, 14.  Mosheim has quite incorrectly understood the connexion between this verse and the preceding.  He thinks that Paul gives occasion for a possible misunderstanding of the words ὁ θάνατος ἐν ἡμῖν ἐνεργεῖται, as if the apostle had no expectation of a resurrection.  But that he did expect this is plainly shown by Paul, vers. 10, 11.  The connexion is rather this : Paul desires to express the opinion that his lowly suffering course of life may prove a source of life to the Corinthians, not only conjecturally, but as a lively conviction imparted from above.  He therefore styles his faith πνεῦμα τῆς πίστεως (in Ephes. i. 17, πνεῦμα σοφίας stands for the same), and describes it in the words taken from the Old Testament, Ps. cxvi. 10 (from the connexion with which the Aorists are derived), as praying him to declare and to acknowledge that it is accompanied by the joyful certainty that he will achieve a perfect triumph for himself and others.  This is indicated by the resurrection and the participation in God's kingdom which stands connected with it.  (In ver. 14 Lachmann reads σὺν Ἰησοῦ, which certainly possesses very weighty authorities in its favour; but the σύν appears to have been only introduced into the text from the σὺν ὑμῖν which follows.—The παραστήσει, according to v. 10, is to be understood to signify, "He will present us, together with you, before the judgment-seat of Christ, as perfected creatures of God.")

Ver. 15.  The apostle in addition expresses the opinion that all things in and by him were for them (i. e. first for the Corinthians, then for all his disciples), in order that their thanksgiving might redound to the glory of God, and be abundant for the grace bestowed upon them through the intercession of mercy.  The passage is entirely analogous with i. 11; the connexion of the διὰ τῶν πλειόνων is also here uncertain, but the joining it with περισσεύσῃ is unquestionably to be preferred, because otherwise διὰ τ. π. would be placed before πλεονάσασα.  In the present passage it would be better to consider περισσεύσῃ transitive;

SECOND CORINTHIANS IV. 16—18.

then the meaning would be, as we have already stated, that the abundance of the grace vouchsafed to much prayer renders the thanksgiving also abundant, *i. e.*, excites to inward thanksgiving. Vers. 16—18. The apostle in conclusion expresses with reference to ver. 1 his readiness to continue to labour without fainting in his apostolic calling; because believers, who looked beyond the temporal and evident to that which was eternal and not seen, would thereby gain everlasting life. The idea in vers. 10, 11, is again repeated here, only instead of the σῶμα, the ἔξω ἄνθρωπος is employed, and instead of the dying, the stronger διαφθείρεσθαι (perishing) is made use of. (Concerning ἔξω and ἔσω ἄνθρωπος, see the observations on Rom. vii. 22). The glorified corporeality is likewise to be supposed existing with the inward man, therefore the ἀνακαινοῦσθαι forms the just antithesis with διαφθείρεσθαι, which would not offer if this state of glorification were excluded; it is similar to the before-mentioned ζωὴ Ἰησοῦ φανεροῦται ἐν σαρκὶ θνητῇ (ver. 11). The expression is based upon a reference to the new birth, the result of which is described by καινὴ κτίσις, καινὸς ἄνθρωπος. (Compare Rom. xii. 2; Col. iii. 10; Tit. iii. 5). The gradual ripening of the new man is plainly declared in the ἡμέρᾳ καὶ ἡμέρᾳ (= יוֹם וָיוֹם). But Billroth errs when he refers the μὴ βλεπόμενα in ver. 18 to the glorified body, because this in v. 1 is called αἰώνια: his view is therefore unsanctioned, for in ver. 18 a general description of faith is given, corresponding with that in Heb. xi. 1. The antithesis of things visible and invisible here, is only the general one of things real and ideal. (In ver. 16, the second ἀλλά is to be received in the signification of "nevertheless," as in 2 Cor. xiii. 4; Col. ii. 5. [See Winer's Gr. p. 421.]—In ver. 17, the τὸ παραυτίκα ἐλαφρόν is to be understood as "the present lightness of our affliction," *i. e.*, our temporal, and *as such* always light suffering.—Paul accumulates expressions in order to describe the gloriousness; to the usual καθ᾽ ὑπερβολήν [i. 8], he adds εἰς ὑπερβολήν, and in the αἰώνιον βάρος he forms the antithesis with the παραυτίκα ἐλαφρόν. In the phrase τὰ βλεπόμενα πρόσκαιρα of ver. 18, the visible does not signify alone the physical visible world, but it rather stands as a synecdoche for all the attributes of mortality, even when not perceptible to the eye, such as fame, honour, &c.)

## § 5. THE GLORIFICATION.

### (v. 1—21).

After Paul has more fully declared his hope in the forthcoming glorification of the body, in which mortality will be swallowed up in life, he further states that the knowledge that all will be discovered before the judgment-seat of Christ, produces a holy fear in him, which impels him to exercise the office entrusted to him as in the sight of God, and without employing any unworthy means to further it. The love of Christ constrains him to preach, for since the Lord died for all, all should likewise live to him ; casting behind the old man, he therefore cries aloud as in Christ's stead: Be ye reconciled with God !

Ver. 1. The connexion of idea between v. 1 and iv. 18, is very striking in its relation to modern knowledge, in so far as the latter is unsupported by Christianity. It appears as if we could look forward to eternity, without having faith in the resurrection of the body. But, as we were already reminded in the Comm. on 1 Cor. 15, the apostle in no respect recognises the idea of a pure spiritual extension of life into eternity; without corporeality there can be no everlasting happiness, or eternity for the creature. But even conceding the scriptural doctrine of the glorification of the body, our passage still retains its obscurity. For we can well understand how the ἐπίγειος = ἐκ γῆς may be opposed to the ἐκ Θεοῦ* i. e. not only abs Deo data, but = πνευματική), and αἰώνιος (in as far as the glorified body is destined for everlasting life ; but it is incomprehensible how Paul can style the glorified body ἀχειροποίητος, seeing that even the earthly is not made with hands, or how it can be asserted that it is ἐν τοῖς οὐρανοῖς, as the clothing upon (ver. 2) must be considered a preparation

* We have likewise no authority for understanding the ἐκ Θεοῦ only synonymous with ἐκ διὰ θελήματος Θεοῦ: but as God according to his nature is a Spirit, all things spiritual have their beginning in his nature. Verse 18 is unquestionably to be understood thus, and it can be received in no other sense in the present passage. It then follows that not only the Spirit, but also the higher corporeality, proceeds from God ; and this by no means agrees with the doctrine of the creation out of nothing, which asserts that the material was of a nature absolutely different from God, and produced alone by his will.

taking place upon earth.  The first difficulty is solved by supposing that a parallel subsisted in the apostle's mind between
the earthly tabernacle made by man, transitory even in its sacred-
ness, and the perfect tabernacle not made by human hands, *i. e.*
the spiritual building of the New Testament.  The former corresponds
with the earthly perishable body, thence οἰκία τοῦ σκήνους, *i. e.*
σκηνώδης, the latter with the new glorified body, which is only so
far styled ἀχειροποίητος, as χειροποιήτου may be added to σκήνους.
The expression ἐν τοῖς οὐρανοῖς is not to be received as implying
that the new body was preserved as it were in heaven, and from
thence descended to man, but Paul anticipates the idea of the
clothing upon, and thinks of the believer as clothed with the new
body in heaven, so that the words are to be understood : with
divine natures alone can we exist in heaven, for with earthly
bodies it is not possible.  As well as ἐκ Θεοῦ, we may likewise say
the new body is ἐκ οὐρανῶν, as in ver. 2, because the transforming power is divine, and manifests itself from heaven.  Another
difficulty which has been imagined in the ἐὰν καταλυθῇ, ἔχομεν (the present is employed with a future signification because
the perfect conviction is expressed that it will be so), from supposing that it compelled us to admit that the apostle was speaking of a physical body received by man immediately after death,
and which he retained until the resurrection of the body, I cannot admit to be such.*  For ἐάν does not assert that the possession
of a new body takes place *immediately* the old one is dissolved,
but only states in general terms that the latter must take place
as a necessary condition of the former.  The apostle also considers the reception of the new glorified body near at hand (see
on 1 Thess. iv. 15), and that he himself would certainly receive
it before death.

Vers. 2—4. This hope is clearly evident in the following verses,

* See Flatt on this passage, and Schneckenburger's Beitr. zur Einl. ins Neue
Tes. (Stuttgart, 1836), p. 124, sqq., in which the views concerning a physical body
are laid down.   Menken (Versuch einer Anleitung, &c., Frankf. 1805, p. 61, sqq.
190) believes that here on earth man possesses a more refined body besides the
earthly one, a view not corroborated by the holy Scriptures, any more than Lange's
supposition that the soul, according to the place of its abode, forms a finer body for
itself (see p. 701, sqq.), the man is never absolutely base.  For were this the case,
the dead could never be called πνεύματα, as in 1 Pet. iii. 18, Heb. xii. 23.  See
further concerning the supposition of a physical body, Groos' work, Der unverwes-
liche Leib als Organ des Geistes und Sitz der Seelenstörungen. Heidelberg. 1837.

in which Paul describes the existence in this mortal body as similar to the longing of the κτίσις after deliverance. (See on Rom. viii. 19, sqq.) The burden of the existence which is only after the flesh, makes the spirit groan for a more elevated condition, and this is indicated by the expression ἐπενδύσασθαι, which is further described in the ἵνα καταποθῇ τὸ θνητὸν ὑπὸ τῆς ζωῆς. (See iv. 10, 11 ; 1 Cor. xv. 54). If the ἐφ᾽ ᾧ οὐ θέλομεν ἐκδύσασθαι did not also stand in the text, we might suppose that it was only the act of the resurrection of the body which was principally indicated. But this sentence unquestionably refers back to the opinion touched upon in 1 Cor. xv. 51, which is authentically interpreted as it were in this passage. Paul regards it as an especial happiness not to taste death, not to be obliged to put off (ἐκδύσασθαι) this body, but to be glorified living, like Elias, drawing the heavenly body over the present mortal body like a garment, but naturally in such a manner that the mortal body is absorbed in the nature of the spiritual body.—In this otherwise clear and simple passage the εἴγε καὶ ἐνδυσάμενοι, οὐ γυμνοὶ εὑρεθησόμεθα is, however, unintelligible. Whether we read with Lachmann and Billroth εἴπερ, or εἴγε with Griesbach, a slight modification of the idea only appears. Certainly in the εἴπερ (if nothing else) a more impressive presentation of the *condition* is contained, but this is precisely the reason it may have been substituted for the milder form εἴγε,* (that is to say, if the idea is not received only as a *presupposition*). The difficulty lies in the οὐ γυμνοί, which further defines the ἐνδυσάμενοι. The Codd. D.F.G. have indeed the reading ἐνδυσάμενοι, and Reiche (Göttinger Oster-Programm, of 1836) declares himself in its favour. But critical authorities at once decide for ἐνδυσάμενοι, which reading has also been inserted by Lachmann in the text; the supposition may therefore arise that a desire existed to avoid the difficulty in the ἐνδυσάμενοι, and this led to the substitution of one letter for another. Now, if we maintain the ἐνδυσάμενοι to be the genuine reading, we must next inquire if this expression is to be accepted literally or metaphorically ?† Usteri defends its acceptation in the first sense, Billroth in the second; according to the

* See Hartung's Partikellehre, pt. i., p. 343, 406. Hermann. *ad* Viger. page 834.

† Flatt has given another explanation of the passage ; this, however, fails in every particular, and we therefore only incidentally mention it. He translates it,

former the meaning is, " If we also are clothed with the garment of
righteousness, not appearing in the presence of God destitute of
the same," while the latter asserts its signification to be, " If we
shall be found clothed with the body, and not without a body."
Unquestionably, Usteri's view is the only correct one,* for even if
ἐνδεδυμένοι is not necessary, as Usteri thinks it would be if Billroth's explanation were adopted, the καί is nevertheless not perfectly reconcilable with Billroth's idea. The fact that the ἐπενδύσασθαι implies that the body is *not* yet put off, is incontro-
vertible ; for the καὶ γάρ κ. τ. λ. (ver. 2) is connected with the
ἐὰν καταλυθῇ (ver. 1) as a heightening of the idea, thus, " For
we know, when our mortal tabernacle is dissolved (*i. e.*, when we
die), that we have a heavenly building ; we therefore groan in
this body, earnestly desiring the clothing upon with the heavenly." It would consequently be perfectly pleonastic if ver. 3
asserted, " that is to say, not being already dead," for when
death has taken place, there can exist no more question of ἐπενδύσασθαι. It only remains to inquire if Billroth's remarks
against the scriptural explanation of γυμνός, and to which Reiche
yields assent, may be disproved. He first observes, that ἐνδύσασθαι must be understood in the same image in which ἐκδύσασθαι is afterwards employed. But the καὶ and the οὐ γυμνοί which
is added, sufficiently shows that the apostle is passing over to
another image ; the words may, therefore, be understood, " It being supposed beforehand that we in another sense shall not be
found naked, but well clothed." Billroth's second observation
states, that we find in this passage no authority for mentioning
the difference between the righteous and the unrighteous. But
as in ver. 10 this is openly stated, it certainly borders upon the
mention of this difference ; otherwise there would have been room
to suppose, that it was perfectly sufficient to be yet living at the

"Although we, if only clothed with it (not clothed upon) shall not be found without a body, *i. e.* will then be in no worse position than they who are changed."
But the "only" and likewise the "although" are not found in the text. It is
also a false notion that the apostle regarded the being changed (1 Cor. xv. 53) as
something evil ; it is rather set forth as an advantage, as great as being clothed,
and of becoming clothed upon.

  * This is asserted of the main point, for in other particulars Usteri has likewise
failed to arrive at a just conclusion, as the following will show. (See Paul. Lehrbegr.,
p. 359 and 391, sq., in the 4th edition). In the chief points, Chrysostom has given
the same explanation.

Parousia of Christ, in order to attain the clothing upon; this
error is refuted by Paul in verse 3, in which he makes it evident
that in order to participate in the blessing, and not to taste
death, a standing in grace at the time of Christ's coming was a
necessary condition. In the third remark Billroth is correct in
opposition to Usteri, but this concerns only an incidental point of
his explanation. The latter incorrectly receives ἐνδυσάμενοι not
as identical with οὐ γυμνοί, but so as to include a reference to
the οἰκητήριον ἐξ οὐρανοῦ (verse 2). But this has precisely the
evil effect deprecated by Billroth, viz., that the distinction between ἐνδύσασθαι and ἐπενδύσασθαι is entirely lost. Without
entering more fully into it, Usteri's view conveys a meaning altogether unsupported. He translates, " otherwise even after we
are clothed, we shall be found naked." But how is it conceivable
that after the clothing with the glorified body has taken place,
any one shall be found naked ? He who is naked, *i. e.*, without
the garment of righteousness, the new nature, cannot according
to the nature of things be clothed upon. The οὐ γυμνοί is,
therefore, only an epexegesis to the synonym ἐνδυσάμενοι, *i. e.*,
clothed, and is applied to those who have put on (the garment of
righteousness). (In ver. 2 the ἐν τούτῳ = to the ἐφ' ᾧ of ver. 4,
cannot be received in the signification of כַּאֲשֶׁר, but according
to ver. 4 σκήνει is rather to be supplied. On the contrary the
ἐφ' ᾧ of ver. 4 is decidedly the conjunction, and not the relative
with the preposition [see on Rom. v. 12], and is best explained
by the Hebrew בַּאֲשֶׁר, Gen. xxxix. 23, Ps. x. 6, and not by the
classic form as = ἐπὶ τούτῳ ὥστε. In those passages of the
New Testament in which it occurs, it would be best expressed
by " because.")

Ver. 5. In order to strengthen this hope Paul continues that
God, who had prepared this heavenly clothing, together with the
mortal body, had also bestowed his Spirit upon them in this life
as a witness. (In the κατεργάζεσθαι regeneration is understood
as a new creation, referring to iv. 6.—The glorification of the
body, as the perfection of man, is the especial idea in the εἰς
αὐτὸ τοῦτο. [See Comm. on Rom. viii. 23].—The καὶ is best
omitted as Lachmann recommends, the ὁ δοὺς κ. τ. λ., can then
be justly understood as in apposition to Θεός.—Whether ἀρραβών

is translated earnest money, or pledge, is quite immaterial, for either would correspond with the idea; the signification is, "The gift of the Holy Spirit, which God has bestowed upon us on earth, is the pledge for our attainment of the object in the future.")

Vers. 6—9. The apostle then states the conclusion, that under all these circumstances, he will ever have confidence, striving only to please the Lord, whether in one place or another. The words πάντοτε θαρροῦντες φιλοτιμούμεθα κ. τ. λ. form the principal idea. A large parenthesis is, however, introduced, containing the accessory idea, in which Paul glances at the στενάζειν of ver. 2, and then connects the whole with the principal sentence, by the words καὶ εἰδότες—κυρίου. The καί has, moreover, from the nature of the thought, the somewhat exclusive, almost adversative signification of the θαρρεῖν: "Since we well know that while on earth we are as it were in a foreign land, in comparison with our true home, which is with the Lord." But the parenthesis has been erroneously restricted to ver. 7, and even by Billroth, believing that θαρροῦμεν in ver. 8 takes up the θαρροῦντες of ver. 6, but on the contrary εὐδοκοῦμεν is the principal verb. Lachmann has properly extended the parenthesis to ver. 6 and 7, whereby the real sense of the passage becomes evident. That is to say, it describes the subordinate nature of the περιπατεῖν διὰ πίστεως, with which necessarily the ἐπιποθεῖν (ver. 2) is given, but even to this condition the θαρρεῖν is added, without, however, denying that the being with the Lord, the περιπατεῖν διὰ εἴδους, is to be preferred. (See Phil. i. 23). In addition the διὰ here expresses the temper that should pervade as it were the life of man. (See Winer's Gr. p. 362). Num. xii. 8 may be compared as an interesting parallel to the antithesis of faith and sight here mentioned. It is there said : וּמַרְאֶה וְלֹא בְחִידֹת, which the LXX. translate ἐν εἴδει καὶ οὐκ δι᾽ αἰνιγμάτων.

Ver. 10. Concerning the subject of this verse see Comm. on Rom. ii. 6, xiv. 10. The apparent contradiction with 1 Cor. vi. 2, 3, John iii. 18, is simply explained thus, that the holy are so far not to be judged, as Christ only knows them in their righteousness. The apostle therefore only makes use of the expression δεῖ ἡμᾶς φανερωθῆναι. The τὰ διὰ τοῦ σώματος scil. πραχθέντα*

---

* Bengel erroneously supplies κομιζόμενα, although he in other respects cor-

plainly refers back to the glorification of the body, and we may, therefore, in the same sense as the apostle supply ἐν τῷ σώματι to the κομίσηται, which would concede an influence upon the future body to offences against morality.

Vers. 11, 12. The apostle was now able to return to the justification of his conduct in his apostolic office. He declares that this must reveal itself to the hearts of men as perfectly true, and that for this reason he needed no self-commendation (iii. 1) towards them; it being only necessary to declare his labours, in order to induce the Corinthians to free themselves from those who panegyrised themselves. Billroth's supposition relative to this passage, who thinks that, according to Gal. i. 10, πείθομεν (ver· 11) implies treacherous persuasion, is deserving consideration, though the connexion by no means sanctions it. It is, however, clear that Paul chose the expression with a view to the accusations of his antagonists, for the δέ in the following sentence corroborates this. The sense might then be this: "As our opponents say, we treacherously persuade men, but our sincerity is manifest before God." The ἀφορμὴ καυχήματος ὑπὲρ ἡμῶν is to be understood thus : Paul desires, by this account of his proceedings, to convince the Corinthians of his sincerity, that they may be able to glory in him as their teacher and defend him against the false teachers. Their falsehood is expressed by the antithesis ἐν προσώπῳ, οὐ καρδίᾳ. Paul boasts himself καρδίᾳ, for God is his glory, as will be presently expressed.

Vers. 13—15. Love alone has been the impelling power to his conduct, Paul continues; and it was manifest to all that he was not eager to appropriate praise to himself either in a moderate or immoderate degree, but that either God (whom he especially desired to honour by his works) or his brethren was ever in his view. The antithesis εἴτε ἐξέστημεν, εἴτε σωφρονοῦμεν, has been correctly understood by Billroth. The different proceeding of the apostle is not here the subject under consideration, for we cannot perceive how it could be introduced by him in this place, but the various judgments passed upon his proceeding by the parties in Corinth. However these may be judged, Paul wishes to say, under no circumstances does he seek his own; and should they

rectly interprets the apostolic idea, *homo cum corpore bene vel male agit, cum corpore mercedem capit.*

regard any praise bestowed as immoderate, he desires it may be
given to God and not to himself; if, on the contrary, they deem
the praise moderate, he wishes therein to consider the weaker
brethren.    Love is with him the element which destroys self.
Therefore the love of Christ (*i. e.*, not love towards Christ, but
that which he bears within himself, and imparts to others) is the
distinction of all those belonging to him; for this reason he died
for all, therefore all (who accept him) must likewise die for him,
*i. e.*, yielding up their substantiality, they live no longer for themselves, but for Christ.—The only difficulty herein is created by
the fact (without taking into consideration the reflections introduced into the Comm. on Rom. v. 12 upon the idea of the Saviour
taking the atonement upon himself) that ver. 14 decidedly
says ἄρα οἱ πάντες ἀπέθανον, which makes the death of all appear the necessary consequence of the death of the substitute for
all; whilst in ver. 15 the ἀπέθανεν, ἵνα κ. τ. λ. represents the
death of all as an act depending upon their own pleasure, as one
may believe.    The difficulty may, however, be thus explained :
without the death of Christ, absolutely none would be in a condition to destroy the principle of self, for that is only possible
by yielding to and self-appropriating the love thereby so abundantly manifested; but the man may always *hinder* by his resistance the power of Christ, which " kills and at the same time
makes alive, from perfecting his work in him.    From this ob-
structing resistance the 15th verse is intended to withhold the
Corinthians.    Before Christ's death it was a subject of reproof to
no man that he lived to himself, but after Christ's death it was a
crime in all those to whom the word of the cross had come.    In
this manner a strict connexion is visible with ver. 16.    (In the
ἐξέστημεν excess and exaggeration are represented as the expression of an ἔκστασις or μανία.—Chrysostom admirably elucidates
the συνέχει of ver. 14 by ἡ ἀγάπη οὐκ ἀφίησιν ἡσυχάζειν με.
See Acts xviii. 5. — The εἰ is wanting in B.C.D.E.F.G., and
is justly omitted by Lachmann; it is only introduced to join the
ἄρα more easily, and also probably in order to remove the apparent pleonasm with ver. 15.    But the hypothetical conception of
a substitution is perfectly untenable; the idea contains not the
slightest reference to it, but only to Christ, who could alone be a
substitute for the whole human race as the second Adam.    The

ὑπέρ plainly stands here = ἀντί, for only upon this supposition does the ἄρα κ. τ. λ. acquire significance. See Comm. on Matt. xx. 28).

Vers. 16, 17. Under this point of view Paul adds, he beholds all believers; he regards the old man in them as dead in Christ, *i. e.* this supposes of course that they conduct themselves as though truly renewed, and he therefore has no occasion to employ any worldly considerations in his intercourse with them as the false teachers do (ver. 12). The οὐδένα (ver. 16) is not to be received absolutely, of every man without exception, it is explained in ver. 17 by the ἐν Χριστῷ. The κατὰ σάρκα (ver. 16) corresponds with the ἀρχαῖα (ver. 17) as κατὰ πνεῦμα is to be supplied for καινά. The entire passage is based upon the parallel between the new birth and a new creation; therefore, the καινὸς ἄνθρωπος is here also styled καινὴ κτίσις = בְּרִיָּה חֲדָשָׁה, as the Jewish proselytes were already denominated. (See Comm. on John iii. 3; Gal. vi. 15.; Ephes. iv. 24). Besides, the τὰ ἀρχαῖα παρῆλθεν κ. τ. λ. contains an allusion to Isa. xliii. 18, 19, a passage which is evidently considered in Rev. xxi. 5. In the passage quoted from the prophet the subject certainly relates to the entire subversion of the condition of the world, and to the foundation of the kingdom of God thereon, but it is equally applicable to individual events as to the circumstances collectively. To this clear view the εἰ δὲ καὶ ἐγνώκαμεν κατὰ σάρκα Χριστὸν, ἀλλὰ νῦν οὐκέτι γινώσκομεν alone presents a difficulty. But if we do not permit the mind to be disturbed by the various significations of our passage, the following very simple meaning of the words is apparent : " I no longer know any man after the flesh, not even Christ himself, of whom it might be supposed that what concerned men could not be applied to him." The words consequently represent the οὐδένα as taken in the most extended sense. Even in Christ a transition took place analogous to that which happened to man in regeneration ; in the resurrection his life κατὰ σάρκα passed over into a life κατὰ πνεῦμα, and in this Paul desires to say he alone knows Christ. The εἰ δὲ καὶ ἐγνώκαμεν might also imply that Paul had already seen the Lord* while staying at Jerusalem before his conversion; but this suppo-

---

* See the general Introduction to the Epistles of Paul, § i., p. 6, note 3.

sition possesses not the slightest ground for support.  By taking
a retrospective glance at the ἐν πρωσώπῳ καυχωμένους of ver. 12,
the words may be easily understood to contain a gentle antithesis
against those who prided themselves upon their *personal* intercourse with the Redeemer while on earth, employing this circumstance in opposition to Paul;* but this reference is certainly only
incidental, and obtains no further consideration in what follows.
But in opposition to our simple exposition of the passage it may
be alleged that Paul generally and especially brings prominently
forward in the immediately following verses, the suffering and
dying Christ ; how, then, can he say here: νῦν οὐκέτι γινώσκομεν
αὐτόν; but the νῦν in ver. 16 contrasts the condition of the conversion with the earlier unconverted state.  Paul was consequently
after his conversion with Christ κατὰ σάρκα, i. e., in his sufferings.
This view is especially held forth by Baur in his article Über die
Christusparthei in the Tüb. Zeitschr. 1831, pt. iv., p. 95.  But if
the apostle speaks of the humiliation of Christ, he decidedly mentions it as passed, representing death as vanquished in the resurrection ; he can, therefore, with perfect justness assert, even attributing due importance to the sufferings of Christ, " I now know
Christ only as the glorified Christ."  This objection, therefore,
cannot materially affect the correctness of our supposition, the
more so as every other explanation of the passage has something
forced in it.  This appears to me especially to apply to Baur's
elucidation of the passage before us, which makes the γινώσκειν
κατὰ σάρκα Χριστόν to refer to the Jewish reception of the idea
of a Messiah, so that σάρξ indicates the national, or that which
is governed by the people's prejudices.  But then it would be
necessary that the article should be used : ὁ κατὰ σάρκα Χριστός
can only indicate the Jewish reception of the idea of the Messiah.
The consequence of entertaining this view would likewise be to
weaken the personal to a simply abstract meaning, under which
Baur asserts that οὐδέν might likewise stand for οὐδένα, but I can
see nothing which would justify such a proceeding.  The con-

* The subject here is by no means referable to a *relationship* with the Redeemer,
although Storr seeks in this passage to gain support for his hypothesis that the
*Christianer* were the brethren of the Lord.  The only inference to be drawn from
the idea contained in this passage is, that if any one imputed so high a value to
conversing only with Christ, the temporal relationship would be yet more highly
rated.  (See concerning this Introd. § 1).

nexion rather requires that the stress should precisely be laid upon the personal capacity, for in ver. 14 the apostle declares that the love of Christ constrained him to judge every person, not according to his exterior, but according to his position relative to Christ. He here employs σάρξ not as signifying sin, but external things in opposition to internal. We must also observe that the idea of an ἀσθένεια cleaves to externals, and this is expressly ascribed to Christ by Paul (xiii. 4).

Ver. 18. This new birth is, however, God's work alone. He has reconciled himself with men through Christ, and given to them the ministry of reconciliation, *i. e.*, the economy whereby the more elevated powers of living, acquired by Christ's operation in men, are extended in a regular manner over the whole race (see on iii. 9). Billroth's opinion that ἡμᾶς refers first to all men, and then ἡμῖν only to Paul or the teachers, is nullified by the circumstance that the διακονία τῆς καταλλαγῆς was certainly not for the teachers alone, but for all. It is true that the one bears itself actively towards it, and the other passively, though inasmuch as the reconciliation was not an occurrence which happened only once, but is continually going on, so likewise in this respect are the teachers passive, for they also require reconciliation and its proclamation. Viewed as objective, the reconciliation is to be regarded as accomplished once for all, therefore it is called καταλλάξαντος.

Ver. 19. This verse confirms and strengthens the idea, by again repeating the subject of ver. 18. (The pleonastic ὡς ὅτι is found again in 2 Cor. xi. 21. (Winer's Gr. p. 548).* It was not necessary here to uphold the divine nature of Christ, therefore ἦν καταλλάσσων is to be understood† = κατήλλαξε, so that here the employment of the præterite signifies the reconciliation to be complete, as, by the use of θέμενος, the ministry of reconciliation which in the form of its utterance is understood as λόγος τῆς καταλλαγῆς, is represented as perfectly established. The opera-

* In the profane Greek authors ὡς ὅτι never occurs, except in the connexion ὡς ὅτι μάλιστα. See Hermann. ad Viger. p. 853.

† The argument employed by Rückert in opposition to this is unimportant. He first says the paraphrase with ἦν is not general with Paul; it is certainly not often employed by him, but nevertheless occurs in Gal. i. 23. Next that the imperfect is not applicable here, but in ἦν the aorist is included as well as the imperfect. And lastly, that καταλλάσσων then requires to be connected with ἦν; but John i. 9 proves that this is by no means necessary.

tion of forgiveness of sin is, on the contrary, received in the μὴ λογιζόμενος τὰ παραπτώματα, as abiding, advancing through the entire history of mankind. It is, however, hardly necessary to state that, with this negative side the positive one of the λογίζεσθαι δικαιοσύνην must be considered connected. (See in the Comm. upon the Epistle to the Romans, p. 146, 1st edition). For that man can only truly believe in the forgiveness of sin in whom the new birth has taken place. The subject of the καταλλαγή and its intention has already been amply treated upon in the Comm. upon the Epistle to the Romans. The present passage is the one which, above all others, sanctions the view that men will be reconciled solely because reconciliation originated with God. But justice and mercy are considered attributes of the divine nature, and also the satisfaction rendered to the Father by the Son, *i. e.*, the love fulfilling the demands of justice.* This view requires the idea of sacrifice which appears in ver. 21, and presupposes a reconciliation with God, even if the expression of it does not occur in the text. (See the remarks on John iii. 16). It is only under this point of view that it can be conceived how the reconciliation may be considered an act for the annunciation of which a ministry with a new economy should be founded. If the reconciliation solely took place on the side of man, it could only be preached that a manifestation of God's love would ensue which would render *possible* the reconciliation of the subject; but the Church has ever taught that the reconciliation was *really* effected upon Golgotha, and its preaching can in this form alone obtain a power to comfort, and at the same time work the necessary change in the individual. (A slight anacoluthon cannot be denied to exist in the participle θέμενος: it depends on the ἔθετο corresponding to the ἦν καταλλάσσων: the participle awakens the idea, as if the insertion of the words relating to the reconciliation were parallel with the μὴ λογιζόμενος αὐτοῖς τὰ παραπτώματα. It is therefore conceivable that interpreters should imagine the words καὶ θέμενος ἐν

---

* The Θεὸς ἐν Χριστῷ is besides to be connected in our passage : God in Christ, *i. e.*, who was in Christ, reconciled the world with himself, not as it were thus : God reconciled the world through Christ with himself. In the first acceptation we are reminded of this passage in John xiv. 9, " He who hath seen me hath seen the Father." The Son is not God *together* with the Father, but the manifestation of the one sole God, of the pure co-existent beam of original light.

ἡμῖν κ. τ. λ. to signify "he hath removed our sins" [λογον
τιθέναι = *rationem inire*]. But this interpretation can require
no special refutation).

Vers. 20, 21. The preaching of the Gospel in Christ's place,*
the entreating men to be reconciled to God, *i. e.* to accept the reconciliation which has already taken place, is decidedly the exercise of the ministration instituted by God.† For on God's part
all is effected, and it is only requisite on the side of man that he
accept the gift of God, and, putting away sin, permit the righteousness of God to be bestowed on him. In conclusion, it must be
evident that the ἁμαρτία indicates a condition; δικαιοσύνη Θεοῦ
also implies the *state* of righteousness (the signification "declaration of righteousness" is thoroughly inapplicable) which the
true καταλλαγή, and the regeneration connected therewith, calls
forth. But inasmuch as this condition is a derivable,‡ growing
state, nay, even one which may be again lost, and which must
ever be drawn fresh from the original source of life, it is not on
the condition itself that salvation is connected, but on the *power*
which creates it, *i. e.*, the objective Christ and his work subjective
to faith. (See upon this subject the copious observations in the
Comm. on Rom. iii. 21). The τὸν ἁμαρτίαν μὴ γνόντα ἁμαρτίαν
ἐποίησε is peculiar to our passage. Gal. iii. 13 is similar: γενό-
μενος ὑπὲρ ὑμῶν κατάρα. The ἐποίησε exposes more strongly the
side of the divine design, which, as may be supposed, does not
imply constraint, but is entirely in concert with the will of the
Son. It is also the same in Rom. viii. 3.—The opinion that
ἁμαρτία here stands for sacrifice for sin, = חַטָּאָה or אָשָׁם, Lev.
vi. 23, Num. viii. 8, occasions some hesitation, as we must then

---

* It is true that ὑπὲρ might here also be understood as "in behalf of the things
which are of Christ;" but the idea of the ambassador, as well as the sentence ὡς
τοῦ Θεοῦ παρακαλοῦντος δι' ἡμῶν, forbid us to receive the idea of substituting.

† This was available not only in reference to preaching to heathens who are yet
to be converted, but also for Christians, who, although such, required not only the
frequent renewal of repentance, but also of the assurance of reconciliation. Without this announcement of the atonement for the world, preaching would possess no
specific Christian character. It is hardly necessary to remind our readers that it
was not sufficient to plant, but it was requisite to water and likewise to continue
to cultivate on right soil; and from consideration towards the necessities of the
church in this respect, preaching naturally included many other objects applicable
to the purpose.

‡ Therefore ἐν αὐτῷ, which is not to be understood the same as δι' αὐτοῦ, but
may be explained by "in case, and so far as we live in his fellowship."

admit that ἁμαρτία has two significations.  The opinion that
ἁμαρτία stands for the concrete ἁμαρτωλός must be rejected, for
it is altogether inadmissible to suppose that God has made the
sanctified to be sinners.  It would be more simple regarding Rom.
viii. 3, analogically to retain the signification " sins."  God
made him who had in no degree an inclination to sin (to say
nothing of the fact that he had never committed it) to be sin,
*i. e.* according to his design, to represent sin.  He then, in agreement with his real unity with sinful man, regarded him as surety
and sacrifice for sin for the whole race, in order in his person to
condemn sin for ever.  See on Rom. viii. 3 ; 1 Pet. i. 24).

§ 6. THE ADMONITION.

(vi. 1—vii. 1).

As the servant of God, the apostle admonishes the Corinthians
not to receive grace in vain, that his ministry may not thereby be
blamed.  He approves himself likewise in all things a servant of
God, because, although overtaken by all kinds of earthly afflictions,
he is nevertheless faithful, and asserts himself victorious over
every opposition (vi. 1—10).  He also expressly warns them
against communion with the powers of darkness, requiring them to
avoid even the appearance of it, and to keep themselves free from
all pollution, as belonging to God's people (vi. 11—vii. 1).

Vers. 1—3.  Paul does not assume a position above the Corinthians, but condescendingly desires to become a fellow-worker
with them, and so to admonish them as they ought to admonish
themselves.  Unquestionably the apostle here considers the possibility of the grace received by the individual being again lost.
The dangerous error of predestination, which asserts that grace
cannot be lost, is unknown to Scripture, and experience confirms
the falsehood of it; as then the conversion of many who at a later
period again became apostates must, according to the views of
predestianism, be attributable only to a *voluntas signi*.  The
apostle felt himself compelled to employ this admonition in order
to avoid giving occasion to the accusation that he fulfilled his
ministry in a sluggish and indifferent manner, as if he had re-

spect unto men.  The quotation from Isa. xlix. 8, with which he supports his admonition, and which he correctly cites according to the LXX., describes the day of grace in which all the promises are to be fulfilled; the mention of it is intended to awaken reciprocal love in believers, and at the same time invite them to make true use of a period so full of blessing.  It is likewise intended to remind them that a difficult hour of temptation may arrive, in which they may not be able to stand, should they not have diligently employed the day of salvation.  (The quotation closely follows the LXX.—Δεκτός has occurred already, Luke iv. 24, Acts x. 35; εὐπρόσδεκτος, Rom. xv. 16.—In ver. 3, προσκοπή = σκάνδαλον).

Vers. 4—10.  Paul then enters upon a full description of his apostolic labours, which must recommend him as a servant of God (v. 12).  Three divisions are evident in the entire passage; the first relates to external afflictions (as far as ἐν νηστείαις); in the next occur expressions of spiritual advantages and virtues, (as far as ἐν δυνάμει Θεοῦ); and then antitheses succeed, in which all the outward afflictions, together with the virtues, are enumerated, and the latter represented as utterly vanquishing the former.  Here, however, without elaboration, no certain foundation can be given for the order pursued with regard to the various particulars; special and general circumstances alternate, without any perceptible reason ; the apostolic discourse presses onward without order, like a mighty stream.  In 2 Cor. xi. 23, sqq., an entirely similar passage again occurs.  In the present passage it is very striking that all the outward things claim mention in the first place ; it might have been expected from the context that the spiritual advantages would have obtained mention first, for, in the exercise of the apostolic office these must first be brought under notice.  But Paul appears desirous of introducing a climax in his relation ; he proceeds from what is outward to things inward, from conflict to victory.  (Concerning στενοχωρία see iv. 8; ἀκαταστασία is found in 1 Cor. xiv. 33, in the signification of " confusion," in which sense it also occurs in 2 Cor. xii. 20 ; it here signifies " disturbed, uncertain life."—In ver. 6 the ἐν πνεύματι ἁγίῳ arrests attention on account of the generality of the expression, for all the preceding virtues are only possible through the Holy Ghost.  For this reason Bengel, Baumgarten, and others,

understand it of the Charismata; but it is not very clear in what
manner mention can be here made of these, as it was possible
for these gifts to be connected with an unlawful striving. It
would be better to consider the expression general, but so that
the following subjects may be understood subordinate to the same).
The antitheses from ver. 8—10 are in strict rhetorical connexion,
and most ingeniously carried out. According to the figure of the
combatant (Rom. vi. 13, xiii. 12; Eph. vi. 10, sqq.), Paul represents himself armed with the weapons of righteousness, wielding
not only weapons of offence ($\H{o}\pi\lambda\alpha\ \delta\epsilon\xi\iota\acute{\alpha}$), but also weapons of
defence ($\dot{\alpha}\rho\iota\sigma\tau\epsilon\rho\acute{\alpha}$, $\phi\upsilon\lambda\alpha\kappa\tau\acute{\eta}\rho\iota\alpha$, $\dot{\alpha}\mu\upsilon\nu\tau\acute{\eta}\rho\iota\alpha$).* With these he
presses forward triumphantly through the most varied circum-
stances. (The $\delta\iota\acute{\alpha}$ is to be understood here "by"; the preposition carries on the figure upon which he entered, although im-
perfectly, by means of the expression $\H{o}\pi\lambda\alpha\ \delta\iota\kappa\alpha\iota\sigma\sigma\acute{\upsilon}\nu\eta\varsigma$). In
what follows Paul places the apparent views of his antagonists
concerning him, introducing it with $\dot{\omega}\varsigma$, in contrast with his own
true character, so evident to the eye of faith. Emmerling like-
wise takes this view of it, but Billroth errs in referring the $\dot{\omega}\varsigma$ to
both the members, thus making the application to the opponents'
views, not particular, but only signified in the connexion with
the whole. The $\kappa\alpha\grave{\iota}$ each time repeated, to which in verse 9 $\imath\delta\sigma\acute{\upsilon}$
is added, and which may always be supplied, entirely refutes this
supposition. Among the antitheses $\dot{\alpha}\gamma\nu\sigma\sigma\acute{\upsilon}\mu\epsilon\nu\sigma\iota$ is striking. This
expression does not imply "mistaken," but "unknown," though
how this could be made a ground of accusation it is not easy to comprehend. Probably it refers to the assertion of his enemies that
he was merely an insignificant teacher in the church; and that
Peter, John, and James were of more importance. To this Paul
replies, by pointing to the acquaintance with him by means of his
extended labours, which had made him well known.—In $\lambda\upsilon\pi\sigma\acute{\upsilon}$-
$\mu\epsilon\nu\sigma\iota$, $\pi\tau\omega\chi\sigma\acute{\iota}$, outward troubles and afflictions are contrasted with
that joy and inward abundance which can be imparted, without in
any degree impairing itself. (Concerning the $\pi\acute{\alpha}\nu\tau\alpha\ \kappa\alpha\tau\acute{\epsilon}\chi\epsilon\iota\nu$, see
Comm. on 1 Cor. iii. 22).

Vers. 11—13. This public statement by the apostle, which
may be construed by his enemies as blindness on his part, he de-

* Bengel observes: *per arma offensiva quum floremus, per defensiva quum labo-
ramus.*

sires to have reciprocated on the side of the Corinthians by a similar proceeding; the reward he alone seeks is love for love. But with this request the reproach is likewise connected, that they are yet reserved and narrow-minded. (In ver. 11 στόμα ἀνέῳγε, καρδία πεπλάτυνται, does not imply conversation generally, but frank confidential intercourse, as Billroth correctly maintains in opposition to Fritzsche.—In verse 12, the apostle contrasts the πλατύνεσθαι with the στενοχωρεῖσθαι, but modifies the idea in a degree. Instead of saying, I am not reserved towards you, he says, Ye are not straitened in us, i. e., I receive you with more heartfelt love. To regard the στενοχωρεῖσθε as imperative, which is suggested by Heumann, Morus, and Schleusner, is unconditionally forbidden by the οὐ.—The accusative τὴν αὐτὴν ἀντιμισθίαν of ver. 13, may be explained with Fritzsche, that without ellipsis it is connected with πλατύνθητε, and signifies τὸ δὲ αὐτὸ, ὅ ἐστιν ἀντιμισθία).

Vers. 14, 15. The admonition with which Paul commences in vi. 1, is now resumed and continued, for by their obedience thereunto the Corinthians are to display the sincerity of their love. But what urged the apostle to take up the general idea in ver. 1, not to receive the grace of God in vain, and to apply it with an especial view to prevent every fellowship with unbelievers? And besides this, connecting the exhortation immediately with the πλατύνθητε καὶ ὑμεῖς, makes it appear that the intention of the remonstrance which follows was, that this mind was to be demonstrated by the separation recommended. But the Christians were already separated from the Gentiles, therefore the exhortation which follows can only be intended to advise them to remain distinct, and to beware of backsliding. Of relapsing into idolatry, it is by no means the apostle's intention to speak, and that which follows contains no allusion to this possibility. Yet if we take into consideration that individual members of the Corinthian church had themselves participated in sacrificial festivals in the heathen temples (1 Cor. viii. 10), it may be safely asserted that there existed at least some ground for dreading a relapse into Gentilism; nevertheless the mention of εἴδωλα in ver. 16 is not to be taken in its real sense, because the antithesis of this, the temple of God, is only employed as a trope. It appears most probable to me, that the reason Paul so decidedly and dis-

tinctly asserts the necessity of an absolute separation from
unbelievers, was in order to signify the danger incurred by
Paul's antagonists (v. 12), if they continued in their present
course. The apostle intentionally alludes to it in an indirect
manner, because he still hoped for a favourable issue, and did not
desire to proceed to extremities with his enemies. By adopting
this view, all that precedes gains strict connexion with the subject
which follows. In addition, it will of course be evident that,
according to the declaration of Paul in 1 Cor. v. 10, the fellowship here forbidden does not apply to every act of association or
living together, but to labouring together for an end. Now, of
labouring with the Gentiles, no party in Corinth had thought,
and the heathen tone which continued to prevail in that city after
the first epistle, could not certainly have given occasion to so
emphatic a diatribe, whilst undoubtedly the enmity of Paul's
adversaries had arisen to so great a height as to render it doubtful whether it would be possible to labour with them for any
length of time, *i. e.* to acknowledge them as members of that
church for whose destruction they toiled. This was to be indirectly brought before their minds, and for that reason Paul expresses the necessity of avoiding all communion with them in the
strongest terms. If the adversaries were not already ἄπιστοι,
σκότος, children of the devil, they were decidedly on the way to
become such. The contrasts of light, righteousness, &c., which
indicate the well-affected, are not to be regarded either as exaggeration, or that which the Corinthians were some day to become, but rather as the true expression of the Christian principle.
The regenerate man in whom Christ dwells, is also sinful and
weak in the old man, nevertheless his true self (*Ich*), which is
alone beheld of God, is holy and perfect, for it is the Christ in
him. The Catholic view of a gradual purification of the new man
in no degree corresponds with the declaration of the Holy Scriptures. See Comm. on vii. 1. (In ver. 14 ἑτεροζυγεῖν which
occurs is a very rare word, the signification of which is not so difficult as the etymology. By some it has been derived from ζυγός
in the signification of "a balance," according to which ἑτεροζυγεῖν must mean "to influence or bias the balance." But it is
undoubtedly better to derive the word from the signification
"yoke," and for this reason ἑτεροζυγεῖν means with various ani-

mals, *e. g.*, oxen and horses yoked together, *i. e.*, working with various powers towards one end.—In ver. 15 βελιάρ is unquestionably the correct reading. It is = בְּלִיַּעַל, but no pure error of transcription, though possibly a provincialism, in which examples are not wanting of the frequent exchange of λ with ρ. βελιάρ is also found in the Testament, xii. *patr. in Grabii spicil.* i. 159.—In ver. 16 συγκατάθεσις, approbation, consenting unto, only occurs in this passage throughout the New Testament. See Cicer. Quæst. Acad. iv. 2).

Vers. 16—18. Paul might consider the image of the temple rather unintelligible to a community formed of Gentile elements; he therefore explains it by quoting from Lev. xxvi. 11, and then proceeds to strengthen his renewed warning against any closer connexion with dissimilar elements by passages from Isa. lii. 11, Jerem. xxxi. 33, xxxii. 38. The application of the first quotation proves how real the apostle desired the image employed should be regarded, for the indwelling of God in man is the object he therein particularly holds forth to view. (See Comm. on iii. 17, vi. 19). In the ἐνοικεῖν, ἐμπεριπατεῖν, nothing may therefore be restricted; the latter expression corresponds to the μένειν employed by John, and stands parallel with the ἄγειν of Rom. viii. 11. In the citation from Is. lii. 11, no allusion is to be discovered to the Mosaic law which declared those unclean who touched a dead body and other objects pronounced unclean. The apostle understands and employs it typically to inward things. The quotation at the conclusion of the chapter contains the promises of grace which shall follow the faithful observance of this admonition, and which are concentrated in those who come under the acceptation of children. (Παντοκράτωρ, except in this passage, only occurs in the Apocalypse, but there frequently. The LXX. render שַׁדַּי and יְ יְ צְבָאוֹת by the same.

Chap. vii. 1. To prove the possession and thankful acceptance of such promises which must assuredly awaken gratitude, Paul again repeats his exhortation that they should preserve themselves free from every stain, and in (childlike) fear of God (see on Rom. viii. 15) perfect themselves in holiness (already commenced). (Concerning the idea of the ἁγιοσύνη see Comm. on 1 Cor. i. 30). According to the connexion of the whole (as already observed in Comm. on 1 Cor. i., and iii. 15), Paul is not desirous of representing σὰρξ καὶ πνεῦμα, i. e., the entire man, inward as well as outward, as unclean and requiring purification; for vi. 14, 15, describes the same objects here addressed as light and righteousness itself, consequently, such as have already received through faith in Christ, forgiveness of their sins, and participation in the merits of Christ. But the sense of the words only bears reference to *keeping* themselves free from all contamination, and to the further growth of the pure new man (1 John iii. 9) already in them, which would have the effect of repressing more and more the death (and not the state of purity) which devolves to the condition of the old man. But, according to appearances, this process of the growth of the new, and dying of the old man, takes the form of a being purified, because the same individual bears within himself the new as likewise the old man. The passages 1 Cor. v. 7, 2 Tim. ii. 20, 21, are to be understood in a similar manner.

## § 7. GODLY SORROW.

### (vii. 2—16).

Turning from the more objective position and bearing of the preceding section, to the concrete circumstances lying before us, Paul first describes his apprehension concerning the manner in which the Corinthians might have received his epistle, in which respect, however, Titus had comforted him (vii. 2—7); he then shows how the godly sorrow of a true repentance is ever the source of inextinguishable joy, for which reason he had been comforted even by their mourning, because it was not a sorrow of the world, working death (vii. 8—16).

Vers. 2—4. This section compared with chaps. x. and xi. proves quite clearly that Paul certainly addressed the entire epistle to the yet outwardly undivided church, but that in the first nine chapters he had internally the well-affected more in view, whilst in the succeeding chapters the adversaries were especially addressed. Yet passages such as vi. 14, sqq., distinctly prove that a reference to his antagonists existed even in the earlier chapters; for without admitting such a supposition, the immediate and animated transition from vii. 1 to 2, and the declarations χωρήσατε ἡμᾶς, οὐδένα ἠδικήσαμεν κ. τ. λ would be difficult to explain.

How could Paul immediately give utterance to the thought " we
have wronged no man," after exhorting them to " cleanse themselves from all filthiness of flesh and spirit," if the latter injunction possessed none other than a strictly general and moral reference? On the contrary, such a transition is easily to be
accounted for, if we admit that it enjoined the necessary and
continual separation from the antagonists, in case they persevered
in adhering to their worldly judgment. (To the χωρήσατε ἡμᾶς,
the πλατύνθητε of vi. 13 may be suitably compared. Love is
represented as a qualification for adoption. In the expressions
which follow, Paul takes into consideration the, to a certain extent, abominable accusations of the opponents. [See particularly
concerning the πλεονεκτεῖν, viii. 19, 20, xii. 14, 16.] We are
not to consider the reference to any distinct individual, the incestuous person, for example.—The προείρηκα refers to vi. 12.—
The plural ἐν ταῖς καρδίαις is again striking, but it refers to Paul
and those of like opinions, to Titus especially [ver. 5, sqq.] The
εἰς τὸ συναποθανεῖν and συζῆν is only circumscribed by the
πάντοτε, so that the meaning is " for ever, and under all circumstances."—In ver. 4, παῤῥησία is not " frankness," but " bold
joyful hope." Ὑπερπερισσεύω occurs again in Rom. v. 20).

Vers. 5—7. In contrast to his present joy the apostle narrates his trials in Macedonia, before Titus brought his intelligence from Corinth, which added yet more to his outward sorrows;
nevertheless through him he received comfort also from God.
The expression ἡ σὰρξ ἡμῶν here indicates the nature of men,
not inasmuch as it is evil, but only as it is weak. Paul intends
to signify that his νοῦς was without care, because he was fully
acquainted with the truth, but that nevertheless the human
element within him was powerfully troubled for his beloved Corinthians. (It would be better to supply ἤμεθα to ἐν παντὶ
θλιβόμενοι, it is not necessary to suppose an anacoluthon). In
this tribulation the God of all comfort consoled him (see i. 3, 4)
through Titus. He describes himself and his friends, as ταπεινοί,
inasmuch as they acknowledged themselves to be in a state of
true spiritual necessity, and because they were not governed by
worldly considerations, but cared for the things of God's kingdom. The ἐν τῇ παρουσίᾳ of ver. 7 must be protected from misapprehension ; not only the coming of Titus rejoiced the apostle,

but also the intelligence which he brought from Corinth, viz., that
his epistle to the church there had made a worthy impression.
(Concerning ἐπιπόθησιν of ver. 7 see the passage v. 2.—'Οδυρμὸν
indicates the affliction caused by the unfortunate state of affairs
in Corinth, ζῆλον the zeal to fulfil Paul's commands; the ὑπὲρ
ἐμοῦ refers to all three subjects.—In the μᾶλλον χαρῆναι* the joy
is compared with the sorrow at first experienced, " I now rejoice
more than I had sorrowed at an earlier period)."

Vers. 8, 9. How extremely doubtful Paul had felt concerning
the result of his letter, is proved by the εἰ καὶ μετεμελόμην: he
had consequently regretted, if only for a moment, that he had
written so strongly; but he no longer entertained the feeling,
he rejoiced truly over the sorrow which his epistle had awakened
in the Corinthians, not that the sorrow itself had proved the
source of satisfaction to him, but the repentance which was connected with it; the godly sorrow which he had been instrumental
in producing, had proved to them of the nature of a blessing.—
In this simple construction of the passage the only doubt which
can arise is relative to the meaning of the βλέπω γὰρ κ. τ. λ. Billroth takes it in the signification of "for I reflect, take into consideration," because it otherwise contains too inapposite a remark.
But the εἰ καὶ πρὸς ὥραν does not agree with this explanation,
which renders subordinate the moment of the λυπεῖν, which the
βλέπω γὰρ is intended prominently to express. If on the contrary we receive the βλέπω γὰρ as representing the above ἐλύπησα ὑμᾶς, not as a supposition, but as a fact experienced, in the
sense of: for I perceive according to Titus' report, &c., the εἰ
καὶ πρὸς ὥραν thereby gains a perfect sense and connexion. It
then expresses the tender love of the apostle, who even when the
sorrow he inflicts is salutary, abridges the period of suffering as
far as possible, in order that godly joy may again shine forth from
the affliction. Thus understood, the idea can in nowise be considered subordinate. (In ver. 9 ἵνα ἐν μηδενὶ ζημιωθῆτε is Li-
totes for ἵνα ἐν παντὶ περισσεύητε, "in order that in every relation, through joy and sorrow, I may bring you a blessing." But,
as Billroth correctly observes, the ἵνα is decidedly to be understood τελικῶς, for Paul sees a divine injunction therein).

---

* Baumgarten considers that the ὥστε με μᾶλλον χαρῆναι ought to be connected with the words which follow; but this would be singularly inappropriate.

Ver. 10. The address which has been of particular application, now extends itself to a more general one. Paul distinguishes a twofold λύπη, the κατὰ Θεὸν, and the τοῦ κόσμου. Both expressions contain something more than a reference, the generality of the subject of the expression must be borne in mind. The κατὰ Θεον signifies not only the divine pleasure, but also the relation to God; and in the τοῦ κόσμου the dominion of the same in the world, and again its relation to the world, are implied. The sorrow of the world, which only deplores sin on account of its unpleasant consequences, has no spirit of life in it; it rather destroys the life which may exist, by precipitating the sinner into a state of despair. Godly sorrow, on the contrary, is the source of everlasting life, for it effects a μετάνοιαν εἰς σωτηρίαν. It might be supposed, that the λύπη was the μετάνοια itself, but the latter already possess faith, the former is the purely negative side of the sorrow, whose subject is not the consequence of sin, but sin itself. (Billroth thinks ἀμεταμέλητον should be connected with σωτηρία, but the epithet could not be applied to the idea of salvation, it does not require to be explained, that salvation is never to be repented of; but it would be perfectly correct to join it to μετάνοιαν, for in a worldly point of view it is possible for man to lament that he must surrender himself to a strict repentance, instead of a cheerful enjoyment of life).

Vers. 11, 12. The apostle exhibits the operation of godly sorrow in the conduct of the Corinthians, with reference to a concrete circumstance, viz., in their proceedings towards the incestuous member of their church (1 Cor. v.) His exhortation had had the effect of arousing in them a mighty zeal, and this was the principal object of his epistle. The mention of their proceedings with regard to the immoral person alluded to is only adduced as an example, and he in no respect enters upon the important questions which agitated the Corinthian community. But the apostle desired to avoid direct mention of the divisions, in order not to diminish the possibility of reconciling them. It is besides very evident that the expression οὐκ ἔγραψα εἴνεκεν τοῦ ἀδικήσαντος is not to be urged; as if it were, that Paul had not had the sinner himself in his consideration. He only intends to say that he desired, *above all things*, to profit by this circumstance to arouse the whole church from its state of slumber, and that this salutary movement might also affect the sinner to his own advantage, was naturally included in the apostle's wish. It has been supposed that the ἀδικηθείς implied the apostle himself, or the church; but this cannot be adopted, because Paul intends expressly to state that his view was not directed to the fact itself; it therefore follows, that the reference can in no degree apply to the church, on whose behalf he declares himself, in the concluding words of the verse, to have written. But had he represented himself alone as the injured party, this would have implied a reproach towards the church, who might thereby have felt wounded; but the context does not justify us in attributing to the apostle any intention of blaming the Corinthians, it is certainly his aim rather to commend them. It is evidently forced in a high degree to receive the εἵνεκεν τοῦ ἀδικηθέντος as neuter (τὸ ἀδικηθέν = τὸ ἀδίκημα), with Heinsius and Billroth, for it is more reasonable to refer it to the father, who, by the conduct of his wife and her stepson, was the really injured party. That we are unacquainted whether he were still living, forms no ground of objection to this explanation, as no moment speaks to the contrary. In ver. 11 the reiterated ἀλλά is again intensive, in the signification of *imo*. The single expressions contain as it were the description of the feeling of the Corinthians, elicited by the apostolic appeal, with reference to the offender, and expressed in the manner of a climax. According to this, the ἀπολογία cannot well imply exculpation through the fact of punishment, as Billroth maintains, for the expressions which succeed bear reference to this, but it indicates the excuses offered for their negligence, in that they had not punished the offenders at an earlier period.—Ἀγανάκτησις [which does not again occur in the New Testament] refers to the exhibition of moral feeling on the subject of the offence, φόβος to God, as the avenger of the wicked persons whom they had tolerated through false clemency. Ἐπιπόθησις and ζῆλος express the sentiments against the apostle himself, and ἐκδίκησις the result proceeding from the objects enumerated.—In ver. 12 the reading ὑμῶν τὴν ὑπὲρ ἡμῶν is unquestionably to be preferred in agreement with Lachmann's opinion. The whole connexion proves that it was undoubtedly the Corinthians' zeal, and not Paul's zeal which was intended, and besides it is easy to account for the existence of another reading. It appeared more natural that the apostle should say, I write in order to prove my zeal to you, than, in order to display your zeal. Nevertheless the critical authorities in favour of this reading are of consequence, which has occasioned Griesbach to hesitate between the two).

Vers. 13, 14. This result of his writing was sufficient to comfort the apostle (retrospective reference to ver. 7), but to the comfort was added the rejoicing over the joy of Titus, who had found everything confirmed which Paul had told him concerning the Corinthians.—In ver. 13 Billroth and Lachmann have already proved the correct reading to be ἐπὶ δὲ τῇ παρακλήσει ὑμῶν περισσοτέ ρως μᾶλλον κ. τ. λ. ; we can only hesitate between the choice of ὑμῶν or ἡμῶν. I prefer ὑμῶν, because it might be inferred from the first person παρακεκλήμεθα that Paul would further enlarge upon his consolation. But Paul's comfort was also that of the Corinthians, they themselves being the origin of it. (Consult Winer's Gr. upon περισσοτέρως μᾶλλον, p. 221). Ver. 14 explains for what cause Titus' joy had so much rejoiced the apostle, viz., that his predictions had been proved correct. Billroth incorrectly concludes πάντα to signify all that Paul had imparted to Titus concerning the Corinthians. The text contains not the slightest allusion to this. It rather signifies everything, without exception, published by Paul in Corinth ; and the whole sentence is intended to contrast him as the faithful preacher of the truth, and whose confidence would not be put to shame by the better portion of the Corinthian church, with the calumnies of the adversaries. (The reading in ver. 14 of ἡ καύχησις ὑμῶν ἐπὶ Τίτου, accepted by Lachmann, is not deserving of recommendation. The ἀλλ᾽ ὡς—οὕτως καί refers to the above κεκαύχημαι, it must therefore mean καύχησις ἡμῶν : for καύχησις ὑμῶν cannot well be said, as the Corinthians had permitted themselves to be deceived. The substitution of these pronouns for each other in the Codd. is so frequent, that their authority can be but slight with reference to them).

Vers. 15, 16. The humble obedience of the Corinthians is represented, as that which above all things especially rejoiced Titus; not though as if they feared the man in the apostle, but God, who proved himself effectual through him. The apostle therefore justly grounds the joyful hope, that all he desires to effect among them will prosper, upon this desirable frame of mind.

## § 8. THE COLLECTION.

### (viii. 1—ix. 15).

The following copious dissertation concerning the collection made by the apostle for the Christians (see Comm. on 1 Cor. xvi. 1), is an energetic exhortation to liberality; but whilst Paul urges this, he does not neglect to secure himself against the probable calumnies of his adversaries, who appear to have been bold enough to endeavour to cast suspicion on the integrity of the apostle. (See viii. 20). He therefore commands that several brethren selected by the church should take charge of the money, and thus effectually put an end to any calumny on the subject.

Vers. 1—4. The apostle commences, by exhibiting the conduct of the Christians in Macedonia, as an example to the Corinthians: they having proved themselves bountiful in a high degree, under very unfavourable circumstances, and entreated the acceptance of a contribution far beyond their circumstances. (In ver. 1 δέ is only to be considered as carrying on the subject. —Χάρις indicates the liberality of the Macedonians, in as far as impelled by Divine grace.—In ver. 2 the mention of the trials of affliction* endured by the Macedonians, only occurs in order thereby to mark more strongly their bountiful spirit. Despite their sufferings, they abounded in joy, at having received, through the Gospel, the heavenly treasure prized so highly by them, and this joy urged them to impart freely of their outward goods. Instead, however, of continuing καὶ ἐν κατὰ βάθους πτωχείᾳ ἡ περισσεία κ. τ. λ., the apostle boldly describes the poverty co-ordinate with the joy, representing both together, as the subject giving occasion to the abundant gift.—It is very possible that χρηστότητος has here been changed for ἁπλότητος, for, according to the general signification, ἁπλότητος may appear inapplicable. But this expression may be used with reference to genuine true liberality and benevolence, as especially appears from ix. 11, 13. The passage Rom. xii. 8 is not to be enumerated also. But in Josephus. Arch. vii. 13, 4 [and

---

* See concerning the persecutions of the Christians in Macedonia, Acts xvi. 20, sqq., xvii. 5; 1 Thess. i. 6, ii. 14.

likewise Tacitus Hist. iii. 86 *simplicitas*], it is employed in a similar sense, also in Isa. xxxiii. 23, Job xi. 13, by the Greek translators.—The αὐθαίρετος of ver. 3 only occurs again in viii. 17 throughout the New Testament. Hesychius explains it by ἑκούσιος: from ver. 5 ἔδωκαν is to be supplied.—In ver. 4. δέξασθαι ἡμᾶς must be erased from the text as a manifest gloss).

Vers. 5—7. Paul employed the unexpected and voluntary sacrifice on the part of the Macedonians, as an argument to animate Titus, intending thereby that he should arouse the Corinthians to a like contribution, in order that they might not in any respect fall short of their brethren. (In ver. 5, ἐποίουν is to be added to καὶ οὐ καθὼς ἠλπίσαμεν.—The ἑαυτοὺς ἔδωκαν τῷ κυρίῳ is not to be understood as of a spiritual yielding up, as if the meaning were, they first gave themselves internally and wholly to the Lord, and then, as a consequence of this commendable frame of mind, offered to the necessitous brethren of their possessions; but the giving here signified is the bestowing everything, and retaining nothing for themselves. If the former were the correct sense of the words, a reference would certainly be made to it in that which follows, and this is by no means the fact. The apostle rather takes for granted, that the entire yielding up everything to the Lord is understood throughout; and that the gifts offered to the Lord were delivered over to him, even to the apostle, is ascribed by Paul to the Almighty's intention and will, as he desired to make them observe that the idea had not originated with himself, —In ver. 6 the προενήρξατο refers to a former abode of Titus in Corinth, when he might also have endeavoured to further the present object. Lachmann has preferred the reading ἐνήρξατο.—In ver. 7 ἀλλά is again to be taken in the sense of *imo*, and ver. 7 is to be closely connected with ver. 6, so that the ἵνα in ver. 7 corresponds with the ἵνα in ver. 6. "Paul requires nothing oppressive from the Corinthians, he only affords them an opportunity of appropriating to themselves another spiritual blessing." Billroth, who has entirely overlooked this, completely errs with regard to the meaning of ver. 7.—Concerning πίστις, λόγος, γνῶσις, see Comm. on 1 Cor. xii. 8. Lachmann reads τῇ ἐξ ἡμῶν ἐν ὑμῖν for τῇ ἐξ ὑμῶν ἐν ἡμῖν ἀγάπῃ. But the usual reading is preferable, because Paul is enumerating the privileges of the Corinthians, consequently the ἀγάπη ἐξ αὐτῶν must be likewise mentioned).

Vers. 8, 9. As in 1 Cor. vii. Paul here also distinguishes between ἐπιταγή and γνώμη, he does not desire to command but to advise, and to test the sincerity of the love professed by his beloved Corinthians; the experiencing Christ's mercy naturally tends to enlarge the heart, and incline the individual to bestow likewise upon others; therefore this grace must be wanting among the Corinthians, if they prove themselves deficient in the particulars named. Ver. 9, as well as Phil. ii. 6, belong to those passages in which Paul plainly brings to their remembrance the humiliation of Christ. The πλούσιος ὤν expresses the eternal existence of the Son in the glory of the Father, and in the ἐπτώχευσε is expressed the voluntary renunciation of the same, out of compassion to the misery of mankind. It is entirely wrong to understand Christ here as a type, though this view is adopted by Billroth and Usteri, making the sense: as Christ, by becoming poor, made others rich, so do ye likewise. The meaning is rather, "As Christ, by becoming poor, made you rich, ye can thus bestow of your abundance upon others, for to this end were ye placed in this condition." The only objection which may be urged against this acceptation, is, that Christ has rendered mankind *spiritually* rich, while the bestowing here recommended regards *outward* things. But as the actual giving presupposes the *intention* to give as the inward motive, which without it could never take place, although the outward possessions as the means might exist, it appears to present no obstacle to our idea. But, on the contrary, a considerable difficulty seems to arise, if Christ is here only considered as a type; for the γινώσκετε γάρ appeals to the Christian knowledge of the Corinthians, presupposing among them that experience of the grace of Christ which makes rich; but its purport is not that they should imitate him, but only that the feeling of their inability to do so should stimulate them to those proofs of grateful love which display themselves in good works, approving themselves thereby not unfruitful partakers of those riches, bestowed through Christ, and not through any merit of their own.

Vers. 10, 11. Paul, however, does not counsel thus with a view to

his own advantage, but to that of the Corinthians, who require
to be led on to the perfection of the work commenced, in order
(as stated in ver. 7) to gain this further blessing.  For the correct understanding of this passage, it is necessary to remark, in
the first place, that according to 1 Cor. xvi. 2, the contributions
to the collection were to take place weekly, and were not to be
made only once ; Paul may, therefore, require that the ἐπιτελέσαι
should succeed the ποιῆσαι.  Then, with respect to the circumstance of the θέλειν following the ποιῆσαι, the expression ἡ προθυμία τοῦ θέλειν (ver. 11), has already explained what was intended, as Winer and Billroth correctly observe, viz., the intention and desire to be well-pleasing to God, which accompanies
the performance.  Paul consequently will say: it shall not only
be done outwardly, but as ye have already begun, it must be
given in the right intention, in fact it must be persevered in
unto the end.  (The ἀπὸ πέρυσι of ver. 10 occurs again in ix. 2.
The expression signifies really, in years past by, also " previous."
Xenophon [Hist. iii. 2, 6] has only πέρυσι.—The ἐκ τοῦ ἔχειν is
to be understood, as shown by what follows, " according to the
possession)."

Vers. 12—15. The relation of the measure of liberality to the
whole amount of possession, is further illustrated in the verses
which follow.  As generosity consisted not in the largeness of
the gift, but in its relative value to the wealth, so it was likewise necessary, that liberality should not be restricted to one side
alone, but among Christ's members, as one body knit together
in the fellowship of love, the giver should receive again, and the
receiver be prepared to bestow where necessary ; in this manner
a true community of goods was produced, which it would be folly
to strive to attain in any other manner.  Love creates freedom
and equality without revolution, a spiritual community of goods.
(See on Acts ii. 44).  Paul very ingeniously applies the passage
from Exod. xvi. 18, which represents that in collecting the manna,
every Israelite found himself upon the same footing.  In God's
kingdom, likewise, none have too much, and none too little, although, according to their various necessities, they have not all
the like quantity.  (In ver. 12 it is preferable to connect εὐπρόσδεκτος to τὶς than to προθυμία.—In verse 13, γένηται is to be
supplied to ἵνα.  This verse shows, besides, that the distress suffered

by the Christians in Palestine was only of a temporary nature,
the removal of which was to be looked for.—In ver. 15 the quotation from the LXX. is made from memory; it runs thus in the
original: οὐκ ἐπλεόνασε ὁ τὸ πολύ, καὶ ὁ τὸ ἔλαττον οὐκ ἠλατ-
τόνησε).

Vers. 16, 17. The apostle then passes from himself to Titus,
who was appointed to conduct the collection, representing him to
be as earnestly solicitous for the welfare of the Corinthians as he
himself had hitherto been; his zeal rendered any exhortation
from Paul unnecessary, for it urged him voluntarily to undertake
the journey.—Billroth's reception of the passage is erroneous, for
he thinks Paul intended to compare the zeal of Titus with that
of the Corinthians themselves; but the sentence ὑπὲρ ὑμῶν contradicts this. The aorist ἐξῆλθε, and likewise those in the following verses, are besides best understood as implying that Paul
wrote as one who had received an epistle, for unquestionably
Titus himself had delivered this to him in Corinth.

Vers. 18—21. In order, therefore, to remove the slightest occasion for malicious accusations, Paul had caused several brethren
to be selected, together with Titus, who were to receive, and
afterwards deliver over, the bountiful collections which were the
object of Paul's exhortation; his wisdom led him not only to act
in a manner free from all suspicion, but also to avoid even the
appearance of it in the eyes of men. This passage is likewise a
remarkable proof of the shameless audacity of some among the
apostle's adversaries; he is not speaking of possibilities; but the
precautionary measures taken by Paul prove that they had really
ventured to cast a doubt upon his integrity.—The description in
ver. 18 might certainly apply to several, but probably Luke is
meant, who is mentioned in the subscription as the person appointed to deliver the epistle, and whose relation of the Acts of
the Apostles xx. 1, sqq. (a passage which belongs to the time of
the drawing up of the second epistle to the Corinthians), ceases
to be in the first person, which implies that he had left the apostle. It will be naturally understood that the expression ψειροτονη-
θεὶς in ver. 19 does not signify here the description of ordination
which it does in Acts xiv. 23; it rather shows that the church in
Macedonia had displayed some degree of activity, with regard to
the choice of the deputies who were to accompany Titus; Paul had

proposed, and the church had accepted them.—Συνέκδημος ἡμῶν refers to the projected journey to Jerusalem, " as our companion." —The πρὸς προθυμίαν ἡμῶν is elliptical, it must be consequently understood as, " a declaration of my willingness." In ver. 20, στέλλεσθαι is employed in the signification of "to withdraw oneself, to avoid." It again occurs in 2 Thess. iii. 6.—Concerning μωμεῖσθαι see vi. 3.—Ἁδρότης = πλοῦτος, περισσεία.

Vers. 22—24. After again making allusion to an estimable brother and companion, all these messengers in conclusion, as his partners and fellow-labourers, are impressively commended to a favourable reception from the Corinthians.—Who the brother is, of whom mention is here made, cannot be determined with any degree of certainty ; probably, however, one of the· individuals named in Acts xx. 4. Paul appears to have included him in the deputation on account of his great confidence towards the Corinthians, *i. e.*, by reason of his ability to arrange something among them. (In ver. 23 the sentence is not regularly formed; it ought to have been, εἴτε Τίτος, or εἴτε ὑπὲρ ἀδελφῶν. We can, with Chrysostom, supply an ἀκοῦσαί τι βούλεσθε to the ὑπὲρ.—Ἀπόστολοι is here, with reference to ver. 19, to be received in the more extended sense of " subordinates."—In ver. 24 Lachmann reads ἐνδεικνύμενοι instead of ἐνδείξασθε, which is certainly preferable to the more difficult reading.—In the εἰς πρόσωπον the tendency of this ἔνδειξις is signified, " in order that it may come before the face of the church, and they may perceive that I have not so praised you without cause.")

Chap. ix. 1, 2. It has been already observed in the Introduction that no interval takes place between chapters viii. and ix., as those commentators have supposed who divide the present Epistle into two parts; but in effect the discussion concerning the collection still goes on. After some information concerning the persons who were appointed to convey the money, Paul returns to the subject of the collection itself, intimating in a delicate manner that it was unnecessary to write more upon that head, as they had ever shown themselves forward in the matter, and he therefore only recommends them to gather the various contributions together as soon as possible.—(Ver. 2. Concerning the ἀπὸ πέρυσι see viii. 10.—Lachmann omits the ἐξ before ὑμῶν, but the usual reading is undoubtedly to be preferred. The zeal is considered as something proceeding forth and issuing from the Corinthians, and really of a communicable nature).

Vers. 3, 4. The sending beforehand of the brethren, according to the declaration of the apostle, appears to have been contrived as the means to secure their fame to the Corinthians, for the Macedonians who accompanied Paul at a later period would not find them unprepared. Something facetious is clearly to be found in the καταισχυνθῶμεν ἡμεῖς ἵνα μὴ λέγωμεν ὑμεῖς, by which the apostle wishes to stimulate the Corinthians to an interest in his undertaking; from the nature of the thing it was not desirable to employ serious command, in urging the display of a charity which would be voluntary. Therefore the ingenious declaration before us was well adapted to prepossess the Corinthians in favour of the thing, since it represented them as disposed towards the collection, and then adds that two brethren should be sent beforehand, in order that the fame of their promptitude in responding to the call made in behalf of their poor brethren, should not suffer in the estimation of the Macedonians who were to follow. Rückert takes occasion from this passage to reproach the apostle with behaviour at once insincere and unpædagogic. In 2 Cor. viii. 2 Paul had represented to the Corinthians that the Macedonians abounded in liberality, and here he declares that the readiness of the Corinthians had stimulated the Macedonians to an exhibition of zeal. But as whole churches, and even entire provinces, are the subject of remark, it would seem possible for the apostle to be completely consistent; Paul might hold forth the liberality of the well-intentioned Macedonians, as an example to the Corinthians, and at the same time produce an effect upon the less benevolently-disposed Macedonians, by the description of the kind feeling existing among the better Corinthian Christians. (In ver. 3 the ἐν τῷ μέρει τούτῳ corresponds to the ἐν τῇ ὑποστάσει ταύτῃ of ver. 4, exactly as in xi. 17. The ὑπόστασις must therefore be received in the sense of "being, thing," which, although it does not occur in this meaning in any other passage of the New Testament, is nevertheless sanctioned by the origin of the word. The word implying "conviction, evidence," which is employed in Heb. iii. 14, xi. 1, is derived from an original signifying "being, essentiality," because the true evidence of an object includes within it its being, according to its degree of potency. The gloss

τῆς καυχήσεως is unquestionably interpolated in this verse out of
xi. 17 of the epistle under consideration).

Vers. 5—7. The brethren sent before (viii. 18, sqq.) were to
close the collections, so that on the apostle's arrival the whole
should be perfectly ready ; all who are inclined to do so might
therefore still richly contribute, but they were, at the same time,
advised to give cheerfully.   (In ver. 5 the collection is styled εὐλογία, inasmuch as it proceeds from benevolent and charitable
minds ; πλεονεξία in so far as obtained with difficulty, and when
alloyed by a covetous spirit.—In ver. 6 ἰστέον is to be supplied
with τοῦτο δέ.—The ἐπ᾿ εὐλογίαις is so contrasted with the φει-
δομένως, that it must be understood "in the manner of a blessing, i. e., abundantly.   Precisely as in 1 Cor. ix. 10 ἐπ᾿ ἐλπίδι
refers to hope.—In ver. 7 προαιρεῖσθαι, to propose to oneself,
to be willing to do something).

Vers. 8, 9. According to Ps. cxii. 9, God is represented as the
rewarder, who ever extends the necessary means to the benevolent,
that under all circumstances they may have the power to exercise
good works of all kinds. (The quotation strictly follows the LXX.—
The ἐσκόρπισε refers to the metaphor of the σπείρειν commenced
in ver. 6, and which is continued in ver. 10.—The μένει εἰς τὸν
αἰῶνα is, according to ver. 8, to be received comprehensively, viz.,
" he continues always, and abounds richly in all good works)."

Vers. 10, 11. The image of the sower is especially employed
with reference to benevolence.   The Almighty who provides seed
for the sower, and bread for food, will also minister that which
is necessary for the growth of the spiritual seed of love, causing
it to increase as the fruits of righteousness, in order that ye may
be rich in all bountifulness to the glory and thanksgiving of God,
through us, by whom ye have been so encouraged.   In this meta-
phorical language, the seed intimates the possession of outward
wealth, but certainly in conjunction with the charitable disposition to employ it to good purposes; and the fruits are the individual acts of charity, proceeding out of these elements.   As Christ
declared, my meat is to do the will of my Father, works of charity
are made to appear in this passage as the meat of believers.   In
the ἐν παντὶ πλουτιζόμενοι this hope is represented as realized;
it stands for εἰς τὸ πλουτίζεσθαι ὑμᾶς.   (In ver. 10 it is unnecessary to seek a distinction between ἐπιχορηγεῖν and χορη

γεῖν; both expressions occur only in the New Testament, in the epistles of Paul and Peter.—The futures χορηγήσει, πληθυνεῖ are to be preferred to the optative; they imply the certain hope which renders any further petition unnecessary.—The form γένημα instead of γέννημα is only found in this passage, in the language of the New Testament, καρπός is more commonly employed for it).

Vers. 12—15. Connecting it with the thanksgiving to God which their charity had called forth, the apostle further declares that this awakening to God's praise and glory, and especially to intercession, are to be included among the good efforts of the collection. The virtues of believers are not to be exercised solely for themselves, or for the sake of the salutary example they may prove to others, for fundamentally the glory of God is the principal object, they being all his work. The apostle himself, therefore, pours forth God's praise (ver. 15). (In ver. 12, either of the two expressions, διακονία or λειτουργία, had been sufficient; nevertheless the employment of both in conjunction is by no means pleonastic, since the διακονία brings forward the application of the relief, and the λειτουργία more especially the collection from the benevolent.—In ver. 13 the διακονία is to be regarded as the test of the intention. The σοξάζοντες refers to those from whom the thanksgiving to God proceeds. He alludes to the ὑποταγή and the ἁπλότης, i. e., to the obedience and the benevolence aroused through the instrumentality of the apostle.—In ver. 14, the καὶ αὐτῶν δεήσει ὑπὲρ ὑμῶν is no longer to be considered dependent on the ἐπί in ver. 13, but is to be connected with διὰ πυλλῶν εὐχαριστιῶν τῷ Θεῷ, rendering ver. 13 of the nature of a parenthesis, and more closely explaining the thanksgiving to God, as well as the intercession by the ἐπιποθούντων κ. τ. λ. — The ἀνεκδιηγητός of ver. 15 only occurs throughout the New Testament in this passage; a form somewhat similar is found, Rom. xi. 33).

# III.

## PART THIRD.

(x. 1—xiii. 13).

§ 9. FALSE APOSTLES.

(x. 1—18).

---

Until now, Paul has addressed himself pre-eminently to the better-intentioned in the Corinthian Church, but from the 10th chap. he directs himself against his adversaries (see Introd. § 3), without, however, making a perfect separation into two distinct classes. Those persons opposed to the apostle had sought to lower his dignity, and weaken his authority, by describing him as weak in personal influence, although courageous and full of self-commendation in his letters. To this representation Paul opposes the declaration, that they would find him to be personally, precisely such as his letters promised; but with respect to the glorying, he boasted not of himself, but of God, who had appointed him to so extensive a sphere of action (1—18).

Vers. 1, 2. The apostle, in order to remove the accusation, that when present he was weak and submissive, although he appeared courageous when absent, commences by beseeching his readers not to render it imperative, that upon appearing among them, he should as boldly assume his apostolic authority as he had done in writing to them. The inference from this is naturally, that evil would arise to them, and they might feel disposed to resent it, if

he were compelled to rebuke them.* That he entreats them to
this by the meekness and gentleness of Christ, evidently implies
that he desires to act in the name of his Master, and would willingly exercise gentleness instead of severity. The words ὃς
κατά κ. τ. λ. are certainly to be understood with the restriction,
"as my adversaries accuse me." In ver. 2 the δέομαι takes up
again the παρακαλῶ, and connects with it the object of the request in the words τὸ μὴ παρὼν θαρρῆσαι τῇ πεποιθήσει. The
form of the entreaty, however, naturally confers upon the μὴ
παρὼν θαρρῆσαι the signification of, "that I may not find it necessary to appear bold when present, or, that ye may not compel
me to appear so." But in order to produce the greater impression, Paul represents this severity which was to accompany his
appearance, as not alone possible, but as already determined
upon, with regard to certain persons. Assuming the standard of
his opponents, Paul is only ironical when he signifies his appearing thus as a τολμῆσαι. It was even that which these men presumed to reprove in him, the κατὰ σάρκα περιπατεῖν, i. e. the being actuated by human views, the fear of man and the desire to
please the world, which was so conspicuous and worthy of blame
in themselves. (In ver. 2 πεποίθησις is forbearingly used; it
indicates severe, serious reproof, as θαρρεῖν does, "to reprove
fearlessly)."

Vers 4—6. In order more forcibly to illustrate this view, Paul
further asserts that, although he might walk after the flesh and
in weakness, he nevertheless warred not with the weapons belonging to the flesh, but with those which were divine and sufficiently mighty to overcome everything contrary to God, and to
bring all into obedience.—The apostle here passes from the idea
of what is sinful in σάρξ, which is most prominent in ver. 2, to
that of weakness, and describes himself as the champion of God,
as not only defending himself, but attacking the strongholds
(ὀχυρώματα) of the wicked. (The κατὰ Θεὸν should be contrasted with the κατὰ σάρκα, but instead of this the idea of what
is powerful is immediately held forth to view, and by means of
the τῷ Θεῷ attributed to God. I cannot receive the dative with
Billroth as "for God," but must consider it "through God," i. e.

---

* At the conclusion of the Epistle (xiii. 2, iii. 10) this idea is again laid down.

according to his will and judgment, in which Winer agrees. See
Gr. p. 193). What he desires to express by the term strongholds is further shown by ver. 5. He mentions the λογισμοὺς
καὶ πᾶν ὕψωμα ἐπαιρόμενον κατὰ τῆς γνώσεως τοῦ Θεοῦ as to be
subdued and brought into subjection to the obedience of Christ,
upon which occasion the πᾶν νόημα is employed in the same
sense as he before uses the λογισμούς. The condition in which
such high proud λογισμοί or νοήματα prevail is called παρακοή,
and is opposed to the ὑπακοή, which Paul desires to call forth.
If we should now inquire what the apostle intended to indicate
by these expressions, it is undoubtedly apparent, according to ver.
7, that he proposed especially to reprove the seeming wisdom of
the *Christianer* party, who took occasion to haughtily exalt themselves in opposition to the true knowledge of Christ promulgated
by the apostle, and claimed for themselves the prerogatives of
true Christians. The theoretical and practical elements may not
be separated in this view, for both necessarily pervade it; theoretical blindness can never remain free from practical consequences. The general deduction from this passage is, that it
asserts the incompetency of human wisdom to pass sentence in
matters of faith; but we must also agree that it is *capable* of
being applied to the adversaries of Paul, whose pride and especial
blindness of heart exalted themselves against the knowledge of
Christ; it may not, however, be denied that the apostle's first and
chief idea regarded a false gnosis (such as is described in 1 Cor.
i. 3) which resisted the true knowledge, and laid claim to reception as the real and genuine Christianity. It is evidently the
design of the apostle (see Comm. on 1 Cor. 1—3) to demonstrate, that the cause of the substitution of false for true Christian knowledge was to be discovered in the fact, that, instead
of seeking the enlightenment of the Holy Spirit which can ex-
plore the depths of the divine Being, man trusted to his own
wisdom. The present passage therefore can only be correctly
understood, when we allow that it proves Paul considered learning incapable of producing the truths of the Gospel out of its own
resources, but that these truths were in effect promoted by the
obedience unto faith, which did not permit itself to be drawn
aside from the simplicity of Christ (xi. 3) by any subtilty whatever. If on the other hand the contents of this passage are to

be extended so as to signify that wisdom is also incapable of receiving and inwardly understanding the truths offered, this
view is decidedly contradicted by the frequent assertion of the
apostle, that mankind are not wanting in the organ necessary to
receive and perceive the divine things revealed to him by the
Spirit (see Comm. on Rom. i. 19); he is simply not to desire to
become his own oracle, to be his own God. (The ὅταν πληρωθῇ
ὑμῶν ἡ ὑπακοή of ver. 6 is very striking ; that is to say, it appears from it, that when the obedience of all is perfected, there
would remain no more disobedient to punish. But Paul only desires thereby to express the necessity of a separation of the elements still existing in Corinth, so that the sense really is : " I
am prepared to punish (viz., by excommunication) all who shall
continue disobedient at the period that obedience shall have perfected itself in you, who form the true church)."

Ver. 7. From this point the apostle addresses his opponents
in a more direct manner, and in the εἴ τις πέποιθεν ἑαυτῷ Χρισ
τοῦ εἶναι alludes above all to the *Christianer*, who laid especial
claim for themselves to the Χριστοῦ εἶναι, while on the other
hand Paul no less strongly vindicates his own right. Baur, however, (Tübing. Zeitsch. 1831, pt. iv., p. 99), correctly denies that
the present passage bears reference to the *Christianer* alone. It
would appear that the apostle was maintaining his authority
against his antagonists, who boasted of a more intimate connexion
with Jesus and his immediate disciples. We must, therefore, conclude that Paul intended to include all his adversaries in the reproof directed against the *Christianer*, their pride leading them
to the assumption that they alone were the true Christians.
This characteristic appeared most strongly in those usually
styled οἱ τοῦ Χριστοῦ, therefore the apostle bore them especially
in mind when dictating his polemic, and employed an expression
which must bring them to remembrance.—The harmony of this
passage has been rendered uncommonly difficult by translating τὰ
κατὰ πρόσωπον βλέπετε, as, " Do ye look on things after the outward appearance ?" Billroth has already, following Ambrosius'
view, received the words correctly as implying, " Behold now what
is so clearly evident," so that βλέπετε is imperative. This agrees
perfectly with what follows, containing an appeal to the simple
sense of the Corinthians, that it was right he (the apostle) should

be considered a servant of Christ, and that his labours should gradually stamp him such. (At the conclusion of the verse the word Χριστοῦ is wanting in so many authorised Codd. that it has been expunged by all the best critics).

Ver. 8. Paul considers his relation to Christ as even closer than the apostolical authority which bestows upon him ? spiritual power. If he have boasted somewhat of this authority, he is by no means ashamed of it, for it is in order to their edification and not to their injury. This requires the addition of the idea, " But the boasting of the adversaries is productive of your destruction. (An anticipation of the idea exists in the construction, since εἰς οἰκοδομὴν καὶ οὐκ εἰς καθαίρεσιν ὑμῶν is immediately connected with καυχήσωμαι, whilst according to the sense it should have been οὐκ αἰσχυνθήσομαι, ἐγένετο γὰρ, κ. τ. λ.—The ἐάν τε γὰρ καὶ περισσότερόν τι καυχήσωμαι only implies, " If I have somewhat abundantly boasted myself," and not " If I would yet more abundantly boast myself.")

Vers. 9—11. To unite ver. 9 to ver. 8 in the manner proposed by Billroth and Lachmann, appears to me entirely unauthorised. Ver. 11 evidently contains a refutation of the assertions relative to the object of his epistles, such assertions being in ver. 10 attributed to his adversaries. The sense in which Billroth receives ver. 9 in connexion with ver. 8 is in the highest degree constrained; it is thus: " I say this to you (that I have received the authority unto your edification), in order that it may not appear that I have desired to terrify you by my letters." But decidedly this impression would not be affected by the course adopted, the contents of ver. 11 can only fully remove an idea of this nature; Paul intends to say, What I state in my letters I am prepared to confirm when present, the severity in my letters is the principle of my entire nature. (In ver. 9 the connecting the ὡς ἂν with the infinitive, instead of the optative, creates a difficulty. Billroth supposes an ellipse by way of diminishing the objections to the connexion of verses 8 and 9. Bretschneider rejects the reading of quasi for ὡσάν, we must therefore suppose with Winer [Gr. p. 285] that it is irregularly employed for ὡς ἂν ἐκφοβοῖμι.—In ver. 10 Lachmann reads φασί for φησί, which must certainly be considered a correction with a view to render the text easier. The singular is not to be understood of any

precise individual, but must be considered impersonal. See
Winer's Gr. p. 339.—Whether the words ἡ παρουσία τοῦ σώματος
ἀσθενής may include a reference to any weakness of bodily constitution, is a question; but it is nevertheless by no means improbable that the weakness which, in the present and following
chapters of the epistle, is mentioned by the apostle as antithesis to
the mighty power of God speaking by him, may be considered
also to bear a corporeal reference).

Ver. 12. The first words of this verse are based upon the idea
which immediately precedes. "Such people might imagine of
us, that being present, we should appear like unto our letters,
for I have not been able to persuade myself to be like unto those
who commend themselves, i. e. I will not praise myself, as my
adversaries do, nevertheless they may be assured that when present, I shall not prove forbearing. (Ἐγκρῖναι and συγκρῖναι are
certainly not synonymous, although, according to the connexion,
very closely allied; the former signifies " to reckon in a number,"
the latter "to place together, or compare with some one."—
Τολμᾶν has, as in Rom. v. 7, 1 Cor. vi. 1, the signification
of sustinere, " to be able to prevail upon oneself.") But the
remaining part of the verse is uncommonly difficult, and has
claimed much particular consideration from annotators. Fritzsche
has made some very acute observations on the passage (Diss. ii.
page 33, sqq.), in which Billroth coincides. Nevertheless I have
not been able to convince myself of the correctness of the explanation sanctioned by these learned men, and Emmerling's views
on the same subject have appeared to me to deserve the preference,* of which Fritzsche himself says : "Emmerlingius eo me
deduxit, ut judicio meo in hoc difficili loco pæne diffiderem." The
view taken by Fritzsche and Billroth is this : they erase the
words οὐ συνιοῦσιν· ἡμεῖς δέ, and connect ver. 12 with ver. 13 in
the following manner : " But inasmuch as we measure ourselves
by ourselves (i. e. our value by the measure of our real perform-
ances, and not by the standard of imaginary ones, as others do),
and compare ourselves with ourselves, we by no means boast ourselves without a measure, for it is according to the measure
which God himself has given unto us." This is, however, doubt-

* See the third Excursis of Emmerling's Commentary.

ful, because the erasure of the οὐ συνιοῦσιν· ἡμεῖς δέ is declared
to be an act of necessity, it being impossible otherwise to explain
the usual reading in a satisfactory manner. It is true Fritzsche
has adduced evidence to prove that the interpolation of the words
in question was in some degree probable, if we could think that
they were wanting in the original text. But the critical authorities so certainly furnish these words, that even Lachmann has
not ventured to omit them. It is only D.F.G. which leaves out
the four words ; some of less weight furnish only the words οὐ
συνιοῦσιν. It is perfectly evident that this omission is only to
be explained by its internal difficulty, for who could have inserted
them in the text if they were originally wanting? Reiche also
correctly makes the same observation in the Programm already
quoted upon 2 Cor. v. 3. In that case the simple meaning of
ver. 12, in its connexion with ver. 13, is apparent, but a new
difficulty arises by the fusion of the two verses. For it is
not very clear, if so intimate a connexion takes place between
the verses, how the apostle should arrive at the μέτρον τοῦ
κανόνος, which God had distributed to him, and to which not
any allusion had been made in the foregoing passage. The
contrast in which ver. 13 is placed with ver. 12, by means of
the ἡμεῖς δέ, extremely facilitates the inference that a new
subject is about to be touched upon. The only question, therefore, is, whether the usual text is capable of a satisfactory
elucidation. As already observed, Emmerling's explanation of
the sense of the passage seems to present a correct meaning; he
considers the οὐ συνιοῦσιν as a participle, belonging to ἑαυτοῖς,
and which the apostle applies to himself as from the adversaries,
so that Paul presents himself in opposition to his opponents in
the words ἀλλὰ αὐτοί κ. τ. λ., in the following manner : " We cannot prevail upon ourselves to compare with those who commend
themselves, but we rather measure ourselves entirely by ourselves (i. e., as may be gathered from ver. 18, by that which the
Lord hath conferred upon us, by Christ's will in us), and compare
ourselves in the like manner, that we may be unwise according to
the opinion of the antagonists, not that we are really so, we do
not boast without measure, but," &c., &c. The ἡμεῖς δέ thus agrees
perfectly; it forms no antithesis with ἀλλὰ καὶ κ. τ. λ., but with
the judgment of the antagonists of Paul, which is contained in

the οὐ συνιοῦσιν. Billroth's remark, that we cannot perceive
for what reason Paul should here consider himself unwise in
the opinion of his adversaries, is incomprehensible. Emmerling has already appealed to chap. xi. 12, in which the same
occurs; and when Billroth remarks upon this, that Paul then does
it inasmuch as he praises himself, but in the present passage he
directly states that he will *not* boast without measure, that commentator appears to have overlooked the fact that the apostle is
here representing the accusations of his adversaries as ridiculous
and contradictory in themselves. One consideration only remains,
viz., that the article is required before οὐ συνιοῦσιν : but as
ἑαυτοῖς precedes, τοῖς might easily have been omitted by the
transcribers, the more so, as misunderstanding the difficult passage, they may not have taken συνιοῦσιν for the participle. Under
any circumstance, this is a far more lenient proceeding than ex-
punging the words οὐ συνιοῦσιν· ἡμεῖς δέ, and, moreover, deserves
the preference from considerably facilitating the understanding of
what follows.

Vers. 13—16. By a very peculiar turn the apostle passes over
in an unexpected manner to a subject altogether new, for which
reason it is advisable to maintain the separation of ver. 13 from
ver. 12 by means of the ἡμεῖς δέ, and not to obliterate it. Paul had
hitherto only guarded himself from the general accusations of his
adversaries, by assuming a high tone throughout his epistles, but
he now comes to a special point, of which the slightest notice had
not yet occurred in either of the epistles, asserting that he had
not intruded himself into a field of labour not his own, but that
Corinth, and not Corinth alone, but all the territory surrounding
that city, had been appointed him by God as the province which he
was to fill with the tidings of the Gospel. From the expression
μετρεῖν (ver. 12) with which in ver. 13 the εἰς τὰ ἄμετρα is connected, Paul passes over, so as to contract the general idea of
the measuring, into the more special one of the limits assigned
to the appointed sphere of activity. We may here inquire, what
can have given occasion to the apostle to enter upon this point
precisely in this place? If Baur rather strongly expresses
his opinion in respect to this question, that the adversaries of
Paul appear to have regarded themselves as the real founders of
the apostolic church (see work already quoted, p. 101), it must

not be forgotten that the assertions of the parties alluded to, according to which they vindicated their claim to authority in Corinth, must have been well known to the apostle. This claim would only have been made with some show of justice if they themselves had been engaged in the work in Corinth *before* the apostle ; for, according to the agreement mentioned in Galat. ii. 9, Paul had, in obedience to the divine will (Acts xxii. 21) received the Gentile world as his appointed sphere of labour. We, therefore, cannot perceive for what reason his adversaries should upbraid him for preaching the Gospel in Corinth ; although if, at the time Paul first appeared there, they were already engaged in the work, they might assume to themselves the right of doing so. But as Christians were already to be found in Rome when Paul appeared there in person, and notwithstanding the rule laid down for him, (Rom. xv. 20), he nevertheless preached there, the same thing might also have occurred in Corinth, no apostle having hitherto appeared there ; and moreover, the persons labouring in that city were by no means orthodox teachers, but rather sought their own honour than that of God. To which of the parties these persons adhered, who were actively labouring in Corinth before the apostle, cannot be discovered from the text before us. In ver. 13 μέτρον τοῦ κανόνος is not pleonastic; the κανών is rather the measure, the scale, whilst μέτρον is the deduction from it. The μέτρον which follows might certainly be omitted, but it is again employed in order to represent the ἐφικέσθαι ἄχρι καὶ ὑμῶν in a heightened degree, as something ordained and commanded by God.—In ver. 14 the ὑπερεκτείνω is significant— it is found throughout the New Testament only in this passage, " to extend beyond the appointed limits."—The ὡς μὴ ἐφικνού- μενοι is to be understood " who should not have come," especially according to the view and assertion of the antagonists.—In ver. 15 the ἐν ὑμῖν is to be connected with what precedes, as Calvin has already correctly stated, although it is perfectly easy to understand in what way the ὑμῶν may be considered to furnish occasion for joining it to μεγαλυνθῆναι. The principal aim of the apostle was to prove that his mission extended far beyond Corinth, and that he, consequently, only waited the perfecting of their faith, in order to proceed further, and bear the Gospel to others.—In ver. 16 τὰ ὑπερέκεινα sc. μέρη, regions beyond, lands

on the other side of the sea, viz., Italy and the more remote Spain.
See on Rom. xv.)

Vers. 17, 18. The apostle now concludes his subject with the
utterance of the fundamental idea of the entire discourse, that
all glory is the Lord's (because all power and all blessing are his),
for which reason he alone can commend men, *i. e.* can approve
him to the hearts of his brethren in the truth. (Concerning ver.
17 see the Comm. on the parallel passage, 1 Cor. i. 31).

### § 10. THE TRUE APOSTLES.

### (xi. 1—33).

In order to lead those Corinthians who were in danger of permitting themselves to be drawn aside from the pure Gospel by
deceivers, to a clearer perception of the distinction between true
and false apostles, Paul is compelled to remind them of his disinterestedness, his sufferings and conflicts; whilst those who
falsely represented themselves as preachers of righteousness,
sought only their own profit, and exacted gifts from the church ;
he at the same time taking occasion to observe, that he regarded
himself in no degree inferior in those points of prerogative which
they claimed for themselves.

Ver. 1. Taking into consideration that which immediately precedes (ver. 17), the ἀφροσύνη whereby the apostle describes the
information concerning himself, can only be taken in the sense
of the opponents. The whole passage hereby acquires an ironical
tinge, and a tendency towards reproach. Paul considers his
readers as entering into the views of his antagonists, and thus
entreats them to permit him to continue yet a little in his foolishness. A comparison with the adversaries in the sense put
forth by Baur (see work already quoted, p. 101), viz., " ye endure
them, bear therefore with me," cannot be acknowledged, as Billroth justly remarks, for this reason, because in that case καὶ
ἐμοῦ would have been employed by the apostle in order more
strongly to indicate its personal application. (Concerning ὄφελον
see 1 Cor. iv. 8. The reading of the *text. rec.* ἠνείχεσθε is decidedly to yield to the ἀνείχεσθε: on the contrary, the dative τῇ
ἀφροσύνῃ presents considerable difficulty in regard to the con-

struction, and it is possible that with Rückert, sanctioned by
B.D.E., the usual reading τι τῆς ἀφροσύνης is to be preferred).

Vers. 2, 3. Paul alleges his sincerity of purpose with regard to
their welfare as the ground upon which he claims their forbearance ; he desires to keep them free from every corruption, although he apprehends that they may have already permitted
themselves to be led astray from the simplicity which is in Christ.
In describing this state of purity, the apostle employs an image
drawn from the state of marriage, but in a peculiar manner. He
seems in it to consider himself in the position of one who selects
the bride, and presents her with all honour to the bridegroom.
It is only thus that the ἁρμόζεσθαι gains a strict connexion, it is
in the sense of " to suit," as employed by the LXX. in Prov. xix.
14; παραστῆσαι may, however, be referred to the Parousia as the
marriage festival of the Lamb. Billroth correctly assumes this
to be the intention of the passage. The ἑνὶ ἀνδρί likewise signifies that she can be no other man's without adultery. In this,
the evil influences are reproved (ver. 4) to which the Corinthians
had yielded themselves. Paul describes this as φθαρῆναι τὰ
νοήματα ἀπὸ τῆς ἁπλότητος εἰς Χριστόν. This ἁπλότης corresponds to the before-mentioned ἁγνότης: it demonstrates the cen-
tralization of the internal impulse to one point, the person of
Christ, just as every thought of the bride is devoted to the object
of her regard. The antithesis exists in the διψυχία, which, according to 1 Cor. i. 3, may here be regarded as the false Gnosis
(ver. 6); for this had even seduced the Corinthians from that
simple faith which Paul had inculcated. This sin is likened by
the apostle to the fall of Eve, who was betrayed through the subtilty of the serpent. We are perfectly justified in concluding
from this mention of the Fall, that Paul spoke of it as the history
of an actual occurrence; but nothing further can be learnt from
the *manner* in which he declares it, or from this brief allusion to
the circumstance. The previous image of the pure virgin led him
to the mention of Eve; under other circumstances he would have
employed Adam, as in Rom. v. 12, sqq.

Ver. 4. The apostle justifies his extreme anxiety for the Corinthians by declaring that he considered them so little grounded
in the faith, that it would be easy to draw them over to another
form of belief were they tempted. The only correct expla-

nation of this verse is decidedly the one in which the ὁ ἐρχόμε-
νος is made to signify the false teachers especially (the article
being only used because the false teacher is considered concrete.
See Winer's Gr. p. 101). Any *decided* personal quality is not to
be supposed. The expressions Ἰησοῦν ἄλλον, πνεῦμα ἕτερον, εὐαγγέλιον ἕτερον, imply only heretical interpretations of scriptural
truth. Paul does not intend to say, Ye may be gained over to
another entirely different form of religion, but only, Ye may permit the correct faith which I have delivered unto you to become
deformed by the admixture of false doctrine, through the instrumentality of unsound teachers. Paul addresses the Galatians in
a similar manner. (See Gal. i. 9). Christianity, disfigured in
its fundamental doctrines, is decidedly no longer Christianity, and
for this reason Paul exclaims to the Galatians, " Ye have lost
Christ!" It does not, however, appear that it had yet proceeded
to such lengths in Corinth. (At the conclusion of the verse I prefer
the reading ἀνέχεσθε, with Billroth and Lachmann. Paul then
more decidedly expresses the opinion, "If the deceiver comes, ye
permit him at best to please you;" ἄν could certainly not well
be omitted with ἀνείχεσθε or ἠνείχεσθε).

Vers. 5, 6. The connexion is restored in the following manner :
If the deceiver comes, ye receive him well, and ye afford already
a hearing to the false apostles. Now, to these stand I in no degree inferior ; but granting that I might be deficient in the words
of worldly wisdom, (1 Cor. ii. 13), nevertheless, I am not so in
true knowledge. Yet, pursues the apostle, correcting himself, I
have been ever manifest before you in all things ; ye are acquainted with my entire proceedings, wherefore should I again
display them before you? Lachmann and Billroth have preferred the reading φανερώσαντες, which must be referred to the
γνῶσις which Paul has pronounced against them. But the passive form appears to me unquestionably to be deserving of preference, for by its use alone an easy and unconstrained connexion
is secured with the succeeding words. Paul then describes himself not in his position as teacher, but in his outward relation to
the church (ver. 6). The ἐν πᾶσι cannot be referred to the
person on account of the εἰς ὑμᾶς which follows, but only to the
thing, therefore, the ἐν παντί is best supposed to relate to the
time. In conclusion, it is plainly to be seen that in the εἰ δὲ

καὶ ἰδιώτης τῷ λόγῳ, an accusation on the part of the ὑπερλίαν ἀπόστολοι and their adherents is implied, which undeniably relates to a more learned education. But Peter, James, and John are not included in this expression (as might be inferred from Gal. ii. 9, where they are styled οἱ δοκοῦντες στύλοι εἶναι); it is rather clearly proved from ver. 13 that the above expression is intended to designate the false teachers themselves. (The form ὑπερλίαν is only to be again found in Eustathius. The apostle in the animation of his description frequently employs accumulated compound words, which he likewise often connects by the repetition of ὑπέρ).

Vers. 7—9. Pursuing his strain of irony, the apostle reminds the Corinthians of the strictness with which he had observed his intention of accepting nothing from any one, in aid of his worldly maintenance, and inquires " whether in this respect he had committed any offence." The apostle, besides states of himself that he had received contributions from other churches, especially from Macedonia (probably identical with that mentioned in Phil. iv. 15, 16), which explains the assertions in 1 Cor. ix. 15, sqq. But he was justified in absolutely rejecting the acceptance of anything offered on the part of the Corinthians, because their feeling was not sufficiently plain and sincere in the matter. His antagonists among them would have put a far worse construction upon his acceptance than they were able to attribute to his refusal. (In ver. 7 the ἵνα ὑμεῖς ὑψωθῆτε is to be understood only as antithesis to the ἐσύλησα: they were considered exalted, and treated nobly, because they were in no degree burthened ; the expression is also in a slight degree ironical.—The second καί of ver. 8 is to be understood emphatically, " although suffering want."—Καταναρκάομαι generally means to " chill." The active form only occurs in the New Testament, and in this Epistle. [See xii. 13, 14.] The LXX. more frequently employs the simplex. It has in this passage the signification of "to burden, to charge," to chill as it were, or weary some one).

Vers. 10—12. The present passage undeniably proves how very important this matter was regarded by the apostle. (See Comm. on 1 Cor. ix. 6, sqq.) He protests that none shall rob him of this boast, i. e. he will absolutely accept nothing from them, not from any feeling of hatred or scorn, but from love, for the sake of those adversaries whom he desires to render conscious of their own untrue and insincere conduct. In ver. 10 the sentence ἔστιν ἀλήθεια Χριστοῦ ἐν ἐμοί is to be understood as the form of oath, " as truly as the truth of Christ is in me," *i. e.* as truly as I am a Christian!—Φράττω signifies first "to stop up." [Rom. iii. 19], and likewise " to deprive of, to defame." The use of εἰς ἐμέ for ἐμοί is striking. It is to be explained from the idea of the hostile party, which is implied in the φραγήσεται.— Concerning κλίμα, see Rom. xv. 23.—In ver. 11, διατι *scil.* τοῦτο λέγω.—The καὶ ποιήσω intimates the steadfastness of the determination, as the καὶ τηρήσω does of ver. 9.—In ver. 12 the ἵνα ἐν ᾧ καυχῶνται κ. τ. λ. is not free from difficulty. It may be inquired if this ἵνα is to be regarded co-ordinate with the one which previously occurs, or dependent on the ἀφορμήν? The first does not appear probable, because had Paul intended an antithesis between ἐκκόψω and καυχῶνται, he would have more strongly marked it by adding ἐγώ and αὐτοί. The τῶν θελόντων ἀφορμήν naturally leads to the conclusion that what follows is to describe more closely the manner of the ἀφορμή. But even admitting the supposition that the second ἵνα is co-ordinate with the first, this does not secure a satisfactory meaning to the idea [we must then conclude that a negation is to be proved], as ver. 20 decidedly shows that they were *not* able to boast themselves of having exerted the same forbearance which Paul had exhibited.* The words alone agree when they express the simple wishes of the antagonists. To these it was in a high degree offensive that Paul should persist in a steadfastness of purpose which made them ashamed; they wished, therefore, to divert him from his resolution, in order that he might have no advantage over them, but be found in all respects the same as they were. The ἐν ᾧ καυχῶνται is, however, so to be understood, that they declare the receiving of money to be a right, a subject of boasting, and an apostolic prerogative, as is plainly to be inferred from 1 Cor. ix. 7, sqq. The entire passage has therefore an ironical tinge, in this manner, " However strongly ye may oppose me,

* Billroth translates : " In order that upon the subject upon which they especially boast themselves (accepting no money), they may be found *(only)* like unto myself." But here it is entirely forgotten that, according to ver. 20, they not only accepted money, but proved themselves highly exacting towards the church ; we can also perceive no authority for the interpolation of the *only*.

ye would gladly embrace an opportunity of permitting me to participate in your boasting, and compel me to accept of a subsistence at the hands of the church; but this would only be for the
purpose of concealing your own shame, and depriving me of my
just fame, therefore ye shall not succeed in your desire!")

Vers. 13—15. Paul now unsparingly removes the mask, and
presents these persons in their true light as false apostles, proving themselves servants of Satan, and, like their master, ever
conducting themselves with hypocrisy. A just punishment was
therefore awaiting them! It is very evident that these can be
none other than the ὑπερλίαν ἀπόστολοι of ver. 5, and it is
equally impossible that the genuine apostles can be signified in
that passage. But it is perfectly possible that these hypocrites
(whose sect is not further defined) may have appealed to the
authority of the true apostles, precisely as the erring teacher
did who is mentioned in Gal. ii. 12. The expressions, moreover, are very strong, and bring to mind the γεννήματα ἐχιδ
νῶν which our Saviour applied to the Pharisees (Matt. xxiii.
33). Had they been members of the Corinthian church, Paul
would undoubtedly have commanded their excommunication; but
we can only regard them as intruding usurpers, who had created
a party to themselves in Corinth, and from whose evil influence
Paul sought to free those who had joined them.—Whether the
apostle, by the expression ὁ σατανᾶς μετασχηματίζεται εἰς ἄγγε
λον φωτός, intended to allude to a decided fact, the history of the
temptation, for example, is not to be discovered with certainty.
However, it is highly probable that the αὐτὸς γάρ signifies it to
be a subject well known to the reader.

Vers. 16—18. After Paul had thus openly and clearly expressed his opinion concerning the false teachers, he returns to
himself and his position, resuming the idea with which he enters
upon ver. 1. These men had brought him into the disagreeable,
though unavoidable position, which compelled him to enter upon
the subject of his rights and privileges. But while doing this,
he judged it necessary to take steps to prevent their regarding
it as right in itself, and worthy of approval; he therefore describes it as an οὐ κατὰ κύριον, ἀλλὰ κατὰ τὴν σάρκα, to which
he was impelled by the conduct of the adversaries, in order to
free them (the Corinthians) from their injurious influence. In

ver. 10 the apostle plays with the idea ἄφρων. In the first place, he prays them not to consider him such because he boasts himself (folly being imputed to those who really do it from pride), nevertheless if they were not willing to be obedient unto him, they were at liberty to regard him even as ἄφρων like other high-minded persons, if it would be thereby permitted him to boast himself in some degree. The latter words are ironical, and convey a reproach that they had suffered the false apostles so to exalt themselves. (In ver. 16 an inversion is to be perceived with the κἂν : it should properly be δέξασθέ με, κἂν ὡς ἄφρονα.—In ver. 17, the ὡς ἐν ἀφροσύνῃ proves that the apostle does not intend to assert that he really speaks foolishly, but that his discourse may present such an appearance. In ver. 18, he speaks more fully of the occasion of his assuming so apparently an offensive line of conduct.—Concerning the expression ἐν ταύτῃ ὑποστάσει τῆς καυχήσεως, see the remarks on ix. 4. It is also here best understood as "object, thing."—In verse 18 the κατὰ τὴν σάρκα is not only referable to national descent, as employed in ver. 22, but to all external privileges, and also such as are enumerated in ver. 23, sqq. The only unusual circumstance is the presence of the article, yet this is by no means incorrect; the antithesis is κατὰ τὸ πνεῦμα, to which in this passage κατὰ κύριον stands parallel, and for which κατὰ τὸν κύριον might also be employed).

Vers. 19, 20. Paul now advances the irony of the discourse, and styles the Corinthians φρόνιμοι, who willingly tolerated the ἄφρονες: to this is appended a description of the insincerity of the false apostles drawn in the strongest colours. Desire of dominion and covetousness are the prominent vices which the apostle holds forth for observation. As to the particular party to which these false teachers belonged, we can arrive at no decided opinion from the present passage; the faults which are the subject of reproof are of a purely moral nature, and such as might be supposed to exist among persons of every denomination. (In ver. 20, according to xii. 16, ὑμᾶς is to be supplied to λαμβάνει: "if any one take entire possession of you.")

Ver. 21. This endurance of unworthy treatment from the heterodox teachers is blamed by Paul, who informs the objects of it that it sanctions the insinuation, that he had proved himself weak (*i. e.*, not possessed of such privileges as the former dared to assume to themselves), whilst he, nevertheless, could exhibit as well-founded a claim as any other could pretend to.   The κατὰ ἀτιμίαν λέγω κ. τ. λ. has doubtless been well explained by Billroth.   It is usually understood of Paul himself in the sense of " I confess to *my* shame that I have proved myself too weak towards such usurpations."   But then πρὸς ἀτιμίαν would have been employed ; and besides, under this view, the ὡς appears entirely pleonastic.   The reference is rather to the Corinthians, " I say this to *your* shame."   The ὡς then represents that which succeeds as the opinion of the Corinthians concerning Paul.   The enumeration of all his privileges which follows is employed as a refutation of this opinion, and this he styles a τολμᾶν, in opposition to the above-mentioned ἀσθενεῖν.

Ver. 22.  The principal prerogative claimed by Paul, and of which he was enabled to boast as well as his adversaries, was that he belonged to God's people ; not only that he was a worshipper of the true God (for the proselytes, in this respect, were equal), but that, being born an Israelite, of the seed of Abraham, he was included in the blessings promised to that people.   Billroth erroneously makes no distinction between the three synonyms, but Ἰσραηλῖται evidently further defines the expression ἐβραῖοι, and the latter again the σπέρμα Ἀβραάμ, in which the idea of being an inheritor of the promise is especially manifested. —Impartiality here compels us to admit that Baur's hypothesis appears greatly supported by this passage.   We have no intimation that Paul here solely attacks the followers of Peter, as seemed to us the case in iii. 4, sqq., but it rather appears that the *Christianer* at least are *also* included, and nevertheless he permits his opponents to appeal generally to their Jewish extraction, which, according to our own hypothesis concerning the *Christianer*, would not be available for them.   (See Introd. § 1).   Nevertheless the far more important obstacle arises in connexion with Baur's view, that the contents of the entire first epistle cannot agree with the Jewish character of the *Christianer*.   If we also suppose that the references to false Gnosis may apply to such Judaizing false teachers as (like those opposed in the Epistle to the Colossians) concerned themselves with theosophist speculations (this characteristic is not specifically observed in them by Baur), there nevertheless does not occur in the relation a single trace of the fact that Judaists had been seduced into that state of false liberty, which the apostle reproves throughout the greater portion of the first Epistle to the Corinthians, but which we may rather take for granted could only be found among Gentile Christians. And as the *Christianer* alone are not signified in x. 7, but all the antagonists generally are condemned, and, in addition, individual parties in Corinth are not distinguished throughout the representation in chap. x.—xii., I am therefore persuaded that Paul's reason for especially alluding in this place to the Jewish descent to which the followers of Peter particularly appealed, was to mark the application to that party, for among the *Christianer* nothing was to be found which intimated a regard for hereditary privileges. *Christianer* and followers of Peter had pursued the controversy against the person of Paul in concert ; consequently the apostle might defend himself against them in the same manner, but making a passing allusion by which only one party could be affected.

Vers. 23—27. In a long series of descriptions such as occur in vi. 4, sqq., the apostle then enumerates the sufferings and necessities endured in his apostolic calling, which, by their number and variety, bear witness to the magnitude of his labours. It is not without an object that Paul exposes, in v. 24 and 26, the treatment he had experienced from the Jews, for he doubtless thereby intended to impress upon them that, in the kingdom of Christ, to be of Jewish descent was not so especial a subject of glorying. This passage proves, besides, how little we really know of the life of the apostle, for the Acts of the Apostles conveys but little information concerning all these perils. See concerning this subject Clemens Romanus (Epist. ad. Cor. i. 5) where a similar recapitulation may be found. (In ver. 23 the παρα-φρονῶν λαλῶ is doubtless stronger than the ἐν ἀφροσύνῃ λέγω of ver. 21. I cannot, however, attribute to the expression the meaning that Billroth does, who thinks it signifies : " I speak foolishly, for I glory in the sufferings which it is my duty to take upon myself ;" for it rather appears to me that the παραφρονῶν λαλῶ is only said according to the standard of the antagonists, " Ye will regard my boasting as inconsistent with common sense." —The conjecture of ὑπερέχω is not wrong, nevertheless the more difficult form ὑπὲρ ἐγώ is to be preferred. Ὑπέρ is here employed adverbially, and is the only example of the sort occurring in the New Testament. [See Winer's Gr. p. 399].—The forty stripes mentioned in ver. 24 are according to Deut. xxv. 3. Josephus relates that they were accustomed to remit one [Arch. iv. 8.]—Of the beating with rods and stoning, examples are to be found in Acts xvi. 22, xiv. 19. Until the present passage no instance of shipwreck occurs.—In ver. 25 the νυχθήμερον ἐν τῷ βυθῷ πεποίηκα doubtless implies the buffeting on the waves after the wreck of the vessel.—Ποιεῖν, applied to time, frequently occurs in the Acts of the Apostles. [See Acts xv. 33, xviii. 23, xx. 3.])

Vers. 28—33. Among these extraordinary vicissitudes and perils Paul includes the existing cares and labours of his charge, so that if he desired to boast himself he would undoubtedly glory in his weakness, which necessarily led him to trust in God's power for the furtherance of his important labours, and must ever be the mainspring of his efforts. (See xii. 9). The apostle, in conclusion, appeals to God for the truth of his account, and mentions in addition, the first danger he was called upon to encounter in his apostolic course. (In ver. 28 τὰ παρεκτός, scil. γενόμενα, " the things which yet occur." Lachmann has erased the comma after παρεκτός, according to which the ἡ ἐπισύστασις μου, "the daily assaults of men upon me," must be received as subject. But this connexion must yield to that defended by Griesbach, according to which the comma is retained after παρεκτός. The things which yet occur must evidently be regarded as of a different nature to those hitherto described, and he only mentions two, the ἐπισύστασις and the μέριμνα, out of many other sources of discomfort.—Billroth gives an entirely mistaken explanation of ver. 29: "Who is weak, that I do not condescend to his weakness [viz., in order to avoid giving him offence], who suffers an offence, that I do not thereby feel myself offended, and burn to free him from the offence, and to reprove him who furnishes occasion of displeasure." The whole context decidedly contains nothing which can be construed to refer to condescending to the weakness of others. Emmerling takes a more correct view of this passage, when he makes ἀσθενεῖν, σκανδαλίζεσθαι, πυροῦσθαι refer to the before-mentioned sufferings. A slight diffi-

culty is alone created by σκανδαλίζεσθαι, but every endurance
is, in a moral sense, a temptation, and may as such give offence.
The sense is then this, "Who suffers, if I do not suffer? who is
tempted, if I do not burn in the fire of temptation? *i. e.*, I suffer more than all others; but of this I am so little ashamed,
that I glory in it, as I must needs glory." In ver. 31 the adjura-
tion is best conceived to relate to all that precedes; the circumstance which occurred at Damascus is only afterwards mentioned
as the first persecution which Paul had to endure [see Acts ix.
24].—Billroth has admirably explained the tautology in ver. 32,
ἐν Δαμασκῷ ἐφρούρει τὴν Δαμασκηνῶν πόλιν by regarding the ἐν
Δαμασκῷ as elliptical; so that the meaning is, likewise in Damascus
I suffered the same;—the Ethnarch guarded the city of the people
of Damascus, &c. Yet the question may arise if ἐν Δαμασκῷ
may not signify the territory of Damascus.—Concerning the occurrence itself, more may be seen in the explanation given on
Acts ix. 24. What is here attributed to the Ethnarch himself
[πιάσαι με θέλων] is there said of the Jews, whom the former desired to please. Josephus relates the wars of king Aretas [Ant.
xviii. 7], during which it is probable the occupation of the city of
Damascus by his troops occurred. The title ἐθνάρχης probably
implies here a military commander, the Commandant of Damascus. It likewise indicates the civil authorities. See 1 Macc.
xiv. 47, xv. 1.—In ver. 33 καί is to be considered adversative,
"But I was let down in a basket through a window, by the
wall)."

## § 11. THE VISION.

### (xii. 1—21).

The endurance of outward suffering which has been related,
can only be subject of boasting to the apostle in an indirect
manner, that is to say, in as far as it is a powerful witness for the
magnitude of his labours. But Paul now adduces as direct proof
of the grace of God which was with him, the mighty visions and
revelations which he had received. In order, however, that he may
not exalt himself from this cause, he declares that God had ap-

pointed him particular personal suffering; therefore it was better
that he should glory in his weakness, for God proves more mighty
in the weak. The apostle then concludes by declaring himself to
be no less an apostle than those arrogant usurpers; God had
authenticated him as a true apostle in Corinth, and the sincerest
love towards the church there filled his heart, which naturally led
him to wish that upon his approaching arrival among them he
should discover the undoubted signs of a suitable frame of mind.

Ver. 1. Commencing with an admonition against boasting, the
apostle passes to that witness which a man can never bear to
himself, but by which the Lord rather boasts and commends
those who are his own (x. 18), viz., to visions and revelations.
It is, however, necessary to distinguish the expressions, so that
in the ὀπτασία the communication from on high may be considered principally, if not entirely, addressed to the sight, consequently that something is imparted by means of an image,
as in the Acts x. The ἀποκάλυψις, on the contrary, is an un-
figurative communication of the divine Spirit to the human. The
two forms may be united, nay, are usually found together, yet
always in such a manner that one or other of these conditions
predominate. The circumstance which the apostle details in
the following verses appear from the contents of ver. 4 to bear
somewhat the form of an ἀποκάλυψις. (Although Fritzsche and
Billroth decide in favour of the καυχᾶσθαι δέ, it is nevertheless a
reading which does not claim to be commended, because it has
only the Codex D. in its favour, and even this hesitates between δέ
and δεῖ, whilst the καυχᾶσθαι δεῖ is authorized by B.E.F.G.
However, the following οὐ συμφέρον μὲν, ἐλεύσομαι δὲ καὶ εἰς,
κ. τ. λ. is so evidently a correction with the object of rendering
the sense easier, that I feel myself compelled to yield the preference to the usual reading καυχᾶσθαι δή. The glorying in himself is brought into antithesis with the glorying that proceeds from
God).

Vers. 2—4. It is universally admitted that it is only owing to
a form of representation, that Paul does not openly declare himself the person adverted to as the object of the grace about to be
described, and this is abundantly and incontestibly proved by ver.
7, sqq. It likewise requires no farther argument in order to
prove that the circumstance under consideration is not identical

with the appearance vouchsafed to the apostle when journeying
towards Damascus.  In the latter, Christ's appearing to him was
for the purpose of humbling the apostle, and convincing him of
his sinfulness, whilst the former was intended to reward his
fidelity and strengthen his faith.  The fourteen years, likewise,
which the apostle states to have elapsed since the occurrence,
would not chronologically agree.*  (See the Chronological Table
at the conclusion of the Introd. to the Exposition of the Acts of
the Apostles).  We may, therefore, only more closely examine the
incident related, without being in a position to elicit anything
further concerning the place or circumstances in which it took
place.   We must *first* observe the remarkable fact, that Paul
twice circumstantially asserts, that whether he was in the body
or out of the body he knew not.   This, taken in conjunction
with the ἁρπάζεσθαι, implies that his witness concerned himself,
and it may be understood that by means of a sudden exercise of
power, he found himself transported to another region or sphere
of existence.   (See Acts viii. 39; 1 Thess. iv. 12; Rev. xii. 5).
These points of information clearly characterise the proceeding
as an ἔκστασις, to which the observations made on Acts x. 9 may
be applied.  The apostle's earthly perceptions were depressed or
in abeyance throughout, and his divine perception powerfully
enhanced through the co-operation of the Spirit.†   It may also
have really happened in this occurrence that a temporary abandonment of the body by the soul took place, as among witches,‡

* The proceeding referred to unquestionably occurred almost immediately subsequent to the conversion of Paul.  Had it been of more recent occurrence, he
would doubtless have referred to it as such.  It also does not appear probable
to me (see the observations thereon which follow), that at a more advanced period
of life Paul was visited by similar revelations.

† Such a proceeding with reference to the apostle Paul was so much the more
striking, as according to 1 Cor. xiv., self-knowledge was very strongly developed
in him, and he could therefore expressly exercise the gift of προφητεύειν.  It is very
probable that at a later period of his life the apostle was less subject to such
trances.  According to the principle that the prophet should have dominion over
the spirit, it is certain that a condition which bordered on loss of consciousness
could but rarely occur among the perfect.

‡ The (in a psychological sense) highly remarkable proceedings against witches
have yet to be fundamentally examined.  The Count von Lamberg has recently
(Nürnberg, 1835) published a very interesting communication concerning the proceedings in Bamberg.  From the perfect agreement of all the witnesses in these
proceedings, we have no choice left us, but to regard such exhibitions as epidemic

and also as it would appear we must admit with somnambulists. But this contains the evil and dangerous fact, that the apostle through the interposition of the divine Spirit attained to the high degree of favour conferred upon the blessed by the act of death. *Next,* Paul states the place to which he was snatched away. That there existed any difference between the third heaven and Paradise (as Irenæus, Clemens A., Origen, Jerome, and also Bengel maintain), is incapable of proof; both the expressions possibly indicate the same thing, that is to say, the most exalted egion of light, the immediate presence of God. For although the Omnipresence of God makes him near to every one of us, on the other hand all created beings cannot be said to be equally near to him. We have likewise no ground for supposing that the representation of several heavens is to be attributed to Jewish superstition, for the same allusion occurs again in the New Testament (see Eph. iv. 10). The rabbinical view of *seven* heavens certainly derives no confirmation from the New Testament (see Eisenmenger's Entd. Judenth. vol. i. p. 460), but the distinction of an upper and an inferior Paradise (same work, vol. ii. p. 296, sq., 318; see also the remarks on Luke xvi. 24) is not unsupported, but rather entirely corresponds with biblical doctrine. The latter represents that which is called Abraham's bosom in Luke xvi., while the former is synonymous with the heavenly temple (Heb. vi. 19, ix. 11; Rev. iii. 12, vi. 9) or the throne, the right hand of God. *Lastly,* Paul signifies what occurred to him in Paradise. In that paradisiacal sea of light he received wonderful impressions, which he describes as rendered perceptive to him through the medium of hearing. He communicates nothing further concerning them, because as a human being he felt himself incapable of adequately doing it. Harmonious, pure spiritual intuition, can never receive expression through the language of man, which receives and communicates in part only. It is not to be considered that any command was issued

creations of the imagination (the great number of which presents a difficulty, there being in Bamberg alone, between 1624 and 1630, 785 processes against witches), or to consider that the defendants believed themselves to have committed the sins under the influence of the spirit (*i. e.*, in an ecstacy). The unholy ever seeks to assume the form of that which is sacred ; the appearances among the former, therefore, notwithstanding their differences, may have been employed as analogy for the latter.

not to communicate what he received, for the οὐκ ἐξὸν ἀνθρώπῳ λαλῆσαι forbids the supposition. These words are not to be translated " it may not be said to a man," for Paul was a man, and it was nevertheless said to him; but " a man has not the power to express it."—It has been already signified in the Introduction (§ 1) in what manner Baur employs these communications in favour of his hypothesis concerning the *Christianer.* (See work quoted, p. 105). His opinion is, that Paul intended throughout to confute the views of his antagonists, who attributed an unseeming value to the fact of having personally known Christ; in opposition to this he therefore desires to make it evident that even on the path of a purely inward experience the Gospel may be propagated. Now the learned man referred to by no means holds that the occurrence here narrated is identical with that which is the subject of Acts ix., and whereby the apostle gained access to Christ and his church, and nevertheless he asserts his conviction, that by this account of a transporting into the invisible world Paul intended to oppose a more spiritual view to the Jewish materialist opinions. In addition to the arguments to the contrary which we have already brought under the notice of the reader (Introd. § 1), this opinion appears to me especially untenable, because with such an end in view it would have proved greatly to the interest of the apostle to relate an occasion on which he had seen the Lord himself, or to call attention to the circumstance that he had beheld Christ in all his glory. But this does not occur, neither is there the slightest allusion to the reference of the relation to the adversaries, but the question rather appears to regard boasting; so that, according to the context, it is solely to be supposed, that the apostle narrates the present circumstance, in order to afford a proof that the grace of God is with him, and also to legitimate his claim to be a true apostle by mentioning the extraordinary gifts of grace conferred upon him.

Vers. 5, 6. Proceeding as if speaking of a stranger, and yet perfectly identifying himself with the individual who experienced what is stated, the apostle continues with reference to ver. 1, " he would only glory in his infirmities (as enumerated in chap. xi.) and not of himself, *i. e.* his privileges, but would only glory in others. Were he, however, desirous of doing it, he had well-founded pretensions, for he stated what was true, but he never-

theless forbore, because he did not desire that any should esteem
him more highly than he should be proved to merit."—The turn
which Billroth gives to ver. 5 is entirely incorrect : " I will only
glory in myself, in so far as I am not myself, not this Paul, but
live in Christ." As to any distinction between his old and new
man, it is absolutely not brought under discussion in this passage;
the ὑπὲρ τοῦ τοιούτου καυχήσομαι applies solely to the fact that
Paul had described the vision as occurring to another.—The οὐκ
ἔσομαι ἄφρων of ver. 6 appears to form a contradiction to xi. 1,
21, 23, xii. 11. But Emmerling has already correctly shown
that the glorying is ironically described in those passages as
ἀφροσύνη, in the meaning of his adversaries; here, on the contrary, the boasting of his opponents is reproved: "They glory
in externals in a foolish manner; I could boast myself in a right
manner of important things if I were so minded." (It would appear that in the ἢ ἀκούει τι ἐξ ἐμοῦ of ver. 6 a twofold meaning is
perceptible; that is to say, the apostle possibly intended to
write εἴ τι ἀκούει in addition to the ἢ ἀκούει, but nevertheless
drew both together in one phrase.—Lachmann's punctuation of
this verse is entirely peculiar. From ἐὰν γὰρ θελήσω—ἐξ ἐμοῦ
he includes all within brackets, and the καὶ τῇ ὑπερβολῇ τῶν
ἀποκαλύψεων is connected with ἀσθενείαις [μου being omitted].
Whether he may have been impelled to the choice of this connexion by critical reasons, I am ignorant, but it decidedly does
not facilitate the comprehending of the passage).

Ver. 7. The apostle now drops the form of description hitherto
employed, by which he had represented the revelation as being
made to another, and continues to say that the God who had so
highly exalted him by this extraordinary grace had also deeply
humbled him, for the purpose of preventing his exalting himself
too highly. Any more particular information relative to the σκόλοψ τῇ σαρκί, or wherein it consisted, is not to be inferred. It
may only be said that it is impossible that the sufferings connected
with his apostolic labours\* in general can be solely alluded to, for
these were detailed fully in chap. xi., and the thorn in the flesh must

---

\* This view, which Fritzsche again defends, derives some degree of confirmation
from ver. 10, and from the assertion of δύναμίς μου ἐν ἀσθενείᾳ τελεῖται in ver. 9;
but the distinct reference to the revelation contained in the σκόλοψ, appears nevertheless to render the grounds for its acceptance insufficient

have special reference to the revelation already related. We are
also as little justified in supposing it implies some spiritual temptation, because τῇ σαρκί is employed in describing it. It is most
likely that it indicates some kind of heavy, depressing, *bodily* suffering, which may besides have exhibited itself in powerful paroxysms,
as expressed in the κολαφίζεσθαι. As in the Old Testament, Job's
corporeal sufferings were occasioned by Satan, so Paul likewise
attributes his thorn in the flesh to the author of all evil, although
the Lord God was able, in the case of his own people, to turn the
enemy's assaults to the advantage of their soul. It must, however,
be admitted that we nowhere else discover a trace of the apostle's
having suffered from sickness of any kind; and even when Paul
recounts all his sufferings and trials, sickness is not enumerated
with them. From this source we may be inclined to suppose
that the expression signifies a temptation to sin, and that from
the addition of τῇ σαρκί it was not displayed in a spiritual, but
rather a carnal form. (Σκόλοψ, a stake, from whence σκολοπίζω,
to impale. See the LXX. in Num. xxxiii. 55; Ezek. xxviii. 24;
Hos. ii. 6.—In ἄγγελος σατᾶν Fritzsche is unquestionably perfectly
right in understanding σατᾶν as genitive; it is in opposition to
σκόλοψ, the suffering itself is in a trope styled an angel of Satan, because it is sent to him from Satan, through the instrumentality of one of his demons. If Satan himself had been intended, the article would not have been wanting. Κολαφίζω =
ὑποπιάζω, 1 Cor. ix. 27, is the figurative expression for "to treat
rudely, dishonourably." It is possible that the suffering which
Paul alludes to, had the effect of entirely incapacitating him for
a time from his work, and this condition (to which was probably
conjoined a sense of inward dereliction) is what the apostle styles
a κολαφίζεσθαι.—The second ἵνα μὴ ὑπεραίρωμαι is certainly
wanting in the best critical authorities; but the omission of the
words is as easy to be accounted for as it would be difficult to
assign a reason for the addition of them, if they were not genuine.
It therefore appears advisable to retain them in the text).

Vers. 8—10. His human feeling led the apostle to entreat to be
freed from this affliction; but the answer to this was, that it was
precisely necessary to his perfecting; that the strength of self-
dependence must be destroyed, in order that God may be able to
work in the man; he must therefore repress any feeling foreign

to that which would lead him to confess, that grace was sufficient for him. For this cause, continued Paul, he gloried most willingly in his weakness, for repeated experience had corroborated the fact, that when he was weak in himself he was strong in the Lord. In the Old Testament it is frequently analogically said that God dwells with those who are broken and humble of heart; but is far from the haughty.—The present passage is by no means to be understood to apply to the apostle alone, nor are we to conclude that the sentence ἡ δύναμίς μου ἐν ἀσθενείᾳ τελεῖται* only concerned the same individual; it is on the contrary to be received as a general truth, specially applied to the apostle upon this occasion, in order to cause him to review his past experience. The natural power of man cannot exist near the divine power of God, therefore should the inward life flourish, self-dependence, the natural life, must decay as a natural consequence; the passive must prevail, when God's power is to be actively exercised. See Comm. on Matt. x. 39. (In ver. 8 there is no authority for receiving τρίς to signify an uncertain number.—Calvin's explanation of the ἀρκεῖ σοι ἡ χάρις μου in ver. 9, which Billroth has adopted, is perfectly unsanctioned. Both consider that χάρις should not signify the grace of God, but metonymically the help of God. But this is precisely what Paul entreated for, and which was refused him. The sense was rather as follows: " Be steadfast in the knowledge of my gracious intention; even if thou perceivest nothing of the feeling of grace, for my strength, in its efficacy, perfects the weakening of the natural life." The ἐπισκηνόω is very expressive, an allusion to the Shechinah is evident [see on John i. 14], because every believer should be a copy of his Lord, Christ, so that Father, Son, and Spirit, can make their abode in him, inhabit him as a temple [see the Comm. on John xiv. 24]).

Vers. 11, 12. Returning to the earlier subject, Paul remarks in an ironical manner (see on xii. 6), that he had permitted himself to be misled, and like the false teachers to boast himself foolishly; that it was not actually necessary, for they (the Corinthians) themselves ought to have undertaken his commendation, being well aware that he was in no degree less than the haughty apostles; God had gradually authenticated him as an

---

* I prefer with Lachmann the reading τελεῖται to the more usual τελειοῦται : the former is sanctioned by A.B.D.F.G.

apostle unto them.   (In ver. 12 the μέν is to be explained by
δέ, as Billroth correctly remarks, "but ye also can relate nothing else of me." — Σημεῖα is first employed in an extended
sense, comprehending in it all and every sign of legitimacy; then
in the more special meaning of one kind of the same.   [See the
observations on Matt. viii. 1].—The ἐν πάσῃ ὑπομονῇ is not altogether easy.   It cannot be doubted that it is to be connected with
κατειργάσθη, and not with that which follows; nevertheless for what
cause does Paul  expressly state in this place that his signs have
been wrought in all patience ?   It appears to me probable that
this involves a reproach to the Corinthians, who, notwithstanding
such signs, have nevertheless shown themselves undecided as to the
reception of Paul's apostolic authority.   In this aspect of affairs
Paul intends to say, he had kindled his light among them, and
patiently awaited the result, secure of the final victory.   This
passage likewise clearly enables us to perceive that the apostle
considered the gift of working miracles and wonders was as indispensable a requisite of an apostle, as it had been to the prophets of the Old Testament).

Vers. 13—15. Paul demands of the Corinthians, with reproving
irony, in what respect they were inferior to any other church ?
Only as far as he had not proved burdensome to them, but had
entirely maintained himself without their aid, and this wrong
they must certainly forgive him.   Indeed, he intended to conduct
himself in the same manner upon the next occasion of visiting
them, which was approaching, for he sought not their goods and
possessions, but themselves; he would rather lay up for them as
his beloved children, nay offer all for them, even his life, although
their love for him was in no degree equal to his for them.   It is
very evident throughout this masterly passage, wherein the deepest
feeling is displayed in a spiritual application, for what cause the
apostle deemed it so important to reject decidedly all offers of support.   His adversaries sought their own advantage, and at least
improved their position by means of the gifts which they received ; Paul's own practice was entirely the reverse of this,
whereby he naturally aroused the hatred of those worldly-minded
persons, because his life tacitly reproved their proceedings.   (In
ver. 13, Billroth correctly assigns to ὑπέρ the meaning of "lower,
in that respect," which is the same as *infra*.—In ver. 14 it was

earlier the custom to connect the τρίτον with ἑτοίμως ἔχω, and not
with ἐλθεῖν. But it has been already observed in the Introduction [§ 2], that in this passage, and likewise in xiii. 1, it is an
actual third coming which is signified, and not alone a third decision on the subject. For it would evidently be very unnecessary to state how frequently the determination had been arrived
at, whilst the τρίτον can very suitably bear a reference to the presence itself; as it consists perfectly with the whole strain of argumentation, that Paul should declare, that what he had already
twice done, he was prepared to repeat upon his third appearance
among them.—In ver. 15 the transition to another idea in the
δαπανᾶν is only imaginary. The θησαυρίζειν certainly implies to
collect treasure, δαπανᾶν to give up the possession, to spend.
The yielding up of his powers for the advantage of believers, is
at the same time spiritual profit for them. Paul proceeds yet
further in the ἐκδαπανηθήσομαι, in which is signified the sacrifice
of life itself. It is by no means to be regarded as a parallel passage with Rom. ix. 3).

Vers. 16—18. Paul draws attention again to the abominable
accusations disseminated by the shameless antagonists, among
which he alludes especially to the charge of catching the Corinthians with guile, i. e., according to the connexion, of having appropriated to himself money received from them, which leads him
to ask, by whom had he been enabled to make a gain of them!
How Titus and the brethren who accompanied him had conducted
themselves, was well known to themselves! (The 16th verse is
to be understood as an observation of the Corinthians: "Ye confess that I have not burthened you, nevertheless ye say, [i. e., the
opponents, and all who allowed themselves to be persuaded by
them] I have caught you with guile."—In ver. 17 is to be supplied, "I, myself, have certainly never received money from you,
have I, as it were, defrauded you by means of a messenger?"
The μή τινα ὧν—δι᾽ αὐτοῦ stands for μὴ διὰ τινὸς ἐκείνων, οὕς.
—With regard to ver. 18, Billroth correctly observes that the
allusion here cannot be to the journey of Titus, which is mentioned in viii. 16, as this had not yet taken place [possibly Titus
himself delivered this epistle], but is rather to the earlier residence of this apostolic assistant in Corinth, which is adverted to
in viii. 6. Upon this occasion Titus had only prepared the way

for a collection, receiving no money himself; the μήτε ἐπλεονέκ-τησεν ὑμᾶς is accordingly to be understood as, "had he therefore the power to defraud you?" Was he not animated by the same spirit of disinterestedness as myself? Have we not walked to-gether in the same steps [as followers of Christ]?)

Vers. 19—21. In conclusion, Paul again remarks, that he speaks not all this to his own commendation, but entirely to their edi-fication; for he feared that, upon his approaching coming among them, they might not be found in a frame of mind such as he could desire, this would cause him to appear severe and not tender towards them. (See on 1 Cor. iv. 21). This possibility he de-sired effectually to remove, for he was equally unwilling to be *again* humbled by the position of affairs among them, or that his abiding among them should be productive of sorrow to the Corin-thians; all, therefore, who were conscious of guilt, were to repent! —In the present passage the πάλιν (ver. 21), as already remarked in the Introduction, § 2, refers to Paul's residence in Corinth at a period distinct from the first presence in that city, when he laid the foundation of the church; upon that occasion he had experi-enced no cause for humiliation, for his preaching had been attended with unusual success. (In ver. 19, it seems to me more forcible to consider the πάλιν δοκεῖτε κ. τ. λ. as a question than as explana-tory.—The general text punctuates after λαλοῦμεν, but it would be better to unite it with τάδε πάντα κ. τ. λ. to a sentence.— It may not be alleged against the reading τάδε, that ὅδε never occurs elsewhere in Paul's writings, for that can only be consi-dered accidental.—A recapitulation similar to that in ver. 20 is also found in Gal. v. 20, in which ἔρεις, ζῆλοι, θυμοί, ἐριθεῖαι suc-ceed each other. See also Rom. i. 29, sqq. A recapitulation must not be too strictly investigated, an accumulation of expres-sion proceeds from copious oratory. In Rom. i. 30 καταλαλία and ψιθυρισμός are found together, but reversed in order.— Φυσίωσις is only found here in the New Testament.—Ver. 21 is not to be understood as if the apostle considered that all the sins named had been actually perpetrated by the Corin-thian Christians, for all who could have been thus guilty, would have been immediately excluded by Paul from fellowship with the church; the emphasis is rather to be laid upon the προημαρτη-κότες. He had observed that many of the Corinthian Christians

did not sufficiently and deeply enough abhor their earlier heathen
abominations, retaining an indifference and laxity of principle in
matters relative to the sexes, which even permitted them to take
a part in the festivals held in idol temples; therefore he wished
to inspire them with a feeling of sincere repentance, and to find
it evinced by their conduct when he presented himself in Corinth).

## § 12. THE CONCLUSION.

### (xiii. 1—13).

Paul concludes his epistle with a very impressive admonition
to the Corinthians not to compel him (the apostle) to exercise his
apostolic power, but to examine themselves strictly relative to
their inward condition, and to give due heed to his warnings,
whilst, in the belief and hope that none will neglect these, he bestows the Christian blessing upon all without exception.

Vers. 1—2. Without adding ἑτοίμως ἔχω, as in xii. 14, Paul
precisely here asserts that he came to them for the third time,
according to which it cannot be denied without constraining the
sense that Paul had already been twice among the Corinthians.
Referring to Deut. xvii. 6, xix. 15, he adduces being present
several times among them, as a witness on his behalf for the truth
of his exhortations, and an argument for the exaction of obedience as a duty on their part. For that purpose he repeats
being absent (and in writing), that which when present (and with
the lips) he had declared to those who had sinned, and to all
others, viz., that upon his next appearance among them he would
not spare. It is consequently evident that upon his second residence in Corinth he had acted with indulgence towards them, and
this had led to the allegation of weakness made by the adversaries. See Comm. on x. 1. (In ver. 1 the σταθήσεται ῥῆμα is
copied from the Hebrew יָקוּם דָּבָר.—If we receive the view that
Paul had already been twice in Corinth when he wrote this
epistle, the words of ver. 2 which Griesbach places in parenthesis,
ὡς παρὼν τὸ δεύτερον καὶ ἀπὼν νῦν are easy of comprehension ;
the παρὼν τὸ δεύτερον refers to προείρηκα, the ἀπὼν νῦν to προ-

λέγω.—Concerning the προημαρτηκότες see xii. 21. The others were, it is true, not so guilty, nevertheless they also needed repentance for having yielded a species of consent to evil influences).

Vers. 3—5. As they required a proof that Christ was in him, they were also to examine themselves, and thereby discover whether they stood in the faith. If they were not entirely reprobate, they would find Christ to be in them, and as such they would be enabled to acknowledge the power of God in the weakness of the apostle, for they had undoubtedly received their faith from him. —This idea decidedly lies in the words of the apostle, although not perceptible at the first view. The introductory sentence commencing with ἐπεί, to which the ἑαυτοὺς πειράζετε of ver. 5 forms the conclusion, is by no means to be understood, as, " for if ye desire to prove, prove yourselves rather than me," for this does not agree with the declaration of Paul in ver. 5, that Christ is also in them except they be entirely reprobate ; he consequently hopes they may find Christ in themselves. According to this, the meaning of these words can alone be, that they (the Corinthians) should argue from that which they found in themselves, upon that which was in the apostle, and in such a manner as acknowledged the apostle to be the source of their own life. The latter is implied by the sentence ὃς εἰς ὑμᾶς οὐκ ἀσθενεῖ, ἀλλὰ δυνατεῖ ἐν ὑμῖν in ver. 3, which brings forward the powerful spiritual influence of the apostle in Corinth, and attributed by Paul to the Christ in him. These words would therefore be better omitted in the parenthesis, and only ver. 4 included therein. The same may likewise be observed of the words in ver. 5, ἢ οὐκ—ἐστιν, which are not to compose a parenthesis, but to be connected with the εἰ μήτι ἀδόκιμοί ἐστε in such a manner as to render perceptible an appeal on the part of Paul to the Christian knowledge of the Corinthians as follows : " Ye will, it is to be hoped, acknowledge that Christ is in you, except ye be entirely reprobates ?"—With regard to the intermediate sentence, Paul there compares himself, as he does in Rom. vi. 4, 5, with Christ, both in his weakness and his strength, to whom also, in conformity to his human nature, an ἀσθένεια is ascribed. It is unnecessary to explain that this includes nothing sinful, but only the *susceptibility for suffering of his nature* is to be understood. This is also the only passage in which an ἀσθένεια is expressly attributed to Christ.

Vers. 6, 7. The greatest advantage was hoped for by the apostle from the examination recommended, viz., the perfect and clear perception of himself which would follow; he therefore entreats the Lord to direct aright the hearts of the Corinthians; he (Paul) desired only their welfare, and not his own honour; he would willingly rather appear unfit, if they would only do that which was honest.—Throughout this passage, which is not altogether easy, it must be borne in mind that καλὸν and κακὸν ποιῆσαι do not solely relate to moral or immoral conduct, for these are in no degree brought under consideration, but they refer to the proper relation to him, the apostle, and to the word of truth which he had preached to the Corinthians. But inasmuch as the moral life is conditionary, it is also certainly included in the reference, though always as the consequence of faith or unbelief. The apostle in verse 6 says he hopes the Corinthians may not find him ἀδόκιμος, i. e., they would find apostolic authority for his severity; and again in ver. 7 he proceeds to state, that he desires that God may permit them to do that which is honest, in order that he may appear as ἀδόκιμος. This is undoubtedly a difficult passage. It might be supposed that we should read ἵνα οὐχ for οὐχ ἵνα, but then the ἡμεῖς δὲ ὡς ἀδόκιμοι ὦμεν which succeeds would be tautological. The passage is thus conceived by Billroth, he again supplies the εὔχομαι to the οὐχ, making the sense, " I desire not that we approve ourselves capable, i. e. severe." But in this construction some scruple is occasioned by the fact that εὔχομαι standing near to each other are construed in a twofold manner, first with the infinitive, and then with ἵνα, under which latter form it does not again occur. The οὐχ ἵνα can only be understood, " I desire this, not with the view that——but." The difficulty is much more easily solved by supposing, that Paul desired that his prayer itself should be regarded as a proof of his δοκιμή. This might be done by him, inasmuch as the μὴ κακον ποιῆσαι, which is the same as the following τὸ καλὸν ποιῆσαι, is precisely what Paul requires of the Corinthians; and, therefore, if the prayer that God would work this in them were fulfilled, it might be regarded as the effect of his powerful intercession. The latter inference is, however, altogether rejected by Paul; he desired their advantage only, and that any connected with himself as an individual should be subservient to his greater object.

Vers. 8, 9. That which follows agrees extremely well with the view just mentioned, for the apostle represents his power as beneficial, and not of a malevolent or injurious nature; if they (the Corinthians) prove strong in the truth, he is content to be weak, for that was even the object of his prayer, their perfecting, not his own exaltation. In the ὅταν ἡμεῖς ἀσθενῶμεν κ. τ. λ. Paul evidently bore in mind a parallel with verse 4; as Christ's weakness, the breathing out of the abundance of his life, conferred a higher power upon the world, so likewise Paul would be content to be weak, and breathe out his life, if his children in the Spirit are only strong. (See Comm. on iv. 12).

Ver. 10. As the aim of this communication Paul in conclusion states his hope, that upon his approaching appearance in Corinth he may be called upon to employ his apostolic authority solely to edification and not to destruction (x. 4, 8), (Ἀποτόμως is found in Tit. i. 13, Wisd. v. 23, in the signification of "sharp, severe." In Wisd. vi. 6, κρίσις ἀπότομος means a sharp sentence).

Vers. 11, 12. In the concluding words the apostle repeats the exhortations rendered especially necessary by the splitting of the Corinthian church into parties, employing for this reason the epithet of God. The fact of recommending them *all* to greet one another with a holy kiss proves that he continued to hope for the re-establishment of unity among them.

Ver. 13. The apostle concludes his epistle with a peculiar invocation of blessing. The ἀγάπη is ascribed to the Father as the source from whence the grace of the Lord Christ pours forth as a stream, producing brotherly communion among believers in the Holy Spirit. That the Son obtains first mention is explained by the fact that the divine nature was first revealed to man in Christ; the Son also first guides him to the Father, and finally perfects man's life in the communion of the Holy Ghost

FINIS.

## 1984-85 TITLES

| | | | |
|---|---|---|---|
| 2202 | Bernard of Clairvaux | The Song of Solomon | 21.00 |
| 4604 | Olshausen, Hermann | A Commentary on Paul's First and Second Epistles to the Corinthians | 14.75 |
| 5002 | Vaughan, Charles John | Epistle to the Philippians | 11.50 |
| 6602 | Tatford, Frederick Albert | The Revelation | 23.00 |
| 8407 | Hamilton, James | Moses, the Man of God | 14.75 |
| 8604 | Haldane, Robert | The Authenticity and Inspiration of the Holy Scriptures | 9.00 |
| 8805 | Morgan, James | The Biblical Doctrine of the Holy Spirit | 19.00 |
| 9519 | Bernard, Thomas Dehany | The Central Teaching of Christ | 16.25 |
| 9520 | Vine, William Edwy | The Divine Sonship of Christ | 9.50 |
| 9521 | Laidlaw, John | Studies in the Parables of Our Lord | 13.25 |
| 9522 | MacLaren, A. & Swete, H. B. | The Post-Resurrection Ministry of Christ (2 vol. in 1) | 17.75 |
| 9807 | Keith, Alexander | Christian Evidences: Fulfilled Bible Prophecy | 20.00 |

## TITLES CURRENTLY AVAILABLE

| | | | |
|---|---|---|---|
| 0101 | Delitzsch, Franz | A New Commentary on Genesis (2 vol.) | 30.50 |
| 0102 | Blaikie, W. G. | Heroes of Israel | 19.50 |
| 0103 | Bush, George | Genesis (2 vol.) | 29.95 |
| 0104 | MacDonald, Donald | Biblical Doctrine of Creation and the Fall: Genesis 1-3 | 18.95 |
| 0201 | Murphy, James G. | Commentary on the Book of Exodus | 14.50 |
| 0202 | Bush, George | Exodus | 22.50 |
| 0203 | Dolman, D. & Rainsford, M. | The Tabernacle (2 vol. in 1) | 19.75 |
| 0301 | Kellogg, Samuel H. | The Book of Leviticus | 21.00 |
| 0302 | Bush, George | Leviticus | 10.50 |
| 0401 | Bush, George | Numbers | 17.95 |
| 0501 | Cumming, John | The Book of Deuteronomy | 16.00 |
| 0601 | Blaikie, William G. | The Book of Joshua | 15.75 |
| 0602 | Bush, George | Joshua & Judges (2 vol. in 1) | 17.95 |
| 0603 | Kirk, Thomas & Lang, John | Studies in the Book of Judges (2 vol. in 1) | 17.75 |
| 0701 | Cox, S. & Fuller, T. | The Book of Ruth (2 vol. in 1) | 14.75 |
| 0901 | Blaikie, William G. | First Book of Samuel | 16.50 |
| 0902 | Deane, W. J. & Kirk, T. | Studies in the First Book of Samuel (2 vol. in 1) | 19.00 |
| 0903 | Blaikie, William G. | Second Book of Samuel | 15.00 |
| 1101 | Farrar, F. W. | The First Book of Kings | 19.00 |
| 1201 | Farrar, F. W. | The Second Book of Kings | 19.00 |
| 1301 | Kirk, T. & Rawlinson, G. | Studies in the Books of Kings (2 vol. in 1) | 20.75 |
| 1401 | Bennett, William H. | An Exposition of the Books of Chronicles | 17.50 |
| 1701 | Raleigh, Alexander | The Book of Esther | 9.75 |
| 1801 | Gibson, Edgar Charles | The Book of Job | 10.00 |
| 1802 | Green, William H. | The Argument of the Book of Job Unfolded | 13.50 |
| 1901 | Dickson, David | A Commentary on the Psalms (2 vol.) | 32.50 |
| 1902 | MacLaren, Alexander | The Psalms (3 vol.) | 45.00 |
| 1903 | Cox, Samuel | The Pilgrim Psalms: An Exposition of the Songs of Degrees | 9.50 |
| 2001 | Wardlaw, Ralph | Book of Proverbs (3 vol.) | 45.00 |
| 2101 | MacDonald, James M. | The Book of Ecclesiastes | 15.50 |
| 2102 | Wardlaw, Ralph | Exposition of Ecclesiastes | 16.25 |
| 2201 | Durham, James | An Exposition on the Song of Solomon | 17.25 |
| 2301 | Kelly, William | An Exposition of the Book of Isaiah | 15.25 |
| 2302 | Alexander, Joseph | Isaiah (2 vol.) | 29.95 |
| 2401 | Orelli, Hans C. von | The Prophecies of Jeremiah | 15.25 |
| 2701 | Pusey, Edward B. | Daniel the Prophet | 19.50 |
| 2702 | Tatford, Frederick Albert | Daniel and His Prophecy | 9.25 |
| 2703 | Wright, Charles H. H. | Studies in Daniel's Prophecy | 13.95 |
| 3001 | Cripps, Richard S. | A Commentary on the Book of Amos | 13.50 |
| 3201 | Burn, Samuel C. | The Prophet Jonah | 11.25 |
| 3202 | Kirk, Thomas | Jonah: His Life and Mission | 12.95 |
| 3801 | Wright, Charles H. H. | Zechariah and His Prophecies | 24.95 |
| 4001 | Morison, James | The Gospel According to Matthew | 24.95 |
| 4101 | Alexander, Joseph | Commentary on the Gospel of Mark | 16.75 |
| 4102 | Morison, James | The Gospel According to Mark | 21.00 |
| 4201 | Kelly, William | The Gospel of Luke | 18.50 |
| 4301 | Brown, John | The Intercessory Prayer of Our Lord Jesus Christ | 11.50 |
| 4302 | Hengstenberg, E. W. | Commentary on the Gospel of John (2 vol.) | 34.95 |
| 4401 | Alexander, Joseph | Commentary on the Acts of the Apostles | 27.50 |
| 4402 | Gloag, Paton J. | A Critical and Exegetical Commentary on the Acts of the Apostles (2 vol.) | 29.95 |
| 4403 | Stier, Rudolf E. | Words of the Apostles | 8.75 |
| 4502 | Moule, H. C. G. | The Epistle to the Romans | 16.25 |
| 4503 | Olshausen, Hermann | Studies in the Epistle to the Romans | 16.50 |
| 4601 | Brown, John | The Resurrection of Life | 15.50 |
| 4602 | Edwards, Thomas C. | A Commentary on the First Epistle to the Corinthians | 18.00 |
| 4603 | Jones, John Daniel | Exposition of First Corinthians 13 | 9.50 |
| 4801 | Ramsey, William | Historical Commentary on the Epistle to the Galatians | 17.75 |
| 4802 | Brown, John | An Exposition of the Epistle of Paul to the Galatians | 16.00 |
| 4901 | Westcott, Brooke F. | St. Paul's Epistle to the Ephesians | 10.50 |
| 4902 | Pattison, R. & Moule, H. | Exposition of Ephesians: Lessons in Grace and Godliness (2 vol. in 1) | 14.75 |
| 5102 | Westcott, F. B. | The Epistle to the Colossians | 7.50 |
| 5103 | Eadie, John | Colossians | 10.50 |
| 5104 | Daille, Jean | Exposition of Colossians | 24.95 |
| 5401 | Liddon, H. P. | The First Epistle to Timothy | 6.00 |
| 5601 | Taylor, Thomas | An Exposition of Titus | 20.75 |
| 5801 | Delitzsch, Franz | Commentary on the Epistle to the Hebrews (2 vol.) | 31.50 |
| 5802 | Bruce, A. B. | The Epistle to the Hebrews | 17.25 |
| 5803 | Edwards, Thomas C. | The Epistle to the Hebrews | 13.00 |
| 5901 | Johnstone, Robert | Lectures on the Epistle of James | 16.50 |
| 5902 | Mayor, Joseph B. | The Epistle of St. James | 20.25 |